The INGENIOUS
Mr. Henry Care

*Lois G. Schwoerer
is Elmer Louis Kayser
Professor of History Emeritus
at the George Washington University,
Washington DC*

The INGENIOUS
Mr. Henry Care

LONDON'S *First*
SPIN DOCTOR

LOIS G. SCHWOERER

TEMPUS

Front cover illustration: The 'Secretarius', Henry Care (detail).

First published 2001 as *The Ingenious Mr. Henry Care,*
Restoration Publicist.

This edition first published 2004 by arrangement
with The John Hopkins University Press.

Tempus Publishing Limited
The Mill, Brimscombe Port,
Stroud, Gloucestershire, GL5 2QG
www.tempus-publishing.com

British Library Cataloguing in Publication Data.
A catalogue record for this book is available from the British Library.

ISBN 0 7524 2883 7

Typesetting and origination by Tempus Publishing Limited
Printed in Great Britain by Midway Colour Print, Wiltshire

Contents

Acknowledgments

This book has been a long time in the making, and my obligations have multiplied accordingly. Colleagues have become accustomed to my obsession with Restoration law, ideology, the press, and that witty, irrepressible rascal, Henry Care, and they have helped me in ways large and small. Among the people on both sides of the Atlantic to whom I extend grateful thanks for sharing their knowledge and insights are Maureen Bell, Charlene Bangs Bickford, Peter Blayney, Jackson Boswell, Kenneth R. Bowling, J.A.I. Champion, Gary De Krey, Mary Maples Dunn, Elizabeth L. Eisenstein, Mark Goldie, Robert Hume, J.R. Jacobs, J.R. Jones, Katharine Lesko, Nancy Klein Maguire, Michael Mendle, John Miller, Howard Nenner, John G.A. Pocock, Leo Ribuffo, Linda B. Salamon, Gordon Schochet, Hilda Smith, Barbara Taft, Melinda Zook, and Steven N. Zwicker.

My ideas about Henry Care and the issues examined in this study were refined in Folger seminars, especially those directed by Steven Zwicker and Derek Hirst, and in conversations with seminar participants and members of the Folger Shakespeare Library community. I am grateful to audiences for their comments when I presented papers that anticipated this book at the annual meeting of the American Historical Association, the Folger Shakespeare

Library, the Institute for Historical Research, London University, the Mid-West Conference on British Studies, Purdue University, and Smith College.

I thank Isabel Witte Kenrick for her research assistance in London repositories. My inability to stay in England for extended periods made her assistance invaluable. Sara Fentress and Bruce Janacek, two former graduate students at the George Washington University, were exemplary research assistants in Washington. I am grateful to Melinda Zook for commenting on several chapters and to Barbara Taft and Isabel Witte Kenrick for reading the entire manuscript. I thank the anonymous reviewer for comments and suggestions, and Christel McDonald for helping with the proofs.

I also want to thank the staffs of the libraries where I worked and those whom I burdened with requests for information from afar: the Bodleian Library, the British Library Manuscript Room and Rare Book Room, the Cambridge University Library, the William Andrew Clark Memorial Library, the Guildhall Library, the Henry E. Huntington Library, the Institute for Historical Research, the Library of Congress Rare Book Room and Newspaper Room, the Magdalene College Library at Cambridge University, and the Public Record Office. I am especially indebted to the Folger Shakespeare Library, where I have labored for so long, always with the patient, cheerful help of the entire staff; I want this time to thank in particular Harold Batie, Carol Brobeck, Georgiana Spiegel, Betsy Walsh, and Laetitia Yeandle.

I am grateful for permission to draw upon the ideas and language of my article 'The Attempted Impeachment of Sir William Scroggs, Lord Chief Justice of the Court of King's Bench, November 1680–March 1681,' published in the *Historical Journal* 38 (December 1995): 843–74. I have also adapted the ideas and language of my 'Liberty of the Press and Public Opinion: 1660–1695,' from *Liberty Secured? Britain Before and After 1688,* ed. J.R. Jones (Stanford: Stanford University Press, 1992), 199–230, with the permission of the publishers, Stanford University Press, © 1992 by the Board of Trustees of the Leland Stanford Junior University.

Permission to use and quote from Roger Morrice, 'Ent'ring Book, Being an Historical Register of Occurrences From April, Anno. 1677 to April 1691,' is given by the Director of Dr Williams's Library on behalf of the Trustees; I have used the photocopy at the Folger Shakespeare Library.

A sabbatical leave helped me to make significant progress on this book. I thank Edward Berkowitz, then chair of the history department, and Linda B. Salamon, then dean of the Columbian School of Arts and Science and the Graduate School of Arts and Sciences of the George Washington University, for approving my request for a leave. I am grateful beyond measure to the George Washington University for its generous subsidy in support of publication and thank especially Carol Spegelman, associate vice president for academic affairs, Lester Lefton, dean of the Columbian School of Arts and Science and the Graduate School of Arts and Sciences, Donald Lehman, academic vice president, and Stephen Joel Trachtenberg, president.

Introduction

The ingenious Mr. Henry Care was among the most important spin doctors in London 320 years ago. The term 'spin doctor' is familiar to us today, but the presence of such folk in late seventeenth-century England may have escaped notice. Yet they were there, and, like many men and women writers in our own time, they tried to shape news, views and events in ways that advanced the cause they wanted to promote. Their skillful writings had such a destabilizing effect on politics, religion and society that Charles II once blamed 'rebellion in the Kingdom and schisms in the Church' on the 'Liberty of the Press' and went on to place controlling the press second only in importance to settling the nation's armed forces.[1] Charles's elevating the press to the level of the military and designating both as basic instruments in achieving the nation's stability was a remarkable, indeed, a unique statement, revealing the king's acute and prescient judgment about the printed word. The fact of the matter is that the torrent of argumentative tracts and pamphlets that poured from the presses did exacerbate contentions over law, ideology, politics and religion in ways that shook the establishment in State and Church.

Learned, witty, irrepressible, irreverent, Henry Care, although little known today, was well known 320 years ago to people in all walks of life because of his leading role in the popular press. People at that time recognized him as a publicist or propagandist who tried to maintain at the boiling point the interest of the reading public in public issues. He had a reputation equal to that of other writers who enjoyed fame then, and who have already found their historians: Aphra Behn, the first woman writer to earn a living by her pen,[2] Abel Boyer, who like Care sought to support himself by writing as a historian, journalist and pamphleteer,[3] Daniel Defoe, who admired Care and confessed an indebtedness to him,[4] and Sir Roger L'Estrange, the official censor of the Stuart monarchy and Care's principal sparring partner in the press.[5] But Care himself has virtually faded from history. To recover Care from undeserved oblivion and give proper place in the historical record to a man whose talents both friend and foe acknowledged and whose accomplishments have made legitimate claims on our attention is a major purpose of this study. Another purpose is to use his life and career to suggest fresh perspectives on Restoration England.

Why have historians neglected Care and why does he merit attention now? One reason Care has been judged unimportant is that he came from lowly social origins; his ancestry is clouded, we do not know exactly where he was born, he held no office in politics or religion. What interest could such a man possibly hold for historians? For years students of history have concentrated on studying elite leaders of politics, diplomacy and military affairs. Only in the mid-twentieth century did people from the lower reaches of the social scale begin to attract serious attention. This new perspective swept onto the stage of history men and women who heretofore had been ignored, among them Henry Care.

Another reason for the neglect of Henry Care is that he was a loser. Care was on the losing side of the two major controversies in which he took part. The first was the Popish Plot and Exclusion Crisis (1678–83) when the issue was whether, in the absence of legitimate royal offspring, James, duke of York, Charles II's Roman Catholic brother, should be excluded from the line of succession to the throne because of his religion. Care was a powerful voice for those who favored exclusion. But, thanks to Charles's political dexterity, exclusion failed, and exclusionists were discredited, Care with them. The second crisis in which Care played a part was the run-up to the revolution of 1688–89, also known as the Glorious Revolution, when the question was whether or not the English people favored a Catholic line of succession to the throne – now assured by the birth of James II's son in June 1688 – or preferred to entrust the nation to the Protestant Prince William of Orange and his wife, Mary, the Protestant daughter of James II. Care had switched sides, placing his rhetorical talents in the service of King James and his policy of religious freedom. James's side lost and Care's death in August 1688 swept him and his writings out of the public arena. Until recently, historians have found little use for losers, a fact that illustrates the limits of so-called 'Whig history' with its focus on winners and its preoccupation with past origins of present conditions.

A little game of counter-factual history shows how different the possibilities could have been. Suppose Care had chosen the side of the Court in the Popish Plot and Exclusion Crisis, as his early printed books suggest he might have done. In those circumstances, he might have won the notice of Charles II and rivaled Sir Roger L'Estrange for royal favor as a writer worthy of taking the Court's message to the public. Or, suppose Care had attached himself to the English partisans of Prince William of Orange in the months preceding the revolution of 1688–89, as persecution during the reign of Charles II and the early years of James II might have inclined him to do. Today he might be known as one of the principal defenders of the revolution in the press. If Care's life had taken these turns, no doubt there would already be studies of Henry Care. But historians of Restoration England, like historians of other eras and areas, have been reluctant to study historical figures who are on the losing side. Now that 'Whig history' no longer prevails, historians recognize that studying a loser can bring valuable insights to light.

Another reason Care has been pushed to the sidelines is that historians today who know of him have disparaged him as a turn-coat and assumed that he converted to Catholicism when he began to write for James II. They find him offensive for those reasons.[6] One historian told me that Care deserved the assessment of his enemies and the neglect of historians, while another spoke so unflatteringly about Care that propriety has sealed my lips. Yet, precisely why he joined James's camp is debatable, and in fact he did not convert to Catholicism. Misunderstanding about Care's religion, especially, has helped undermine further interest in him, for until recently historians of England have been disinclined to study Catholics. The individuals and issues of James II's reign have, with a few exceptions,[7] been relegated to the dustbin of history, Care along with the rest. But now, historians have undertaken to revisit King James and his era.[8] This present concern for the larger issues of James's reign is reason enough to justify interest in Care and in what his experiences may tell us about this short-lived Catholic reign.

Today many of the reasons for ignoring Henry Care have vanished. Readers are now interested in historical figures who do not come from the higher reaches of society. Studying Care and his career offers an exciting opportunity to penetrate the anonymity of lower-middle-class life in London 320 years ago. Care's experiences provide a window on how a man without formal education, social connections, family background, or ready money, but who was smart, ambitious, hard-working and blessed with a 'golden pen' might become visible to contemporaries – and to historians. Care's 'scribbling' was his only path to upward social mobility in a hierarchical society based on class, occupation and money and to a circle of interesting and important men and women in politics and literature. His choice of topic and publishing strategies shows how he got into print, provides insights into print culture and exposes features of his personality.

A further reason why Care merits our attention is that he is one of few identifiable authors who wrote in quantity during the major Restoration press wars. His voice and ideas were before the public more than anyone else's on the side that he was championing – the Whigs in the Popish Plot and Exclusion Crisis, and James II's Catholic policy of religious freedom in the revolution of 1688–89. He was able to achieve this distinction because in both crises he brought out weekly papers: the *Weekly Pacquet of Advice from Rome*, accompanied by the *Popish Courant*, appeared every week but one from December 1678 to July 1683, and *Publick Occurrences Truely Stated* appeared every week from February 1688 until Care's death in August of that year. At the same time, he also wrote a number of tracts and contributed actively to several newspapers. Care's productivity and dominance alone justify using him and his writing as a prism to illuminate the era.

Moreover, study of Care and his career complements the work that has been done on the print culture of the era; to date, historians have focused attention on printers and publishers. An author, however, provides as good or better evidence for understanding this new institution; as a judge remarked, apropos of Care himself, 'One author found is worth twenty printers found.'[9] Attention to the individual brings center stage the part played by Care and his counterparts on the Court side – L'Estrange with his *Observator*, Edward Rawlins and his *Heraclitus Ridens*, and Nathaniel Thompson with his newspaper the *Loyal Protestant* – in restyling political rhetoric during those years and opening up a public space for the discussion of political and religious issues by the commonalty, not just the middle classes.

Still further, Care was arguably the most important 'popular historian' of the seventeenth century.[10] His *Weekly Pacquet of Advice from Rome* marked a new departure in the writing of history; it was a serious account of the history of Roman Catholicism and Protestantism presented in weekly installments and avowedly aimed at a marginally educated audience. He used this history as a propaganda instrument in political polemic in his attack on popery, the Church of England, and the idea of a Catholic succession to the English throne. The subtle, yet obvious, sub-text of the *Weekly Pacquet of Advice from Rome* was that it showed what might be expected from a Catholic king of England. Contemporaries well understood this fact, and for us to understand it now brings a sharper vision to Restoration culture.

Investigation of Care yields other advantages. For example, it enhances understanding of the Popish Plot and Exclusion Crisis, highlighting a dark and brutal side of Restoration government. A Care perspective uncovers the central role in that crisis of the feared threat to the sanctity of law and the legal power of Parliament. Care himself, and other men and women in the print world, were harassed by the government, brought to trial and punished in one way or another. This is a matter of importance on two counts. First, the steps that the State and Church took to control the press and its members suggests that the 'potential for absolutism,' as it has been called, was greater than sometimes thought.[11] Second, men in the House of Commons invoked harassment of Care and others as one of the grounds for trying to impeach Sir William Scroggs, Lord Chief Justice of the Court of King's Bench. For the first and only time in English history, the charge of repressing the press and harassing its members was central to an attempt to impeach a minister of the Crown.

Additionally, studying Care brings the short reign of the Catholic king James II into new perspective. Although neglected to date by historians, James's propaganda campaign was actively supported by the king and his ministers, and vigorously pursued by Catholic and Dissenting writers. Care, a Dissenter to the end, wrote more than anyone else for the king's cause; a modern historian has called him the 'hardest working horse' in James's journalistic stable.[12] Bringing the press and the propaganda effort into focus changes our understanding of James's effort. Care's increasingly sharp criticism of the Church of England provoked a brutal response and provides a hard perspective on the Church and its attitude toward toleration, religious liberty and Dissent during these years.

A concentration on Care, who has been described as the 'brain of the opposition,'[13] confirms and expands the nature of Whig ideology that predominated during the Exclusion Crisis. His tracts highlight Whig claims for religious toleration and constitutional-ism and their specific fears for the sanctity of juries and Parliament. Care, however, went beyond the Whigs in arguing for freedom of the individual religious conscience in terms that were virtually identical to those of John Locke. It is worth noting that Care was in print with those ideas before Locke printed his *Letter on Toleration*. With those of contemporaries, Care's tracts helped to create a 'jury ideology;' that is, an abiding respect for law and juries. Care's *English Liberties: Or, The Free-Born Subject's Inheritance* played a prominent role in the transmission of ideas about the jury and other fundamental laws, and the rights and liberties of Englishmen to eighteenth-century England and the American colonies. William Penn, among others, was deeply indebted to this essay.

Finally, the ultimate reason for a book about Henry Care is my fascination with him. Care's *English Liberties* introduced me to a man of rhetorical skills, wide knowledge and, so it seemed, ardently held principles. A splendid fellow, I first thought. Then I began to think that Care was really a spin doctor who shaped his writings to serve a range of political and religious causes; he was probably nothing more than a Vicar of Bray. Closer reading, how-ever, revealed continuities in his thought; here was a man of strong intellect who changed sides but retained some basic political and religious principles. He now became even more interesting and our enduring relationship began. Care's story has, to my mind, a timelessness that can illuminate the press of all eras. Indeed, rough parallels between Care's print world and that of the early twenty-first century are not difficult to find: spin doctors, *ad hominem* attacks, ambitious and profit-driven writers and publishers, writers of abiding and undeviating principles, and turn-coats occupy both. I hope that readers will find these identities and enjoy them as instructive, enlightening, and sometimes, amusing, as I have.

Early Life
and
Writings

Henry Care, nicknamed 'Harry,' was born in 1646 and died at the age of forty-two on 8 August 1688.[1] These are two prominent and certain facts among the many uncertainties about his early life. We do not know the day of his birth nor anything of his mother or father, nor whether he had brothers or sisters. Care spelled his surname *Care* rather than *Carre, Carr, Carey,* or *Cave*, as it sometimes appeared, but there is nothing to link him with other men named Care who lived when he did. An unidentified man, said to be Care's uncle, won notice because he put up £100 in 1682 to assist Richard Janeway, a radical publisher.[2] If this unknown man were really his uncle, he apparently did nothing to help his nephew. This story offers the only inkling of wealth in Care's family. The preponderance of evidence, however, indicates that Care came from an impoverished background and that he struggled with poverty until the latter years of his life. Anthony Wood's sneering remark that Care's 'breeding' was that of 'a little despicable wretch'[3] is unwarranted, but a contemporary described

Care's house in 1679 as quite modest and in 'no ways agreeable to the Greatness of his Mind and spirit.'[4] Care himself mentioned renting 'a little House' in St Sepulchre's Parish.[5] Writing within fifteen years of Care's death, Daniel Defoe also noticed the 'poverty of circumstance' in Care's life.[6]

Marriage did not improve Care's status. Although the record of the marriage is lost, other evidence shows that Care married a woman named Bridget or Brigitta, whose surname is unknown, in 1680 or 1681[7] when he was thirty-four or thirty-five years old. With her Care may have had a daughter.[8] Bridget died in 1699, eleven years after Care.[9] Whatever Care's precise social background, he was intent upon improving it and enhancing his prospects.

Where Care was born is also unknown, but it was almost certainly England. If he was not a Londoner by birth, he was one by choice. Except for a period of about eighteen months, in 1683 and 1684, he lived in London from young adulthood – at least from 1670, when he was twenty-four years old and began to publish – until his death. He changed his residence several times, but always lived within the vicinity of St Sepulchre's Church and Old Bailey Street.[10] Old Bailey Street, also called 'court of the Chamberlaine of London,' was in Faringdon Ward Without, which stretched along the wall of the city to Ludgate and was known as 'Fleete lane' where it turned toward Fleet Street. St Sepulchre's Church was in the Bayly, by 'Chamberlaine gate.'[11] This area of London was downscale in Restoration England.

The London where Care lived was a mixture of commercial, public and residential buildings. His neighborhood may hold the key to two puzzles: how a young man of indifferent background got a start in the print world and how he came to the notice of people highly placed in politics and law. With its population of about 700,000 and its well-articulated wards, London was a place where a person could know his neighbors and be drawn into a network of people who attended the same church, drank and talked at the same coffee house or tavern, and carried on their

business affairs in or near their residence. Care lived close to St
Paul's Cathedral and Churchyard, where numerous bookstalls and
printing establishments were located, and where printers, publishers, and booksellers resided. Among them were the men and a few
women with whom Care, as an aspiring writer and later as a recognized author, did business. For example, among his publishers
and printers over the years were Langley Curtis, who had his shop
first in Goat Court on Ludgate Hill and then at the Sign of Sir
Edmundbury Godfrey, near Fleet Bridge, and Francis Smith,
whose shop, the Elephant and Castle, was in Cornhill near the
Royal Exchange. One may easily imagine Care as a young man of
intellectual bent haunting the bookstalls and meeting people in the
print trade. Neighborhood networking may explain how Care got
to know the publisher and printer of his first book and persuaded
four men to 'puff' it.

Care also lived near law courts and law offices, the Old Bailey
prison and the Guildhall, where trials of print people were held,
his own among them in July 1680. Such places were magnets to
people prominent – or otherwise – in law and politics. The Green
Ribbon Club, famed for its promotion of Whigs and Whiggish
principles, was located nearby at Chancery Lane End. Roger
North describes the house as 'double balconied in the Front' so
that members could saunter out with 'pipes in their Mouths,
merry faces, and diluted Throats, for vocal Encouragement' of
people below. The club supported Care in 1679 and 1680, when he
was in trouble with the law, so it is certain that he was known earlier by some members. No doubt he was among those persons
whom the club welcomed in the course of their efforts to 'make
Proselytes' and spread news and views.[12]

Further, Care lived close to the parish of St Botolph, where in
1676 Anthony Ashley Cooper, the first earl of Shaftesbury and a
leader of the Whigs, bought his London residence, Thanet House,
located on Aldersgate Street. Although West London was the
section of the city where most men and women of wealth and
position lived, some noble families, like those of the duke of

Lauderdale and the marquis of Dorchester, owned houses on Aldersgate Street. Shaftesbury chose Thanet House for financial reasons but reaped political benefits from the location because it facilitated his contacts with members of London's middle class and artisans, who could easily slip in and out unnoticed.[13] Perhaps when Care was in the eye of the storm over Exclusion and other 'hot' topics he was invited to Thanet House.[14]

Care's residences may also shed light on his eclectic interest in religion. The parish of St Sepulchre's Church was near the city wards that were heavily populated by Dissenters: Aldersgate Without, Bishopsgate Without, and Cripplegate Without.[15] Moreover, he lived not far from 'The Mouth,' a Quaker meeting-house, and in the neighborhood of Milton's house.[16] Youthful awareness of Protestant sects may have sparked Care's later interest in religious doctrine and discipline.

Care's London residences may also have influenced the topics he chose to write about. Living close to Blackfriars, Care would have had intimate knowledge of the Great Fire of 1666, perhaps from his own experience or from the recollection of neighbors. If he wrote narratives of the fire with the aim of laying responsibility for it on Roman Catholics and the English Court, as he was charged with doing, his descriptions could have drawn authority from his own or reported memories. A short distance from Blackfriars were the wharves on the Thames where goods from internal and external markets were brought. When Care wrote an essay in 1686 about the merchant and his habits, he may have derived information from his personal observation. He would also have seen, and perhaps known, artisans, carpenters and stonemasons furiously engaged in rebuilding St Sepulchre's Church, which was severely damaged in the Great Fire. The new St Sepulchre's was re-consecrated in 1670. [17] Care's avowed aim of helping people, especially young artisans in London and Westminster, who were without formal education or time to understand the complexities of religious and political history no doubt reflected a common social background and a personal relationship with many of them.

There were numerous taverns and coffee houses in Care's neighborhood. In 1676 Care mentioned the 'Blew Ball near Kings Printing House in Black Fryer.'[18] Care also patronized the Queen's Tavern near Ludgate, Sam's Coffee House, the Widdow Coffee House in Ave-Mary-Lane, and Brittain's Coffee House in Goat Court near Fleet Bridge. Since Care loved to drink and talk politics and religion, taverns and coffeehouses were important to his life.

Although centered in London, Care was neither unaware of nor unknown in counties outside London and countries outside England. He kept an eye on events in the counties and was present at and reported as an eyewitness the election in Essex in 1679.[19] He and Curtis had their 'correspondents' on the spot in Chichester to report on a law case against a prominent Whig.[20] He wrote as if he were familiar with libraries in Cambridge and Oxford, in effect as if he had done research there.[21] His writings touched persons outside London. In May 1682 partisans of the king in Norwich celebrated Charles's birthday with a bonfire of opposition tracts and effigies of 'several Factious and Seditious Libellers,' of which Care was the only author.[22] He had vision enough to be aware of the New World, referring to it several times, and to write on the 'most proper Method of Preaching the Gospel among the Heathens.'[23] His tract *English Liberties* was reprinted in the colonies. One colonist asked his London bookseller to send him a copy of volume 5 of Care's *Weekly Pacquet*.[24] Care's intellectual cosmopolitanism extended to the European continent as well. Skilled in French, Care not only translated the work of a French author[25] but may have visited France in the course of writing *The Grandeur And Glory Of France*. He was deeply knowledgeable about European history and religious ideas from antiquity to his own time.

Mystery surrounds Henry Care's education. He did not attend a well-known grammar school, but his knowledge of Latin (the staple of grammar-school instruction) and of classical, Renaissance and religious thinkers makes it almost certain that he had some grammar-school training. He had no university training, nor did he attend one of the Inns of Court or the Chancery Inns. This negative evidence shows that he was largely self-educated and that his family was not sufficiently well connected for him to win the post of servitor at a university. That post has been described as a way for men of humble circumstances to advance their education and career prospects.[26] In any case, Care developed a love of the life of the mind and somehow accumulated a remarkable store of knowledge. He became well informed about the history of England and Europe, English law, canon law, rhetoric and litera-ture. Above all, he read books about religion, including the doc-trine and discipline of the Church of England, the Roman Catholic Church and Nonconformity, as well as Judaism and Islam. Interested in astrology and medicine, he was familiar with an impressive range of authors, mentioning by name or alluding to major and minor writers in the European and English intellectual tradition up to and including his own time. Besides Latin and French, Care knew Greek. He did not master Hebrew, confessing that he depended upon 'those skill'd' in that language.[27] Remarking with some sarcasm that it did not take seven years to learn Latin,[28] Care was proficient enough to prepare and publish three translations of books from Latin to English.

Early twenty-first-century readers may be surprised at the intel-lectual range and achievement of this self-educated man, but men far more distinguished than Henry Care were informally educated in the early modern period. Shakespeare and Ben Jonson are prominent examples. Also, a host of self-educated women, among them Lady Rachel Russell, Dame Eleanor Davies, Margaret Cavendish, the duchess of Newcastle, and Aphra Behn may be recalled. Even in the House of Commons during the Restoration about 28 percent of the members had not attended Cambridge, Oxford, or the Inns of Court.[29]

Still, self-education that results in genuine breadth and depth of information and understanding is remarkable. It requires three things: native intelligence, which Care had in abundance, encour-agement and some guidance from an educated person or persons, and access to an extensive library. I conjecture that Care received encouragement, guidance and access to books from the Reverend William Bell (1626–83), the vicar at St Sepulchre's Church from 1 October 1662 to his death on 19 July 1683. This hypothesis rests upon the fact that later in life Care named Bell as a man with whom he had kept in touch and who knew his mind on religion.[30]

I also surmise that one or more lawyers guided Care's early education and supplied him with books. Contemporaries referred to his legal connections: John Gibbon, a writer on heraldry and, interestingly, the famous Edward Gibbon's great-great-uncle, reported the rumor that Care was 'Bred an attorney.'[31] In Restoration England an attorney was a member of the 'lower branch' of the legal profession, a man who had received his early training as a clerk to a senior person, not through membership in one of the Inns of Court. [32] This hearsay explained to Gibbon how Care could be so knowledgeable about the law as well as other things. Other men also thought that Care held some kind of inferior position in the legal profession.[33] Care's extensive knowledge of the law gives credit to the point. For example, two of his tracts, *Draconica* and *English Liberties* copiously display this knowledge. Also, his use of legal analogies suggests a deep familiarity: in explaining why he had 'epitomized' some passages in the medical book he translated, he said that 'too many words both confound the understanding, and clog the memory... The effect of a Chancery Bill is sooner apprehended in a small Breviat, than in the swelling Tautologies of a hundred sheets.' [34] He also expressed profound respect for the law, describing it as 'the Kings High-way,' almost the equal of the Bible: 'It bears so much Analogy (at a humble distance) with the Gospel' that people who follow it 'cannot Err.'[35] Care did not reveal how he earned a living before he turned to writing, but at the end of his life he referred to 'the Profession (no way Dishonorable) he was bred to' from which he 'might get... a Comfortable... Living.' The comment is oblique, but not incompatible with the evidence just adduced.[36]

Finally, Care was on friendly terms with attorneys and others in the legal world. In 1680 Samuel Astrey, a clerk in the Court of King's Bench, 'leaked' word to him about a controversial ruling on the *Weekly Pacquet*.[37] In late 1681, as proof of a story he had recounted, Care named three men in the Augmentation Office who held 'originals' of leases pertinent to the account.[38] The next year Care spoke knowingly of the views of certain judges.[39] In an undated letter written when he was living outside London, Care asked his correspondent to send a reply to a Mr John Sutton, 'an attorney at Law in ye Blackfryars,' who would forward it to him.[40] These details support the idea that some lawyers took a helpful interest in him and that he worked for lawyers until he established himself in the print world.

Care had access to a large number of books through four channels. First, he no doubt patronized those shops that acted as lending libraries; he even advertised one of them as 'next door to the Queen Head [Tavern].'[41] Second, he referred to the 'publick' libraries in Oxford and Cambridge as if he had worked in them, and it is possible that an admirer arranged admission for him. Third, as just mentioned, Care's minister and his legal associates may well have made books available to him. Fourth, on 23 May 1679 Care was admitted to the library at Sion College[42] a college and almshouse for Anglican clergy. Sion College required a recommendation from a London clergyman to admit a nonclergyman;[43] Care's sponsor was in all probability the Reverend Bell, who was affiliated with Zion College in various capacities, becoming president in 1672–74 and again from December 1682 to his death. He took a special interest in the library, giving and raising money and overseeing the library's operation.[44] Apparently Care used the library a lot, for a contemporary remarked upon his connection with Zion College.[45]

However it was that Care became educated, his intelligence and learning were recognized by contemporaries, who dubbed him 'Little Luther,' and by L'Estrange's biographer, who described him as the 'brain' in the press of the Whig opposition.[46]

Henry Care's appearance and manner were caricatured by his enemies in notably consistent terms, and no doubt there are nuggets of truth in their remarks. Contemporaries referred to him as 'this little Gentleman,' ridiculed him as 'Monkey-faced,' commented upon his 'Black Muzzle' and described his body as 'Rat-like.'[47] One author, in airing his suspicion that Care was about to leave the Whig cause 'as Rats do a rotten Ship,' remarked, ''Twas not for nothing that nature shap'd [Care] like that Vermin.'[48] Although these terms were intended to demean rather than describe, taken together they add up to a picture of Care as a man of modest height with a slender and angular build, flat features, and a black beard.[49] We also know that he was right-handed.[50] Alas, Care's expressed desire to have an early work adorned with his portrait came to nothing.[51]

In manner Care was feisty, quick tempered, and given to extreme and unguarded language, traits that his alleged love of drink probably magnified.[52] He liked jokes, humor – the light touch. As he put it, 'Everything is big with Jest, if we have but the wit to find it out.'[53] Delighting in verbal swordplay whether orally or in print, Care did not suffer fools easily. Early in his career, Care defended himself from an attack in print, saying that he would not retreat from his enemies 'like a snail' but would 'go on and use' his pen against them.[54] In an undated unpublished piece Care defended his 'more than ordinary severity' against a critic who had savaged a book that he, Care, admired. He had described the critic in coarse terms as un unknown 'saucy Libeller' whose face was embossed with pimples, and he had demeaned his intelligence as insufficient to understand the complexity of the work in question.[55]

This extreme language reflected Care's exuberant intellect and personality, his love of wordplay, and his rhetorical strategy. Perhaps Care really felt, as he once wrote that 'Fortune... always loves to help the bold.'[56] A man in his position had to be bold if he were to be noticed. At the same time his reckless rhetoric conformed to the practice of the verbal polemical culture in which he participated. No doubt the print culture influenced him even as he contributed to it. Taken together, these characteristics enabled him to exploit developments in politics, religion and society, and to make a name for himself.

I

Care entered a print world that, in theory, was firmly regulated. The centerpiece of the government's attempt to control the press was the Licensing/Printing Act which was in force from 1662 until 1679, when it was allowed to lapse.[57] The Act banned all 'books or pamphlets' that were 'heretical [or] seditious' – in short, that maligned Christianity or the Church of England or 'the government or governors' of the nation. To achieve this end, an elaborate system of pre-publication censorship and licensing was set up aimed at preventing offensive material from ever coming on to the market: a secretary of state was to vet books on politics and history; the Lord Chancellor, law books; the archbishop of Canterbury and the bishop of London, religious, philosophical, and all other works. When a censor signified his approval, the work was entered into the Stationers' Company register and a fee of ten pence was paid to the company. Penalties were supposed to be imposed on persons who failed to register their writings. *All* material, whether heretical or seditious, or neutral and inoffensive, was to be licensed.

The Stationers' Company, as is plain to see, played an important part in the licensing process.[58] Chartered as a London guild in 1557 by Queen Mary I, the Company theoretically possessed a virtual monopoly over all the printing and sale of books; the *quid pro quo* for this lucrative arrangement was its cooperation in administering the government's orders regarding the press. To carry out their duties the stationers were empowered to search for and seize prohibited material, and to arrest the suspected printer or anyone who interfered with the search. This provision gave the company virtually the same power as the secretaries of state who themselves were authorized to issue general and specific search warrants.

These weapons, the 'soul' of the Licensing/Printing Act, one commentator thought,[59] were indeed powerful, but their use was controversial and had the effect of undermining support for the government.[60]

The Licensing/Printing Act also attempted to control the press by limiting and regulating the craft of printing. The law reduced the number of printers to twenty-four – twenty master printers of the Stationers' Company, the king's printer, the printers of the two universities, and the printer at York. The fewer the printers, the fewer the pieces of printed material, was the idea. Control over master printers was in theory comprehensive; for example, they were permitted only two apprentices and two presses, were required to post a bond of £300 against unlawful printing, to ascertain the names of authors and to give those names to the authorities upon demand. Vacancies that occurred among master printers were to be filled by nominees of the archbishop of Canterbury or the bishop of London. Finally, the act imposed heavy penalties: for a first offense, suspension from printing for three years; for a second violation, a fine, imprisonment, and/or corporal punishment 'not extending to life or limb' and total disbarment from the craft.

The appointment in 1663 of Roger L'Estrange as 'Surveyor of the Imprimery' was designed to strengthen these overlapping procedures. L'Estrange himself recommended the creation of this office and campaigned to be appointed to it by printing in 1663 a much admired pamphlet, *Considerations and Proposals In Order to the Regulation of the Press.*[61] He argued that the Stationers' Company had failed to eradicate offensive material and to supervise and control the number of printers. He promised to rectify this situation. He also set himself up as an arbiter of politically correct ideas, providing a lengthy list of abhorrent ideas and an 'Index' of books to be banned. He opposed reprinting books on grounds that the style of earlier writers was more powerful than that of recent authors; he had in mind the tracts and pamphlets from the Civil Wars, which he believed were still spreading sedition and blasphemy. In essence, he advocated a spy network of persons open to bribery and set out a program designed to impose thought control by rigorously limiting the number of presses and printers, and by tightening the surveillance of the craft.

The idea of creating an officer to supervise the press found favor, and Charles appointed L'Estrange to the new position, placed him under the supervision of the secretaries of state and ordered him to report to the king and the Privy Council.[62] L'Estrange received the authority to 'search for and seize' unlicensed books and papers, a responsibility that brought him into direct competition with the Stationers and the Secretaries of State. He also won the right to license books and tracts that did not already fall to one of the licensors, and hence licensed Care's *Weekly Pacquet of Advice from Rome*. Messengers of the press, called 'instruments for discovery and intelligence,' were appointed to assist him. Finally, L'Estrange received a royal patent for the sole right to print and publish news, and for the next three years he brought out *The Intelligencer, Published for the Satisfaction and information of the People* and *The Newes*, which he wrote with a verve that won admirers. L'Estrange, then, already had experience and success in publishing a newspaper before he undertook *The Observator* fifteen years later, in 1681.

Using these powers, L'Estrange embarked on a professional and personal vendetta against press people who criticized the government or Church. The *Calendar of State Papers* teems with general and specific search warrants that he requested, and stories abound of his discovering secret presses and tracking down and arresting printers, booksellers and publishers. It has been said that he 'gagged the London Press then, as it has never been gagged before or since,' that his 'animus and zeal' made press control 'vindictive,' 'partisan,' and 'menacing.'[63] L'Estrange was responsible for the financial ruin or lengthy imprisonment without trial of many press men and women.

II

With his nimble intellect, desire for recognition and need for money, Care maneuvered his way through the shoals of this print culture. He adapted style and subject to the market and from 1670 to 1678 wrote on nonpolitical subjects. His first two books were about women: in 1670 a translation of Agrippa's provocative sixteenth-century essay on women, *De Nobilitate & Praecellentia Foeminei Sexus*, whose title Care rendered as *Female Pre-eminence*, and in 1671 a collection of letters entitled *The Female Secretary: Or, Choice new Letters*, ostensibly designed to assist women of all classes in letter-writing.

Care's probable reason for translating Agrippa's essay is that he and his publishing associates hoped to profit from the well-established market for translations and at the same time exploit an earlier public interest in the 'woman question'.[64] The target was also the growing number of literate women in London; about 50 percent of women were literate by the end of the period.[65] To excite interest in his project, Care *invented* a literary quarrel in the English press. No such quarrel actually existed during the 1660s; indeed, of the approximately 154 tracts written by, for and about women only five, scattered over the decade, directly addressed the question of women's qualities.[66] Conspicuous among them was *A Discourse of Women Shewing Their Imperfections Alphabetically* (1662), a translation of a French book printed earlier in 1617. Moving through the alphabet, starting with avarice, bestiality, concupiscence and so on, the author (Jacques Olivier) showed that women excelled men in each of these undesirable qualities. Although the tract was not incompatible with commonly held views of women, its vituperation was extreme. Sensing this, the author expressed the hope that one day 'praises and encomiums' to women would be published. But no rebuttal appeared until Care picked up the gauntlet, eight years later. In a gesture of self-importance, Care described himself as a champion of women who wanted to 'put some check to the rude, undeserv'd reproaches cast on [them] by the Men.'[67]

His admirers reinforced this point, one crediting him with rescuing women from the 'foul aspersions' which soiled 'th'whole Sexes Honour' in the *Discourse of Women*.[68] These remarks made it seem as if a genuine literary quarrel was already in progress, when in fact nothing of the sort was true.

Care himself offered another reason why he translated Agrippa's essay; he said that he found the idea that women were superior to men challenging. 'Extravagant opinions' appeal to 'this giddy Age,' he added, perhaps hoping that good sales would follow. He expressed admiration for Agrippa's intellectual courage in handling an unpopular argument; 'like all great Wits,' Agrippa took pleasure 'in stemming the impetuous Tide of popular opinion...'[69] Care apparently wanted to cast himself in this mode of resisting popular opinion.

In an effort to secure a patron, Care boldly dedicated *Female Pre-eminence* to Queen Catherine. Of course, there is nothing unusual in an author dedicating a book to a wealthy person in hopes of creating a patron. But for someone like Care to dedicate his book to the queen was presumptuous; clearly, he hoped to win notice through the queen's patronage. A near-contemporary remarked that printing had put monarchs at the mercy of aspiring authors; by achieving royal favor, a 'Plebean... can Vault into the view of the Most Exalted Wits, and Most Renowned of Men.'[70] Brazenly, Care explained that since Agrippa had dedicated *his* book to a princess, he (Care) had 'derived an ambition' not to have 'less than Sovereign Patronage.'[71] With a flourish, Care declared that only the queen's stamp of approval on his book (like Charles's effigy on the nation's coin) would assure the public's acceptance of it. There is no evidence that Queen Catherine was ever aware of Care's book.

Care sought endorsements of his translation and persuaded four people of minuscule reputation to write testimonials. These 'puffers,' who cannot be positively identified, expressed unbounded admiration for Care's literary talent. One of them, Philogynes, commended Care's 'choice Words,' which he said were arranged in the 'most harmonious Cadencies,' and pronounced the whole a 'charming stile.' Lamenting the decay in 'our English Prose,' he declared that Care gave promise of restoring English literature. He continued that 'such fair Blossomes in your Youth presage/No common Fruit from your maturer Age.' [72] These commendatory verses are important for two reasons. First, they link Care to persons of literary pretensions, and through them to a literary circle of some kind. Second, they probably called Care to the attention of other writers of larger reputation and may help explain how he became acquainted with Dr Samuel Pordage and Elkanah Settle, both prolific authors and playwrights.

Hope of profit again drove Care and his associates to compile a collection of letters for women, which appeared the following year. Printed letter manuals had long been a popular literary genre, their roots reaching back to the familiar letters of Cicero, Petrarch and Erasmus, to 'courtesy' books (which flourished in the Italian Renaissance and migrated north), and to the equally venerable how-to books that dealt with such matters as midwifery and cooking.[73] In England books on the epistolary arts had enjoyed steady sales for almost a century, from 1586, when the first original letter manual in English, Angel Day's *The English Secretorie,* appeared.[74] In early seventeenth-century England James Howell's *Epistolae Hoelianae: Familiar Letters* is said to have made 'the penning of fictitious correspondence a fashionable art.'[75] A 1657 catalog of 'the most vendible books' in England included letter books.[76]

Care's collection of eighty-three letters pointedly designed only for women was the largest model letter manual of that type to date. Only one previous collection, Jacques DuBoscq's *Secretary of Ladies* (translated from French and first printed in England in 1638), offered letters for women alone. Although Care speaks of serving 'each degree of Women,' he specifically removed noble ladies from his audience and, with one exception, aimed his model letters at the 'Gentlewoman.' He explained that the 'unhappy Education or Inexperience' of these gentle ladies had failed to provide them with a 'competent Skill and Dexterity in managing the Pen.'[77] Although (as already noted) there was a steady improvement in female literacy in London during the Restoration, the general level of female education had declined.[78] Thus, even literate gentlewomen might find it difficult to frame letters to meet their epistolary needs, and it was this market that Care hoped to exploit.

The letters vary in character. Some are genuine sympathy letters appropriate to send on the death of a husband or child. But others were meant to amuse, surely men as well as women. The most entertaining is one advising a young woman how to reject a proposal of marriage from an old man. The letter-writer confesses that she would not mind being 'Mistress of a Fortune,' but at the same time she expresses belief in true love as the basis of marriage. She explains that she is unfit to be a nurse and also that she could not possibly go to bed with a man whom she might confuse with her grandfather. Advising her suitor to think about his approaching death, this artful lass voices the hope that he will remember her in his will.[79] The letter is frankly heartless and grossly materialistic. It is not written for a young woman seeking epistolary guidance on how to reject an aging suitor. It is meant to make the reader, whether a woman or a man, laugh at the aging swain and the heartless but romantic young miss.

Other letters on current social issues and attitudes hold interest for what they tell us about Care's intellectual vitality and acute social observation. They discuss the current fashion of wearing black patches (a 'monstrous fashion/till of late never practiced'), present arguments against women who are proud because they are chaste, offer pro and con arguments respecting learned women, describe the countryside (perhaps to demonstrate his descriptive talents), and discuss the Tunbridge Waters (perhaps to show Care's scientific bent). Bawdy verses about whether to love all women or to be faithful to one lady are included, aimed obviously at men.

A cover letter introduces the verses. The reader is invited to believe that it was written by a 'Gentlewoman,' otherwise unidentified. She introduces 'Mr. C' [i.e., Henry Care], a lover of poetry and of drink, as the author of the verses and suggests a comparison between him and the Water Poet, John Taylor. She explains that 'Mr. C' fell into a 'Fitt' when she 'did but deny him a little Drink' and began 'a scribbling with as much Rage & transport, as a Quaker comes to hold forth in.' After an hour 'his teeming fancy' had produced the verses. The 'Gentlewoman' sends them to her friend to amuse her: 'The simple Water-Poet mak[es] us sometimes as merry as the worthily admired Dryden.' This cover letter shows Care eager to situate himself in the limelight and to show that his talents extend to writing verse. He creates an opportunity to link his name with much better-known writers, John Taylor, the Water Poet and John Dryden. It is also worth noting that the remark about denying him drink spurring him on is the first indication that he was fond of spirits.

The concluding section of the letter manual, entitled 'Directions for the Indicting, Writing, and Superscribing Letters,' provides evidence of Care's skill as a teacher.[80] Saying that he had 'consulted the best Authors,' Care set down sound advice for the aspiring writer. In an age when flowery language was rampant, Care recommended plainness of expression, clarity, and brevity as 'necessary qualit[ies]' in good writing. Avoid 'tedious prefaces,... long Parentheses, wanton Circuits of Figures and Digressions' and popular turns of phrase, such as 'to value oneself upon such a thing;... to cajole; to engage in Amours.' Care praised wit and humor, in effect celebrating his own style of writing. 'The truth is,' he said, a 'certain briskness and Gayety of Humor' make prose sparkle, even when discussing the 'most important matters.' Such advice was as useful to a man as to a woman, again suggesting that Care's intended audience included men.

Care took an interest in marketing and sales. Remarking that a reader's 'tickling delight' in criticizing a book was sometimes the only thing that inspired a purchase, Care confided that criticism did not hurt so long as critics bought the book.[81] Francis Kirkman, an essayist, translator, publisher and bookseller, was the only other author to employ such a gambit.[82] Kirkman's and Care's use of such a tactic marks a new departure in press history.

The press run of Care's first two books is unknown, but scholars generally agree that the average run during the Restoration was between 1,000 and 1,500 copies.[83] Each book sold for one shilling, so if Care sold the lot, he and his publishing associates would have realized 2,000s–2,500s, or £100–£150. It was a sum of money worth striving for.

III

With these two publications Care's interest in writing about women came to an end. He turned to very different subjects, their variety attesting to his intellectual curiosity and interest in realizing a profit. In his third book, *The Grandeur And Glory Of France* (1673), Care dealt with a public issue for the first time. The Third Dutch War, begun the year before, aligned England with Catholic France against the Protestant Netherlands, England's perennial commercial rival. The war provoked criticism of Charles II, his Court and ministers, his naval and military leaders, and his foreign policy. The King's Declaration of Indulgence, issued two days before the declaration of war, had aroused deep misgivings because it suspended the execution of penal laws against Catholics and thereby hardened the fear that the Court was riddled with Catholics, and strengthened the suspicions of a secret deal between England and France. In this context, Care, noting the people's 'greediness after News,' offered 'Triumphant Portraitures' of the major leaders of France, which he declared filled a void in the literature on the war.[84] Attentive to marketing strategies, he and his publisher packaged the book attractively with a handsome portrait of Louis XIV. In 'To the Reader' Care promised that if this book were well received he would write another on the campaigns and the 'turns, counterturns and windings up of every Act... in this Tragedy.'

The Grandeur And Glory Of France shows Care's interest in research, his respect for evidence, and his keen observation of contemporary developments, strengths that would inform his later polemical writings. He insisted on the accuracy of his book, saying that he had consulted many authors and intimating that he had visited France.[85] Describing his book as a 'Landskip,' not an 'exact Map,' Care introduced the biographies with a comprehensive account of France, including geographical features. Anecdotes and stories vivified his stories of great French leaders.

Care shaped this book to ingratiate himself with the English Court. He chose as his dedicatee James, duke of Monmouth, Charles II's illegitimate and at this time beloved son. As captain general of the English forces, James fought under the French king and the French general Turenne against the Dutch in 1672 and according to all accounts distinguished himself. Care heaped praise on the young man, using the same kind of flowery and extravagant language that he had used in his dedication to Queen Catherine. The book reinforces Care's earlier monarchist leanings: he characterized the Dutch as insolent and perfidious, showered sympathy on the French king, government and ministers, and distanced himself from ill-informed 'little people,' who he predicted would criticize his book in 'their Coffee-Conventicles.' He described a royal court as the 'Epitome of a Kingdom,' which lesser mortals imitate, and the king as the 'soul' animating the Court. Despite these efforts, there is no evidence that anybody at Court noticed him or his book.

Care introduced himself in this book as 'H. Care, Gent.' Of course, he had no legal claim to this mark of gentle status. Forms of the title *gentleman*, whether legitimate or spurious, rarely appeared on printed tracts in Restoration England.[86] Although many people bestowed on themselves the title of gentleman,[87] possibly only one other *author*, Francis Kirkman, elevated himself to gentle status during this era. In a tract printed in 1673, Kirkman explained that he used the 'honoured Word Gent. to import that the Translator was a Gentleman' and declared that 'printing that word on the Title of the Book did as much to entitle him to Gentility, as if he had Letters Patents for it from the Heralds Office.' Indeed, it was 'more authentic because more publick.'[88] Care continued to use the press to improve his social standing. He subscribed himself as 'Gent.' again on the frontispiece of his history of England in 1678. He had some success with this ploy: at his trial in 1680 he was arraigned under the name of 'Henry Care, gent.,' the printed version of his trial in 1680 called him 'Gent.', and so too did a lengthy tract printed after his death. Also, Robert Watt listed him as such in his bibliography.[89]

Although Care's book on France was attractive, readable and instructive, it did not generate sufficient public interest to warrant the promised sequel. Care turned on a dime – the dedication of his next publication is dated 10 November 1673 – and for the first time took up a religious topic. *The Jewish Calendar Explained* aimed to assist persons of 'weak Capacities' to read the Bible with understanding and to grasp 'obscure' aspects of 'sacred Antiquity.'[90] Persons of 'weak capacities' would have found the topic demanding and the book difficult. Admitting a debt to 'the Judicious observations of the most Loyal, Learned, and Ingenuous George Wharton, Esq.,' Care explained at length the meaning of time, how ancient peoples reckoned time, and the significance of the Sabbath and numerous feast days. Along the way he underlined identities between Christianity and Judaism, illustrating his points with parallels in language. Emerging from these complexities at the end of the tract, he offered a sermonette advising readers to live each day as if it were their last.

The Jewish Calendar Explained shows Care's knowledge of biblical esoterica and his fascination with etymology. His interest in astronomy and astrology was reinforced by his praise of Wharton, an astronomer and author of almanacs from the 1640s through to the mid-1660s. The book is also noteworthy because the dedicatee was 'the worthily accomplished Mr. William Kiffin of London, Merchant' (1616–1701). Kiffin, a major spokesman for the Particular Baptists, had won a case brought against him in 1670 for keeping a conventicle and had extracted favors for the Baptist community from the court. A man of wealth who was well respected in mercantile circles, he had won the high regard of Charles II.[91] Care used the dedication to testify to his respect for Kiffin and thereby to counteract what he called 'some Immerited aspersions,' which remained unexplained. This dedication is the first hint of Care's sensitivity to the Nonconformist community.

Care turned next to another new topic: medicine, or 'physick.' Books on medicine were popular, figuring among the 'most vendible' books in 1657 and 1660 and were well represented in catalogs of books printed between 1666 and 1674.[92] No doubt Care and his publishers were trying to take advantage of this demonstrated interest. In 1676 he printed a broadside titled *A most Safe and Effectual Cure for the Rickets*,[93] using it to promote the sale of a medicine that 'both Cures and Prevents' rickets and was available only through him 'at the sign of the Blew Ball near King's Printing House in Black Fryer.' Bluntly entrepreneurial, Care chastised parents for 'loving Money too much and their Children too little' if they failed to buy his elixir. He also advertised as forthcoming two other books of his on medicine. One, to be entitled 'A Guide for Nurses wherein the Causes and Cure of all Diseases commonly incident to Children are plainly set forth and discussed' apparently fell by the wayside. The second, however, came out in 1676. Entitled *Practical Physick: Or, Five Distinct Treatises Of the most Predominant Diseases Of these Times*, it was a translation of a treatise on five major diseases written by Dr Daniel Sennert, a professor of medicine at the University of Wittenburg, that had originally appeared in Latin in 1637.[94] Again targeting an unlearned audience, Care told his readers that in the first three treatises he had 'epitomized' some of Sennert's complexities and removed the tedium to save them 'time and charge.' Care's labors no doubt were eased by a translation of Sennert's works by Nicholas Culpeper (1616–54), the well-known physician and writer on medicine and astrology, whose wife had published the translation posthumously, in 1674. Care was almost certainly accused of plagiarizing; the introduction to the last two treatises stresses that they were first translated by Culpeper, and when a second edition of *Practical*

Physick came out in 1679, Culpeper's name appeared along with Care's on the title page.

Care bestowed on himself a new persona: 'student of Physick and Astrology.' Used by Culpeper and other compilers of almanacs, the label elevated Care to their company.[95] It also linked him publicly with Henry Coley, the protégé of the well-known, now aging astrologer William Lilly.[96] In 1676 Care praised Coley's *Clavis Astrologiae Elimata* in a commendatory poem. Calling Coley his 'Honoured Friend,' Care wrote appreciatively of his work in astrology and made unmistakable his belief in the 'ancient glorious art' of astrology and in Providence.[97] This rather startling new self-identification was probably intended to herald some future writing that he had in mind. It also suggests the posturing of a young man on the make, anxious to identify himself with established writers and to ensure that his own work would find acceptance. Care never returned, at least in print, to the role of 'student of Physick and Astrology.' His interest was passing: he had an opportunity at Lilly's death in 1681 to memorialize the old man in the *Impartial Protestant Mercury*, but only a brief mention appeared.[98]

The years 1676 and 1677 were busy ones for Care. At the end of March 1676 he launched his first weekly newssheet, *Poor Robin's Intelligence*, a single sheet printed on both sides that appeared every Tuesday from 28 March 1676 until 2 October 1677, followed by two final issues, on 23 October and 6 November 1677. It was revived in 1679, when it had a run of ten weeks from September to November.[99] *Poor Robin's Intelligence* was printed, it said on the mast head, 'for the Profit of the Seller and the Pleasure of the Buyer.' Attributed to Care or William Winstanley (1628–98), the author of the original *Poor Robin* series,[100] which began in 1661 or 1662 and continued until 1776 at intervals, written by various people, this *Poor Robin's Intelligence* was almost certainly written by Care. The precise title does not appear in the list of Winstanley's works in the *Dictionary of National Biography,* but it is used again in 1688 for a series that Care indisputably wrote. A contemporary,

Edward Rawlins, stated flatly that Care 'wrote *Poor Robins Intelligence...*'[101] Finally, in the 1678 list of inhabitants, lodgers and recusants in St Sepulchre's Parish appears the entry 'Hen Car or poor Robin.'[102] I suspect that Care listed himself as 'Poor Robin' in an impulsive effort at humor and that he 'borrowed' the title to tap into an established genre in hopes of profit.

Poor Robin's Intelligence reported news from Europe, London and other parts of England in the form of amusing stories, many of them silly or bawdy or both. Stories about sexual escapades of gallants and loose women abound. Care demeaned women's intelligence, chastity and morality to win a laugh, suggesting that he did not hold women in high regard, as he would have readers of *Female Pre-eminence* believe.[103] Always reaching for a smile, Care provided 'Divertisements' instead of 'Advertisements' in *Poor Robin's Intelligence.*

This collection, though slight, was significant. It may have advanced Care's prospects with the Whigs. Rawlins, mentioned above, explained that Care wrote *Poor Robin's Intelligence* 'for the edification of the men of Smithfield' and that 'upon his success in those performances, [he] is now made one of the Secretaries of the Prince of Whigland,' that is, William Lord Russell, the leader of the Whigs in the House of Commons.[104] If the remark is true, it helps to explain how Care came to the attention of the Whigs and locates him in a circle about Lord William Russell.

The last thing Care printed before the Popish Plot broke was *The Plain Englishman's Historian.* Licensed in August 1678, this history was in the bookstalls at the same time as his tracts on the Plot. It is notable on two counts. First, the book was the first collaborative effort between Care and Langley Curtis, with whom he was to have a long-term relationship. Curtis, described as 'a middle-sized Fellow... the Bridge of his Nose somewhat lower than ordinary,' was a bookbinder at this time who also did some printing; we know for certain that in February 1669 he printed *The Quaker's Spiritual Cort proclaymed,* a book that marked him as a bold man, even a religious radical.[105] What brought Care and Curtis together is unknown, but, as already noted, the two men lived in the same neighborhood and perhaps met there.

The second significance of *The Plain Englishman's Historian* is that it gave Care experience in writing history, a new undertaking for him. Regretting the deplorable reading preferences of the young, Care eulogized the study of history as 'pleasant,' 'useful,' and inspiring. Promoting his book as a 'very brief Epitome of English history,' he promised his readers that it would 'neither weary nor... impoverish' them. It would offer the 'plain Englishman' who lacked the time for 'tedious reading' more knowledge of his nation's history than any other book of its kind, and at a cheaper price.[106] The book was not a success. Although Care took some pains to break up the chronological narrative, sometimes interlarding it with striking stories, the long chronological survey defeated him. As the account progressed, it sank into a bare recital of events without comment. Still, as we shall see, *The Plain Englishman's Historian* anticipated several features of the *Weekly Pacquet of Advice from Rome*.

Care had achieved modest success as a writer by the fall of 1678 when the Popish Plot broke and his career took off in another direction. Although only one of his publications, *Practical Physick*, had a second edition, *Poor Robins Intelligence* lasted for over a year. *The Female Secretary* did not fade entirely from sight; it was availabe at an auction in December 1685.[107] Bathusa Makin's reference to *Female Pre-eminence* in her *Essay To Revive the Antient Education Of Gentlewomen*, published in 1673,[108] brightened the visibility of that book. The republication in 1672 and 1673 of *A Discourse of Women Shewing Their Imperfections Alphabetically* and the reprinting of verse translations of Agrippa's *The Glory of Women* were no doubt connected with *Female Pre-eminence*. Further, at least seven defenses of women came on the market, the most notable being François Poulain de la Barre's *The Woman as Good as the Man: or, the Equality of Both Sexes* (1677) and James Norris's *Haec and Hic: or, The Feminine Gender More Worthy than the Masculine* (1683).[109] In some measure, then, Care was successful in creating a literary contretemps.

Care's choice of topics and publishing strategies reveal how an ambitious writer without academic or social standing managed to get into print. Taken together, his publications reveal a brash fellow without deep and abiding interests in any one subject. On the eve of the Popish Plot, the man who was to become a polemicist of uncommon skill, passion and coarseness was on the outer fringes of the London world of print – visible, to be sure, but certainly inconsequential.

The WEEKLY PACQUET
of
ADVICE from ROME

The Popish Plot and Exclusion Crisis turned Henry Care's life upside down. Within the context of these momentous events, Care achieved fame in some quarters and notoriety in others as the most persistent polemical voice against Catholicism, the Church of England, and the Stuart Court and, increasingly, as the most passionate proponent of Dissent, religious toleration, law (as he saw it) and exclusion. Shedding his former persona as champion of women, student in physic and astrology, and commentator on the French Court, Care took on a new identity as 'a Lover of true Protestants.'[1] This one lasted for the rest of his life. Continuing his early interest in history, he brought out every week but one, from 3 December 1678 to 13 July 1683, the *Weekly Pacquet of Advice from Rome,* a history of Roman Catholicism written for a popular audience presented in weekly installments and accompanied by the *Popish Courant,* a lighthearted sheet of jokes and stories demeaning popery and libeling contemporary persons and events.[2] Although neglected by historians, the

Weekly Pacquet was the most important popular history of the seventeenth century in England.

Moreover, the *Weekly Pacquet* was much more than a popular history. With the *Popish Courant*, it was a polemical missile that repeatedly hit high-placed targets with punishing force. Because of its popularity and effectiveness, it gave Care enormous visibility, bringing him to the notice of other print people, the royal Court, the Anglican Church, and Whig critics of State and Church. Throwing himself into partisanship for the first time in his career, Care built on the style and rhetorical devices that he had used earlier. Apparently, he initially aimed, in his *Weekly Pacquet* and *Popish Courant*, to do no more than defame popery and the Roman Catholic Church for the larger purpose of discrediting the idea of a Catholic's succeeding to the English throne. But in reaction to events and the policies and practices of monarchy and Church, within eight months Care had broadened his target to include the Court, the bench, Lord Chief Justice Scroggs and the Church of England. At the same time, he defended the Dissenting community and broached a theory of religious liberty that he articulated more fully later as a defender of James II's policy of religious toleration.

The *Weekly Pacquet of Advice from Rome* made Care the most important popular historian of early modern England. It was so central to Care's career and so important in the bitter press contest that it requires close attention.

I

Care was among the first to exploit in print the journalistic opportunities of the Popish Plot, and his immediate response paved the way for the appearance of the *Weekly Pacquet*. For several weeks in the early fall of 1678, 'government sources' had 'leaked' rumors about the tale Titus Oates and others had been pouring into the ears of the king and members of the Privy Council since late August. By 1 October newsletters were carrying reports to

THE
WEEKLY PACQUET

OF

Advice from Rome:

OR,

The Hiſtory of POPERY.

A Deduction of the
Uſurpations of the Biſhops of Rome,

AND

The ERRORS and SUPERSTITIONS

By them from time to time brought into the Church.

In the Proceſs of which,

The Papiſts *Arguments* are Anſwered, their *Fallacies* Detected,
their *Cruelties* Regiſtred, their *Treaſons* and *ſeditious Principles* Obſerved,
and the *whole Body of Papiſtry Anatomized.*

Perform'd by a SINGLE SHEET,

Coming out every *Friday,* but with a continual *Connexion.*

To each being added,

The POPISH COURANT:

OR,

Some occaſional Joco-ſerious Reflections on Romiſh Fopperies.

The Firſt Volume.

Sicut veſtra *intentio eſt* Semi-chriſtianos *quos* decipiatis *inquirere ; ſic* noſtra
eſt intentio, Pſeudo-chriſtianos *vos oſtendere ; ut non ſolum Chriſtiani peritiores
vos* Convincendo *prodant, ſed & imperitiores vos* Cavendo *proficiant.*

London : Printed for , and are to be ſold by *Langley Curtis,* on *Ludgate-hill,*
either ſingly any Sheet by it ſelf, or *Whole Sets,* containing them
all together ſince they firſt came out. 1 6 7 9.

Title page of Henry Care's *Weekly Pacquet of Advice from Rome*, volume 1. Care's most
widely known publication appeared every week but one from 3 December 1678 to
13 July 1683. The *Popish Courant*, a sheet of jokes and stories demeaning popery and
libeling contemporary persons and events, accompanied it.

counties outside of London that a horrific Catholic conspiracy, orchestrated by Jesuits and blessed by Rome, was under way to murder Charles II, install the Catholic duke of York on the throne and restore Catholicism to England.[3] Although some skeptics dismissed the stories as inspired by Charles II's Lord Treasurer, Thomas Osborne, earl of Danby, to detract attention from his own political problems, many people were deeply troubled by the tales, their anxieties magnified by the government's arresting priests and disarming papists without giving a reason.[4]

Reports of Catholic plots were not new, nor was the belief in their reality.[5] The fact that similar rumors had circulated in the spring of 1678 fed the gossip in the fall.[6] But in the fall of 1678 conditions promoted public hysteria. Faith in the government had been severely compromised during the 1670s by domestic and foreign policies, which the press, although technically under the authority of the Licensing/Printing Act, exposed. Cynicism, confusion and suspicion were widespread.[7] Charles II's critics feared that his foreign policy concealed a conspiracy to link England with Catholic France, impose an absolute form of government and restore Catholicism.[8] The pamphlet *England's Appeal From The Private Cabal At White-Hall To The Great Council of the Nation, The Lords and Commons In Parliament Assembled* written by the Dutchman Pierre Du Moulin and in circulation in London during 1672, hammered home the idea that English religion and economic interests were ill served by fighting on the side of Catholic France against Protestant Holland. Anxieties were further exacerbated when, following peace with Holland in 1674, the government failed not only to pursue the expected war against France but also to disband the army raised for that war.[9] London merchants and artisans were drawn into opposition to the king because of French competition and erratic financial strategies, like the Stop of the Exchequer in 1674.[10] In addition, the publicly acknowledged conversion to Catholicism of James, duke of York, the king's brother and, absent legitimate royal offspring, heir to the throne, fanned suspicion and censure. Another reason for disgust was the

Court's effort to influence members of Parliament through bribes and threats, an approach developed by Danby.[11] Country party members, led in the House of Lords by Anthony Ashley Cooper, first earl of Shaftesbury, and in the House of Commons by his protégé, William Lord Russell, also aired their own charges and suspicions. Because of this immediate background, the rumors that flew around London and the countryside in September and October were all the more believable.

In the months before the Popish Plot broke the press played a part in arousing fears of Catholic-inspired disasters. *Trap ad Crucem; or, The Papists Watchword*, a collection of unverified statements and depositions that charged Catholics with torching London, was published in 1670. It terrified the unsophisticated, and it and other lurid pieces, such as *London Flames*, help to explain why Oates's outrageous stories were so readily accepted.[12] Andrew Marvell, a poet and parliamentarian from Hull, aired arguments in his *Seasonable Argument to persuade all the Grand Juries in England to petition for a New Parliament* that became part of the national hysteria (1677). A severe and deeply embarrassing assault on the Court party, it listed the names of members who allegedly had received bribes or otherwise disgraced themselves in the period 1661–72. It so angered the court that a reward of £200 was offered to identify the author.[13] Marvell's *Account of the Growth of Popery and Arbitrary Government in England*, also published in 1677, lifted the attack even higher, claiming that the Court was involved in a scheme to change the monarchy into an absolute tyranny, return the Church of England to popery and place the nation under French influence.

Marvell's *Growth of Popery* drew a response from L'Estrange. In *The Parallel; or, An Account of the Growth of Knavery* he argued that the reformers of 1677 were counterparts to those of 1641 and bluntly declared that Marvell's *Growth of Popery* was sedition clothed in religion, the first link in a chain of events leading to the nation's misery.[14] He continued his rebuttal in 1678 in *The Reformed Catholique or The True Protestant*, stressing that the

Dissenters' railing against popery concealed their real target, the Church of England. Excoriating their clamor for religious liberty as 'frivolous' and 'utterly unlawful,' L'Estrange maintained that if toleration were granted, Dissenters would impose a tyranny on all who disagreed with them.[15] These points were reinforced in his *Tyranny and Popery...* (1678), in which he insisted that Presbyterianism, like popery, was 'Inconsistent' with monarchy. What difference was there, he inquired, 'betwixt the Papal Tyranny... and the Presbyterial?'[16] Although Care made no reference to this press warfare, it is reasonable to think that he was aware of it. The lines of argument over which he and L'Estrange would battle were already being drawn.

Care's *Character of A Turbulent, Pragmatical Jesuit and Factious Romish Priest*, licensed on 15 October 1678, was among the first printed tracts to play off the stories about a plot.[17] Langley Curtis, the publisher with whom Care had already established a connection, published it.[18] Two days later, on 17 October, when the discovery of the body of Sir Edmund Berry Godfrey, the magistrate before whom Oates and Bedloe had made their depositions about the plot, transformed the rumors into 'political dynamite,'[19] another tract directly related to the plot appeared: Reverend Gilbert Burnet's *Letter written upon the Discovery of the late Plot*. People rapidly came to believe that Catholics had murdered Godfrey to silence him. Two weeks later Care was ready with a second piece, this one relating to Godfrey's alleged murder: *An Elegie Sacred to the Memory of Sir Edmund-bury Godfrey Knight*, also published by Curtis.[20] By then the press was teeming with printed sermons and pamphlets excoriating the plot and Roman Catholics.

Character and *Elegie* are important for understanding Care and the print world. First, they show Care using the press, as he had done before, to exploit public interest in topics that he perceived were 'hot' and would generate sales. Second, *Character* presented him as a man violently opposed to Roman Catholicism and deeply knowledgeable about it, an entirely new posture for him, demonstrating his intellectual malleability and agility. Third, these two pieces confirm Care's talent at adapting his style to the subject and the need of the moment. Care's *Elegie* was a restrained lament in verse form, in which he described Godfrey as a 'Loyal Patriot' whom 'a weeping Nation shall just Honours pay.' By contrast, *Character* attacked Jesuits in extreme and unguarded language. Devising memorable analogies, Care vividly portrayed Jesuits as the Pope's learned 'Janizaries,' who insinuated themselves into royal cabinets as 'gently as malevolent Stars dart their influence, or blasting Mildews slide into the bosom of a flower.'[21] The common popish priest was just as bad; he 'uses an unknown tongue, transacts most of his business in Hugger-Mugger, comes in secretly, and crawls up and down in Corners like a Serpent.'[22] In its virulence against the Jesuits *Character* anticipated the *Weekly Pacquet*. Fourth, *Character* and *Elegie* no doubt brought Care and Curtis into a still closer relationship – it must have pleased both of them that *Elegie* had a second edition in 1678 – and strengthened the foundation for their partnership.

II

The *Weekly Pacquet* was launched by Care and Curtis on Tuesday, 3 December 1678, the day when London saw the first execution at Tyburn, of a man Oates had accused: Edward Coleman, secretary to the duke and duchess of York. Thus, the first issue reached the city's booksellers at a propitious moment for sales. Indeed, immediate events had created a context favorable for the *Weekly Pacquet*'s introduction. Since convening on 21 October, parliament had engaged in a frenzy of activity, summoning Oates and Bedloe to testify, barring all Catholics but the duke of York from the two houses, trying (unsuccessfully) to call up the militia and bringing in articles of impeachment against Danby. The trial of Coleman in the venerable Westminster Hall before a special commission presided over by Scroggs[23] and the anticipation of trials to come of

Jesuit priests accused of high treason[24] fanned hysteria about the Popish Plot. So, too, did a multitude of sermons, tracts and pamphlets decrying and explaining the plot, the 'murder' of Godfrey, the history of the Roman Catholic Church and the papist doctrine of 'king-killing.'[25]

In this setting the *Weekly Pacquet* initially met with the government's approval. Its purpose was entirely suitable. Proposing to present an account of 'the Usurpations of the Bishops of Rome,' it promised to unfold and answer the arguments of papists and to record their 'Cruelties... Treasons and Seditious Principles.' All this was to be published each week, 'but with a continual Connexion.' The *Popish Courant*, described as 'Some occasional Joco-serious Reflections of Romish Fopperies,' would accompany the *Weekly Pacquet*.[26] In the early winter of 1678, who could object to a project such as this? No one! In fact, it may be that Care, who had tried earlier to identify himself with the Stuart Court, hoped that this new project would advance his prospects there. In any case, the *Weekly Pacquet* won a license from L'Estrange, but not without (so Care later charged) Care and Curtis's paying him five shillings instead of six pence each month from December 1678 until the lapse of the Licensing/Printing Act at the end of May 1679.[27]

Care later took credit for conceptualizing and inaugurating the *Weekly Pacquet*. In a contentious public statement at the time he and Curtis parted company, in August 1682, Care declared that he 'alone began' the *Weekly Pacquet* and implied that he had initiated arrangements with Curtis to publish and sell it.[28] These points Curtis never denied. Furthermore, after the break with Curtis, Care, acting as if he owned the *Weekly Pacquet,* made arrangements with two successive printers to reproduce it. In addition, a contemporary described Care as 'the Author and Beginner' of the *Weekly Pacquet*.[29] Care's earlier ambition, aggressiveness and interest in humor make it reasonable to credit him with the idea of a weekly containing serious history accompanied by a sheet of amusing, politically pointed remarks.

Care's proprietary claim merits attention for two reasons. One, it shows that no political figure was involved in initiating the project. Care's relationship with Whigs in and out of Parliament and in the press came later. Two, it opens an interesting question: what moved him, a quick-study artist who went from topic to topic, a person of several persona and multiple interests, to choose on his own the historical mode and undertake the awesome task of researching and writing about 1600 years of religious history? How did he know what to do and where to start? After all, he might have adopted other approaches to engage in the controversy, such as pamphleteering. There are several possible answers. First, Care's writing the *Plain Englishman's Historian* a few months before inaugurating the *Weekly Pacquet* gave him useful experience in writing history. He had gained practice in reading rapidly about unfamiliar topics, abstracting what he had read and writing up the results 'as in miniature' or 'as in a landskip.'[30] He had used anecdotes and two- or three-word summaries to describe personalities or issues, devices he carried over to the *Weekly Pacquet*. This training may also have shown him the attractions of historical research, discovery, reflection and composition. His experience with the law and lawyers would have reinforced respect for evidence and for a logical, rational approach to history. It is reasonable to think that a highly intelligent man like Care might find the craft of history intellectually satisfying and that he wanted a project in which he could expand this newly discovered interest.

Second, classical and humanist texts, with which he had shown ample familiarity during the 1670s, may have played a part in introducing him to history. They would have familiarized him with questions of historical evidence, objectivity and 'truth' in historical scholarship. They also would have shown him how useful knowledge of history could be as instruction and inspiration. Third, contemporary histories emphasized the didactic role of history,[31] and Care's reading of them may have given him the idea of using a historical approach. His major purpose, he said, was to fortify unlettered Protestants against the blandishments of smooth-talking

Jesuits, 'to furnish meaner Capacities with... Arguments... [that] every Judicious Christian' should have.[32] The history of popery and Roman Catholicism, unfolded over a long timeline, would add weight to assertion and reason. No other approach could do that so effectively.

Fourth, as a writer keenly alive to popular currents in the book trade and keenly interested in turning a profit, Care would have been aware of the popularity of historical manuals and histories on all subjects and hopeful of taking advantage of that interest. Histories and manuals, according to Daniel Woolf, appeared in 'bewildering number' after 1660; the market for them was 'virtually limitless.'[33] Two histories of popery, one published in 1674, the other in 1677, almost certainly provided Care with data. Historical manuals would have been particularly useful to a fledgling historian like Care, who took chronology very seriously. *The Historian's Guide*, printed in 1676, provided a chronology of world events, and its companion piece, *England's Remembrancer*, a chronology of English events. Cheap, short epitomes and abridgments of history also flooded the market; they were, in Woolf's words, 'perhaps the most successful genre of history-writing.'[34] Care himself vigorously disparaged epitomes and abridgments, which shows, of course, that he knew about them. Taken together, these considerations may help explain how and why Care conceived the idea of writing a history of popery. His preparation for this massive project was thin. That he nevertheless launched it underscores his brash self-confidence and quick intelligence.

The *Weekly Pacquet* marked a new departure in press history and in the writing of history. First, the *Pacquet* was the first *weekly* publication to appear at the time of the Popish Plot. It anticipated by seven months all the other serials; the *Domestick Intelligence*, published by Benjamin Harris and regarded as the first 'real' newspaper, did not start until 7 July 1679.[35] Second, although it was a serial in the sense that it appeared weekly, the *Weekly Pacquet* differed from earlier and later serials in that it was not a newspaper or newsbook – it did not report foreign and domestic *news* – but rather a kind of journal offering a history of Christianity, accompanied by a sheet of jokes and ribald commentary. Third, the *Weekly Pacquet* was the first history of any subject to be presented in installments, in effect, as a series of short tracts. Fourth, although Care was not the first author nor the only one during this crisis to target an unlearned middle- to lower-class audience and write for them in a learned fashion, nor the first to write history aimed at that group, his emphasis on the 'vulgar' was so strong as to set the *Weekly Pacquet* apart from others. Fifth, Care used the *Popish Courant* to tell funny stories and make political jokes, first at the expense of Catholic clerics and doctrine, then, within six or seven months, at the expense also of men and policies of the State and the Anglican Church. Political humor certainly did not originate with Care – it appeared in the late sixteenth century in the Marprelate tracts, in pamphlets during the Civil Wars, and in exchanges in the early 1670s – but he was among the first to bring political humor into a much broader arena, the world of journalism, and use it to discredit persons and institutions. Without question, he was the first to link a joke sheet that became pointedly critical of the establishment to a sober, pseudo-learned history. Part of his purpose in doing so was to reach a broad audience and thereby increase sales.

Sixth, the *Weekly Pacquet* was published on a continuous basis longer than any other Whig serial during the Popish Plot and Exclusion Crisis. It appeared week after week (but one) for four and a half years, numbering 240 *Pacquets* (twenty-two of them under a slightly different title) and 240 *Courants* (also with variant titles).[36] When bound, these issues filled five volumes in four sturdy books totaling 1,920 pages. By reason of the quantity of material, its unique format, and its targeted audience, *The Weekly Pacquet of Advice from Rome; or, The History of Popery* was the most important of all the 'popular' histories.

Care and Curtis followed several strategies aimed at establishing the *Weekly Pacquet*, turning a profit, and keeping and expanding a readership, strategies that reveal aspects of Restoration print culture. First, the title was no doubt designed to attract readers. The words *Weekly Pacquet* would have had a familiar ring; over the past few years several pamphlets with the word *Pacquet* in their titles had appeared.[37] The words *from Rome* intimated that the author was writing from that iniquitous city of papists, which added an exotic and provocative note. The subtitle conveyed a seriousness of purpose: to present a *history* of the *Usurpations* of the *Bishops of Rome*, a topic of enormous public interest. Second, the initial decision to print the *Pacquet* anonymously may have been a marketing strategy rather than an attempt to avoid reprisal or licensing fees. Care explained later that he had hoped that the absence of the author's name on the title page would assure the 'better Esteem of the Book, and so render it more serviceable.'[38] This explanation surely concealed the fear that his name would detract from sales by revealing an author without formal education who lacked the credentials of a historian of religion. Why would an educated person buy a history of the Catholic Church written by such a person? Why should an uneducated person trust his account? Concealing his authorship was a way of circumventing these negatives.

A third marketing tactic was to price the weekly single sheets at one penny and from time to time to bind the sheets together into a volume selling for one shilling.[39] This 'Pamphlet-course' had numerous advantages. As Care explained, it assured that the *Pacquet* would 'most likely fall into Vulgar hands' and be read by people 'who have most need of such Assistance.'[40] A compelling proof that the single sheets did so is their present-day rarity[41] and the fact that Care and Curtis decided to reprint them in a single volume. Care's sensible assumption that the marginally educated would prefer a short piece to a learned, lengthy book is reflected in a contemporary comment on the reading habits of the 'vulgar': 'Two sheets is enough in all Reason for a Dose for the Strongest Constitution, and one for the Weaker.'[42] Another advantage was that the single sheets put Care's views – and his name too, after it was known for sure that he was the author – before the public regularly, thereby stimulating interest in him and his ideas. The bound volumes reinforced that interest by making the sheets available in a more permanent form. In addition, the procedure multiplied profits; Carolyn Nelson and Matthew Seccombe concluded that profit was a major reason for the popularity of the strategy among press people.[43]

A fourth tactic that Care used was the direct sales pitch. As he had done earlier, Care entreated readers to buy the *Weekly Pacquet*. Appealing to their sense of responsibility to inform themselves about popery, he promised that he would complete the 'whole Anatomy-Lecture on Popery' if they bought the *Pacquet*, and he implied that if they did not, the project would fail. In his brash way, Care said that the investment was small, adding that most men spent a penny a week on less worthwhile things.[44] Fifth, Curtis assisted in the sales effort by advertising: in each bound volume was an announcement that copies of all single sheets and of the successive bound volumes were available at his shop. And advertisements for the *Weekly Pacquet* also appeared regularly in other Curtis publications. Sixth, if common practice was followed, some single sheets were scattered about the streets of London free of charge, posted on lampposts and in doorways, and left in coffeehouses and taverns for people to pick up. Other sheets and bound volumes were carried by peddlers to places outside of London.[45]

A seventh tactic was to target a wide, diverse, even national, audience. Care signaled his hopes for a national audience by addressing the first issue to his 'Countrymen.'[46] Underlining the seriousness of his intention, within three weeks of launching the *Pacquet*, Care adjusted the print schedule because of competition from an unidentified source. Explaining that 'divers Protestant-Gentlemen in most counties of this Kingdom' wanted to buy the *Weekly Pacquet*, Care shifted the day of publication from Tuesday to Friday to avoid 'prejudice to other Intelligence.'[47] This concern over a national audience stayed with him: he continued to address his countrymen and expressed pleasure over their interest.[48] That he and his *Weekly Pacquet* were a presence in several areas we have already noted.

Care identified other specific groups that he hoped to reach on a national level. After initially discounting the 'learned,' he was soon hoping to remind 'better-learned Protestants' of what they might already know.[49] He referred to the 'satisfaction' he took in knowing that 'learned' and 'Sober persons' looked with 'favour' on his work.[50] He also believed that the 'young clergy' of the Church of England would find his 'Discourse... not unacceptable.'[51] When he first started the *Weekly Pacquet*, he even aspired to persuading 'modest and impartial Romanists' of the truth of his account and occasionally referred to Catholics.[52] Interestingly, his announced audience outside of London was socially upscale and literate; apparently Care did not expect to win readers from among yeomen, tradesmen and husbandmen, whose literacy rate was low.[53]

His principal focus, however, was London and Westminster. He paid special attention to members of Parliament and was reviled by his enemies for dedicating volume 2 of his *Pacquet*s to them in the autumn of 1680 and for appealing to them for protection and assistance. But above all, Care aimed his *Pacquet* at young middle- and lower-class Protestants, singling out 'all true English Protestants' or 'unbyassed Protestant Readers' and specifying 'the Younger or more Mechanick sort' of 'middle or meaner Rank.' Using language that had appeared in *Plain Englishman's Historian*, Care avowed that he hoped to reach the 'plain honest-hearted Protestant Reader,' who knew nothing of the intricacies of religious controversy, and to fortify him with knowledge to defend Protestantism. His *Pacquet* was for persons without money to buy, leisure to read, or education to understand learned and 'tedious' books; it did not compete with such books, Care said.[54]

Care's emphasis on the 'Younger or more Mechanick sort' of 'middle or meaner Rank' invites two questions: who exactly did he have in mind, and why did he focus on that group? Care no doubt meant principally apprentices and journeymen among the artisans and tradesmen in London. Figures on the number of journeymen in mid-Restoration London are not available, but social historians reckon that there were approximately 30,000 apprentices out of a total urban population of about 550,000.[55] Apprentices thus constituted about 5 percent of the city's population. Together with journeymen they would have totalled approximately 45,000 persons, a respectable pool of potential readers. The social origins of apprentices varied. For the years immediately preceding the Restoration, about 18 percent were sons of gentlemen or esquires, about 23 percent came from yeomen families, and about 43 percent were artisans, professionals or businessmen.[56] Clearly, the 'Mechanick sort' did not come from the bottom of the social scale. (In the absence of research on the point for Restoration London, I have assumed that the pattern did not change greatly.) This meant that such men could afford to pay a penny a week for the *Weekly Pacquet*. Although the average wage for London journeymen and apprentices in late Stuart England is not available, the daily wage rate for building craftsmen in southern England was between eighteen to twenty pence, or approximately £22 to £23 a year.[57]

A sizable portion of London's tradesmen and craftsmen were able to read. Their literacy rate – 78 percent in London, 63 percent in Middlesex – was much higher than elsewhere in the country.[58] Literacy, however, varied with specific occupation and residence. For example, London apothecaries and grocers were 100 percent literate, whereas blacksmiths, bricklayers and joiners were only 62 percent literate. The highest degree of literacy was among Nonconformists and those living in the center of the city, with the rate dropping sharply in the outer parishes or suburbs.

Care could count on his 'Mechanicks' being interested in politics. Actively involved in the lower reaches of city government, apprentices voted in ward elections and served as constables, watchmen, beadles and militiamen. They were already politically conscious before the frenzy generated by the Popish Plot and Exclusion Crisis. They predominated in the crowd demonstrations and other projects organized by both Whigs and Tories, activities which reinforced their interest in public issues and hence in buying printed matter. Further, Care's targeted audience was among those who frequented the taverns and the new coffee houses in both London and the counties, where politics was a usual topic of conversation. These data suggest that, while the *Weekly Pacquet* was a 'popular' weekly that avowedly addressed a non-elite audience, it was a potentially lucrative undertaking for Care and Curtis.[59]

Although Care assumed that his 'Mechanick sort' were all 'true English Protestants,' there was, in fact, as Tim Harris has demonstrated, nothing monolithic about their political and religious inclinations. Since the early years of the Restoration, this group had reflected and expressed differences over such issues as the Church of England and its relationship to other Protestant denominations, taxes and the moral degeneracy of the royal Court.[60] The attitude they had in common was fear of popery. Thus, there was an initially favorable response to Care's *Pacquet*. But dislike of popery did not automatically translate into a specific political or religious commitment, and as the *Weekly Pacquet* came to be identified with radical Whiggery and criticism of the Church of England, it antagonized Tory Anglicans among Care's 'true English Protestants.' Care's unsophisticated equation of class and religion was one reason for his ultimate failure.

Why did Care focus on middle- and lower-class groups when earlier he had aspired to become a client of Queen Catherine and the duke of Monmouth? There were several reasons. First, the social background of Care's major audience was similar to his own, and their residence in London and Westminster made them his neighbors. Yet Care stood apart from this audience because of his learning, intelligence and writing skills. Having mastered classical literature, Latin, scholastic philosophy, Renaissance Humanism, Catholicism, Anglicanism and sectarianism not as a scholar but as a journalist, he was aware that persons whose education was minimal could not readily understand those matters.[61] Although Care protests too much that he had no 'base Interest, or Vanity' or 'low aim at paltry Profit' in writing the *Weekly Pacquet*,[62] one should grant that he was genuinely concerned for people whose slim education made 'celebrated' volumes of history 'fruitless.' Care regarded his *Weekly Pacquet* in part as a means of empowering the 'Mechanick Sort' with an understanding of the history, religion, law and politics of elite culture. This sense of social responsibility undergirds some of the books that he published in the 1670s.

A second reason for focusing on persons from the 'middle and lower ranks' was no doubt the hope of profit. If a sizable portion of approximately 45,000 'Mechanick sort' purchased the *Weekly Pacquet*, Care would make a tidy sum of money. He appealed directly to a group that many writers slighted or ignored. When the press controversy began to heat up in 1680, Roger L'Estrange expressed disdain for the 'vulgar,' writing that the people were 'to be menag'd, with Invisible Wires like Puppets; and not to know either the Why or the What of things, but to do as they are bid.'[63] Such a comment offered a beautiful opening for Care.

Another consideration was connected with his criticism of the Catholic Church, namely, that papists aimed to keep the common people ignorant of Christian history and doctrine. Using the English translation of the Rhenish Bible as an example in point, Care railed against its use of 'uncouth words and phrases,' which the 'common Englishman understands no more than Arabic.' As a result, he said, the common people regarded the Bible as 'hard and obscure' and were made dependent upon 'dumb images or dumb priests.'[64] Later he leveled the same charge against the Church of England. By seeking to inform the unlearned, Care defied the established Church, whether Catholic or Anglican. At the same time he underlined his belief, stressed at length in *The Darkness of Atheisme* (1683), that a mind informed by reason was essential to a person's religious experience and belief.

In sum, Care's intended audience included country gentlemen throughout the nation, 'some clergy' of the Church of England, 'better-learned Protestants,' whose understanding would be reinforced and above all, 'true Protestants' of 'middle or meaner Rank' in London and Westminster.

III

Since Care's avowed major target was Everyman, the question is, Did he really try to reach Everyman? The answer is yes, in both the *Weekly Pacquet* and the *Popish Courant*, as well as in many of his tracts. His attention to order, syntax and clarity of expression – the precepts of good writing outlined earlier in *The Female Secretary* – along with the rhetorical devices he employed, would have had wide appeal to readers, whatever their social standing or educational background. This fact warns one against exaggerating the distance between elite and popular culture in the Restoration. Yet, certain stylistic features seem to have been fashioned with the marginally educated in mind. Such strategies help us to understand how Care's rather esoteric topic would have appealed to the undereducated and how the practice of reading history penetrated the middle and lower classes.

Although Care made no effort to lighten the burden of comprehension by using pictures, a device that R.W. Scribner maintained was the most important one an author can employ to reach the so-called common man,[65] he was attentive in other ways to the needs of uneducated readers. Care almost always translated into English the many Latin (and occasional Greek) phrases and words that he used.[66] Anticipating confusion, Care frequently clarified terms or concepts that he thought might puzzle his readers. For example, he explained that *fifth century* refers to the years *before* AD 500.[67] He took the time to define concepts, such as annates and words like *Homeousians*.[68] Care's interest in the etymology of words also served the minimally educated. For example, he was at pains to decipher the word *cross*, supplying four meanings. Citing Erasmus, he ridiculed Catholics for maintaining that the wood of the cross was sacred because Jesus hanged on it, saying that then everything else Jesus touched should be sacred, including, he delighted in pointing out, Christ's ass, Jews and Judas.[69] The example shows Care combining etymology and the lessons of a famous Renaissance figure with ribald humor. Who could fail to respond, whether unlearned or learned? Such devices accomplished two ends: they informed the minimally educated and also established Care's own *bona fides*.

In still other ways Care showed his concern to reach the common folk. It was his practice (as it was that of other Restoration authors) to address his audience directly, drawing them into a close relationship with him. 'The Reader is to be reminded...,' he wrote. 'Let the Pious Reader observe...,' he counseled. Guiding his readers, he exhorted them in a charming turn of phrase to 'Prick up the Ears of your Attention.'[70] Encouraging readers to bear up under the weight of details, Care said that he took no delight in 'wearying' them but advised that he would rather 'seem tedious to the Curious, than defective to the Judicious,'[71] a comment suggesting that he had several audiences in mind. Further, he supplied a table of contents for each bound volume of *Pacquet*s except volume 5. His simple, short tables would have helped readers to locate quickly subjects of interest and also, significantly, would have drawn attention to topics he wanted them to notice. For a person whose knowledge of the esoteric subjects of the *Weekly Pacquet* was slight such assistance would have been invaluable, and it would have helped the sophisticated reader as well. Similarly, Care's practice of providing frequent summaries or overviews would have helped all readers, whatever their social or educational level. He used an arresting analogy to invite the reader to pause and reflect on his account of the first 600 years of the Catholic Church. Like 'weary Travellers' who 'in the heat of Summer,' having climbed halfway up a mountain, stop and look back and then, 'with renewed vigour, and brisker pace, ascend the rest of the mountain,' he wrote, so his readers too should recollect what they had learned.[72] Showing concern that his readers should not lose their way in moving from a discussion of events on the Continent to a discussion of events in England, he signaled, 'We shall... here make an Halt, and (according to our Method) retire homewards' to take up what had happened there in the meantime. To assist further, he obligingly gave the exact number of the *Pacquet* in which he had digressed to Continental affairs.[73]

Care was also attentive to chronology, which, he opined, was the 'only Thred to guide us in the Labyrinths of History.' Counseling his readers time and again not to forget 'to keep pace with us in time-reckoning,' he warned that 'without keeping time, there is little good Musick to be expected.'[74] Changing the metaphor, he declared that forgetting chronology is like putting to sea 'without either Compass or Rudder.'[75] But his history was not a mindless narrative of one thing after another in chronological sequence. Nor was he a slave to chronology. When he heard that some Catholic readers were unsatisfied by his account of a point, he decided to revisit the issue: 'I love Order as well as any Man,' he wrote, 'but had rather make bold with Method, than not do my business.'[76] Again he would tell his readers that he would 'briefly speak of' a particular issue, in this case the Pope's claim that he alone had the authority to declare persons saints, and here he went on to say that he was 'anticipating History in point of time, rather than break... the thred of our discourse.'[77] Paying attention to chronology, however, went beyond a concern for clarity; it was directly connected to one of his main theses: that the Catholic Church and doctrine were entirely different in modern times from their primitive origins. By using 'good Records and Authors' and keeping the chronology straight, Care promised to map 'the respective times of alteration [in the Catholic Church's original practice] with the circumstances.'[78] This essential element in his argument was inextricably linked with his methodological assumption and practice.

Care used various stylistic devices to enliven his text. First, popular or common expressions appeared in the serious, sober *Weekly Pacquet* just as they did in the *Popish Courant*; they gave the text a sense of immediacy and relevance. For example, Care dismissed a person who disagreed with him with the question, 'Can any Man be of so thick a Skul as once to imagin...?'[79] Criticizing Roman Catholics for disrespecting the Bible, he remarked that they made the Scripture into a 'Nose of Wax'; that is, they gave it any meaning they chose.[80] Denigrating the papacy, he described one of the

Popes as a 'most holy Infallible Ghostly Father fit for a Bib and Muckinder'; that is, he had the intelligence of a child.[81] These everyday expressions, unheard of in conventional histories, testify to Care's way of lightening the text and thereby drawing along his readers. His colloquialisms have the added benefit of revealing something about ordinary conversation in the Restoration.

Second, proverbs, epigrams and verse also animated Care's text, providing variety and offering refreshment to the reader. A proverb of special interest to this study was a favorite of 'Bookmen': 'The drier the Subject, the more Brains are required for Sauce.' Care used the proverb to ridicule the efforts of Catholic Churchmen to prove the existence of purgatory.[82] He left it to his readers to infer the superiority of his brain power in dealing with the complicated history of popery. A striking epigram derogated in amusing terms papal rule in Rome by connecting the origins of that rule, not with the biblical story, but with the founding of the city by Romulus, who had sucked a wolf.[83] Care obligingly translated the epigram from Latin into English so that no reader could miss the point. One of the most effective verses focused on 'Abhorrers Abhorr'd,' those persons who opposed petitions for calling a Parliament in the winter of 1680. In it Care addressed them as 'Monsters more base than Africk can affor'd' and advised them to 'Be gone... to France, and there enslave/Yourselves and Spurious off-spring.'[84] Written at the end of December 1680, when the fortunes of Whig Exclusionists were at a low ebb after the failure of the second Exclusion Bill the month before and leaders of Parliament were frantically seeking ways to force Charles to call a new Parliament, this piece shafted the Court and Tories by implying that they lacked understanding of English freedoms and linking them with France and 'Popish Bondage.' No reader could have missed the point.

In one instance, however, Care offered a ballad that defeated his audience. Presented in 'Oldfashioned Rhymes' and described as 'an Ancient Poeticial description of the Babylonish Whores Pedigree,' this poem evoked the image of the 'Silver Tibris' swimming in

'Golden Sands' and told how once proud spirits had come to 'change Caesars for Fryars, a monarch for a Monk.'[85] People contemned the poem, apparently because of its obliqueness, and Care replied to the criticism; his response is interesting because of the light it sheds on his personality and his impatience with less learned critics. 'What Law,' he inquired disdainfully, 'obliges an Author to find his Readers Brains, as well as Rhymes?' All that was needed to understand the poem was 'a Competent Acquaintance with Scripture, and a very little History.' Showing his strong ego, he wrote: 'We may with modesty say, There is not only Sense, but some Wit and a Great deal of Truth' in the lines. Defiantly, he proceeded to add further verses of like denseness.[86]

A third device that Care used to maintain the interest of his readers was the bawdy story. An example is the tale of a nun, Beatrix, who becomes enamored of a young priest and forsakes her calling for him. He satisfies himself and throws her over, and she, having no other skills, becomes a whore but is rescued from her life of sin by the Virgin Mary.[87] Another gross story concerns a monk who, while traveling on an English ship from Jerusalem to Italy, develops a passion for the boatswain's boy, whom he offers money to commit sodomy. The child reveals all to his master, who advises him to take the money, arm himself with a knife and 'circumcise the devout Devil in the heat of his Lust.'[88] Care apparently relished these tales, and he did not spare his reader obscene details.

Fourth, Care also employed metaphor, similes, analogies and parallels. Several striking examples illustrate his skill and show his confidence in a Bible-literate audience. Care compared the creation of the 'Present Popish Church' to the erection of a huge building involving the work of many people. He summoned the image of 'Canonists,' who 'like Blacksmiths blowing with the Bellows of their Decrees... hammer'd... in the Coals of the Pope's Constitutions.' Vulcans, such as Gratian, Pope John and Pope Boniface, added their contributions, while the part of 'Apprentices and Journeymen' was played by Hostiensis and Panormian, among others. Monks and friars served as carpenters. Aquinas and Scotus gave final shape to the building by using 'the leaden and flexible Compasses of their Logick and Philosophy.'[89] To underscore the dangers Catholicism posed to true Christianity, Care concocted a 'Catholick Pill.' He invited his readers to imagine a pill made of lay ignorance mixed with drams of monks' devotion, combined with a score of plenary indulgences to provide a tincture and completed by a dash of penance. The mixture is wrapped in the Pope's infallibility. He who swallows it should do so blindfolded with a cup of absolution at the hour of death.[90] Possibly because of his earlier interest in medicine, Care used the pill metaphor more than once, and it got him into serious trouble with the government and the law. These stylistic mechanisms enlivened his points, related them to things with which his readers could readily identify and thus fixed them in their minds.

Care also delighted in explaining religious esoterica. For example, he inquired of his readers, 'Would you like to know why Cardinals wear red hats?' Care had at the ready several explanations drawn from learned authors, which he presented before advancing his own, a moral about pride.[91] One of the most engaging explanations concerned the meaning of *Peter's pence*. Care took his readers back to Saxon times, providing them with the etymology of the phrase, and then drew them along a historical overview, showing how a gift of alms became an annual absolute tribute until it was removed by Henry VIII. Spicing up the whole with pointedly derogatory comments about avaricious Popes, he ended with the calculation that Peter's pence over 700 years had drained £5,250,000 out of England and the request that his readers think how much more those popish 'Horseleeches' had 'sucked' off by other means.[92] It is easy to be beguiled by such tales and fascinated by the details that pour from Care's store of information. He told his audience things they had always wanted to know but had been afraid to ask. In doing so, he no doubt aimed to reach the unlearned, who did not have a clue about the topics, as well as the learned.

IV

Care promised his Everyman audience that he would provide them with the history of the Roman Catholic Church from its beginnings up to the present time. And he almost succeeded. Each bound volume of pamphlets covers roughly 500 years of history. Volume 1, comprising thirty-one *Pacquets* and *Courants*, opens with the question whether St Peter was ever really in Rome and continues the story of the Popes down through the first five centuries. The *Pacquets* in this volume are dated 3 December 1678 to 4 July 1679. Volume 2, with forty-seven *Pacquets* and *Courants*, continues on to the year 1000, focusing on the Popes, their evil lives and usurpations. These *Pacquets* are dated 11 July 1679 to 28 May 1680. Volume 3 contains eighty *Pacquets* and *Courants* dated 4 June 1680 to 16 December 1681 except for the absence of a pacquet during the week of Care's trial, on 2 July 1680. The volume covers religious history from 1000 to 1370. Volume 4 focuses on the 150 years from Wycliffe to Luther in thirty-five *Pacquets* and *Courants* dated 23 December 1681 to 18 August 1682. Volume 5 also contains thirty-five *Pacquets* and *Courants*, dated 25 August 1682 to 13 July 1683. This volume covers the history of the Reformation in England, but the account was aborted; when Care ceased publication in July 1683, he had reached only the reign of Queen Mary I.

During these four and a half years Care never lost sight of his stated mission: to reveal the 'usurpations' of the Popes. At first, from December 1678 through June 1679, Care did no more than defame popery and the Roman Catholic Church. By the summer of 1679, however, by implication and direct comment he was using the history of popery for partisan ends: to underscore the excellence of true Protestantism (that is, Dissent), the moral necessity of freedom of the religious conscience, the evil prosecutory practices of the Church of England, and the corruption and Catholic sympathies of the monarchy and the bench. These are the basic themes that Care advanced from one perspective or another in the *Weekly Pacquet* and in all of his subsequent writings.

Care's central argument, in brief, was this: the Catholic Church had departed from its origins, gone grievously wrong, and distorted the terms of its original doctrine, dogma and role. Following an interpretation common among Dissenters, Care explained that initially the Catholic Church had practiced a true Christianity, very like that of its early critics, the Waldenses and Albigenses and of Protestant Churches after the Reformation.[93] Over the centuries corrupt Roman pontiffs, out of greed and ambition, had seized authority in the Catholic Church, used money that had poured into their coffers to sustain opulent and self-indulgent living, laid claim to supremacy over secular powers and distorted the doctrine, discipline and organization of the true Christian Church. The authentic heirs of that true Church were the present Dissenting communities; their progenitors had appeared in the past under the leadership of men like John Wycliffe, John Hus and Martin Luther. These were the men 'who sound[ed] the Trumpet of the Reformation,'[94] and the facts stated just above were the answer to the Catholics' taunting question, 'Where was your church before Luther?'

The foundation of the argument for papal supremacy was that Christ had built his Church on St Peter, bishop of Rome, and through the laying on of hands that authority had been transmitted through the ages. At the very outset, in the first two chapters of the *Weekly Pacquet*, Care attempted to destroy this claim. Using reason, logic, and copious citations from both secular and religious histories, Care maintained that the bishop of Rome had been only one among several leaders of the young Church, that St Peter had never been in Rome, and that the idea of the transference of authority down through the ages through the laying on of hands was a myth constructed by self-interested Popes. History showed how ridiculous it was, argued Care, pointing to the presence of a woman Pope and to the Great Schism, when there had been more than one Pope. The importance of Care's argument that St Peter had never been in Rome cannot be overestimated, for it undermined the foundations of Catholic doctrine. Care returned to this thesis later – significantly, during his tenure as James II's propagandist – when he restated it in a tract called *A Modest Inquiry*.

Another point in Catholic dogma that Care sought to disprove was the infallibility of the Roman Catholic Church. Care emphatically declared that 'notwithstanding all their vapours, the Churches of Rome have no Rule of Faith whatsoever, that can pretend to lay any tolerable claim to the Title of Certainty.'[95] His point was that an individual using reason and prayer cannot be absolutely sure that he is right. Since only God knows the truth, fallible human beings should respect the views of others. It followed logically as another theme that persecution for religious conscience was wrong: no one can know with absolute certainty what is the Truth; the understanding of religion is an individual and spiritual matter of conscience, and conscience cannot be touched by force. Care argued further that the laws against Dissent were not legitimate. Their original purpose had been to prevent sedition; since Dissenters were not seditious, the laws were not applicable to them. To drive home condemnation of Catholic persecution, he introduced a discussion of Mohammedanism, which was well known for its tyrannical government but tolerant in matters of religion, saying that it was better for a person who 'would enjoy Liberty of Conscience' to live under Mohammedanism than under Catholicism, which cruelly punished Dissent and tried to force men to convert.[96] These and other points about religious liberty he developed more fully when in the service of James II.

Care bitterly condemned still other aspects of Catholic discipline and doctrine. For example, he ridiculed the use of the sign of the cross as 'palpable idolatry,' comparing it sneeringly to the Egyptians' worship of garlic and onions, a metaphor that he obviously expected his Bible-literate audience to understand.[97] In truth, Care pointed out, the sign of the cross was nothing more than an identifying mark of early Christians. Drawing upon the 'famous Durandus,' Care explained 'the worthy reason why Fish is preferred [during Lent]:' it is because God never cursed the waters, an explanation that Care regarded as a 'folly and impertinence.'[98]

Care also discussed in insulting terms the central doctrines of Roman Catholicism. For example, he called the Mass a 'prodigious heap of Confusion' whose unfolding ceremony he dismissed as a 'Theatrical' piece. Describing the ritual in great detail, he stressed with contemptuous humor the use of Latin (which made everything unintelligible to the people), the elaborate vestments and the 'Apish and profane Gesticulations.' Reaching for a laugh, he described how the priest 'holds out his Cup for more Wine... licks his fingers... washes his hands;... takes up the Chalice [again]... licks it, and tries if he can get any good out of it.'[99] He treated such concepts as saints, angels and the Virgin Mary, all sacred to Catholics, in like manner, in effect making Catholic religious practices and ceremonies grotesque. As we saw in reviewing his efforts to reach the marginally educated, Care presented many examples in illustration of what he regarded as the stupidity of Catholic beliefs and ceremonies.

V

Care's approach to writing history was similar to that practiced by traditional Restoration historians. Like them, he insisted upon his 'objectivity' and love of truth.[100] He was attentive to detail, correcting an error (caused by the press, he said) so as 'not to Die in the Readers Debt.'[101] Although his avowed mission was to reveal the 'usurpations' of the Popes, Care maintained that he had used documentary evidence with integrity, protesting 'in the presence of God' that he had not to his 'knowledge falsified or wrested one of the Authors cited, nor wilfully lessen'd any of their Arguments.'[102] Underscoring his respect for documents, and in keeping with the general emphasis during the Restoration on documentary evidence, Care included documents in whole or in part, translating them for the unlearned.[103] To prove his impartiality, Care pointed out that he had drawn upon Roman Catholic authors so that 'none may tax us with partiality or ill-will.'[104] It is true that he cited numerous Catholic writers, most particularly Bellarmine, whom he dubbed the Church's 'Thirteenth Apostle,'[105] as well as Baronius, Cressy, and Platina. If a Catholic historian wrote something negative about the Pope or the Catholic Church, it must be true, Care inferred. Justifying further his use of Catholic histories, Care explained that 'truth is a spark of Light, that we often come at by the Collision of opposite Flints.'[106] The remark aptly reveals how Care reasoned.

Care did not claim that his research was 'original,' but he did insist that he did not 'traffick with Epitomes, Abridgments, and Common-Place-Books.' These he dismissed as 'the usual Refuges of vapouring ignorance, and lazy Auxiliaries of Pocket-learning.' Instead he went to 'the Well-head, and consult[ed] the best and most approved Authors.'[107] He contended that his 'Citations ... have generally been examined, and faithfully transcribed from the Original Authors quoted' except in a 'very few' instances when the original books were unavailable.[108] His remarks were no doubt partly intended to set the *Weekly Pacquet* apart from the popular 'Epitomes' and 'Abridgments' that he may have feared competed with his history. They also reveal Care's method: he read histories and essays written by the 'best and most approved Authors,' checked citations to material that interested him, and then wrote up a condensed account citing variously the histories and the original sources he had found therein. His respect for data that were contemporary to the event suggests that he had thought about the nature of evidence: that kind of evidence was 'so much the more to be valued,' he commented.[109] Finally, a spot check of his citations shows them to be accurate.

The number and range of his citations are impressive. In addition to the Bible,[110] Care referred to the work of the major classical, Renaissance and Reformation authors on the Continent and in England up to his own time, including Erasmus, Luther, Calvin, Melanchton, Shakespeare, Bellarmine, Baronius, Platina and Onuphrius. He described many writers with one or two words, as he had done in *Plain Englishman's Historian*, referring, for example, to the 'eloquent Chrysostome,' the 'learned Hierome,' and the 'Laborious and Judicious Augustine.' He showed his intellectual reach by mentioning that Raphael, 'the famous painter,' had replied to criticism that he put too much color on the faces of Peter and Paul by saying that he intended to show them 'Blushing in Heaven' to see their successors.[111] Whatever the true depth of his reading, his reputation as 'learned' has some validity.

Care was actively involved in tracking down books and manuscripts. He got at least one manuscript from 'an eminent and worthy Citizen of London,' who had found it among the papers of his uncle, Lord Bacon's chaplain.[112] He consulted with someone in the Augmentation Office and was assured that a transcript of a particular lease was under seal there.[113] Someone else gave him a copy of a warrant issued by Danby that he cited as evidence of the Jesuits' confidence in England's conversion to Catholicism in 1678.[114] As noted, Care may have worked in Sion College Library in London. He also seems to have known about the holdings of libraries in Cambridge and Oxford. He informed his readers that a certain manuscript was 'to be seen in the publick Library at Cambridge.'[115] An interlocutor in the *Popish Courant* advised another to 'get... down to Cambridge Library,' where he could 'read *The Observator*' (L'Estrange's weekly publication).[116] When reproducing some passages from Wycliffe's printed work, Care noted that 'one [of the originals was in] Bennet [*sic*] Colledge Cambridge, the other [in] the Publick Library at Oxford.'[117] Care was also aware of the riches of the Bodleian Library.[118] Whether he used these libraries in Oxford and Cambridge is unknown, but it is possible that someone sympathetic to Care's arguments arranged admittance for him. At the very least, Care was sufficiently knowledgeable about the holdings of these libraries to recommend them to his readers.

Notwithstanding such efforts to establish his credentials, Care faced criticism as a historian on four counts, all of which reflect a hierarchical society's social and intellectual snobbery. First, Care's authorship was questioned. It was said that he had written only the *Popish Courant*s, while the difficult 'sober part' had been composed by either a 'Club or Cabal'[119] or a single author identified as 'one Mr. Robinson.'[120] Robinson (or Robertson) was a bookseller and successful newswriter thought to be 'bred to the law' who served 'several coffee-houses' and a 'considerable quantity' of customers in the country. He had the reputation of giving 'as good an account, especially in term time, as any [writer]' of public affairs. A friend of Nonconformists, he was one of Dr Bates's booksellers. Known for his 'easy and unruffled' temper, he was considered 'Ingenious and of quick Parts.'[121] Although Care does not mention Robinson, he no doubt knew of the rumor and must have taken satisfaction in having his work assigned to such a well-respected man. Care's rejoinder to the charge that someone else had written the history part was that he had been convicted (at his trial in 1680) of writing the whole and that he had sought to conceal his authorship so as to advance the prospects of the *Pacquet*s.[122]

Second, Care's enemies criticized the format of the *Weekly Pacquet*. Calling it nothing more than a 'Fardle of Pamphlets,' they implied that the format of weekly installments rendered the *Pacquet*s unworthy of serious attention. Care rebutted this charge as the 'very scum of Impertinence;' he said that it was beneath an 'intelligent Man' to suggest that 'Sense and Reason were confin'd to Folio's.'[123] Third, enemies disparaged Care's lack of experience and his social and academic credentials. Scorning his deficiencies, ridiculing him as a 'meer Ignoramus, never of any University,' his detractors dismissed him as a 'Mechanick sort,' one who should not venture into divinity or subjects of state, and demeaned him as 'some Presbyterian, of the Tribe of 41... a sawcy nonsensical Rascal.'[124] Care made a splendid rebuttal. Professing a 'Veneration and Esteem for learning and Science,' he admitted that he himself possessed little knowledge but contended that he was learned enough not to be 'so ignorant as to boast of Knowledge.' He pointed out that university training can result in conceit, impatience and display, as in a mind-less 'sputter of Latin and Greek.' And with rollicking and devastating humor, Care, who had written more week after week than anyone else on the evils of Roman Catholicism, inquired:

If such a pitiful lay ignorant unread fellow [like me] can say so much against Popery, what might an Hero in Cap and Gown, circled with Postiles and Polyantheas, and all the Ammunition of Pocket-Learning; or a man of Parts and Leisure, a Reverend Divine, with ten Cartloads of Books, and three Spiritual Preferments, the helps of Conversation and bountiful Patrons, the assistance of the Bodlean [sic] Library, and the prospect of promotion, to spur on flagging Industry, what, I say, might such an one have wrote upon this Subject?[125]

He summed up his point, writing proudly that his *Weekly Pacquet* had given 'the vulgar Englishman as much insight into the Mystery of Iniquity, perhaps as any one single work whatsoever.'[126]

In other direct ways he undertook to counter the charge that he was an 'ignoramus.' His sprinkling the *Pacquet*s with Latin and Greek words and phrases and, even more to the point, translating them into English demonstrated his knowledge of classical languages.[127] Care also went to lengths to show that he knew that in the Bible the articles – *the*, *a* and *an* – are used in diverse ways.[128] Similarly, he was at pains to point out that he 'was not ignorant' of learned disagreements over the meaning of the number 666 and over whether the letters *ei* in the word *Lateinos* were pronounced as a diphthong.[129] In such ways Care reassured his readers, both learned and unlearned, of his qualifications and thus of the reliability of his historical account. A conventionally educated person writing history would have found such defenses unnecessary. But Care's establishing his *bona fides* helped him to make a mockery of his critics' scorn of his lack of formal training. His competence was self-evident.

The fourth charge was that Care had plagiarized, either by stealing 'Verbatim' from a work or by stitching together a 'Collection' of stories drawn from other books. Was there any truth to these charges? So far as I can determine, there is none to the charge of copying word for word from a text. Care's detractors did not specify the book(s) they charged him with copying from, and Care turned aside the accusation with an indignant denial and a scornful challenge to produce the references.[130] As we have seen, Care had not been above appropriating another's translation and had recognized that literary 'borrowing' was common, but he seems to have taken care to avoid plagiarism in the *Weekly Pacquet*. For example, he called attention to his naming a source, saying that it was 'more than every Courant-Monger can do.'[131] He was at pains to rectify some minor error in a citation.[132] He correctly paraphrased and cited texts,[133] and when he used verbatim several paragraphs from a book, he announced that he was doing so and transcribed the portion faithfully.[134] His procedure is appropriate even by the standards of the late twentieth century.

To the criticism that his *Pacquet* was nothing but a collection of stories taken from other books, Care responded in remarks that further reveal his method and understanding of the historian's craft. He admitted that the 'matter' of his *Pacquet* was not new, but his 'handling of the same things in another manner' justified his effort. In his *Pacquet* the reader could find the 'substance and choicest notes of several Authors, like a Posy made up of several Flowers,' as he put it.[135] His defense went to the heart of how he conceived of writing history. 'What can it be else [but a collection of data from other books], as far as 'tis Historical. Would they have me forge Stories, as Popish Legend-Scribblers do?'[136]

Care's responses invite one to rephrase the charge and ask, were there any books to which Care was especially indebted as he went about assembling material? Anthony Wood was confident that he had discovered Care's major source: *Fiscus Papalis... A part of the Popes Exchequer*, translated by William Crashaw and published in 1621.[137] Drenched in sarcasm, *Fiscus Papalis* mocked indulgences and relics and generally ridiculed the beliefs of Catholics. Care readily acknowledged a debt to Crashaw,[138] and there are obvious identities in purpose and substance between *Fiscus Papalis* and the *Weekly Pacquet*. Other books were even closer to Care's polemic: outstanding among them was *Synopsis Papismi, That Is, A Generall View Of Papistrie: Wherein The Whole Mysterie of Iniquitie, and Summe of Antichristian Doctrine is set downe* (1592), written by the prolific, learned and widely admired Andrew Willet. The *Synopsis Papismi* covered such topics as whether Peter had been at Rome, the prerogative powers of Popes, ceremonies of the Church, angels and transubstantiation, and also laid out a general conceptual framework of Church history that probably aided Care in the theoretical design of the *Weekly Pacquet*. Care specifically drew on the *Synopsis Papismi* in answering a point made by Bellarmine, and he adopted words that appeared in Willet's title, referring to the 'Mystery of Iniquity.'[139]

Another book markedly close to Care's work was *The Romish Horseleech; or, An Impartial Account of the Intolerable Charge of Popery to this Nation*. Written by Thomas Staveley, an antiquary and lawyer, and published in London in 1674, *Horseleech* could also have furnished Care with illustrations of the evilness of popery.[140] Like *Fiscus Papalis, Horseleech* stressed that popery had drained the wealth of the English nation and sent it off to Rome. A third book was William Hughes's *Man of Sin: Or a Discourse of Popery*, printed in 1677.[141] Warmly recommended by Care as 'an Exquisite piece... very much worth... Reading,' and one he kept by him,[142] *The Man of Sin* was a compilation of stories about papal miracles, lusts and forgeries, which would have served Care's purposes very well. It may have encouraged Care, who liked the light touch, to use humor to illustrate the evils of popery. A fourth book that Care surely knew and that was probably also central to his project was Reverend Gilbert Burnet's *History of the English Reformation*, the first volume of which was published on 23 May 1679. It focused on the corruption of Catholicism as a faith and an institution. The English Reformation, presaged by John Wycliffe in the fourteenth century, was a reaction to Roman clericalism, superstition, ambition and popery. Insisting upon Henry VIII's imperial authority and the right of the Church in England to undertake reform, Burnet presented the English Reformation as a restoration of the rights of the crown, of the doctrine and practice of the early Church, and of the monarchy's rightful property, thereby justifying the Dissolution of the Monasteries.[143] These themes are basic to the *Weekly Pacquet* and are directly and extensively addressed in volume 5. Finally, Foxe's *Acts and Monuments*, which was available in multiple issues in Latin or English and also in abridgments and selections, offered a useful compendium of stories about the cruelty and corruption of papists during the reign of Mary I, which Care drew upon.[144] In sum, I suggest that this quick-study artist had at his elbow these six books – *Fiscus Papalis*, *Synopsis Papismi*, *Horseleech*, *The Man of Sin*, Burnet's *History of the English Reformation*, and Foxe's *Acts and Monuments*. Of course, he also used the many other books that he listed in reference notes. This hypothesis helps us to understand how Care could have written his popular version of 1600 years of Church history. No trained historian, he would have had to have the help that such books as these offered.

Of course, Care was not a dispassionate researcher seeking the 'truth.' Like traditional historians of the Restoration era, he searched the written evidence for 'proofs' that buttressed his a priori beliefs and prejudices about religion and religious institutions.[145] Citation of the evidence provided the 'proof' of his contentions. His *Pacquet*s were not a history as a modern historian understands the term but a polemic that drew upon historical data to provide depth and solidity to his argument. Recent studies have maintained that such an approach accurately describes the general 'practice of history' in the Restoration period.[146] Those 'tedious' and 'fruitless' tomes that Care said he wanted to spare his audience the trouble of reading did the same kind of thing.[147] One may conclude that Care conducted historical 'research' with integrity. He read widely, and where possible, he checked the originals of references that interested him. Care's research was not 'original' research, and he did not suggest that it was. Care's method of gathering material resembles, essentially, the approach of a well-trained and intelligent novice historian.

Does this attention to evidence, documents and citation in research, and to clarity, order and chronology in presentation mean that the new interest in science had influenced Care's understanding of history and how to practice it? Barbara Shapiro has argued that science deeply influenced the writing of history in late Stuart England.[148] Care's earlier publications show his interest in the 'soft' aspects of science: medical texts, etymology, his concern to achieve order and clarity in expression. But there is no sign that he was preoccupied with the new science.

It seems more likely that the fount of his preoccupation with exactness was the tradition of classical and Renaissance rhetoric, just as it was for Restoration historians of much larger reputation.[149]

VI

What kind of sales did the *Weekly Pacquet* enjoy? Although no sales or profit-and-loss balance sheets exist, indirect evidence and some speculation indicate that sales were brisk and profits satisfactory. That the *Pacquet* had such a long and continuous run – four and a half years, longer than any other Whig serial – suggests that Curtis and Care were well pleased with the profit from it. That in two instances (explained below) Curtis tried to retain control of the *Weekly Pacquet* speaks to the same point. Care and Curtis made money from selling the *Weekly Pacquet* as a single sheet and then again from selling bound volumes of the same single sheets. Thereby, Care was assured of an income each week and a bonus at the time of selling the bound volumes. Carolyn Nelson has figured that a profit margin of 'at least 40%' could be expected from a serial, enough to 'provide an income for author, printer and publisher, week after week.'[150] Two years into the project Care remarked with evident pride that the *Pacquet* had fallen into 'many thousands hands.'[151] The playwright Aphra Behn, who was a Tory sympathizer and therefore no friend of Care's, wrote in similar terms, saying in 1682 that the *Weekly Pacquet* 'clogs the nation.'[152] Care and Curtis made an effort to promote the *Pacquet*. In London it was advertised and sold by Curtis, and it was also advertised as sold by 'most' booksellers at their stalls in St Paul's Churchyard and other places. If one assumes that its distribution was similar to that of other tracts and mercuries, the *Pacquet* would have been hawked about the streets of London and also sold at coffeehouses and taverns.[153] No doubt, the *Pacquet* was sent by the penny post to the counties as a part of Care's determined effort to reach those 'divers Protestant Gentlemen in most counties' who were interested in buying the *Weekly Pacquet*. Curtis and many other booksellers used the penny post to send out their products.[154] Tessa Watts found that in the early seventeenth century 'regular carrier services' and 'chapmen's routes' were already established and that in effect a 'national market for the cheap print' existed.[155] Surely those routes and services continued in the Restoration era. That partisans of the king in Norwich celebrated Charles's fifty-second birthday with a bonfire of opposition tracts and effigies of 'several Factious and Seditious Libellers,' including Care, shows that Care and his *Pacquet*s were known there.[156] Possibly the *Pacquet*s could be found in the 'public library in Cambridge,' where there were copies of L'Estrange's *Observator*.[157] Arthur Annesley, first earl of Anglesey, who kept a collection of 'all remarkable [tracts] relating to Government,' which he allowed others to consult, owned all the bound volumes of the *Weekly Pacquet*.[158] John Evelyn's library contained at least three of Care's publications, including four volumes of the *Weekly Pacquet*.[159] The libraries of the first and second dukes of Newcastle contained two volumes of the *Pacquet*.[160] The library at Sion College held the volumes covering 1679 through 1680.[161] Care's fame even spread to the colonies, where at least one interested party wrote asking his London bookseller to send him a copy of volume 5.[162] That Care was a target of attack also suggests that the *Weekly Pacquet* enjoyed lively sales. As Care put it, if his *Pacquet* had not made a difference, it 'would never have been so smartly pelted, nor had so many Stones flung at it.'[163] That both the single unbound sheets and the bound volumes are rare today suggests that they were bought up.

One may only speculate about how many 'thousands hands,' as Care put it, actually paid for the *Pacquet*s. A total of 240 *Pacquet*s and *Courant*s were printed. The average print run for tracts printed between 1679 and 1681 was 2,300, a figure larger than the generally accepted average of between 1,000 and 1,500 for the Restoration era.[164] If one conservatively takes the average of 2,300 as the print run, then a total of 542,800 *Weekly Pacquets* were on the market over the four and a half years. They sold for a penny a piece. In addition, the five bound volumes of *Pacquets*, selling for a shilling each, were also on offer. If the print run was 2,300, then 11,500 copies were on the market over the years. If every one of the separate sheets and the bound volumes were sold, they would have fetched a total of £2,768 (£2,261 for the single sheets, £507 for the bound volumes). To put that figure in perspective, the average yearly wage for London artisans was £22 to £23. The late twentieth-century multiplier, now figured at eighty, would put the total income from sales at £220,880.[165] Such an income over four and a half years, however it was divided between Care and Curtis, would have laid a foundation for financial security. And, of course, Care would have enjoyed income from his other publications as well.

However, not all the single *Pacquets* or the bound volumes were sold. As we saw, some single sheets were distributed free of charge about the streets of London and in coffee houses. Bound volumes remained available for sale after Care's death. In January 1689 Curtis announced that he had in stock copies of all five volumes. In response it was said that Care's 'true' volume 5 could be had only at the home of Care's widow, Bridget.[166] So the total brought in by the *Weekly Pacquet* was less than the calculation above. Still, it must have been considerable. This little calculation helps to explain how it was possible for Care to become a 'professional writer' earning his living by his pen.

VII

The *Weekly Pacquet* was the most important of the popular histories that sprung up during the Restoration and targeted a marginally educated audience. Care did not have the usual education or social background of those who wrote conventional history, but he was well equipped for the task of writing popular history. Possessing the instincts of a historian, such as concern for the validity of evidence, a desire to explain, and interest in organization and clarity – Care was at pains to make his history interesting and understandable to the 'Mechanick sort.' The devices that he used assisted them and may also have appealed to the educated. The distance between popular and elite culture was not as great in the Restoration era as sometimes suggested. Although his influence was not lasting, Care altered the style of history writing for the broad public. Moreover, the weekly installments of history and commentary provided opportunity for a kind of regular political participation, different from that offered by newspapers, for people who had only a limited role in the political process. Care's work empowered readers with a knowledge of the history of the Roman Catholic Church, which was otherwise very difficult for them to obtain. The history he imparted was soundly grounded. As Kitchin observed years ago, if one sets aside the blatant prejudice against Catholicism that permeates the *Pacquet*s, what is left is an excellent account from a Protestant perspective of the history of the Christian Church, Catholic and Protestant.[167] The *Weekly Pacquet* modified the political culture of Restoration England by adding a new dimension – history.

The *Weekly Pacquet* decisively enhanced Care's reputation as a skilled and effective writer, propelling him into the limelight as the best-known and most widely identified of the anti-establishment authors. The *Pacquet* also played a central role in intensifying and spreading anti-Catholicism at all levels of Restoration society. Under cover of robust anti-Catholicism, Care used the *Weekly Pacquet* and especially the *Popish Courant* to criticize the policies and practices of the Court, the Church of England and the bench. This proved to be his undoing.

3

The ACQUITTAL
of
Sir George Wakeman

T he acquittal on July 18, 1679 of Sir George Wakeman, Queen Catherine's Catholic physician, and three Benedictine monks on a charge of high treason was a defining moment in Care's career. His defamatory response to it in the 1 August 1679 issue of *The Popish Courant* was the first in a string of libelous pieces against Lord Chief Justice Sir William Scroggs, the presiding judge at Wakeman's trial, that came tumbling from the presses. It was this vicious print campaign in late summer and early autumn of 1679, made possible by the lapse of the Licensing/Printing Act in May 1679, that sharpened the government's determination to try to control the press and press people by using the courts and the law. Chapter 3 focuses on the responses in the press to Wakeman's acquittal, the beginning of the war in print between Care and L'Estrange, and the government's use of law and judicial rulings in the autumn of 1679 and the spring of 1680 to try to hamstring the press.

Sir William Scroggs (1623–83), Lord Chief Justice of the Court of King's Bench, 1678.

I

Care's scurrilous attack on Chief Justice Scroggs signaled a turn-about in his attitude toward the establishment, a significant change in light of his earlier efforts to ingratiate himself with the Court. One would expect that events of the spring of 1679, such as Charles II's pardoning Danby or proroguing Parliament and then dissolving it by proclamation, thereby aborting the first Exclusion Bill, would have provoked Care.[1] They did not. No doubt he approved of the handling of the thirteen Popish Plot trials from November 1678 through June 1679. Scroggs, the presiding judge in all the cases, had intimidated the accused, overlooked inconsistencies in the testimony of Titus Oates and William Bedloe (his confederate), and expressed satisfaction at the guilty verdicts rendered in all but one case.[2] Furthermore, in February, Scroggs ruled that 'one positive single witness against a plotting papist was sufficient to keep them in prison,' a ruling that made it easy to deny bail to a papist.[3] Scroggs also made clear from the bench how profoundly he loathed Catholicism, describing it as a 'religion that quite unhinges all piety, all morality... They eat their God, they kill their king, and saint the murderer.'[4] Such a remark was typical of the vitriolic anti-Catholicism in the *Weekly Pacquet* and surely won Care's favor.

Two things, however, suggest that in the early summer of 1679 Care was moving into circles that opposed the court: one was his publicly stated disgust that anyone should express sympathy for Catholics who were executed. Emphatically he insisted that 'whoever' sought to 'lessen the Plot, or [Catholics'] Guilt, because they pretended Innocence is undoubtedly either a Party in the Conspiracy, or so silly that he almost deserves a Fifth of November Breakfast... to rectifie his foolish Credulity.'[5] The second was his possible involvement in writing Popish Plot narrative accounts and his near certain authorship of *A Narrative and Impartial Discovery of the Popish Plot: Carried on for the Burning and Destroying the Cities of London and Westminster* (1679), addressed to 'The Surviving

Citizens of London.' [6] *A Narrative and Impartial Discovery* named Bedloe as the author, featured his picture as the frontispiece, and promoted him as one 'lately engaged in that Horrid Design, and one of the Popish Committee for Carrying on such Fires.'[7] L'Estrange responded to the tract in *Lestrange's Narrative Of The Plot* (May 1680), and later, in the *Observator*, continued to excoriate it. He claimed that a group of booksellers had met for the purpose of finding a topic that would sell and had selected the subject of the London Fire, no doubt because of its earlier popularity, and chose Bedloe to 'own it.'[8] They picked him because he was well-known, had not previously written a 'narrative,' and had been a true 'witness' to the fires (having set some of them himself), a circumstance that would authenticate the account. [9] They each paid him £10 to sign on as putative author, but on the recommendation of Benjamin Harris, the radical Anabaptist bookseller, asked Care to write the piece. They helped Care by 'furnish[ing] him with Libells for materialls,' namely *Trap ad Crucem*, which had terrified margianlly educated persons when it first appeared in 1671, and *The History of the Fires*.

Care accepted the commission, incorporated the 'Libells' into the text, and also made 'Alterations... [out] of his own Head,' even after the manuscript had gone to the printer.[10] L'Estrange described the resulting tract as full of lies and riddled with plagiarism, an 'Insolent and Scandalous Cheat.' [11] A late twentieth-century reader would concur. The tract did not contain the 'Divers Depositions and Informations... Never before Printed,' promised in the extended title. Rather, the tract was drawn almost verbatim from *Trap ad Crucem*. By innuendo and insinuation *A Narrative and Impartial Discovery* implicated the king, the duke of York, the king's Guards and others, in the fires, implying in one outrageous example that the king had given a man authority to burn the city.[12]

No corroborating proof of Care's authorship has survived, but three considerations buttress L'Estrange's charge. First, although Care denied that he was the author, he grudgingly admitted that he had helped Bedloe. Second, there are similarities between *A Narrative and Impartial Discovery* and the *Weekly Pacquet*: the harangue in the former against people whose belief in the plot was shaken by the speeches of the condemned conforms with the same outrage expressed at about the same time in the latter. Also, the language of the preface of *A Narrative and Impartial Discovery* is similar to that of the *Weekly Pacquet* in momentum and vehemence. Third, the commission would have brought Care significant advantages which may have been compelling at this point in his life: a chance to oblige some booksellers whose favor would be useful in the future and an opportunity to make money. How much he would have made is unknown, but the profit from the 'Narratives' was said to be sizable and the sum given Bedloe just for the use of his name provides an approximation. [13]

If Care was the true author, *A Narrative and Impartial Discovery* is important, for it marks the first time that Care was noticed by a group of radical press people, the first time that his integrity was seriously compromised, and the first time that he directly assaulted the entire Court of Charles II. If he was not, L'Estrange's account holds interest for the light it sheds on how tracts were written and printed, even read. The process by which *A Narrative and Impartial Discovery* was commissioned shows the printer/publisher/book-seller acting as a patron, commissioning the writer, and supporting him with ideas and money.

Within two months of the appearance of *A Narrative and Impartial Discovery*, Care's denunciation of Scroggs in the 1 August issue of the *Popish Courant*, which appeared on the Friday after Wakeman's trial, made his alignment with critics of the Court unmistakable. Although news of the trial and verdict had appeared earlier, the *Popish Courant* was the first to offer comment.[14] Invoking the same kind of medicinal simile he had used before, Care announced the discovery of a marvelous medicine with which Scroggs and others had dosed themselves.[15] It had the power to make 'Justice deaf as well as blinde,' remove 'spots of deepest treason,' and induce people to 'behold nothing but Innocence in the blackest Malefactors.' This medicine 'makes Fools wise men, and wise men Fools; and both of them Knaves.'[16] These defamatory words propelled Care into the limelight.

Why did Care write this inflammatory paragraph? Perhaps he was genuinely suspicious of Scroggs's integrity. One has only to compare Scroggs's handling of Coleman's trial with Wakeman's, as Luttrell recommended, to find the judge 'to be infinitely chang'd... even in the same things.'[17] It is true that the judge's public face had seemed to change in the Wakeman trial. His harassment of Oates and Bedloe, the major witnesses against Wakeman, and his summing up the evidence in favor of the accused inclined many people to think that the court had instructed him to secure an acquittal and spare the queen embarrassment.[18] There is no proof of that intimation.[19] Indeed a dispassionate observer would find reason to praise Scroggs for resisting the 'politically correct' Whig view of those scoundrels Oates and Bedloe. But the charge against Wakeman came so perilously close to the queen that the suspicions are understandable. The news that Charles wept with joy and relief upon hearing the verdict would have reinforced misgivings.[20] More damaging, because more public, was the unfortunate courtesy call that the Portuguese ambassador (Queen Catherine was a Portuguese princess) paid Scroggs and the rumor that bags of gold were left at his house.[21] Suspicions gained further credence from Wakeman's departure for France after his trial[22] and from the flight in the fall of the duke of Buckingham, who feared the worse because he had accused Scroggs of being under orders to protect papists.[23] Jurymen too felt the hostility and 'some' contemplated moving to avoid it.[24]

No doubt contributing equally to Care's slanderous denunciation of Scroggs was his hope of capitalizing on the interest the trial and verdict had generated. The government anticipated that interest by announcing in the 17–21 July issue of the *London Gazette* that a printed account of the trial would immediately appear to 'prevent all false copies.'[25] *Domestick Intelligence*, the first unlicensed newspaper, fanned the concern by featuring on the front page of its 22 July issue a news account of the trial and the names of the jurors.[26] Coming a week later, Care's attack on Scroggs may be seen as swinging his *Weekly Pacquet* into a spotlight that was already bright.

Further, it is possible that the attack was an effort to avenge his publisher, Langley Curtis. Curtis had been called before the Privy Council in July for printing and dispersing *Advice to a Painter*, a piece described as a 'Scandalous and Seditious Libell.' He was discharged on 30 July after being required to enter a bond of £200 and to promise never again to do anything 'prejudicial' to the king and government.[27] Two days later Care's blast appeared. Coincidental timing suggests that the two men or Care alone saw the public humiliation of Scroggs in the popular *Weekly Pacquet* as a revenge for the treatment Curtis received at the hands of the authorities.

Finally, one may suggest that Care's attack on Scroggs signaled an effort to identify himself with and assist Shaftesbury and Whig partisans and thereby win their notice. Anything denigrating Scroggs was presumptively pleasing to Shaftesbury, for it was public knowledge that enmity between the two men was personal and long standing, antedating the Popish Plot.[28] It was also clear that the Wakeman verdict was a serious setback to Shaftesbury's political designs, for it dashed hopes of persuading Charles to divorce the queen and marry a Protestant woman.[29] Multiple reasons, then, help explain Care's unguarded attack on the Lord Chief Justice.

The idea that Care used his assault on Scroggs to attract the attention of Whigs is strengthened by another move that contemporaries thought he made at about the same time, namely, the publication of a blatantly partisan version of the 12 August parliamentary election in the county of Essex. Allegedly an eye-witness report, *Essex's Excellency: Or The Gallantry of The Freeholders of that County*,[30] praised those honest Whig candidates who refused to defile the election by bribing electors with meat and drink, as corrupt Tory candidates allegedly did. The result was the return of poorly qualified men who destroyed the integrity of Parliament.

'Nothing can so soon enslave you and your Posterity,' advised Care, 'as the Choice of Ill Members in parliament.' Observing that too long Parliaments and too frequent elections threatened the 'Free-born English man's Liberty,' Care accused members of Parliament who had voted to continue the Parliament of 'almost [selling] the [nation] for slaves.'[31] Although Whig candidates were the clear victors, Tories demanded a poll, which over three days occasioned melees and fisticuffs. In the end the Whigs prevailed, providing an example of probity which Care hoped would inspire other electors.

Essex's Excellency holds interest on three counts. First, it propounds ideas about bribery and other kinds of political corruption and employs vocabulary such as 'Free-born Englishmen' that reappeared in Care's subsequent writings, especially *English Liberties*. Second, the tract stands as the first *printed* evidence of Care's identifying himself with the fortunes of parliamentary Whigs. Thirdly, *Essex's Excellency* made sufficient noise to draw a response, further underscoring Care's growing reputation. Within a fortnight appeared *A Faithful and Impartial Account Of The Behaviour of a Party of the Essex Free-Holders...*[32] The anonymous author, said to be Dr Edward Fowler, expressed himself as 'horrified' by *Essex's Excellency*, saying that it was worse than what happened at the election because written in 'cool blood.'[33] *A Faithful and Impartial Account* defended the clergy from aspersions cast upon them at the election and excoriated their Nonconformist critics for acting like 'Turks and Barbarians' and Scottish Presbyterians while deceitfully championing toleration. While regretting the necessity of writing, the author remarked that 'we would not be run down by either extreme, if God... should put an end to our fears of Popery.'[34] The comment is significant because it places the author among the first to dare to suggest that the hysteria over popery had gotten out of hand.

Care's defaming Scroggs in the *Weekly Pacquet* was the first of a torrent of anonymous scurrilous tracts and single sheets abusing the Lord Chief Justice. For example, *A Satyr Against Iniustice: Or,*

Sc—gs upon Sc—gs provided six triplets of abuse of Scroggs, one saying, 'Our Judge to Mercy's not inclin'd/Unless Gold change Conscience and Mind.' Jane Curtis was tried for publishing this piece. Another offensive tract, in print before 25 August, *Some observations upon the late trial of Sir George Wakeman... By Tom Ticklefoot,... late Clerk to Justice Clodpate,* observed that Scroggs suffered from Clodpate's disease, that is 'to sham up an evidence' according to who was with him that morning. The tract also reported a rumor circulating in coffee houses that jury men were bribed to bring in a verdict of 'not guilty.'[35] The well-known book seller Francis Smith was charged with publishing it. *A New Year's Gift,* which appeared at the end of the year, so offended Scroggs that he committed Smith's son for selling it to a coffee house. [36] One can understand why: this piece accused Scroggs of bribery, said he was unworthy to be a judge, and added a postscript about judges under Edward III and Richard II who were sentenced to death for taking bribes. It reported Scroggs's 'scurrilous threatenings' and his 'clinching his fist at... the booksellers and scribblers' and described his 'furious language' like the noise of 'a bear robbed of her whelps.' So extensive was the press campaign that insinuations about Scroggs's role spread far beyond London.[37] On circuit in the fall of 1679 the judge suffered terrible indignities, including having a half-dead dog being tossed into his carriage and having his sleep disturbed as he was driven along by a man rapping on the top of his coach and calling out 'A Wakeman, A Wakeman.'[38] The only thing he seems to have been spared was to be savaged in the forty-three prints or cartoons that appeared from 1679 through early 1681.[39]

II

This unrestrained outpouring from the press was possible because the Licensing/Printing Act of 1662 had lapsed with the dissolution of Parliament in late May 1679. The interesting question is: how could Charles II's Court have allowed this to happen? It was not the result of mindless inattentiveness on the part of the Court or its critics in Parliament, as is sometimes suggested.[40] On the contrary, interest in press control in the spring of 1679 was widespread. The Court, no doubt alarmed by the large number of hostile tracts in circulation, publicly signaled its concern over licensing printed matter.[41] On 6 March the Lord Chancellor, Sir Heneage Finch, recommended that Parliament 'think of some better remedy of regulating the press' than was available at present.[42] Danby, the Lord Treasurer, who was not above using the press in his own interests, prepared a memorandum in February or March regarding possible steps to control seditious pamphlets.[43] The politically conscious public also took an interest, a few men arguing in printed pieces for the first time in the late seventeenth century that freeing the press would have signal advantages. Thomas Hobbes, contradicting an earlier opinion, complained in 1679 that the monopoly of the Stationers was a 'great hindrance to the advancement of all human learning.'[44] Charles Blount, a deist and republican, wrote at length in *A Just Vindication of Learning:... In behalf of the Liberty of the Press* (1679) adamantly opposing pre-publication licensing on grounds that it was unworthy of Englishmen and unnecessary in view of the laws already on the books. Playing to the anti-popery prejudice, Blount declared that censorship was nothing more than a 'relique of Popery.' Drawing heavily, but without acknowledgment, upon John Milton's *Aeropagitica*, Blount declared that a censored press obstructed learning, offended reason, insulted the 'common people' and 'endangered the government.'[45] Another author, William Lawrence, a Dissenting minister, condemned a fettered press on grounds that a free press would 'bring... very great benefits and advantages to the People,' including profit to English printers.[46] A few individuals, then, recognized the value of a free press but none developed a principle of liberty of the press.

In parliament, where the issue of renewing the Licensing/Printing Act would be decided, the debate had everything to do with partisan politics and nothing to do with principles. Whigs wanted a free press to help them enlist public support for the Exclusion Bill. In the House of Lords Lord Wharton and unidentified Nonconformists probably worked for the lapse of the Licensing/Printing Act.[47] In the House of Commons the committee responsible for recommending re-enactment used delaying tactics, probably in hopes that their failure to recommend renewal would prevent the king from proroguing Parliament. One of the opposition's aims was to keep Parliament in session and thus preserve it as a protected forum in which they could attack the government.

It is not certain that had the government pressed for renewal, it would have succeeded. But in the event, the Court's concern over the press retreated before its anxiety over the Exclusion Bill (introduced on 15 May), and blocking that bill took precedence over all other matters. To save his brother, Charles prorogued parliament on 27 May and then dissolved it in July. With these steps, the apparatus of pre-publication censorship came tumbling down.[48] The 28 May 1679 issue of Care's *Weekly Pacquet* was the last to bear a license.

The government's failure to achieve renewal of the Licensing/Printing Act was a tactical failure of deep significance. In the absence of the legal authority provided by the Act, the Court was at a severe disadvantage in dealing with a rambunctious press. The government's response to the lapse will show how erratic was its reaction and how vulnerable it was to the charge of illegality.

Almost immediately following the lapse of the law, the Court and Privy Council engaged in damage control, taking steps that lay bare their concern and faltering response. Meeting the day after the prorogation of parliament, the Privy Council, upon hearing a report that the number of seditious pamphlets was likely to increase, summoned L'Estrange and the masters and wardens of the Stationers' Company to meet with it and others to figure out 'fit Directions... against unlicensed Bookes.'[49] It soon became clear, however, that deciding on 'fit Directions' in the absence of a statutory law was no easy matter. Several stratagems were developed.

One of the first steps the Council took was to try to contain the circulation of printed matter by controlling the hawkers who dispersed books. Following royal orders, the lord mayor of London, the aldermen and the wardens of the Stationers' Company considered the matter in August 1679 and ordered the marshal and constables to bring hawkers before a city official for questioning. The penalty for peddling seditious material was hard labor at Bridewell Prison. In October the Privy Council, having ordered the judges to devise an 'expedient' to limit the hawkers, issued a proclamation offering a pardon to hawkers who reported the name of the bookseller or printer who had supplied them with seditious material to sell.[50] Neither approach seems to have worked; in December the council turned to Court officers to get rid of hawkers who were plying their trade at the gates of Whitehall,[51] but unlicensed hawkers continued to appear on the streets of London.

The Privy Council also tried to improve the Stationers' performance. The king's bookbinder, Samuel Mearne, was installed as a master for 1679, and he used his influence to persuade the company to impose a fine for failure to abide by licensing rules.[52] The council also asked the Stationers and L'Estrange to prepare fresh proposals for 'regulating the abuses and libertyes of the Presse.' L'Estrange, in an about-face of an earlier attitude, recommended that the printers be incorporated as a separate company, declaring that 'ye Presse may be Regulated this way and no other.'[53] Among his reasons was that printers' superior knowledge of the craft made them more effective than anyone else in uncovering violations of printing laws. Booksellers will never implement the law, for their 'interest runs directly agt. it.' Nothing came of the idea; opposition from the Stationers killed the proposal.[54] Later, in 1681 and 1683 when the Court embarked on a more systematic effort to restrain the press, the Stationers' Company, under Court direction, drew up supplementary ordinances imposing fines for violating regulations that had appeared in the old Licensing/Printing Act.[55] The continued closeness between Court and Stationers showed during the *quo warranto* proceedings against London companies. The

Stationers' Company was the first to surrender its charter and the first to receive a new one. The Stationers were rewarded with clauses, as requested by the company, that, for example, gave royal approval to the company's register (to reinforce the Stationers' effort to provide a kind of copyright), and limited the binding and sale of books in London and environs to company members. Charles and his successors continued to depend on the Stationers until the lapse of the Licensing/Printing Act in 1695.[56]

The Privy Council took another step in late September: it called upon L'Estrange again, ordering him to collect suspicious tracts and assign them to legal officers to read for treasonable content. The purpose was to identify titles and authors of seditious tracts to use as evidence when a case should be brought in future against a press person.[57] The Council itself selected certain tracts for special attention, and a quantity of them are preserved in the Public Record Office; among them issues of *The Weekly Pacquet*.[58]

Rather surprisingly in view of later developments there is no evidence that the Council at this time considered commissioning writers to defend Scroggs and the establishment. However, L'Estrange, on his own initiative, undertook to fortify the government by writing on its behalf two major tracts. One, *The History of the Plot* (printed in September and published 'By Authority') was the first piece in print to express skepticism of the Popish Plot and the trials of Roman Catholics. The danger of directly questioning the validity of the plot and the trials led L'Estrange (as he later explained) to cast doubt on the evidence by 'slanting, hinting... trimming' and on the witnesses by 'bantering betwixt Jest and Earnest.'[59] His approach was understated and subtle: for example, he painted an amusing picture of the divisions that the Plot had caused among the English: 'A man must be fierce and violent to get the reputation of being well-affected, as if the calling of another 'damned heretic' and 'Popish dog' was the whole sum of controversy,' he wrote.[60] But he was deadly serious in blaming the press for the current hysteria and in ridiculing the 'mercenary scribbler' who 'take[s] upon him[self] to handle matters of Faith and State [and] give laws to princes.' Stressing a favorite point – that anti-popish hysteria concealed criticism of the Church of England and the monarchy, just as in the Civil War – he insinuated that there was a Protestant plot, not just a Popish Plot. With respect to the Catholic trials, L'Estrange intimated that brutality had moved Miles Prance to turn king's evidence.[61] All this was laid out with such studied impartiality that his *History* undermined the received assumption that the accused were guilty. Of course, this approach again opened him to the charge of sympathy for Catholics. The opposition recognized that L'Estrange's *History* threatened their position, and Care, whether on his own initiative or commissioned by Whig parliamentary leaders (as some thought),[62] answered it.

In the meantime, the government was rendered nearly apoplectic by *An Appeal from the Country to the City, for the preservation of his Majesty's Person, Liberty, Property, and the Protestant Religion*, the most offensive of all the pamphlets published in the autumn of 1679. It appeared anonymously (signed 'Junius Brutus,' now identified as the deist and republican Charles Blount) in mid-October and with no indication of the printer or publisher.[63] The major purpose of the tract was to promote the exclusion of the Catholic duke of York from the line of succession to the throne and advance the claims of the Protestant duke of Monmouth. It may well have been inspired by recent events: the king's serious illness in August, the return of the Catholic duke of York from his enforced exile, and the exile of the Monmouth; no doubt it aimed to prepare the way for the hoped-for reappearance of Monmouth in November in disobedience to the king's orders. *An Appeal* opened with an hysterical description of what would happen to London and its citizens should Popery prevail.[64] Go to the top of the Monument to the Great Fire, readers were advised, and from there survey the city. Then, 'imagine you see the whole Town in a flame, occasioned this second time, by the same Popish malice which set it on fire before.' Tickling his readers' imagination further, the author painted a picture of their wives and daughters ravished by papist troops, their parents and other relations burned at the stake, their churches turned into stables and their ministers of God 'torn in pieces.' In sum, whatever the Devil would do were he prowling the earth will 'infallibly be acted by his Agents the Papists.'

The tract then scolded the king for dissolving or proroguing Parliament 'whenever they come to redress the Grievances of the Subject' and threatened him with disaster if he did not allow Parliament to sit. It identified the enemies of the people as 'young beggarly Officers' who favor a standing army; 'Courtiers' who tax and oppress the people for their own advantage; 'over-hot Churchmen' who favor popery and downplay the plot and throw suspicion on the Dissenters. The worse enemy of all was the papists who aim to bring in popery, a design which they can effect either by a popish successor or French arms. If one were forced to choose the agent, continued the tract in a remark deeply insulting to the duke of York, one should 'submit to a foreign Power,' because it has not fought against his own subjects, will be less vengeful, and also 'more likely to let us enjoy our own Religion and Liberties, than any Popish Successor will.' More dirt was shoveled on Charles and James by invoking the story of Sejanus to drive home the point that a king may be deceived by trusting favorites, especially a brother.[65] The solution to this dire situation was to depend upon a person able to lead the nation against a French and popish army, and 'no person is fitter than' Monmouth. Remember, readers were urged, that kings with defective titles make the best rulers for they are 'constrain'd by a gracious Government to supply what [they] want in Title.' Its advocacy of replacing James with Monmouth in the line of succession to the throne could not be more plain.

Understandably, the government was alarmed and angered by *An Appeal* and took immediate steps. Lord Chief Justice Francis North and Attorney General Sir William Jones were asked to evaluate it for the Council.[66] Within a few days 'several Persons' were called before the Council and two female press people and two clerks in the Letter Office were arrested.[67] Benjamin Harris, the Anabaptist book seller, who was later tried for publishing the

Appeal, was not questioned at this time, although the government may well have had him in their sights. There is no evidence that the authorities asked L'Estrange to reply to the tract, and it was probably on his own initiative that he did so in *An Answer to the Appeal from the Country to the City*, a powerful rejoinder that answered line by line the fantasy of popery that *An Appeal* had spun out, substituting the words 'Schismatical and Republican Malice' for Popery.[68] Playing on themes that he had used in earlier tracts, L'Estrange heaped blame on the press, identified the 'Regicidal Principles of Seventy-nine' with the 'Regicide itself of Forty-eight,' and painted present-day critics as filled with the 'Venom of the Old Cause swallow'd and Spew'd up again.' Offering a historical perspective, L'Estrange compared the author of *An Appeal* to Wat Tyler the fourteenth-century radical. The regicides, he went on, had created a government following the Civil War that was a 'Persecuting and Non-sensical Presbytery' – worse than the papacy. Unwisely for his reputation, L'Estrange drew further contrasts between the regicides and papists that was favorable to the latter. Admitting the danger of popery, L'Estrange insisted that 'safety' was in a 'mean, betwixt' it and 'Libertinism.' His civility towards Catholics provided ammunition to his enemies to charge him with being a secret Catholic. Clearly, in the autumn of 1679 the Court already had in L'Estrange an effective and intrepid champion to meet this new challenge in the press. L'Estrange had created this role for himself, just as earlier he had created other roles.

Also in October, the Council, moving with greater assurance, issued general search and seize warrants as well as specific warrants.[69] The use of general search warrants was illegal, a blatant misuse of power. Care and Curtis were the first of the press people to be called before the Privy Council on such a warrant; they appeared on 15 October in response to a summons of 13 October.[70] No evidence of what happened at that interview has survived. But the encounter holds interest for it raises the question why the Council wanted to talk with Henry Care, this low-level tract writer. Although they already knew the publisher Curtis, they could not have been absolutely certain that Care was the author of the anonymous *Weekly Pacquet*. One may speculate that their suspicions were aroused by an exchange in the press in mid-September between Johann Gibbon and Care under the title *The Touch of the Times, Or Two Letters Casually Intercepted. The First, From the Author of a late Pamphlet Intituled, Day Fatality: To the supposed Author of the Weekly Packet of Advice from Rome. The Second. the Answer thereunto.* In the first letter, dated 12 September, Gibbon bitterly complained about a scurrilous attack that he said Care had made on him in the 5 September issue of *The Weekly Pacquet*. The second letter, dated 17 September and signed by Care, made sport of the idea that Care was the author of *The Weekly Pacquet*. Gibbon rejoined with *Flagellum mercurii Anti-Ducalis*, a short piece addressed to Care in which, on evidence reportedly supplied him by one of the king's Officers at Arms, declared 'You are the Author of the Packet.'[71] Interestingly, Gibbon warned Care against opposing the duke of York, saying that he endangered himself. These pieces are the earliest printed evidence linking Care to *The Weekly Pacquet* and they may have prompted the Council to summon him.

If suspicions were aroused that Care was the author of *The Weekly Pacquet*, the authorities' fury no doubt doubled when they read the continuing brash and taunting criticism in the 12 September issue of *The Popish Courant*. Care recycled the idea of a transforming medicine, this time calling it an '*Oleum Matchivellinum*, or the Tincture of Dissimulation.' This medicine had the power to transform 'Traytors into Martyrs' and enable papists to assume the shape of a Protestant.[72] The next week, Care was at it again, this time introducing a Roman Catholic spokesman who made the points that were emerging as Care's quintessential themes: Catholic delight over how violently they have enraged people against Nonconformists who are 'in all points, of their own Religion' and over Catholic friends 'in Masquerade,' men thought to be the 'White-boys of your Church, ' who in the press 'raise irreconcilable as well as causeless Jealousies [among Anglicans] and divide [their] Affections.' The result is wonderful for the Catholic cause: anyone who speaks of the papist dangers is branded 'odious.'[73] These themes — that Protestants who express sympathy for Catholics and hostility towards their critics were really Catholics hiding behind a mask of Protestantism and that they were prominent in the Church of England — would become constants in Care's polemic. This particular issue of *The Weekly Pacquet* must have struck home, because someone placed it among the State papers.[74]

Equally audacious was the issue of *The Popish Courant* printed on 10 October, just three days before the Privy Council's summons was issued. In it the Roman Catholic spokesman announces that Catholics have 'made it [their] business to cast an odium upon *[The Weekly Pacquet]* and hope shortly to crush it.' They are resolved to 'roast' the 'Miscreant Author in a Bonfire of his own Heretical Pamphlets.'[75] In its prescient anticipation of the government's intention to summon Care, this tale slandered the authorities by evoking the memory, kept green by John Foxe's *Acts and Monuments*, of Protestants burned at the stake by the Catholic Mary I. Such gratuitous insults no doubt hardened the resolve of the government to move against the press on several fronts.

The most effective move the Privy Council made was to seek the assistance of the judges (who, it will be remembered, held their tenure at the pleasure of the king). On 17 October 1679 the Council ordered the judges and the king's learned counsel to consider 'what Expedients may by Law be made use of to remedy the great Mischeifs that dayly arise from ye Licenciousness of the Presse.'[76] Responding within a fortnight on October 27, 1679, the judges (Scroggs, Sir William Ellis, Sir Thomas Jones, and Sir Francis North were among those who signed the ruling) handed down a ruling that the king's authorized officials might seize printed libels against the government or against public or private persons and jail the persons responsible pending trial 'according to law.' The judges did not say that the government had the power to censor books before publication nor arraign printers for unlicensed printing. No comment has survived on what the judges meant by 'according to law,' but they were no doubt referring to the law of seditious libel, which, as we have seen, empowered the government in precisely the way the judges specified.

The ruling was controversial from the beginning and became increasingly so with time. Three judges – Sir Robert Atkyns, Sir Francis Pemberton and Sir William Dolben – dissented, and Atkyns expressed his opposition in an angry 'public squabble' with Scroggs: to Scroggs's assertion that the king 'might prevent printing and publishing whatever he chose by proclamation,' Atkyns rejoined that 'such matters were fitter for Parliament, and that if the king could do this work of parliament, we were never like to have Parliament any more.'[77] Atkyns may have been criticizing the procedure used in reaching the ruling rather than the ruling itself, for, although contemporary critics charged otherwise, this ruling neither illegally extended the law nor made new law; rather it reinforced the terms of the old law of seditious libel. Rulings, however, carried substantial weight. Sir Matthew Hale under-scored the power of judicial rulings in *The History of the Common Law of England* when he wrote that, although only king and Parliament can make law, rulings have a 'great Weight and Authority in Expounding, Declaring and Publishing what the Law of this Kingdom is.'[78] Although the government could not have been entirely pleased with this ruling, they proceeded to employ it immediately in a royal proclamation dated 31 October which included a reward system for informers.[79] To assure wide circula-tion, the proclamation was printed in the 3 November issue of the *London Gazette*.

The October ruling and others that followed were vitally important to the government; press law was in disarray and the need for clarification – in the interests of the Court, of course – was acute. But the rulings also engendered genuine fear among Court critics. Atkyns had put his finger on the sore point: fear that the judges were usurping the authority of Parliament in the law-making process. Politically sensitive people came to regard the judges' ruling and the resulting royal proclamation as tantamount to making law without Parliament. Scroggs's harassment of print persons in interviews in the autumn and in subsequent trials intensified the consternation. In effect, a 'crisis of authority' developed from the contest over restraining the press. This 'crisis of authority,' born of a perceived threat to the integrity and independence of the law and to the power of parliament to make law for the nation, adds still another dimension to the Popish Plot.

The 27 October ruling was crafted at a time when Scroggs (undoubtedly the major figure behind it) was seething with rage over the printed attacks and other indignities heaped upon him by what he regarded as low-life scribblers. His anger was surely all the more heated because he was, in fact, vulnerable to the suspicion that king and Court owned him. Contemporaries recognized that he owed his advancement from one high legal post to another to the patronage of a man at the center of affairs in the mid-seventies, the earl of Danby, the Lord Treasurer. Even in 1676, when at Danby's insistence, Scroggs was appointed to the Court of Common Pleas (his first major advancement) pranksters posted papers about town saying that judgeships were up for sale and young lawyers might apply to the Lord Treasurer.[80] Two years later he became Lord Chief Justice of the Court of King's Bench, again supported by Danby.[81] Unfortunately for him, Danby's impeachment and removal in 1678 deprived him of a friend and left him exposed as a protégé of a discredited minister. Moreover, Scroggs's printed speeches gave direct evidence of his deep loyalty to the throne; an admirer told the king that Scroggs's public address upon his appointment to the Court of Common Pleas 'taught' the people more loyalty to the crown than all the sermons together printed since the Restoration.[82] Celebrating his elevation to King's Bench, Scroggs asserted that loyalty to the king was the 'Heart and Life' of the legal profession, that the crown must be 'guarded by lawyers as well as Laws,' and that in his court lawyers could expect favor to be 'measured to them by their Loyalty.' [83] The charge that he acquitted Wakeman at the behest of the king to spare the queen embarrassment was consistent with what was already known of him.

The Lord Chief Justice responded publicly to the insults hurled at him in the press on the very first day of the court term, 23 October (just before the ruling was announced). Not only did he have entered two informations of *Scandalum Magnatum* against a detractor, but also he delivered before the Court of King's Bench a 'long harangue' against his enemies and in vindication of his legal and personal honor.[84] Firmly denying all the insinuations about the Wakeman acquittal and announcing his views in unmistakable terms, although 'sometimes with hesitations & stammerings,'[85] he lashed out at 'hireling Scriblers... who write to Eat, and Lye for Bread.' Warning them that it was the 'proper business of this Court... to prevent and punish the mischiefs of the Press,' he anticipated the royal proclamation by disclosing that there was a law now to 'punish a Libelous and Licentious Press' 'overrun with Lies and Libels,' and that he intended to use it. Ironically, Scroggs contributed further to the uproar by ordering his speech printed, thus using for his own ends the press that he despised. He made certain in the title of the printed speech that the world should know that his remarks had been in response to the 'many Libelous Pamphlets which are publisht against Law, to the Scandal of the Government, and Publick Justice.'[86] To underscore the unity of the court, two highly respected fellow justices, Jones and Sir William Dolben, defended Scroggs and applauded his points in brief statements appended to the tract.

Scroggs put into practice the judges' ruling and his threat against the press that he had trumpeted in his speech, and Henry Care and others suffered. On 23 October (the day of his speech), Scroggs used his warrant to call in Care.[87] Upbraiding him in furious language for writing the *Weekly Pacquet*, Scroggs called him 'Rogue' and said that he would 'fill all the Gaols in England with such Rogues, and pile them up as Men do Faggots.'[88] The interrogation must have been persistent and severe, for Care confessed to writing the *Weekly Pacquet*, whose authorship he had heretofore tried to

keep secret. Refusing to accept bail, although Care offered good
sureties, Scroggs remanded him to King's Bench prison. Four days
later a newsletter writer referred to Care as the author of the
Weekly Pacquet, thus establishing that his authorship was certainly
accepted from October 1679, although strongly suspected before
then.[89]

Members of the Green Ribbon Club hearing that Care had
been thrown in jail, promptly came to his aid. They agreed to a
weekly assessment of twelve pence each to assist him. They justified the step on grounds that 'in a full society' the club had 'in a
most particular manner' recommended the *Weekly Pacquet* to all
persons who warmly favored the Protestant religion, 'wch by ye
Pacquet the author has expressed himself a bold Asserter.'[90] This
gesture by Green Ribbon Club members is of uncommon interest
because it is the first unequivocal and concrete piece of evidence
linking Care to Whig political radicals, as distinct from evidence
about his association with radical political press people. Clearly,
Club members looked with favor on *The Weekly Pacquet* as an
effective statement of views they endorsed and on its author
whom they volunteered to assist.

Despite Scroggs's announced intention to 'fill the jails' with
'rogues' like Care, the Lord Chief Justice's power to do so was limited by the fact that he could not legally keep Care (or anyone else)
in jail indefinitely because in May 1679 (the same month the
Licensing Act lapsed) the *Habeas Corpus* Act had passed. The Act
further strengthened the writ of *Habeas Corpus* by, for example,
requiring the court to release a prisoner on bail within two days. [91]
The passage of the *Habeas Corpus* Act protected authors, printers
and publishers who antagonized the government, against lengthy
imprisonment, if they were willing and financially able to purchase
a writ of *Habeas Corpus*. In 1681 the writ, including fees to numerous court officials, cost approximately £2 6s, a considerable sum
when one considers that the average yearly wage for a craftsman
was about £12.[92] Still, the writ did provide a shield. A contemporary noted its importance respecting the press: 'Swarms of

impudent licentious libels upon all sorts of persons, and upon all subjects... will continue whilst the *Habeas Corpus* is still in force, [for press people] are sure to be bailed.'[93] Care purchased a writ of *Habeas Corpus*, and Scroggs, taking the same bail he had refused before, released him on 25 October, after two days in jail. Within a week Care was at it again, promising if God would give him 'Liberty *once more*,' to write in behalf of the 'Protestant interest' against the 'Corruptions' of the age.[94]

Scroggs made life as difficult for Care as he could by requiring him to report each day to the court to answer an Information, 'if any should be brought.'[95] On 11 February 1680, the week after the government had successfully prosecuted Benjamin Harris, Francis Smith and Jane Curtis, an Information was filed in Court of King's Bench against Care, charging that notwithstanding the fact of a 'traiterous conspiracy' of Catholics against the kingdom he had 'maliciously and unlawfully' published a 'false, scandalous and malicious' book, *The Weekly Pacquet of Advice from Rome*, with the intention of 'scandaliz[ing]' the government and bringing it into contempt. The Information specifically cited the defamatory remarks of August first directed against Scroggs.[96] Appearing on behalf of Care on 12 February, an attorney, one Benedict Brown, entered a plea of 'Not Guilty,' and the court ordered Care 'To stand bound in his recognizance to appear the next Term to Answer thereunto.'[97] After additional judicial rulings virtually assured his conviction, Care was brought to trial on 2 July 1680.

In the meantime, on 24 October, the day after Care's bruising encounter with Scroggs, two other press people felt the wrath of the Lord Chief Justice. One was Francis Smith, the Baptist preacher, known as 'Elephant Smith,' a nick-name designed to distinguish him from other Smiths and derived from his shop, the 'Elephant and Castle,' located first near Temple Bar and after 1670 in Cornhill.[98] A generation older than Harris and Care, Smith was already well-known to the authorities as a man of radical religious and political views and a pesky bookseller of iconoclastic material, publishing, for example, *Trap ad Crucem* in 1670, on which Care

probably drew (as we have seen). Smith was brought in for questioning about *Some Observations upon the late Tryal of Sir George
Wakeman... By Tom Ticklefoot.*[99] Messenger of the Press Stephens
deposed that he had seen 'Parcels' of it in Smith's shop.[100] In the
interview, according to Smith's account, Scroggs insisted that he
identify the author, which Smith said he was unable to do. Smith
urged that his case was bailable and pointed to the many 'citizens
there present' who would stand bail for him. Scroggs rejoined that
unless Smith told him the name of the author of 'that seditious
pamphlet,' he would send him to jail.[101] Smith was adamant and so
Scroggs refused him bail, upbraided him in the same coarse language he had used against Care, and ordered him remanded to
King's Bench prison, thereby forcing him to gain release through
the expense of a writ of *Habeas Corpus.* At the same time Scroggs
filed an information in the Crown Office, thus laying the groundwork for a trial later on.[102]

Jane Curtis, Langley Curtis's wife and one of many print women
who promoted partisan political interests, was the second person
who appeared under warrant before Scroggs on 24 October.
Her offense was selling another scurrilous tract that deeply
offended Scroggs, *Satyr Against Iniustice: Or, Sc—gs upon Sc—gs.*
Understandably, Scroggs ached to punish Jane Curtis. His summoning her before him created some legal problems, however, for,
given the legal status of a married women as a *femme couverte*,
Curtis could not be legally prosecuted. Thus, Scroggs, in effect, had
to indulge in a pretence that she was a *femme sole* and thus liable to
prosecution. Whatever his intellectual gyrations, Scroggs treated
Curtis just as miserably as he did all press people, swearing at her
and her friends who had gathered in her support, declaring that he
'would shew no more Mercy than they could expect from a Wolf
that came to devour them,' refusing her bail, and forcing her also to
the expense of buying a writ of *Habeas Corpus* to obtain release
from prison.[103] She was called to trial later in February 1680.

'A while after' – the date was 7 January 1680 – Francis Smith's
son, Francis Smith, junior, also felt the wrath of the judge for

selling to a coffee house still another tract, *A New Year's Gift*.[104] This piece so incensed Scroggs that he charged Smith, junior, with publishing a seditious libel and jailed him. In terms that he had used before, the furious judge fumed at Smith, declaring that 'he would take no Bail;... he would ruin them all.' [105] But the next day Smith, junior, used a writ of *Habeas Corpus* to win his release and the matter was dropped without explanation.[106] The people involved in these interviews (except Francis Smith, junior) felt the further displeasure of the bench later, in 1680, when they were brought to trial on the same charges. These interviews and subsequent trials took on great significance in the autumn of 1680 when they were used as charges in the abortive impeachment proceedings against Scroggs.

On 29 November, Scroggs took a further step to try to ruin press people by issuing a warrant to Messenger of the Press Stephens and a large group of local officers. The warrant ordered the officers to assist Stephens to seize all seditious and treasonable books and pamphlets that they might find in the shops of booksellers or printers and empowered all of them to arrest 'the Author, Printers, or Publishers' and bring them before a Justice of the Peace 'to be proceeded against according to law.' The stated purpose was to reinforce the king's 31 October proclamation. The warrant laid bare Scroggs's view, which, in effect, reiterated the attitude Charles II had expressed in 1662 that 'ill-disposed Persons' were 'daily' printing seditious and treasonable books and pamphlets for the purpose of inciting the king's subjects to 'Sedition and Rebellion' and that the press must be controlled. After this flurry of activity, Scroggs and others took no further legal action against press people for the next couple of months.

Two days later, on 1 December, an indecorous incident occurred which is worth reporting because its political overtones were unfortunate for Scroggs. The Lord Chief Justice encountered Shaftesbury and friends at a dinner with the Lord Mayor of London. Obviously still smarting under aspersions cast on him regarding the Wakeman trial, and much in his cups, Scroggs provoked a fracas. Shaftesbury was conciliatory, even conceding that Scroggs had not accepted a bribe, but it took two or three hours to mollify Scroggs.[107] The incident did nothing to soften the earlier hostility between Shaftesbury and Scroggs. Possibly Shaftesbury heard that Scroggs, almost certainly in the autumn of 1679, had advised the Court to attempt to divide his followers to leave him 'without shelter' and to commission a piece about him that would spoil his 'political intentions.'[108] When a deposition containing new information about Wakeman's guilt was transmitted to the Privy Council in December 1679, Shaftesbury, in a tit for tat, declared that Scroggs was 'no longer fit to serve either King or nation.'[109] This enmity is a part of the background of the attempted impeachment of Scroggs a year later.

At about the same time, critics took several steps to register their dismay at the government's high-handed tactics and try to embarrass the king and his friends. One move was to mount a massive effort to petition the government to call a new Parliament. Starting in early December 1679, Shaftesbury and his men organized the so-called 'Monster Petition' and presented the longest of the petitions to the king on 13 January.[110] Widely circulated in London and the counties through a well-organized campaign at the grass-roots level, the petition focused not on Exclusion but on the king's failure to call Parliament and to try offenders like the earl of Danby and the five Catholic lords still held in the Tower for alleged complicity in the Popish Plot. It asked the king to allow Parliament to reconvene on 26 January, the day to which it had been prorogued. Although moderate in language, the petition was inherently provocative, for it implied that Parliament alone could redress the grievances of the nation and that the king should follow the advice of his subjects. Charles regarded petitioning as a design to overturn his authority and sovereignty; he issued a royal proclamation that forbade petitioning the government and damned the act of signing as seditious.[111]

Although about 18,000 persons signed the London petition in defiance of the royal proclamation, the strong negative reaction of the Court dampened the initial enthusiasm for the petition and left it dominated by radical Whigs. A recent analysis of the petition shows that although a 'wide cross-section' of society was represented, the signers were (as loyal contemporaries charged) heavily Nonconformist and included a large component of Baptists and independents, political malcontents inclined to radical Whiggery and members of political clubs, notably the Green Ribbon Club. Prominent examples of the latter included Henry Cornish, Vincent Alsop, Charles Blount and Robert Ferguson.[112] The signature of John Locke was in 'close proximity' to these,[113] opening the admittedly remote possibility that Care and Locke at least knew of each other. Care and persons with whom he was, or would become, closely associated were also among the signatories: James Astwood, a printer of opposition tracts who became Care's printer after he split with Curtis, and Slingsby Bethel, a republican and member of the Green Ribbon Club, who would eulogize Care at his death and attempt to revive *The Weekly Pacquet* at the time of the revolution of 1688–89. The fact that Care signed the petition on the sheet marked 'St Botolph Aldersgate' – the ward in which Shaftesbury lived – would seem to indicate that he wanted to identify himself with residents of that ward. That Care should have signed the petition, a project so emphatically opposed by the government and so closely identified with Shaftesbury and Whig political radicals, reveals how far he had traveled in the last four or five months towards associating himself with the Whigs as a critic of the establishment.

Despite the numerous signatures, the Whig-sponsored petition did not achieve its goal. When Parliament met on 26 January 1680, the day to which it had been prorogued, Charles simply prorogued it again, thereby deepening the tensions between himself and his critics.

An indication of Care's growing public reputation and influence was an attack on his house in the Old Bailey on 31 December, during the period when the petition campaign was in progress. At about 2:00 a.m., according to the *Domestick Intelligence*, seven or eight persons thought to be of the 'Popish Party' climbed the 'pales before [Care's] door,' shouted obscenities and broke his windows. Neighbors raised the cry and the ruffians fled. Harris explained that the intruders aimed to murder Care, the 'supposed' author of *The Weekly Pacquet,* because he had become a 'continual and severe scourge unto them.'[114] Although the 'Popish Party' is named, it could not have been lost on the politically sensitive reader that Care had also become a 'scourge' to the government. Through his writings and his brush with the law this little-known scribbler had achieved sufficient public visibility and notoriety over the last few months for some people to try to harm his person and property with the obvious aim of scaring him into silence.

A second step taken by critics of the government was to assail the man most closely associated with a growing fear that Parliament was being pushed aside as the law-making institution, namely, Scroggs. As would be publicly revealed within the year in the attempted impeachment of Scroggs, his detractors regarded the judges' ruling, the resulting royal proclamation, the Chief Justice's use of warrants, and his treatment of press men and women as tantamount to making law without parliament. I call this fear that the integrity of the law and the lawmaking powers of Parliament was threatened a crisis of authority, and I argue that it would form an important part of the Exclusion Crisis. With their customary audacity, on 21 January 1680, just a week after the furor over the 'Monster Petition' and only days before the appointed meeting of Parliament, Oates and Bedloe presented to the Privy Council thirteen *Articles of High Misdemeanours* against Scroggs. The substance of the *Articles* was similar to and in some cases identical with those that would be used later to try to impeach him. Articles 4 and 5[115] charged Scroggs with oppressing the king's loyal subjects by wrongfully imprisoning and refusing them bail, naming specifically Care, Jane Curtis and Francis Smith, senior. Praising the *Weekly Pacquet* as 'very useful' to 'Loyal and obedient Protestant Subjects' in its uncovering of the 'Impieties of the Romish Church,' article 4 insisted that Scroggs had been unable to identify

anything in the *Pacquet* that demeaned the kingdom's laws or government. Article 5 further complained that Scroggs had illegally
imprisoned Jane Curtis, a *femme couverte*. It was during this meeting
that Oates introduced an obscene and demeaning charge that
Scroggs had danced naked.[116] The Council, with the king present,
heard the charges, listened to Scroggs's defense (which they gave
him six days to prepare), and dismissed the case, saying that Scroggs
was free to proceed against his accusers 'according to law,' meaning
he could invoked libel law or the laws of *Scandalum Magnatum*.
Perhaps one reason for this decision was that King Charles recalled
his promise to Scroggs five months earlier that he would never
desert him.[117] Although some thought that Oates and Bedloe had
lost ground, Scroggs did not take them to court, no doubt because
his reputation was fragile and because (it was said) he feared defeat
– an indication of his weak position.[118]

This affair had a public dimension: Oates and Bedloe's charges
and Scroggs's defense were printed (in three editions), and further
printed interventions followed, notably a tract in Scroggs's defense,
Innocence Unveil'd that summoned before the public's mind Henry
Care. Linking Care with two publishers, it exulted that 'Those
Scriblers Harris, Smith, and Care, will quake, For their Foundation
doth begin to shake.' It warned all three men to 'beware... /Of him
you aim'd to catch within your snare.' This piece rejoiced that now
justice was restored and Scroggs's 'great Integrity is fully known.'[119]
The effect of the printed material was, of course, to spread widely
news of the event and keep 'Those scriblers' before the public eye.
For Care the public accounts of the trial enlarged his name
recognition.

The Court and its friends, already outraged over the 'Monster
Petition' and the effrontery of Oates and Bedloe at the meeting
of the Council, were all the more infuriated at the continued
appearance of tracts opposing the government. One of the most
exasperating was Henry Care's *History of the Damnable Popish Plot*,
which answered L'Estrange's *History of the Popish Plot*. With a
timing that could not have been fortuitous, it came 'Piping Hot'

from the press on 26 January 1680, the day appointed for parliament to meet and also, as it turned out, the day on which it was again prorogued.[120] The *History of the Damnable Popish Plot* is of uncommon importance, for it marked the first direct exchange between Care and L'Estrange and laid the groundwork for some of the rhetorical devices that these two men perfected in their later exchanges. It won the warm praise of L'Estrange's biographer, who described its author as 'formidable' and pronounced its preface as 'worthy a piece of invective as exists in the [English] language.'[121] And it riled L'Estrange who responded in kind.

To discredit L'Estrange's account, Care charged that it was no 'history' at all, ridiculed it as incomplete and inaccurate, and pronounced it dangerous because it might lead readers to discount the popish menace.[122] To demonstrate a true historical approach, Care placed the current plot in an historical continuum, linking it with 'those [plots] under which our Ancestor have laboured' (80). Drawing upon papal decretals, canons, and the work of Catholic historians and spokesmen, Care lingered over popish treasons during the reigns of English monarchs since the Reformation. Only then did he present the proceedings of the recent Popish Plot trials, underlining those omitted by L'Estrange. He explained why there was no universal abhorrence of the Plot: the king trod in the 'merciful steps of his Ancestors,' 'good men' were 'charitable' and 'fashionable' men about town turned the Plot into a jest, as they turned 'all things, though never so serious and sacred, into Drol and Ridicule' (116, 180; see also 319). The book ran close to 400 pages, the length itself implying how much more was needed beyond L'Estrange's eighty-eight-page account to set the record straight.

Care used to rhetorical advantage the strong anti-Catholicism in English society, playing off and feeding it in other ways. One was to emphasize how dangerous the principles and practices of Catholics were to Protestant princes; Catholics can never be 'faithful subjects' of a Protestant prince, asserted Care, quoting king James I (78-79). He sought to discredit Catholic claims of loyalty to the English monarchy by recalling the Irish Rebellion, stating that Catholics were 'mainly instrumental' in stirring up the Civil War, and declaring that they were not loyal to Charles I (ch.4). Catholics tracts, written by 'desperate Bigots' to 'poyson the minds... and divide the affections' of good Protestants were despicable (329 [second page so numbered]). Catholic authors dealt in lies, reporting, for example, that the king did not believe in the Plot, a thought which, of course, Care circulated more widely by the retelling (347; see also 322). Yet, interestingly, as we saw in the early issues of the *Weekly Pacquet*, he reached out to English lay Catholics, begging them not to give up their 'natural English Birthright' for a religion that was tantamount to 'Slavery' and urging them to convert to Protestantism and become loyal subjects (363). This gesture is worth noting: even for the violently anti-Catholic Care, there was hope that English Catholics might yet accept Protestantism.

Care seized the opportunity of his *History* to forward a discussion of two interrelated topics: (1) the relationship of the Church of England and Dissent and (2) the failings of the Anglican clergy. Although these two themes had appeared in the *Weekly Pacquet*, this was the first time that he had addressed them in an extended essay. Eight years later, in unsparingly bitter and vituperative terms, Care made them the main thrust of his *Publick Occurrences*. But in the *History of the Damnable Popish Plot*, he used moderate language and careful reasoning. Addressing the Church of England, he advised this venerable institution to be 'cautious' about enforcing matters of indifferent significance, for the times were dangerous, and not only was such rigor contrary to 'Prudence and Charity' and repugnant to apostolical doctrine but it threatened unnecessarily the Church's unity. Care carried the point further, declaring that what was coercive beyond 'bare Excommunication, is in truth a branch of Civil authority' (354, 356), thereby broaching an idea that he later developed: that Church and State are separate and thus punishment by the Church can not affect a person's standing in the State. In 1680 he did not cultivate his idea of religious toleration;

rather, in a reflection of his personal experiences and hopes, he advocated comprehension: the Church should change certain ceremonial requirements and 'comprehend' those Dissenters who wanted to remain within. For all his intellectual exuberance and use of filthy language in other writings, Care preserved a part of himself inviolate for the worship of the Christian God and came to believe genuinely that each person should be able to worship according to his conscience. Later he would say that he had always subscribed to that view.

The second motif was a strongly worded but essentially sensitive critique of the Anglican clergy. Blaming the clergy's 'scandalous coldness in religion' and its 'worldly-mindedness' linked with the harsh enforcement of matters indifferent as the most powerful reasons for separation, Care argued that godly people in particular judge a minister's doctrine by his actions (355). He counseled the clergy that the 'onely' way to acquire and maintain authority was to practice the 'great Evangelical Virtues, 'which he listed as 'Humility, Meekness, Heavenly-mindedness, ardent Love of God, and zealous endeavours for the salvation of Souls.' With a touch of contempt, Care observed that the practice of 'ordinary moral vertues' was no more than 'heathen Civility,' not Christianity (356). Continuing this harsh assessment, he pointed to men who 'turn the sacred Profession into a kind of Trade' and use it to win preferment and 'delicious Living.' To redress this situation and help the nation to confront fanaticism and popery, he boldly recommended that the Church advance those clergymen who practice true Christianity (357).

Care looked to Parliament to save the nation and dedicated his *History of the Damnable Popish Plot* to the two houses of Parliament, calling them 'Worthy patriots' and 'illustrious Great council.' He bracketed his text with fervent expressions of hope that Parliament would be allowed to sit long enough to uncover continuing popish designs. Not so subtly insulting the government, he cast himself at the feet of Parliament, begging for protection from the 'Snarlings of malicious Slanderers' and the 'Frowns of mighty

Criminals.'[123] His intentions seem patently clear: to associate himself with the parliamentary opposition at a time when his own legal future remained problematic.

Care's *History* so deeply angered L'Estrange that he promptly folded an outraged answer into his *Citt and Bumpkin in a Dialogue over a Pot of Ale, concerning Matters of Religion and Government.*[124] The main purpose of this tract was to deride and decry the late petitioning campaign, ridicule the political principles of court critics and defend himself. The format was notable, for it was the first of L'Estrange's Popish Plot tracts in dialogue, and it presents its serious message with a light, humorous touch.[125] A conversation takes place in a tavern between 'Citt,' a cosmopolitan Londoner, and 'Bumpkin' an unsophisticated fellow from the country. Speaking in colloquial language, the two reveal all the fraudulent things that they have done to get signatures on the petitions. Says Bumpkin, 'I fill'd up all those spaces with Names that I either Remember'd, or Invented myself, or could get out of two or three Christening-books.' Along the way 'Citt' instructs 'Bumpkin' in political principles and how to avoid jail if arrested. The tomfoolery between them is funny, even 300 years later. After Citt and Bumpkin are well established, a third character, Trueman (L'Estrange's mouth-piece), is revealed. Trueman, who has overheard their exchange, stands for truth and morality seen from a Tory vantage point, and his role is to defend the Church of England and the government of Charles II. Castigating Dissenters for their 'uncharitable bitterness,' Trueman insists that they conceal censure of the Church of England in their criticism of priests and Jesuits. To defend himself against Care's *History of The Damnable Popish Plot*, L'Estrange answers one by one the charges Care leveled against his *History of the Plot* and then, in a burst of vitriolic language, describes Care's book as a 'slanderous... arraignment of the government,' a 'Medley of Rags and Solecisms pick'd up out of Rubbish,' and, although admittedly 'most suitably put together,' comprised of little that had not been said before 'thirty times over.'[126] He treated Care himself in like fashion: Care was 'a little Grubstreet-Insect,' 'a Hackny sollicitor against both Church and State.' 'Calumny and False Witnessing is [sic] the best part of [his] Trade.'[127] In this rebuttal, the *ad hominem* attack which figured in Care's *History* became a feature of the L'Estrange–Care sparring in the press. *Citt and Bumpkin* was much more popular than Care's *History*; it had gone through four editions by June 1680 and a fifth appeared in 1681. It provoked several replies, none from Care, who contented himself with snide remarks in the *Weekly Pacquet*.[128]

That L'Estrange seized the opportunity of a tract that apparently was initially designed for another purpose to respond to Care suggests L'Estrange's sensitivity to the calumnies Care had heaped on him, his delight in battling an adversary in the press and Care's growing reputation. L'Estrange certainly knew, or knew of, Henry Care, but this was the first time that he responded to him directly in print. His doing so reinforced the dialogic relationship between the two men, which Care had initiated with the *History of the Damnable Popish Plot*.

This activity in the press coincided with a further attempt by the government to control printed material. On 28 January the Privy Council turned again to the judges to help restrain the 'present exorbitancy of the Presse.'[129] It seemed clear that the judges' October ruling and the king's proclamation of 31 October did not provide sufficient restraint. The judges had not said that the king could 'by law' censor material before it appeared nor arrest persons for unlicensed printing. Further, the ruling had made no reference to newspapers which had begun to appear and bedevil the establishment with critical accounts of current events. The response of the judges, however, was disappointing. The bench was divided, Burnet relating that 'Three, some say Four' judges opposed Scroggs about how to help the King 'in the Intervalls of Parliament.' The 'rest did not speak,' which a knowledgeable observer attributed to Scroggs's 'officiousness.'[130] Later it was reported that the judges had agreed that 'they knew not of any way to prevent printing by law; because that act for that purpose was expired.'[131] They handed down a ruling that denied the crown the authority of pre-publication censorship, but recommended that the court use the old medieval laws of *Scandalum Magnatum* against the press. The court was so disappointed in the ruling that it forbade the clerk of the Privy Council to enter it in the Council's official *Register*, probably because it feared that registering the ruling would compromise efforts to achieve an opinion allowing pre-publication censorship.[132] But, the opinion was used to bring Benjamin Harris, Francis Smith and Jane Curtis (all friends of Care's) to trial in February and other rulings brought Care to trial in July. The rulings and the trials were central reasons for the downfall of Scroggs.

4

CARE'S TRIAL
and
Sir William Scroggs's
IMPEACHMENT

our major press persons infamous for their criticism of the establishment – the publishers and printers Benjamin Harris, Francis 'Elephant' Smith, Jane Curtis and Henry Care, the only author among them – were brought to trial in the first half of 1680. Held in February and early July against a backdrop of judicial rulings and lively exchanges in the press, these four trials variously illustrate the problems and strategies of the government, the bench and press people in their contest with one another in the law courts. They reveal the difficulties the establishment had in shutting up press people who irritated it almost beyond endurance and, in Care's case, in shutting down a publication it detested. The court procedures at the trials, the behavior of the prosecution, and the law on which the prosecution grounded its cases were subject to criticism, and the parliamentary opposition used all these in their bid to impeach Scroggs in the autumn of 1680, an extraordinary development in the history of the press.

The trials also highlighted the weapons the lower-middle-class people were able to marshal on their own behalf: distinguished Whig lawyers, weaknesses in the law, problematical judicial rulings, uncooperative witnesses sympathetic to the defendants, and a large and highly vocal audience. As the earl of Anglesey commented, 'The old civil war had... transformed itself into a judicial war – men fought with one another in judicial battle.'[1] The 'judicial battle' that took place in Care's trial and in the attempt to impeach Scroggs is the major focus of this chapter.

I

There was a long runup to Care's trial, held on 2 July 1680. An information had been filed against Care in February,[2] but while the trials of Harris, Smith and Curtis went forward immediately, proceedings against Care were delayed without explanation. It is a guess that the government wanted to test public reaction to the other trials; it is a certainty that the authorities waited until the judges had crafted favorable rulings respecting the press before going forward. The trials of Harris (5 February) and of Smith and Curtis (7 February), each in the Court of King's Bench, held at the Guildhall, are instructive for several reasons. First, the government's seriousness of purpose is evidenced by the assignment of distinguished legal figures to manage the trials: Scroggs as presiding judge at the trials of Benjamin Harris and Henry Care; Sir William Jones at those of Smith and Curtis; Sir George Jeffreys, the acid-tongued, tough-minded recorder of London, as leader of the prosecution at the trials of Harris, Smith and Care.[3] The lowly defendants were far from helpless: their defense was in the hands of Sir William Williams, a highly visible and well-respected Whig lawyer, joined in Harris's case by Sergeant Thomas Strode and in Care's case by a powerful Whig, Sir Francis Winnington, a former solicitor general. Their presence underscored the Whig partisan interest in the cases, an important feature at a time when

Parliament, to which the Whig press people looked for protection, was not in session.

Second, the trials generated a lot of popular partisan attention, with 'great multitudes' on hand, their attendance almost certainly promoted by Whig interests.[4] The huge crowds at Harris's trial punctuated the proceedings with 'halloos and shoutings,' and when the 'guilty' verdict came in, onlookers responded with 'a very great and clamorous shout.' These antics deeply disturbed Scroggs. 'What shall become of us,' he thundered at the end of the trial, when 'for such a base book [*An Appeal From The Country To The City*] such clamorous noises shall be made?' 'Our lives and fortunes are at stake.'[5] The crowds were undeterred. Whigs turned out again on the day Harris stood in the pillory, arranging themselves around him to deflect missiles thrown at him, and 'hollowed and whooped.'[6] Harris's vocal friends, however, were disinclined to support him financially by contributing money to pay his fine. At Care's trial Scroggs attached political significance to this, contending that the 'hummers' were 'false' to the 'interest and men that they seem to espouse'; they were really 'enemies to the government' who appeared 'only to affront a court of justice.'[7] He used this interpretation of the noisy crowd to justify the severity of the government's response.

Third, the government faced another difficulty in proving that the law covered the offense with which the defendants were charged. For example, Harris was accused of printing and selling *An Appeal From The Country To The City* 'maliciously to scandalize the king and government with it.' Three witnesses for the prosecution readily showed that the miserable pamphlet had been sold in Harris's shop. This Harris's defense counsel admitted, but he insisted that Harris had had no 'malicious design.' Rather, he, like others, had sold the tract 'in a way of trade' and 'only... to get money.'[8] That concession and explanation were the standard defense of press people. Apparently one of the judges voiced his doubts that 'the mere selling of such a book' was actionable, and in front of the court Scroggs undertook to set him straight. Insisting that 'except for the writer of it,' there was no worse offender than sellers of seditious material because for 'trivial profit' they compromised 'the peace and quiet' of the nation, he asserted that 'all the judges' had recently met, not once, but twice, and each time they had declared 'unanimously' that anyone who wrote, printed or sold a pamphlet that was 'scandalous to public or private persons' might be punished, and the book seized.[9] This reading echoed a ruling made almost twenty years earlier on the law of seditious libel: in 1663 Chief Justice Hyde and Chief Justice Kyling had declared that 'tho' printing be a trade, and selling of books also, [printers] must use their trade according to law, and not abuse it, by printing and selling of books scandalous to the Government or tending to sedition.'[10] Scroggs was on sound legal ground, a fact recognized by the House of Commons: none of the articles of impeachment respecting the press suggests that Scroggs misconstrued the law.[11] The present point is that not all the judges at the trial agreed that the law covered the offense – no more than they had earlier – and Scroggs's emphasis upon their unanimity caught him in a falsehood. Scroggs knew full well that three or four judges had dissented in October 1679 and that there had been no unanimity in January 1680. Scroggs's lecturing the justices revealed a fissure in the government's position.

Fourth, Scroggs's irritation with the jury was a further sign of weakness. He refused to let the jurors take a copy of the *Appeal*, which was in the courtroom, with them when they retired, and he upbraided them for their verdict – 'guilty of selling the book' – which intimated that Harris was not guilty of a design 'maliciously to scandalize the king and government.' To qualify his guilt in this way, Scroggs complained, was 'not their business.' Rebuking them for even retiring to consider a verdict when the evidence was so full and he had instructed them so particularly in the law, Scroggs scolded them for their 'scruples' and for giving the 'party... advantage.' 'It was not so prudently done as might have been done,' he growled.[12]

Fifth, Scroggs's remarks that the justices aimed to restrict newsbooks was another sign of disorder. Announcing in confused language that even though the stories in newsbooks were 'not scandalous... yet if they are writers (as there are few others) of false news,' they were subject to punishment, Scroggs declared that 'all' domestic intelligences are 'factious.' The offense of printing news was also 'punishable in the seller, though in the way of his trade,' he added.[13] Scroggs's remarks referred silently to the laws of *Scandalum Magnatum* and show that he conflated those laws and libel law to strengthen the position of the government. Since the laws of *Scandalum Magnatum* made it illegal to defame the monarch or the great men of the realm by spreading orally or in writing 'false news,' they were useful in the present circumstances. The comments suggest how desperate Scroggs was to cobble together rulings and readings that would give the government a stronger position against the press. They lend additional credence to the partisan fear that a crisis of authority had opened up in the nation's government.

Sixth, the difficulties of the court were also evident in the treatment of the defendants. Thus, Scroggs tried to bargain with Harris, offering favor for Harris's naming the author. Nothing came of the overture, and the frustrated Scroggs in the end treated Harris with great severity.[14] In Smith's case, the defense admitted publishing *Some Observations Upon the Late Tryals of Sir George Wakeman*, and Smith's wife apologetically described her husband, who was absent because of illness, as contrite and eager to submit. The court, delighted with the admission of guilt and the apology, imposed only a small fine, a gesture surely calculated to avoid a reaction against the government.[15] Similarly, Jane Curtis, tried for publishing *A Satyr Against Iniustice: Or Sc—gs upon Sc—gs*, escaped harsh treatment. Again Williams admitted the record, and this time the court did not proceed to trial but called Jane Curtis to stand before it. Curtis, who in reality was feisty and obdurate, presented herself as a wife who had not known what she was doing, as 'ignorant in the matter,' explaining that her husband had been, and remained, out of town.[16] His sympathy aroused, Jones promised to intercede on her behalf with Scroggs. Curtis's ploy, which depended upon social stereotypes and legal assumptions about women, worked; this time Jane Curtis avoided jail. Although the court's leniency was calculated to avoid a reaction against the government, in Curtis's case the legal awkwardness of jailing a married woman under *coverture* was an additional consideration. The charge that Curtis's *coverture* rendered her imprisonment in October 1679 illegal appeared in the articles of misdemeanor against Scroggs that Oates presented to the Privy Council three weeks before her trial. And in the autumn of 1680 the same charge was included in the impeachment drawn up against Scroggs. The court in February was clearly sensitive to the problem.

A seventh challenge to the government was to silence the defendants, who had the resources – their own presses or those of friends – to continue to print obnoxious material. Overseeing his affairs from prison, Harris printed an account of his trial[17] and kept his *Domestick Intelligence* going for several weeks with the help of his wife and Nathaniel Crouch. Another outrageous remark in the 30 March issue of the *Domestick Intelligence* forced him out of business on 16 April.[18] But Harris was back again in December 1680, secure for the time being in the protection of the Second Exclusion Parliament. Smith also saw to it that an account of his trial appeared: *An Impartial Account Of The Tryal Of Francis Smith*, which included a report of Jane Curtis's trial. The effect was to exculpate the defendants, while painting the government as prosecutory. In the end the February trials did little to advance the interests of the government; indeed, they weakened its position, a remarkable testament to the power of press people and of printed material.

II

Still faced with patent difficulties of reining in the press, the court remained intent upon winning a legal opinion favoring pre-publication censorship. Two months after the February trials, on 14 April 1680, the court made a third appeal to the judges for a ruling about its legal power to regulate the 'abuses of the Presse by pamphlets and newes Bookes.'[19] It did so with greater confidence because the judiciary had been newly reconstituted. Disappointed by the 28 January ruling on the press, aware, surely, that the 'discourse amongst the Judges' following that ruling was 'much talked of,'[20] and incensed over some judges' attitude toward petitioning, the king had dismissed Sir Robert Atkyns on 6 February and Sir Francis Pemberton on the 16 February. Charles could, of course, legally take this step because their tenure was at the king's pleasure. Atkyns understood well enough that he had been dismissed because he had offended Scroggs and North by opposing censorship by proclamation and upholding the right of petitioning.[21] Pemberton was at a loss to explain his removal, but Burnet felt that he had been 'turned out entirely by Scroggs's means' because of his moderation and his refusal to sign earlier rulings respecting the press.[22] The new bench handed down a third ruling on 5 May that went a great distance toward meeting the needs of the court.[23] Although the ruling did not apply to all printed material, it declared that the king may 'by Law prohibit the printing & publishing all News Bookes & Pamphletts of News whatsoever not licensed by [his] Authority as Manifestly tending to the Breach of the Peace & Disturbance of the Kingdome.'[24] Ignoring the absence of statutory law in support of this opinion, the judges used the idea that unlicensed news tended to breach both the peace of the nation, which it was the responsibility of the king to preserve, and the king's prerogative power to grant printing monopolies.[25]

This ruling proved useful to the government, which employed it in Care's trial, in the ban issued in November 1682 against the publication of all news sheets except the *London Gazette* and the *Observator*, and immediately, on 12 May, in a royal proclamation 'For Suppressing the Printing and Publishing Unlicensed News-Books and Pamphlets of News.'[26] Insisting on the importance to the State that printed news be accurate, the proclamation declared that 'Evil-disposed Persons' were circulating idle and malicious reports to 'Scandalize the Government or for other indirect Ends.'

The judges had 'unanimously' declared that such practices endangered the peace of the kingdom. Thus, the king and his Privy Council had decided 'strictly to prohibit... all persons whatsoever to print or publish any News-Books or pamphlets of News' without a license. Offenders would feel the 'utmost Severity of the Law.' Two weeks later, on 28 May, Scroggs issued a warrant that sought to implement the proclamation, empowering Stephens and certain local officers to seize unlicensed newsbooks and arrest the persons responsible for them.[27] By these steps the prerogative power of the crown to license the press with respect to news was reinstated. Theoretically, the government now had the power to decide what the public should read about daily news events. And, in fact, the authorities almost prevailed, for almost all newspapers ceased publication.[28] Care, however, defiantly continued to publish the *Weekly Pacquet*.

The government was still unsatisfied with what the bench had offered, and it took a further extraordinary step to close in against Care. On the last day of Easter term, 28 May, the judges issued a ruling that specifically targeted Care's *Weekly Pacquet* and banned the future printing or publication of it 'by any person whatsoever.'[29] The ruling was genuinely controversial. Even so devoted and loyal a supporter of the king and the royal prerogative as Roger North admitted some years later that the order was an arbitrary use of legal power; he described it as 'controvertible' and not 'a clear case.' Still, there was some legal precedent: Roger North reported that his brother Francis had explained that the order was 'grounded on that Law which takes away the Star-Chamber' and located in the Court of King's Bench all residual law that the Star Chamber might have lawfully exercised to prevent 'great Offences.' There was 'ground enough' for it, North concluded.[30] But the ruling against the *Weekly Pacquet* sidestepped statutory law and located the power to control the press in the bench reinforced by royal prerogative.

This was the consideration that animated Scroggs's critics; they were furiously opposed to the ruling and used it to charge the

Lord Chief Justice and the bench with usurping Parliament's law-making authority. Care later put the worst possible construction on the ruling, arguing that if the court could ban the *Weekly Pacquet* on so little authority, it could also ban the Bible and 'any other Books.' Describing the ruling as 'meer Arbitrary will and Pleasure,' Care underlined the absence of a clearly stated complaint, reason or condition for disallowing publication of the *Weekly Pacquet*. In contrast to statements that all the judges had concurred in the opinion, Care laid the blame squarely on the Lord Chief Justice. ''Tis said, none of the other Judges knew of it,' he wrote.[31] My point is that the justices, with the court's approval, wrote a special ruling that they no doubt knew would be disputable, which underscores how important they thought Henry Care and his *Weekly Pacquet* were in the print contest and the lengths to which they were willing to go to suppress them.

Why were the judges, led almost certainly by Scroggs, so intent upon silencing Care? First, Care was the only author the government had in its snare – Smith, Harris, and Jane Curtis were publishers and booksellers. Pointing out the difficulties in finding an author, Scroggs remarked that 'one author found is better than twenty printers found.'[32] Second, the 5 May ruling applied only to 'News Books and Pamphlets of News'; however, the *Weekly Pacquet* was not a newsbook but a history, together with a sheet of nasty remarks on public events. Strictly speaking, it did not fall under the 5 May ruling. A further technical point was that since the *Pacquet* was published each week, it did no good to convict the author of violating the law just one week, for the condemnation would not extend to the sheet printed the next week; it was a far surer thing to ban the publication entirely. A friend of the court, Roger North, was convinced that 'no ordinary judicial Order could reach it' and hence a special ruling was required.[33] Third, Care, a darling of the Whigs and of the Green Ribbon boys, had deeply offended Scroggs and others by the subtle but outrageous fare the *Weekly Pacquet* served up each week about the Court and the Church. As Roger North put it, beneath the 'outward

Pretence' of showing the inanities of Roman Catholicism, the weekly sheets 'continually reflected on the Government.' North shrewdly explained that 'all this [the historical evils of popery] you are to expect from the Duke of York, and... the King and the Duke are one.'[34] A fourth difficulty was that since the *Weekly Pacquet*'s anti-Catholicism was so robust and met with such general approval, it was awkward to criticize it and its author; it was more effective to get rid of it entirely. For all these reasons, the bench issued its most problematical ruling against the press, dedicating it to erasing Care's *Weekly Pacquet*.

III

In the meantime, the furor in the press over the Popish Plot, now shifting to the exclusion of the duke of York from the succession to the crown, was unabated.[35] Much to the alarm of the government's friends, the opposition seemed to be riding a wave of popular approval: L'Estrange lamented that the 'faction has gotten so much the Command of the People, as to make them believe every thing that They Say, and approve of everything that they do.'[36] Although there was real urgency, the government took no initiative to present its side in print. It was L'Estrange, confessedly writing for money, who came forward as the government's ardent champion.[37] A number of his tracts, six new and four reprinted ones, were circulating in the spring of 1680, devoted to vindicating the court's interests, defending himself against charges of popery, and rebuffing insults and slights hurled at him, especially by Henry Care.[38]

The press contest in 1680 has been investigated by Mark Knights, but two features that he does not mention are pertinent to this present study. One is the hardening of the animosity between L'Estrange and Care. The scurrilous remarks that Care flung at L'Estrange seem to have wounded him deeply. A contemporary noticed Care's ability to rile L'Estrange, reporting that while the latter dismissively called Care a 'little Creature,' that 'little

Creature... has been a Goad in his side.' He has 'prick'd the Bull so hard, as has made him bellow full loudly' and be 'Splenetik at Mr. Care.'[39]

A particularly insulting example of Care's irrepressible nasty wit is a phony advertisement that appeared in the *Courant* for a soon-to-be-released treatise that would show 'How a Decayed Gentleman may live by his Fingers-ends; Scribble thred-bare Extravagances two and forty times over, and each time Answer them himself, and so... Reply, Rejoin, and Surrejoin all alone... as his pinching, Necessities shall require.'[40] If readers missed this in the *Courant*, they could have found it in *Citt and Bumpkin answered*, by EP (Edward Phillips?), which quoted it verbatim and identified it as targeting L'Estrange. For a man of his position, reputation, experience and age, L'Estrange was surprisingly sensitive to Care's insulting comments. Instead of ignoring the comment, L'Estrange fell into a rage and answered in print, justifying his writing for money to serve the king and in a bid for sympathy, admitting that he was old, too old to start a new career.[41] This ranting only magnified the incident. L'Estrange, moreover, kept the exchange of insults going, heaping opprobrium on Care, portraying him as a 'pitiful Cause-Jobber,' a 'Small Thred-bare Solicitor in the Old Baily.'[42] He also revisited the criticisms Care had leveled against his *History of the Plot*, answering each charge, reiterating points he had made in part 1 of *Citt and Bumpkin*, and again showing himself to be markedly thin skinned. Further, he opened the matter of Bedloe's *Narrative of the Fire*, setting out the essentials of his understanding of its origins. Although he did not accuse Care directly of writing it, he laid the groundwork for doing so in the future. Clearly, the hatred between L'Estrange and Care was well in place before the press battle between them began in earnest in 1681.

The second feature of the print warfare central to this study is the prominent part assigned to Care in a print, *The Committee; or, Popery in Masquerade*. L'Estrange wrote the accompanying text, conceptualized the picture and got someone to draw it for an engraver. His publisher, Henry Brome, published it on 15 April 1680. The most effective publication of that spring, *The Committee* has been called a 'landmark in the history of English satire'; it represents the first time both sides used pictures in their exchange and the first time L'Estrange engaged in a graphic battle.[43] Costing six pennies, this large broadside measured fifteen by twenty inches and featured an engraving across the top and an 'Explanation' written in rhyming verse across the bottom. Letters key the verse to the picture, making the meaning of the picture plain to all viewers, whatever their political sophistication. The 'Explanation' tells the viewer that the print is a 'satyr' on those who killed Charles I, and the iconography illustrates exactly points that L'Estrange conveyed in his tracts. The picture shows a Presbyterian as a leader of a group of Nonconformists seated as 'The Committee' at a table strewn with papers marked 'Church and Crown Lands,' 'Sequestration's,' and so on. On the floor, at the left lies the head of Charles I, murdered by 'Rebels,' and on the right is a priest of the Church of England, vomiting his living. These and other pictorial details invited the viewer to understand that the current turmoil stemmed from the Civil Wars and would lead to like results, the destruction of monarchy and Church.

In the very center of the picture, marked 'F,' sits a man holding a paper bearing the words 'Ps Narrat: Nar:of Fires Corrante. Tom & Dick.' On his left is a 'Babby,' a little figure with a monkey's tail and arms outstretched.[44] On his right are a pot and an inkwell. The man looks up as if to receive instruction from the figures at the table. The 'Explanation' at 'F' reads:

> *Now wash your Eyes, and see their Secretarius*
> *Of Uncouth Visage; Manners most Nefarious,*
> *Plac'd betwixt Pot and Pipe, with Pen and Paper;*
> *To shew that he can Scribble, Tope, and Vapour:*
> *Beside him, (Craving Blessing) a Sweet Babby;*
> *(Save it!) the very Image of the Daddy!*
> *He deals in Sonnets, Articles, takes Notes,*

> *Frames Histories, Impeachments, enters Votes,*
> *Draws Narratives, (for Four Pound) very well;*
> *But then 'tis Forty More, to Pass the Seal.*
> *Beside his Faculty, at a Dry Bob,*
> *That brings him many a comfortable Job.*[45]

The figure represents Henry Care. Attributes associated with him make the identification unmistakable: he was known as the secretary to the 'Faction' in the press;[46] L'Estrange referred to him, and none of the others, as a 'monkey,' noticed his fondness for drink, underscored his braggadocio and accused him of writing narratives of the Fire. Care was indisputably the author of the *Courant.* Capping proof is that on the British Library copy of the print at the couplet 'He deals in Sonnets, Articles, takes Notes/Frames Histories, Impeachments, enters Votes,' there is a note in Luttrell's hand: 'Touch on Mr. Henry Care.'[47]

The Committee inspired a sharp rejoinder from two sources. One was Stephen College, the 'Protestant joiner,' who later was tried, found guilty, and executed as a traitor for seditious words and actions at Oxford. College himself designed and engraved a large broadsheet of text and pictures that came out on 26 October 1680. The reader is told that the dog Towzer stands for L'Estrange and the broom tied to its tail is Henry Brome, his bookseller. A devil drives him on to Hell, past the hangman and his friends, the Pope and the duke of York.[48] The second answer came from the author of *Citt and Bumpkin Answered.* Mincing no words, he characterized *The Committee* as 'seditious,' 'libellous and scandalous,' and misrepresenting basic truths and said that its author deserved punishment.[49] L'Estrange promptly responded in *A Short Answer To A Whole Litter of Libellers*, where, pointing to the last three lines of the 'Explanation,' he declared that his purpose was to show that liberty of religious conscience portended great danger: 'License is like a Sea-Breach to your Grounds;/Suffer but One Flaw, the whole Country Drowns.' The metaphor is worth noting, for Care used an identical one in his *English Liberties* later in 1682.

The Committee; Or Popery in Masquerade (1680), a political print with text by Sir Roger L'Estrange, said to be a 'landmark in the history of English satire.'

MITTEE,

Masquerade.

COVENANTING PEOPLE

Wee'l be true to you

Little Isaack. Pope

A Solemn
LEAGUE
and
COVENANT
Come and let us joyn our
selves unto the Lord, in
a perpetuall Covenant, ỹ
shall not be forgotten.
Jer. 50. 6.

Indepen   Fifth Mon   Nailor   Idamite

Court of Justice   Humilia:

No Bishop Lord   No evill Counsellors

Army Account

widowes teares

Blood of Ireland

a Cordiall for ỹ D.

Sequest:
1643
1648

Biblia Sacra

against Fishers

Hooker

The Colchester Wedding

Canons
Surplice
Apocrypha   Com: Prayer
+ in Bapt

Ill *Accidents*, and *Humours* to *improve*,
Under the fair Pretexts of *Peace*, and *Love* ;
To ferve the Turn of an *Ufurping Power*.
But read their *Minutes*, and *They'l* tell ye *More*.

[*E*] Take a view, next, of the *Petitioners*.
But why, (you'l fay) like *Beafts* to th' *Ark*, in *Pairs* ?
Not to expofe the *Quaker*, and the *Maid*,
(By Luft to thofe Brutalities betray'd)
As if *thofe two Sects* more addicted ftood
To *Mares*, and *Whelps*, then *other Flefh and Blood* :
No, But they're coupl'd Here, only to tell
The *Harmony* of their *Reforming Zeal*.

[*F*] Now wafh your Eyes, and fee their *Secretarius*
Of *Uncouth Vifage* ; *Manners* moft *Nefarious*,
Plac'd betwixt *Pot* and *Pipe*, with *Pen and Paper* ;
To fhew that he can *Scribble*, *Tope*, and *Vapour* :
Befide him, (craving Bleffing) a *Sweet Babby* ;
(Save it!) the very *Image* of the *Daddy!*
He deals in *Sonnets*, *Articles*, takes *Notes*,
Frames *Hiftories*, *Impeachments*, enters *Votes*,
Draws *Narratives*, (for **four Pound**) very well ;
But then, 'tis **forty more**, to Pafs the *Seal*.
Befide his Faculty, at a *Dry Bob*,
That brings him many a comfortable Job.
                                    (*Rout*

[*G*] Mark, Now, Thofe *Club-men* ; That *Tumultuous*
Crown, *Bible*, *Magna Charta*, under Foot !
Thofe *Banners*, *Trophies* ; and the Execrable
Rage, and Tranfports of an *Incenfed Rabble* !
Here, the *Three States* in *Chains* ; and *There*, the Head
Of a *Good King*, by *Rebels murthered*.
And all this while, the Creatures of Thofe Knaves,
That blew the Coal, themfelves, the greateft Slaves.
What Devil could make Men Mad, to This Degree ?
Only *miftaken Zeal*, and *Jealoufie*.
Liberty, *Confcience*, *Popery*, the *Pretence* ;
Rapine, *Blood*, *Sacrilege*, the *Confequence*.

Marginalia from *The Committee; Or Popery in Masquerade* (1680) identifying Henry Care as the 'Secretarius.' A note in Narcissus Luttrell's hand near the couplet 'He deals in Sonnets, Articles, takes Notes,/Frames Histories, Impeachments, enters Votes' reads, 'Touch on Mr. Henry Care.'

In sum, L'Estrange's tracts and the print, published in the spring of 1680, during a period when Care published only his the *Weekly Pacquet*, were of uncommon importance. The court's former censor and continuing champion had in effect acted as Care's press agent: by naming him, by answering him, by featuring him in *The Committee*. L'Estrange's singling out Care for this special attention would seem to indicate that he regarded him as his major adversary in the press; he alludes to no other press person. This mark of recognition would have elevated Care's reputation and enlarged his visibility in political and press circles. But Care's prominence could have cut both ways, hardening the resolution of the government to rein him in, as in legal rulings, and at the same time underlining the potential problems involved in doing so.

IV

From the perspective of this study, Care's trial on 2 July 1680 in the Court of King's Bench, held in the Guildhall, was a climax to events of the past six months: the trials of other press people in February, the judges' rulings and the prominence of Care in L'Estrange's publications. The most interesting of the press trials held in 1680, Care's trial offered the public exciting political theater – strongly defined characters, brisk dialogue, and an active and 'numerous auditory.' Scroggs presided, even though his conflict of interest was blatant: the offensive printed passage cited in the information had implicitly savaged him and he had been responsible for harassing Care in the fall of 1679, for entering the information against him in February 1680 and almost certainly for initiating the controversial ruling about the *Weekly Pacquet* in May. The same lawyers as in earlier press trials battled each other: Jeffreys for the prosecution, and Williams, this time joined by Winnington, for the defense. Indirect evidence places Care in the courtroom, but he took no part and said nothing.[50] Contrary to what is usually thought, Care was charged at law, not for publishing a seditious libel, but for publishing an issue of the *Weekly Pacquet* without license from the government. Like the previous trial, Care's trial showed the strengths of press people.

The government made careful preparations immediately prior to Care's trial. At about the time of the 28 May ruling, Scroggs took a step aimed at banishing the *Weekly Pacquet* from the face of the earth: he sought to intimidate the printer. Interestingly, Scroggs summoned, not Langley Curtis, but Jane, his wife, and interrogated her about the printing of the *Weekly Pacquet*. Why did he call in Jane rather than Langley? Did he think, in view of her performance before the court three months earlier, that she would be more easily manipulated? If so, the Lord Chief Justice must have been disappointed. Jane Curtis justified the printing of the *Weekly Pacquet* at length, insisting that it had been licensed, paid for and entered in the Stationers' Company records. Scroggs thundered back that the *Weekly Pacquet* was a 'scandalous libel and against the king's proclamation' and threatened to 'ruin her if ever she printed any more.'[51] 'Soon after' this encounter, she, Care and 'other printers' were served with the 28 May ruling.[52]

Second, while the choice of the Guildhall for the trial served Care well (it located the trial virtually in his neighborhood and facilitated the appearance of men at his trial who by their number and vocal intervention signaled their support), the date of the trial, 2 July, favored the court; it could not have been fortuitous.[53] At the London shrievalty elections held in late June, two ardent Whigs, Slingsby Bethel and Henry Cornish, had defeated the two incumbent Tory sheriffs, Sir Simon Lewis and Sir Jonathan Raymond, but they had not yet been sworn in. Since London sheriffs had the power to influence the selection of juries, holding Care's trial before the Whig takeover of the London shrievalty meant that Tory-inclined jurors would be empaneled by the still incumbent Tory sheriffs. This was surely the court's calculation, and it paid off: of the twelve jurors chosen, only one was a Whig, eight were Tories and three are unknown.[54]

The date of Care's trial also meant that it followed hard on the heels of two striking events in London, one involving an unknown, the other touching people at the high reaches of politics. The first was the public punishment on 30 June of an Essex yeoman who had been convicted of uttering defamatory words about Scroggs's role in the Wakeman trial. He was fined £200, imprisoned pending payment, ordered to post bond for good behavior for three years and commanded to stand in Westminster Hall with a paper pinned on him explaining his offense.[55] One effect was to refresh public memory of the Wakeman trial and the widespread denunciation of the acquittal. Further, the stiff punishment no doubt alerted observers to what lay ahead for persons like Care convicted of a similar crime. The second event was the judges' peremptory dismissal of the Middlesex grand jury during the last week in June, before the end of its term. By dismissing the jury, the judges scuttled a scheme orchestrated by the radical Whig leadership to indict the duke of York as a popish recusant.[56] The Whigs had calculated that Charles II would void the indictment, giving them the opportunity to charge that there was no justice respecting papists.[57] All the judges concurred in the dismissal of the jury, but Scroggs took the brunt of the blame, and the dismissal figured in his attempted impeachment later in the year. This incident highlighted the bench's use of legal powers that seemed arbitrary and unjust to court critics and underlined the arbitrary nature of the legal opinion that was central to the prosecution of Care.

The charge against Care stated that he had 'maliciously' published a 'scandalous and malitious Book, Intituled, *The Weekly Pacquet of Advice from Rome*' at a time when the kingdom was shaken by a terrible conspiracy of Catholics. The information specifically cited the passage in the 1 August issue about an 'Incomparable Medicament' that 'makes justice deaf, as well as blind, and takes out spots of the deepest Treason more cleverly than Castile-Soap does common stains.'[58] Since the information was dated February, there was no reference to the subsequent legal rulings. The challenge for the prosecution, according to the Information, was to prove Care's authorship and his malicious intention.

At the outset, however, Jeffreys shifted the spotlight to another legal question – 'whether or no rascals may have liberty to print what they please?' – the question that had brought out the large crowd, he said.[59] Answering the question in the negative, Jeffreys referred to the 5 May ruling, which he said had been passed by 'all the judges of England' and prohibited any person from printing anything 'concerning the affairs of the public without licence from the king.' Since the 'affairs of the public' could be almost anything, this remark implied that the licensing authority of the government was extensive, indeed overwhelming. Addressing the jury, Jeffreys declared, 'That is the matter, gentlemen, that you are to try.' In other words, the legal issue was the violation of the licensing requirements spelled out in the ruling. Reinforcing the point, Scroggs stressed later in the trial that whether the subject matter was malicious or not had no bearing on Care's guilt or innocence. Curiously, no-one specifically referred to the 28 May ruling targeting the *Weekly Pacquet*. But Jeffreys's comment regarding the 5 May ruling extended the royal prerogative over the press and deeply alarmed the Whigs, who complained, with reason, that the judges had made new law, and they cited this ruling in the articles of impeachment drawn up against Scroggs later in the year.

Advancing a broad and penetrating denunciation of people who wrote against the government, Jeffreys charged such critics with using a 'specious pretence:' they called a person 'a papist, or but popishly affected' to provide a cover for libeling that person. Their prey was anyone who did not agree with them. Henry Care was patently guilty of such actions; he 'thinks he can scratch the itch of the age' and 'libel any man in government' that he wished to. Distinguishing between a person who tried to suppress popery and one who was 'transported with [that] zeal because he is of a party,' Jeffreys insisted that Care had dishonestly used antipopery in the interests of partisan political ends and thus placed before the court a response to the claim that Care's only aim was to discredit Catholicism.

Uncooperative witnesses undermined the prosecution's effort to prove Care the author. The exchange between Mr Stevens, a printer, his unidentified servant and the lawyers was protracted and repetitive, with both witnesses giving inconclusive and contradictory answers: they only assumed that the author was Care; they would not swear that the offensive paragraph was in the papers they had been given to print; they had not dealt directly with Care but with the publisher, Curtis, or with Care's nameless 'boy.'[60] At one point when Stevens answered deviously, an irritated Scroggs was heard to say, 'What tricks we have in this world!' (7: col. 1117).

The defense team seized on the weaknesses in the testimony. Describing the evidence that Care was the author of the *Weekly Pacquet* as 'remote and conjectural' (7: col. 1122). Winnington argued in a 'learned speech' that even if that authorship were granted, there was no proof that he had written the offensive paragraph as the information charged.[61] Pointing to the 'shams' and 'artifices' of the age and to Care's reputation as a 'satirist against popery' who was 'very liked for it,' he suggested that a Catholic might have 'shuffled' in the insulting words to get Care in trouble with the authorities (7: col. 1121). This conjecture brought out 'Hems' from the people, which prompted an angry intervention from Scroggs: 'You see what a case we are in gentlemen; you see what a sort of people we are got among' (7: col. 1122). The prosecution, however, retreated to the idea that the witnesses' 'private opinion' and the 'general report of all' held that Care was the author. It answered the hypothesis that the sheet was 'shuffled' in by a Catholic by arguing that had two *Pacquet*s come out the week of 1 August – one by Care and one by the alleged papist – the hypothesis might carry weight, but since there was only one *Pacquet* and no papist had been identified, Care was surely the author (7: col. 1125). It was not a strong showing.

Care's defense team also argued that even if Care were shown to have authored the offensive paragraph, there was no proof of malicious intent. Rather, the paragraph was 'indiscreet,' reflecting 'some little extravagances in... writing.'[62] The defense called three character witnesses to prove that Care was in love with the policies of both Church and State and would not commit a malicious act. Jeffreys and Scroggs insistently swung the questioning around to Care's authorship, but the witnesses refused to say unequivocally that Care had written the *Weekly Pacquet* (7: cols. 1122–24).

Scroggs's comments during the trial revealed, significantly, ambivalence in his attitude toward the case and even toward Care.

Without explanation in the record, the Lord Chief Justice commended the 'prisoner' for his 'modesty,' a most peculiar description of the usually ebullient Care and quite at variance with the verbal abuse Scroggs had heaped upon him in their interview the previous October (7: col. 1115). Seemingly astounded at the popularity of the press, Scroggs marveled that men were 'so fond' of printed pieces that 'they will deny their children a penny for bread, [and]... lay it out for a pamphlet.' Because of this passion for news, especially news criticizing the government, 'no man could keep two-pence in his pocket,' he said (7: col. 1128). Furthermore, irritated and perhaps somewhat intimidated by the crowd of 'hummers,' he blamed these noisy people for elevating the case to a 'public concern.' Their 'shouts and noise' gave it greater importance than he had initially thought it deserved, he confessed. There were a great number of 'people that do espouse [Care's cause], and the government is hereby concerned much more than by any one action that this Carr [sic] could have done' (7: cols. 1125–26). Confiding his innermost thoughts to the court, Scroggs divulged that 'the truth of it is, I did not look upon [this cause] to be of this nature and moment, when it was opened' (7: col. 1126). Of course, the words were malicious but 'not so insolently done as some persons do conceit' and 'not so apparently appropriated, that a man might observe an extraordinary design in them.' This was what he had thought, he acknowledged, but 'really the case is altered even by those men.' If Care was found guilty, the severity of his sentence would be their fault since 'they have undone [him],' Scroggs declared. And the same thing would happen in other cases, 'whenever there is popular attendance upon public causes that concern the government.'

Turning to the matter of Care's authorship, Scroggs admitted that the evidence was 'not plain.' Insisting that justice and fairness would prevail in his court, he declared that he would prefer that Care 'with all his faults ... and his hummers' be released rather than wrongly convicted. These reflections led him into a lengthy and careful statement about probable and conjectural evidence, presumption and reasonable inference, absolute certainty and 'human frailty.' At the end he reassured the jury that their verdict need rest only on 'reason and the probable evidence of things.' 'For,' he explained, 'you do not swear, nor are you bound to swear here, that he [Care] was the publisher of this book; but if you find him guilty, you only swear you believe it so' (7: cols. 1127–28). These were obviously curious digressions for a man who nine months earlier had thundered that he would use the law to pile print people up like faggots.

Jeffreys was less guarded; he announced that anyone who voted to acquit Care 'must be a man of a humming conscience.'[63] But he too backed and filed, saying that the prosecution did not intend to charge Care with 'particular words' – 'That is a mistake of the Information,' he explained – but rather with printing the entire book in which such words appeared (7: col. 1124). Jeffreys's admission that the prosecution had made a 'mistake' in drawing up the information underlines the weakness of its case against Care. The question of malicious intent did not detain either the Lord Chief Justice or Jeffreys. The latter dismissed proving malicious intent by saying that 'the thing itself is a sufficient indication of the malice and depravity of it.' Both men insisted that the import of the words was clear, Jeffreys saying, 'We must debauch our understandings, and be as great Doltheads as they would make all men that will not be of their party, if we don't plainly see into the [words'] meaning' (7: cols. 1127–28). Both emphasized the judges' 5 May ruling that it was illegal to print or publish any newsbooks or pamphlets of news without authority. It made no difference whether the subject matter was malicious or not; if the book was published without permission, it was illegal. Understandably, he did not comment on the fact that the *Weekly Pacquet* had been licensed and that the ruling had been handed down after the date of the offending passage. Speaking directly to the jury, he told them that they must decide only whether Care was the author. If they thought he was, he had violated the law, and the judges would then decide whether the matter was malicious or not and shape the sentence accordingly.

What is one to make of this seeming about-face on Scroggs's part? Given his record of persistent harassment of Care, his remarks catch him in a lie about his initial reaction to Care and the paragraph in the *Weekly Pacquet*. Did he soften his rhetoric to show the magnanimity of his spirit and to try to recover his reputation as a dispassionate judge? He went so far as to recognize the weakness of the prosecution's case, admitting that the evidence was 'not plain' and delivering a homily on the nature of evidence. Was he laying the groundwork for the government to try to coopt Care (the only surely known author of antigovernment tracts at this time), to win him over to the court side? Care's sentence reinforces this hypothesis. The comments may also expose a genuine concern that the 'people' (i.e. the London populace) had come out in force in the courtroom as well as in the streets because they were so disenchanted with the government. Without doubt, Scroggs's harangue was an effort to intimidate the crowd and try to persuade people that their 'hemming' and 'shouting' damaged their interests and those of their friends.

Following these two hours of testimony and comment, the Tory-inclined jury withdrew; after deliberating for 'nigh an hour,' they returned with a verdict of 'guilty.'[64] Sentencing was deferred until the autumn.[65] The immediate reaction favored Care. Morrice, the Presbyterian diarist who was sympathetic to Care, was skeptical of the outcome. 'No full evidence' that Care had published the sheet or even that the remark referred to Scroggs had been presented, Morrice said. 'Yet such was the Jury that it brought him in guilty.'[66] Luttrell, who had no reason to admire Care, kept in manuscript his opinion that 'the evidence against him was very slender.'[67] Care's reaction to the verdict was, predictably, defiance, as it had been to the ruling. Defiance served him well. He brazenly continued to produce the *Weekly Pacquet* each week (except for the week of his trial), concealing it under the thin veil of a slightly different title, *The New Anti-Roman Pacquet: Or, Memoirs Of Popes and Popery Since the Tenth Century*. He made a couple of cosmetic changes to reinforce the fiction that it was different from the

Weekly Pacquet: he renumbered the issues, starting *The New Anti-Roman Pacquet* with the number 1, and he also gave the *Popish Courant* a new title, *The Popes Harbinger, By way of Diversion.* Losing no opportunity to embarrass the government, he explained to his readers that the *Weekly Pacquet* had been banned, but since he was 'ignorant' of the crimes of the author or authors, he would not excuse them. He would only say that the 'main design' of the *Pacquet* had been to 'expose the Roman Villanies, and arm Protestants against the insinuating Attaques of Jesuitical Emissaries,' which purpose was neither 'illegal or offensive, but rather a Work very necessary and of good use in the present Juncture.'[68]

Care's *New Anti-Roman Pacquet* was the only opposition 'newspaper' to appear until the end of the year; it lasted for twenty-one weeks. Care and Curtis should be credited for their brash bravery in keeping the *Weekly Pacquet*, however titled, before the people in defiance of the government when all the other opposition papers had ceased publication.

Care further signaled his defiance by identifying himself publicly with the opposition. First, in August 1680 he was present at a hearing at the Old Bailey when Whig leaders were attempting to humiliate an Anglican minister, the Reverend George Hickes, whom they had charged with idolatry.[69] Second, on 22 October, the day Parliament reconvened, he addressed it in verse in extravagant words of praise:

> *Hail, Glorious Senate, welcom as the Day*
> *To wearied Pilgrims that have lost their Way.*

He called upon it to make England

> *A Match for haughty France, and treacherous Rome.*
> *But first subdue the Monsters here at Home.*
> *Monsters! that would our Sacred Faith and Laws*
> *Or'e-turn... ... ...*
> *Enslave our Persons, and destroy our King.*[70]

The subtext of his verse, that chicanery and treachery respecting religion and law flourished in the state, was all too plain to see.

Despite his intransigence, on that same day, 22 October, when Care appeared in the Court of King's Bench expecting to be sentenced for the crime of printing the *Weekly Pacquet* without permission, nothing happened. An observer reported that 'no motion' was made and 'it's thought it will be forgiven him.'[71] Apparently, however, the defense did enter a motion to dismiss, for Care himself recorded that after all he had suffered at the hands of the authorities, 'upon a fair motion at the King's Bench Bar... the Court adjudg'd... for the Defendant.'[72] No evidence survives respecting why the Court of King's Bench – that is, Scroggs – should have decided to favor Care this way. No doubt Scroggs wanted to avoid a renewed outcry of support for Care and protest against the government at the opening of Parliament. The king himself had urged a softer approach, telling L'Estrange in August that he should be more restrained in attacking the court's critics.[73] Care himself openly suggested that Parliament's presence accounted for his good fortune. Perhaps the feeling had grown that the evidence of fact and the law were too problematic in Care's case to proceed further. Maybe the step was another attempt toward silencing Care by coopting him. Whatever the reason, Care escaped both a fine and imprisonment. Moreover, on 3 December 1680, with the new Parliament furiously engaged in attacks on the king's ministers, Scroggs among them, the *Weekly Pacquet*, 'under the auspicious Influences of a Loyal Protestant Parliament,' appeared with its original title in place and with renumbered issues, just as if there had been no interruption. Care heaped fulsome praise on 'that great and wise Assembly' for lifting the ban on his *Pacquet.*[74]

By now it was clear that Care was known in parliamentary circles. On 26 October 1680 Winnington cited the 'case of one Care, who was indicted for Printing a weekly Intelligencer' and reflected upon the dire implications of the ruling handed down against Care's *Weekly Pacquet*, saying that he thought it amounted 'to little less than a total prohibition of printing any thing against Popery.'[75]

He lamented that lacking a Parliament and forbidden to petition or write for the Protestant religion, English Protestants had used the 'old way of presenting Grievances by Juries,' and juries too had suffered interference. Clearly, Winnington was strengthening the case for bringing impeachment charges against Scroggs. But he went on to praise Care in terms that measured the reputation this lowly man had achieved, declaring that Care 'had a strange knack for writing extraordinary well upon that subject [popery]' and that the *Weekly Pacquet* 'was by most persons thought not only very ingenious, but also very useful at this time for the information of the people, because it laid open very intelligibly, the Errors and Cheats of that Church.' All this was high praise, and it made a strong enough impression that two of the Royalist propagandists brought it up a year later.

Either at the direction from Whig leaders or on his own, Care wielded his pen even more sharply against the establishment. His purpose undoubtedly was to help make the Whigs so offensive that the king would prorogue Parliament and then call another in which a third Exclusion Bill would be brought forward. Responding in hysterical language to the Pope-burning procession in London on 17 November 1680, Care asked his readers to imagine what it would be like to live under popery and supplied his own description. Daringly using language almost identical to that of the infamous *Appeal from the Country to the City*, he declared that Englishmen

> will be dispossessed of your Estates,... turn'd out of all your places, your Trades and Employments lost, your Houses fired about your Ears, your selves forced to flie destitute of Bread and Harbour, your Wives prostituted to the lust of every Savage Bog-Trotter, your Daughters ravish't by Goatish Monks, your smaller Children tossed upon Pikes,... whilst you have your own bowels ripped up, ... or else Murdered with some other exquisite tortures, and... never more to see a Bible, nor here [*sic*] again the joyfull sound of Liberty and Property.

He ended this diatribe with a flourish: 'This, this Gentlemen is
Popery... true bred barefac'd Popery, in its Natural complexion.'[76]
This was what the nation might expect under a Catholic king,
and this, in view of the defeat of the second Exclusion Bill on
15 November, might well occur. It was a bold slap at the court and
the bench, which had prosecuted Harris less than a year earlier for
printing *An Appeal from the Country to the City*. It hit with special
sharpness Lord Chief Justice Scroggs, who had taken such offense
at the *Appeal*.

Three weeks later, when the court's critics were still wallowing
in disappointment over the defeat of the second Exclusion Bill
and continuing to scheme how they might distress the government, Care directed the same kind of hyperbolic language against
the king's friends, whom he called Tories. A Tory, he wrote on
10 December 1680, is

> A murdering Bog-trotter transplanted... A Christian Canniball,...
> that gnaws out the Heart of Liberty, and Property... . His boasted
> Loyalty reaches [no] further than a drunken Health;... His skill in
> History begins and ends in Forty one; urge never so modestly Legal
> Rights, and he cries out, you Arraign the Government; speak of the
> Commons of England, and the General Sense of the Nation, and he
> Exclaims, Damn the Mobile;... Magna Charta he values no more
> than an old Almanack, swears the Statute-book is only good for a
> Loosness, because its Contents are said to be very Binding.[77]

This diatribe invites comment. There is no doubt of Care's orig-
inality; it well demonstrates his skills in manipulating language, his
wide reading and his ability to zero in on the points that stung the
king's sympathizers, especially L'Estrange. His language became
pervasive; phrases from his unflattering description of a Tory reappeared in a later tract, *The Character of a Tory* (n.d.), which Sir John
Somers regarded as of sufficient interest to include it in his 1750
collection of pamphlets.[78] Further, Care's use of the word *Tory* was
possibly the first time that word had appeared in Exclusionist

prints.[79] Through such writing as this, Care contributed to the deepening polarization in English politics. This kind of name-calling would become very popular when a genuine contest in the press between friends and critics of the government took off the following year.

Finally, Care resumed his attack in one of his most effective verses, written at the end of December 1680, when leaders of Parliament frantically continued to seek ways to embarrass the court. Addressing 'Abhorrers Abhorr'd,' that is, those persons who opposed petitions for calling a Parliament in the winter of 1680, Care characterized them as

> Monsters more base than Africk can affor'd.
> What? Not Petition to our Soveraign Lord,
> That PARLIAMENTS might sit, and save the
> KING and KINGDOM too, ...
> Be gone ye Fopps to France, and there enslave Yourselves and Spurious off-spring;
> For a Knave Is fit t'Engender Vassals; but too Brave Is this Rich Isle, which only owneth those,
> That Popish Bondage do resolve t'oppose.
> Was thou in ENGLAND born, and there born FREE?
> Thou profane Esau! Nay more vile than He
> To sell thy Birthright to the French and Pope.[80]

This piece, as any politically savvy reader would readily see, shafted the Tories, although not naming them, by implying that those who opposed petitioning lacked a sense of true 'Englishness' and English freedoms and by linking them with France and 'Popish Bondage.'

Not only his writings but also the appearance on 18 February 1681 of a printed account of his trial kept Care and his problems before the public.[81] Neither Care nor Curtis took the initiative in getting the account in print. Their unaccustomed restraint is baffling. But one John Combe, a publisher whose shop was located near the Royal Exchange in London, petitioned the House of Lords on 28 October 1680, less than a week after they had reassembled, for permission to print and publish several trials, among them Care's. Combe averred that he had recorded the proceedings 'carefully in Short Hand.'[82] He was granted permission but was instructed to submit the copy to the crown's legal officers for approval and correction. It took Combe more than three months to get the material on the market. Perhaps the February publishing date was intended to capitalize on the excitement generated by the slow-moving proceedings against Scroggs and to refresh memories about how the law had been bent. The printed trial record is further notable because the title refers to Care as a gentleman – *The Triall of Henry Carr, Gent.* – a designation that also appeared in the indictment. One remembers how Care earlier had practiced self-promotion by laying claim to the title; the term must have delighted this socially ambitious fellow. That Care was regarded as a 'gent' in some quarters in 1681 shows how far this unknown, armed with his pen, had traveled.

Care, then, was very much on the scene during the weeks when Parliament was engaged in a frenzied effort to 'bring down the government' by attempting to remove several of the king's ministers by the quasi-legal procedure of impeachment. Of all the ministers threatened with impeachment, only Lord Chief Justice Scroggs was actually charged, and on grounds that included his treatment of the press and press people.

V

The press trials and press persons, including Henry Care, played an unprecedented role in the attempted impeachment of Sir William Scroggs. Although the impeachment procedure itself failed, the indirect consequence was King Charles's removal of Scroggs from his position as Lord Chief Justice of the Court of King's Bench. That the relatively new institution of the press had a part in ousting a minister of the crown is a signal development, a testament to its power in Restoration England. The event shows how significant in politics was a public that included nonelite persons. It also lays bare the fear animating many people that judge-made law (i.e., the rulings about the press) would overwhelm Parliament, England's traditional lawmaking institution.

The Scroggs impeachment has been studied recently, and my discussion will be confined largely to the part the press played in it.[83] That the press would be conspicuous was predictable, given the inclusion of Sir Francis Winnington, one of Care's defense attorneys, on the committee the Commons appointed to investigate the proceedings of the justices and other ministers of the crown. No doubt Winnington's presence helped to focus attention on the sufferings of press persons. The committee carried out a thorough investigation of the conduct of the justices, focusing in part on the press. Making use of its authority to send for 'Persons, Papers and Records,' the committee took informations from and/or interviewed more than fifteen witnesses, plus an unspecified number of printers and booksellers, among them Henry Care (the only author), Francis Smith, Benjamin Harris and Jane Curtis. Robert Stephens, the messenger of the press, was also interviewed. Other witnesses included the three clerks of the Court of King's Bench, one of whom, Samuel Astrey, provided court documents, including the ruling banning publication of the *Weekly Pacquet*. The committee also referred by title to seven tracts and pamphlets that had offended the court, including Care's *Weekly Pacquet, A Satyr Against Iniustice: Or Sc—gs upon Sc—gs,* and *Some Observations Upon the Late Tryals of Sir George Wakeman,* and no doubt had those tracts before them.[84] The expert witnesses and the records enabled the committee to compile a very detailed and well-documented report, on which the eight articles of impeachment against Scroggs were built.

The articles of impeachment damned Scroggs for, among other things, his handling of the press. The first article was connected indirectly to that question. Cast in provocative language reminiscent of that used in the impeachments of William Laud, archbishop of Canterbury, and Thomas, Earl of Strafford, the article accused Scroggs of 'traiterously' attempting to 'subvert the Fundamental Laws and Establisht Religion and Government' of the nation with the aim of introducing 'Popery and Arbitrary and Tyrannical Government against Law.' Although the language of 'fundamental laws' could be seen as almost routine, part of the time-honored discourse of the ancient constitution heard throughout the century, in Scroggs's indictment these words were not formulaic.[85] Rather, evoking the words from 1641 in the very first article before a House whose members were well read in English history, and law was a powerful rhetorical and strategic move.[86] That the language was deliberately chosen is shown by Winnington's remark reminding the venerable John Maynard (1604–90) of his part in Strafford's trial, where 'that article was a great Crime.'[87]

Winnington made the comment to persuade the House to elevate the charges against Scroggs to treason, but there was also a second purpose to his remark. Twenty-five years ago Conrad Russell identified the main fear driving the treason case against Strafford: that Strafford aimed to alter the constitution by substituting the king's will for law. Russell wrote, 'The English parliament was afraid of losing control of legislation.'[88] Fear of losing control of the legislative process is exactly what concerned the Commons forty years later. Members were emphatic and expansive on the point, and the basic reason for their alarm was the judges' handling of the press. For example, Henry Powle declaimed that the 'two great pillars of the government are Parliaments and Juries'; they conferred the title 'free-born' on Englishmen. 'Free-born,' he explained, meant that Englishmen were 'ruled by laws of their own making, and tried by men of the same condition with themselves.' The judges had invaded these two rights; they had 'grasped legislation power into their own hands as in that instance of printing.'[89] A month later, on 23 December, Winnington referred specifically to the ruling respecting Care's *Weekly Pacquet* and intoned that by it 'the Judges make a Law for the whole

Kingdom' and that 'therefore' the act justified the charge of 'assuming to themselves a Legislative Power, etc.'[90] Clearly, central to the crisis of authority that alarmed members so deeply was the treatment of the press. That and the dismissal of the Middlesex grand jury (the subject of article 2) formed the foundation of the fear.

Four closely related articles (3–6) directly concerned Scroggs's handling of the press in ways that were detrimental to the legal rights of press people, the nation's law and legal processes, and the legislative role of Parliament.[91] Article 7 was also inextricably linked with these four articles. Article 3 cited Scroggs and the 'other Judges' of the Court of King's Bench for the ruling that banned Care's *Weekly Pacquet*. The House committee had investigated this matter carefully. They had examined Astrey, who deposed that Care had been 'informed against' for writing the *Pacquet* and had pleaded to the information. Astrey explained that before Care had come to trial, 'all the Judges of [the] Court... none dissenting' had ruled against the printing or publishing of the *Weekly Pacquet* by anyone at all. Expressing astonishment that 'Protestant Judges should take Offence' at a book whose purpose was to discredit popery, the committee recounted that it had interviewed Jane Curtis and Care himself. Curtis had told of her encounter with Scroggs in May, and Care of his exchange with the Lord Chief Justice in October 1679. On the basis of this information, the committee concluded that the ruling against Care's *Weekly Pacquet* was 'illegal and arbitrary.'

Article 4 charged the Lord Chief Justice and his colleagues with unfair levying of fines on persons they had found guilty to the disadvantage of Protestants, including publishers. Working from a list of all fines imposed by the Court of King's Bench since Easter term, supplied to them by the ever-obliging Astrey, the committee ran through the stories of several persons. For example, they named Benjamin Harris, noting that he had been fined £500 and that, unable to pay the fine, he was still in prison. To drive home their point, they cited cases wherein the Justices had shown compassion and mercy, and so concluded that the judges had acted 'arbitrarily, illegally, and partially,' favoring papists and persons popishly affected, and oppressing Protestants.

Article 5 condemned Scroggs alone for refusing legitimate and sufficient bail, 'onely to put them to Charges' of purchasing a writ of *Habeas Corpus*; and imprisoning writers and booksellers, among them Care, Benjamin Harris, Francis Smith and Jane Curtis, and verbally abusing them. Ignoring the fact that Jane Curtis was a *femme couverte* with children, Scroggs had prosecuted her 'to her utter ruin.' His actions in committing persons who were bailable by law had been 'illegal, and a high Breach of the Liberty of the Subject.'

Article 6 complained that Scroggs had used general warrants for 'attaching the Persons and seizing the Goods' of the king's subjects. Although no specific examples were named in this article, the warrants the committee identified in its report related to the press, especially to the activities of Messenger of the Press, Robert Stephens. Significantly, the information about Stephens had come from 'several Printers and Booksellers,' who informed the committee of the 'great Trouble and Vexation given them unjustly' by Stephens. Stephens's defense was that he had proceeded by the authority of two warrants issued by Scroggs, which he handed over to the committee. The warrants, dated 29 November 1679 and 28 May 1680, empowered Stephens to seize seditious or unlicensed newsbooks and pamphlets, and apprehend those persons responsible for them. It was these warrants that the committee adjudged to be 'arbitrary and illegal.'

Article 7 concerned Scroggs's 'defaming' and 'disparaging' the evidence of witnesses, thereby encouraging the Popish Plot, a silent reference to his handling of Titus Oates and William Bedloe in the Wakeman trial. The Wakeman trial was not named in the indictment, but the ensuing uproar in the press, which had formed the core of the information against Care, and Oates and Bedloe's presenting charges of misdemeanor against Scroggs before the Privy Council ensured that no politically conscious person could fail to connect it and article 7.

VI

The impeachment of Scroggs holds special interest because for the first and only time in the history of impeachments for high treason, the press and press people played a significant role in the charges. Four out of the eight articles of impeachment (articles 3–6) were connected directly with the press, and another two (articles 1 and 7) were indirectly related. Scroggs's handling of Care and other press people provided the hardest evidence that he had acted illegally. Scroggs, with the approval of Charles II, bent the law to achieve censorship and punishment of the press, and he was guilty as charged in articles 3–6. The event expressed members' genuine fear that the bench and the crown were threatening law, legal processes and the legislative role of Parliament. This concern, although expressed in extravagant language, was not just rhetorical window dressing. The court and Scroggs's attitude toward and handling of the press gave proof of the government's willingness to make law not through Parliament but by judicial rulings and royal proclamations, just as it had done prior to the Civil Wars. The attempted impeachment symbolized a crisis of authority; it highlighted profound legal issues that the prospect of a Catholic king on the throne magnified. The debates on the impeachment were wide ranging and drew in several political concerns (such as judicial tenure, the force of royal proclamations, the right to petition the king and the independence of juries), but the most important concern was the threat to law and Parliament's role in making it. And the most important evidence was that provided by the press. Although Charles II's dissolution of the Oxford Parliament aborted the impeachment proceedings and spared Scroggs a legal judgment that certainly would have gone against him, Scroggs's career was finished. The tribulations of a bunch of lowly press people exploited by a Whig-dominated House of Commons brought down a Lord Chief Justice of the Court of King's Bench. The attempted impeachment severely embarrassed the government and no doubt figured in the king's determination to try to recoup his position. To the steps he and his friends took we now turn.

5

Restyling POLITICAL RHETORIC
in the
Exclusion Crisis

The years 1681 to mid-1683 marked the apex of Care's writing career. During that period he engaged in a ferocious battle in the press with his Royalist enemies, L'Estrange, Rawlins and Thompson. Care was defeated. In the course of this print warfare these men kept interest in political and religious issues at boiling point and enlarged the public space much earlier than Habermas would have it. They also restyled political rhetoric during the Exclusion Crisis, employing with renewed intensity and imagination the time-honored devices of dialogue, humor, *ad hominen* attack, invective, code words, myths and poetry. Although used notably by Tim Harris and Mark Knights but otherwise generally neglected by modern historians, their weekly serials – Care's *Weekly Pacquet* and *Popish Courant*, L'Estrange's *Observator* (the major combatant in these exchanges), Rawlins's *Heraclitus Ridens*,[1] and Thompson's *Loyal Protestant* – were read by more people than any other piece of propaganda. These superb examples of the popular press during the

Restoration offer an unrivaled resource of what both sides wanted the 'people' to read during these frantic years and, although more difficult to prove, what the people *were* actually reading.

The genuine press war that occurred was the result of a change in policy at the highest reaches of government. A brief review of that change is required before we examine the rhetoric and ideas of the new serials and explain how it happened that the Royalists won.

I

Sometime in the winter of 1680–81 Charles II gathered himself for a concerted battle with his major enemies in the Whig Party,[2] the Nonconformist community, and the opposition press. Within two years all three were decisively routed. The king had been forced into action: the court and its friends had suffered intolerable indignities and setbacks in the parliamentary session that previous autumn. Although they had achieved the defeat of the second Exclusion Bill in the House of Lords, they could not stem the frenzied activity of disappointed Whigs who tried to impeach the king's ministers, pardoned and released from jail their friends in the press (Harris and Smith), and took the unprecedented step of ordering the printing of their votes, giving Harris the lucrative right to do so. The court's apparent effort to placate the press by dropping charges against Care did not work; Care boldly resumed publishing the *Weekly Pacquet* and the *Popish Courant* under their correct names and volume numbers. The Whigs' underlying goal was to coerce Charles to dissolve Parliament and call for new elections so that they might introduce a third Exclusion Bill.[3] Ultimately, to their regret, Charles did exactly what they wanted.

The king's adroitness in destroying his enemies by subtle and sophisticated political maneuvering and manipulation was remarkable. First, Charles summoned Parliament to meet in Oxford on

21 March 1681, and once there, he managed it with consummate skill. After some feinting and dissembling, he suddenly dissolved the Parliament on 28 March and immediately departed, leaving the disgruntled Whigs no viable option but to depart themselves. The king's move ended the Whig effort to pass a new Exclusion Bill, aborted the impeachment proceedings against Scroggs, thereby preserving him from a near-certain verdict of 'guilty,' and, since Charles refused to call another Parliament, deprived parliamentary Whigs of a forum and radical press people of a champion for the rest of his reign. Financially secure because of French money and swelling customs revenues, Charles was able to rule comfortably without Parliament.[4]

Charles followed the dissolution of the Oxford Parliament with a second masterful step: the publication on 8 April 1681 of a justification of his measures with respect to the two last parliaments, *His Majesty's Declaration To All His Loving Subjects, Touching The Causes and Reasons That Moved Him To Dissolve the Two Last Parliaments* (hereafter *Declaration of Reasons*), which he ordered read from every pulpit.[5] Blaming the two Parliaments for their own dissolutions, the declaration detailed the 'unwarrantable proceedings' of the Westminster Parliament and underscored the failure of the Oxford Parliament to heed his instructions to 'make the laws of the land their rule.' These and other steps, the *Declaration of Reasons* stated, had brought the king reluctantly to the decision to dissolve the Oxford Parliament. In contrast to members' 'restless malice,' Charles, in a gesture evocative of his father's *Answer to the Nineteen Propositions* (in June 1642), pledged himself to rule by law and promised to call frequent Parliaments.[6] The king's declaration provides additional evidence of the court's recognition of the power of public opinion and its determination to try to mold it. In blaming Parliament and emphasizing the king's devotion to law, it added new ingredients to the court's efforts to capture public opinion. The extensive efforts made to respond to the declaration by addresses of thanks and pamphlets (both pro and con) indicate how powerful an effect it had.[7]

A third move the king made was to ally himself with the lieutenancy and depend upon it to impose the court's will in the
counties. As Victor Stater has shown in detail, the Lords Lieutenant
were willing agents of the crown; by and large Royalist and
Anglican in outlook, they undertook enthusiastically to harass
Dissenters and suppress their meetings while at the same time promoting the interests of Church and State by organizing loyal
addresses or bonfire celebrations. Stater argues that the partnership
with the lieutenancy enabled Charles II to save the constitution,
but at the cost of binding himself so closely to Anglicans and
Royalists that his Catholic brother was unable to break the relationship between the two.[8]

A fourth way in which Charles assumed the unaccustomed role
of a take-charge king was to renew efforts to rein in lowly press
people. In a stunning admission of the damage that the opposition
press had done to his government's 'approval rating' and of the
importance of nonelite opinion, he and his ministers took steps to
make the Stationers' Company a compliant ally, used the power of
quo warranto to control the composition of London juries and
therefore the fate of men brought up on charges,[9] turned to
informers to track down Nonconformists, prosecuted obdurate
press people (among them Care) and ruthlessly capitalized on the
Rye House Plot crisis in 1683 to persecute the court's enemies.[10]
The effort to control printing hurt the opposition badly, for in the
absence of Parliament, the press was the major outlet for the opposition's ideas.

And that was not all. In a fifth step that recognized the limita-
tions of imposing authority from above, acknowledged the power
of ideas and admitted the need to try to mold public opinion by
persuasion through the printed word, the government decided to
undertake its own propaganda campaign. This notion of designing
new measures for dealing with the seditious press came from several people at court. Danby had expressed interest in propaganda
and used the press himself, as we saw. Secretary of State Sir Leoline
Jenkins, whom Knights describes as a kind of 'co-ordinator or

protector of Court propagandists,' preserved among his papers an outline of a pamphlet aimed at swinging public opinion around to the court.[11] Sir Francis North, Lord Chief Justice of the Court of Common Pleas, took the initiative, however, according to his brother and biographer, Roger North. Roger recounted that Francis reasoned that persecution was useless; it made libels more popular and hurt the 'poor wretches' that sold them for money. He recommended that the king abide by the law, not show that he was 'touched to the quick' by pamphlets, and set up 'counter writers' to rebut every libel that came out and thereby keep the opposition off balance.[12] He advised further that the court improve the dispersal of 'ingenious books wrote for the Governmt.'[13] North also suggested using the 'light touch' of humor and ridicule rather than rough suppression, but at the same he recommended swift and severe punishment for anyone who clearly violated the law.[14] Finally, L'Estrange had been so often consulted by the government regarding the press that it is reasonable to think that his advice was solicited again.[15] Indeed, in the spring of 1681 he encapsulated the apparent opinion of the court, writing, "Tis the Press that has made 'um Mad, and the press must set 'um Right again.'[16] Someone had to select the 'counter writers' that Roger North mentioned, and L'Estrange's experience and knowledge of the press would have recommended him for that. Whoever did the choosing, L'Estrange (ever adept at self-promotion), Rawlins and Nathaniel Thompson were, Roger North explained, 'employed... for a constancy, and others, with them, occasionally.'[17]

These three writers did indeed provide 'a constancy' in the press war. *Heraclitus Ridens*, the first off the mark, on 1 February 1681, appeared once a week until 22 August 1682. Thompson's *Loyal Protestant* followed on 9 March 1681 and, with the exception of the weeks between 16 November 1682 and 20 February 1683, continued until 20 March 1683; it was published twice a week until 3 November 1682 and three times a week thereafter. *The Observator in Question and Answer* made its debut on 13 April 1681. On 6 July L'Estrange changed the title to *The Observator, In Dialogue*, and he kept the journal going until 9 March 1687, producing issues twice a week until 6 July 1681 and three or four times a week thereafter, for a total of 861 issues.[18] It was the longest-lived of any serial.

The three Royalist writers were exceedingly well qualified to present the case for the court. Like Care, they were blessed with intelligence, literary talent and flair, sharp wit, and quick humor. In temperament they were unscrupulous, vulgar, mean-spirited, scurrilous, ambitious and aggressive. L'Estrange, his biographer concluded, was 'vindictive,' filled with 'petty vengeance' and 'habitually meanly cruel.'[19] Self-importance and self-confidence marked their attitude; L'Estrange actually apologized one time for his arrogance.[20] In social background and status, Rawlins (b. 1646) and Thompson (1648–87) were similar to Care. Neither came from a distinguished family nor felt the burden of social pretensions, as did L'Estrange. Thompson, a Catholic, began his career as a printer in Dublin; he allegedly accepted financial assistance from Langley Curtis when he moved to London and never repaid the loan. Masquerading as an Anglican, Thompson was probably close to the infamous informer John Hilton.[21] In 1679 he printed the *True Domestick Intelligence*, a newspaper critical of the government; in 1681 his interests seemed better served by printing the *Loyal Protestant* on behalf of the court. Such political turns earned him the reputation of a 'mercenary fellow for any side that pays him well.'[22] Knights uses Thompson as an example to warn against too readily identifying press people as Whig or Tory.[23] Thompson's career also puts Care's shifts in allegiance into perspective.

Rawlins was a 'dissolute' Cambridge graduate, proud of his degree but confessedly possessing a 'very small estate' and a love of drink.[24] Apparently he worked as a 'Correcter to the Press.'[25] His loud and scurrilous remarks uttered in coffee houses about the Plot, Titus Oates and petitioning that Care reported in the *True Protestant Mercury* may have called him to the attention of the court.[26] L'Estrange's background was quite different, as we have seen. The very fact that Kneller painted his portrait in 1684 says something about the social standing he enjoyed at the time of the

Sir Roger L'Estrange (1616–1704), appointed surveyor of the press by Charles II, was Care's principal sparring partner in the press.

press wars (see fig. 5). Deploring the 'Indecency of a Gentleman Entering into a Street-Brawl... with the Sink of Mankind, both for Quality, and Wickedness,' L'Estrange expressed the fear that 'the Profession and Business of a Pamphleteer' would ruin his family name.[27] But these misgivings did not deter him.

Rawlins and Thompson went about their business with the enthusiasm and energy of men in their mid-thirties. L'Estrange, their senior by thirty years or more, was conscious of a generational divide between him and his press enemies: 'What makes these youths have such a spight against L'Estrange?' his interlocutor queried.[28] Nonetheless, L'Estrange, whom Burnet described as the 'Manager of all those angry writings,'[29] had energy equal to that of his fellow writers. Even severe illness in January 1682 and again in March 1683 failed to interrupt the flow of *Observators* or other tracts.[30] As he put it, he was so proud to have a part in breaking the neck of that 'Villanous Cheat of a Plot' that he would die happy if success attended his efforts.[31]

Government writers were well supplied with news. A group of young Tory men, joined in what has been called the 'first press club,' assisted Rawlins,[32] while L'Estrange and Thompson had 'correspondents' on the scene in places outside London.[33] L'Estrange had the closest relationship with the government: he regularly sent issues of the *Observator* to both secretaries of State before publishing them, and Secretary Jenkins supplied both L'Estrange and Rawlins with news and information.[34] At least once, the king himself ordered that a certain paper appear in either the *Observator* or *Heraclitus Ridens*.[35] Furthermore, these men were alive to what was being said by others; they advertised contemporary books; they drew upon parliamentary debates.

Such talented polemicists produced very attractive papers. Thompson in his newspaper and Rawlins and L'Estrange in their commentaries covered the daily and weekly news of London, the counties, Scotland and Ireland. L'Estrange's comment about the *Observator* is broadly applicable: 'Every day Started New... and Every Paper was to be Accommodated to the Accidents and

Emergencies of the Season.'[36] Political and social minutiae were
included along with major happenings: tavern brawls, prosecu-
tions, presentments, trials of such figures as Shaftesbury, Fitzharris
and College, ignoramus juries, religious persecutions, petitioners
and abhorrers, processions, political activities of London apprentices and polemical tracts. Accounts of all these events and
developments make the serials, it may be repeated, an unrivaled
source for street and social life in the early 1680s.

Thompson's was the only true newspaper. The other two serials,
by L'Estrange and Rawlins, did much the same thing as Care had
done for more than two years in the *Popish Courant*; that is, they
offered a varied fare of news, commentary, ballads, stories, what
passed for poetry and farcical as well as genuine advertisements.[37]
In like manner, *Heraclitus Ridens* varied its commentary with
Pindaric odes probably written by the poet and miniaturist
Thomas Flatman,[38] amusing advertisements[39] and, a hallmark of
the journal, a 'Queries' section containing barbed rhetorical questions designed to shaft the opposition.[40] L'Estrange also advertised
meetings and, like Care, sermons and books. Thompson featured
letters to the editor. Their main drawing card, however, was the
discussions of political and religious events and principles. These
necessarily brief but pointed discussions tutored the less well read
and reminded the sophisticated and politically elite of theories that
underlay attitudes toward events. Their importance lies in their
providing an index to what a broad section of society was reading
as the essential issues and principles in the Exclusion Crisis. They
enable us to consider whether the large audience of the serials was
getting anything basically different from what the readers of more
serious and lengthy pamphlets were getting.

The serials won the Royalists public affection and esteem. An
admirer praised L'Estrange for his 'Flashy Wit,' saying, 'I'de turn
Towzer loose to any Whelp in Christendom, ay,... it makes a man
fit for any company.' He reported that a fellow confided that he
would rather listen to the *Observator* read once than Richard
Baxter, the Presbyterian divine, preach sixteen times. Another man

wanted only three books in his library: the Bible, *The Whole Duty of Man* and the *Observator*. The man knew of a church warden who always took a copy of the *Observator* to church, 'partly as an antidote to Whiggism, but chiefly to read if the Minister should chance to be Dull.'[41] Rawlins too had his followers. His 'Queries' became so popular that an anonymous person inquiring about an issue in London said that he wanted to 'imitate the new mode of instruction lately made current' by posing some queries.[42] As Care himself said, meaning to be derisive rather than complimentary, some country parsons 'study [*Heraclitus Ridens*] more by half than the Bible.'[43] Burnet reckoned that *Heraclitus Ridens*, the *Observator* and L'Estrange's tract *Dissenters' Sayings* (discussed below) supplied the Anglican clergy with material to turn against and ridicule Dissenters.[44] Following in the wake of admiration and imitation came a change in public opinion.

The court defenders were successful in putting opposition press people unaccustomedly on the defensive and forcing them repeatedly to answer charges and defend their opinions. In response, the booksellers and publishers Smith and Harris took up the cudgels. Smith produced, for example, *Democritus Ridens: or, Comus and Momus, A New Jest and Earnest Pratling concerning the Times*, and Harris brought out *The Weekly Discoverer Strip'd Naked*. But their principal newspapers – Smith's *Protestant Intelligence; Domestick and Foreign* and Harris's *Protestant (Domestick) Intelligence* – closed down in April 1681, and both men were jailed. The other papers that started up on the side of the Whigs were also short-lived.[45] Other writers, such as John Phillips and Elkanah Settle, also joined in the attack on the Royalist serials, and many Whig writers engaged in the full-blown press war against Royalist tracts. But Henry Care, while also writing important tracts, carried the major burden of answering the Royalist serials, a heretofore unnoticed fact that bears emphasis because it further justifies his claim on our attention. Long ago Kitchin observed that 'with the exception of Harry Care's learning ... in the *Weekly Pacquet of Advice*, there is nothing to set against [the] Royalists journals.'[46]

Care's leadership role in responding to L'Estrange, Rawlins and Thompson came about because both sides wanted it that way. The Royalists chose Care as their adversary in the press; he was the only opposition *author* whom court writers repeatedly targeted by name. In so doing they not only practically invited him but relentlessly goaded him to respond. That Royalist propagandists made Care the major figure testifies to how deeply he had riled them. L'Estrange's biographer judged that Care was the 'one man more obnoxious than all the rest put together.'[47] Thus, while it is true that court writers desperately wanted to knock out the major opposition publishers and booksellers – for if they could do that, the problem would be virtually solved – they attacked Care with the same vehemence. Calling him 'Squire' did not mean that they regarded him as inconsequential.[48] Indeed, they placed Care equally in the limelight with the publishers and booksellers. For example, L'Estrange used a memorable analogy to lump together publishers and author Care: in his inimitable way he compared them to the mythical three-headed dog Cerberus, who guarded the entrance to Hell. This creature had three mouths: a 'Protestant-Mercury' one (Langley Curtis), an 'Impartiall Protestant-Mercury' one (Richard Janeway), and a 'Popish Corrant' one (Care), at least two of which worried the *Observator* every week.[49] He continued the equation, writing again about 'my Cares and Curtis'es, My Janeways and Harrises.'[50] The linkage of these names appeared also in tracts by other government sympathizers.[51]

Court writers also addressed Care directly. L'Estrange was so fixated on the damage he felt Care had done that he laid blame for everything on Care.[52] He made Care such a central figure in the first volume of the *Observator* that next to Care's name in the index he wrote 'Et Ubiq.' following a single page reference.[53] He called one of his interlocutors the 'Courantier' for six issues, from 1 November through 11 November 1682. He opened the eighty-fifth issue by inquiring, 'What says the comical Courantier to the world now?' *Heraclitus Ridens* targeted Care with similar frequency, mentioning him in thirty-four of the eighty-one issues.

Nathaniel Thompson also chose Care as his target. No other author received this attention. The consequence was that in the minds of court polemicists, other Royalist writers and therefore the politically sentient public Care stood out as the only identifiable *author* among opposition press people.

Another reason for Care's leadership role is that he was responsible for writing in whole or part three different serials: his own *Popish Courant* and two newspapers, the *True Protestant Mercury* (published by Langley Curtis and, in his absence, Jane Curtis) and the *Impartial Protestant Mercury* (published by Janeway). Describing Care and Thomas Vile as the 'writers,' 'editors' and 'true proprietors,' Sutherland judged that the *Impartial Protestant Mercury* carried on a 'serious campaign against the government.'[54] Although Care received some help with the *Impartial Protestant Mercury*,[55] he was largely responsible for these serials each week, so he had pressing reasons and ready opportunities to answer his critics. Care put himself on a punishing schedule to do so: the *Popish Courant* came out every Friday. *The True Protestant Mercury* appeared on Wednesdays and Saturdays (28 December 1680 to 25 October 1682, with a lapse of two weeks in April 1681). The *Impartial Protestant Mercury* was on the streets every Monday and Thursday (27 April 1681 to 30 May 1682). Therefore, Care had only Tuesdays free to work on the tracts on constitutional and religious subjects that he produced during these years. Overwork may account in part for the illnesses he suffered in August 1681 and reportedly in July 1683.[56] But like L'Estrange, Care allowed no interruption in the *Weekly Pacquet* and *Popish Courant* nor in the two newspapers.

Finally, Care was no doubt driven by hope of money to undertake this leading role in the press war. Rawlins alluded to this motive when he remarked that Care found the pence rolling in and so 'blundered on.'[57] To sum up, public pressure, hope of profit, concern to defend his side, and responsibility for three different publications help to explain why Care wrote more in defense of the Whig cause than anyone else in 1681–83.

With these partisans ranged against one another, a hard-fought and protracted press battle ensued. During the months it lasted a dark, ugly, even violent side of Restoration England was revealed not only in individual human suffering but also in the hyperbolic language of printed controversy.[58] Each side suffered scurrilous charges from the other, distortion of their views, and defamation of their character and that of their wives. As long as London's city government and hence juries were controlled by the Whigs, pro-government writers were presented by the grand jury and suffered imprisonment, the pillory and fines, while ignoramus juries protected opposition writers and leaders. When control of London's city government and therefore juries fell to the Tories, the tables were turned.

Opposition press people were no match for a government determined to use its persecutory and legal authority; equally to the point, critics met their match in the energy and talent of royal propagandists. As fear of fanaticism gradually replaced fear of popery, public sentiment shifted to the side of the court, and support for the opposition receded. Roger North relished the success of the Royalist writers: 'They soon wrote the libellers out of the pit,' he exulted. 'The trade of libels... fell to nothing.'[59] By the end of 1682, and in some instances earlier, radical press people were in retreat. Care himself had begun to waver in October 1681, but he did not cease publishing the *Weekly Pacquet* until 13 July 1683.[60] The fall of the *Pacquet* marked the total collapse of press resistance.

II

The Royalist writers were early spin doctors; their aim was to dislodge the prevailing argument that the court, the Church of England, the bench and the Tory Party were infected with popery and determined to destroy English liberties. They sought to replace this argument with two principal ideas: one, the thought, long promoted by L'Estrange, that Whigs, the Nonconformist community and their allies in an uncontrolled and subversive press were radical fanatics who fostered sedition and rebellion and were intent upon upending the monarchy and the Church, and returning the nation to 1641; and two, the notion that the court stood for law, liberty and property, while the Church of England stood for the true Protestant religion (as by law established), an idea that had assisted Charles I and was now newly stressed. They faced an enormous challenge. But with their serials appearing every week, reinforced by loyalist tracts, they were remarkably successful. How did they do it? By persuasive substantive arguments, many of them timeworn; by rhetorical devices, also timeworn, such as dialogue, humor, invective, *ad hominem* attacks, fables, poems and ballads; and by targeting a vastly expanded audience. The result of the rhetorical strategies employed by Royalists and Care was a restyling of political rhetoric during the Exclusion Crisis.

The announced audience of the court writers was diverse – they intended the entire spectrum of society – but they placed emphasis on the nonelite. There was serious political purpose in targeting a broader audience, and for court writers it marked a new departure. Less than a year earlier L'Estrange had iterated his long-held view that it was 'not the Common Peoples Province to dive into the *Arcana imperii*'; their ignorance rendered them incapable of judging the 'Mysteries of Government.'[61] But, persuaded of the 'Absolute Necessity' of doing so, he did a turn-around and specifically announced in the *Observator* that he intended to address the 'Common People' and 'the Ignorant.'[62] A month later, one of Rawlins's interlocutors remarked ruefully that 'now all the care is... to satisfie the People without Doors; if they be but pleased, it is no matter for any body else.'[63] Rawlins exaggerated, for propagandists on all sides hoped to reach elite subjects as well. We have seen that that was the case with Care, and the Royalists betrayed the same intention in various ways. L'Estrange harbored lingering misgivings about the 'people,' expressing the fear three months into writing the *Observator* that 'Ignorant common People' will 'ruin the King and the Church and subvert the Government.'[64] He surely hoped to touch persons other than them in his *Observator*. Further, court writers assumed a familiarity with literary, political and religious writers that marginally educated persons could not be expected to have. Thus, for example, Rawlins referred to Milton, Shakespeare, Dryden, *Don Quixote*, Suarez, Bellarmine, Mariana, and the recently printed *Plato Redivivus* and *Jani Anglorum*.[65]

Even so, L'Estrange was conscious (as he had not been previously) of reaching out to a large audience. Following Care's practice in the history part of the *Weekly Pacquet*, L'Estrange introduced 'Headnotes' (starting with number 112 of the *Observator*), which provided the reader with a synopsis of each issue. Further to assist the reader and again like Care, he supplied a table of contents for each printed volume of *Observators*. He took pains with these tables, dividing them into several sections to make them 'Short, Plain, and Methodical' for the 'Readers Ease, and Satisfaction.' They also would have directed attention to the issues that L'Estrange wanted all his readers to notice. Although his tables would have assisted any reader, they no doubt reflected L'Estrange's new sense of responsibility to reach the commonalty.

The most striking rhetorical device used was the dialogue – both between authors of works and between interlocutors within a serial or tract. As a literary device, the public dialogue between Care on the one hand and Rawlins, Thompson and L'Estrange on the other was, of course, not new. There had been printed dialogic relationships between authors before, from the Reformation forward, and especially during the Civil Wars. What was new was the regularity and frequency of the dialogue, so frequent that the participants were able to engage in printed repartee. Replies and rejoinders usually came within days of each other, making the conversation so rapid and specific that a reader would have no trouble following nor feeling a sense of participation in it. One has only to read the serials together to see that Care relentlessly carried on this kind of literary back-and-forth with all three Royalist writers.[66]

The Royalists also initiated the dialogue between two or more literary creations. Rawlins was the first of the court campaigners to employ the device in the first issue of *Heraclitus Ridens*. L'Estrange, whose *Citt and Bumpkin* had been such a success the year before, fell into dialoguing again in the *Observator* starting on 13 April. Within a fortnight, on 22 April, Care jumped on the bandwagon, his new interlocutor explaining that 'since folks are so set upon Dialoguing, let you and I have a touch [at it].'[67] As a genre the dialogue was, of course, not new; Plato springs to mind, and less distantly so do Erasmus and sixteenth-century English figures like Thomas More, Thomas Starkey and Thomas Elyot, all of whom used the dialogue to write on political and religious issues.[68] In the 1640s, pamphlet dialogues, mimicking play scripts and responding to the circumstances of civil war, emerged as a subgenre for purveying news and commentary on political and religious issues. Perhaps, as Susan Wiseman suggests, their influence may be discerned in Harrington's *Valerius and Publicola*, a theoretical discussion in dialogue of the merits of a commonwealth, and in Hobbes's *Behemoth*, a dialogue on events in the Commonwealth.[69] But the dialogue was not much in vogue in English popular printed political writing after the Restoration, and in the context of the Exclusion Crisis it appeared only rarely before 1681: apart from L'Estrange's *Citt and Bumpkin* there was only Care's (?) *Clodpate's Ghost*, dated 25 August 1679. What was new in 1681 was its popularity and its use for designedly jocose-serious purposes.

Rawlins was the only serialist who created realistic and memorable interlocutors. The names and personalities of his two figures, 'Jest' and 'Earnest,' never changed. Over the months he endowed them with distinct characteristics rather than opposite viewpoints. Earnest was sober, serious, deliberate and prone to extended explanations of principles or theories. Jest was a perfect foil with his merry wit, impatient nature, irreverent spirit and quick tongue. Jest prepared the reader, saying to Earnest, 'Well, you have a mind to be grave a little, pray don't be tedious.' Then Earnest launched into a theoretical discussion.[70] The two of them were unmistakable.

Neither L'Estrange nor Care developed unforgettable characters. L'Estrange started out in an unimaginative way with the prosaic Question and Answer. After three and a half months, they became Whig and Tory, and then at various times Trimmer and Observator. Care's interlocutors stood for a viewpoint, and their names exemplify the outlook he was emphasizing at a particular time. He began with Papist and Masquerade (i.e., a Catholic masquerading as a Protestant) and then introduced John Indifferent (to emphasize Care's impatience with Dissenters who declined to take a firm stand against popery), then Tory and Papist. Tory and Trueman (representing Care himself) began dialoguing on 11 November 1681 and had a long run, until 1 September 1682, when Moderate Tory, followed the next week by Whig, joined them in a three-way exchange. Later the dialogue was between Trueman and Observator alone, no doubt to underscore Care's adversarial relationship with L'Estrange. From the end of November 1682 until July 1683 Care alternated the dialogue form and essays.

Whatever the success of these writers in crafting striking interlocutors, their dialogue did what effective dialogue always does: it created a sense of intimacy, immediacy and verisimilitude, lured the reader into identifying with one or more of the interlocutors, lowered the intellectual temperature of the discourse and then slipped into a discussion of some serious question. L'Estrange was especially skilled at drawing the reader into a believable situation. For example, Whig and Courantier meet in secret, hoping that Observator will not find them; but Whig promises that if he should find them, he (Whig) will put Courantier out the back door. Thus prepared, they settle down to talk.[71] Tory announces to Whig that so-and-so has a speech impediment and is going to Oxford to be cured. Whig is curious: 'How an Impediment? Does he stammer? Or is he Tongue-Ty'd?' Some people cannot pronounce an *S* or an *R*, he says helpfully. What *could* be the matter? By now the reader wants to know too. So Tory tells him, making political points the while. It turns out that the fellow is not 'Lisping and Wharrling' over certain letters but rather stammering over invoking God's blessing (as in the Litany) on the *entire* royal family (including the duke of York). In addition (this in a swipe at the ignoramus juries) it seems that he cannot 'for his hearts bloud pronounce *Billa Vera*.'[72] Habermas recognized the dialogue form as important in the fashioning of a 'political public sphere' in the late seventeenth century;[73] these serialists offer important examples of dialoguing. Freist has made the same point for mid-seventeenth-century print culture, pointing out that dialogue has some of the features of a theatrical play.[74]

III

Humor was another hallmark of the propaganda campaign. Care, who had been self-consciously using humor every week for more than two years in his *Popish Courant*, was disdainful of the banter in the work of his enemies. His disdain, of course, was a measure of their success, a way of chiding them for making light of a serious matter, and perhaps an expression of fear that they were more amusing than he was. 'Some people think,' wrote Care scornfully, 'that Englishmen are to be caught like trouts, by tickling.'[75] 'Tickling' is exactly what the royal polemicists did. *Heraclitus Ridens*, in keeping with its title, was always exuberantly merry: Rawlins made Jest into a stand-up comic, one who announced belief that 'an ounce of mirth is worth a pound of sorrow!'[76] and found the droll in whatever the point under discussion. 'Reason or Fooling alone won't work,' said L'Estrange, who explained that he chose a middle ground between playful humor and solemn rationality and tried to 'Season the One with the Other.'[77] In fact, although full of merry nonsense, the *Observator* was less rollicking than *Heraclitus Ridens*, and a just mean between jocularity and seriousness may have pleased some readers better.

Care, for all his disdain of his enemies' humor, promoted the value of humor in persuading readers to a point of view. His Catholic interlocutor remarked that a 'pretty Droll [i.e. a jest, a joke]... does us more service than Bellarmine,' whose 'Reason and Argument [are] the worst course in the world to defend' Catholicism.'But droll and Impudence... are weapons irresistible.'[78] In the *Popish Courant* Care almost always gave his readers something to make them smile or smirk. His dubbing the Pope 'His Unholiness'[79] can bring a smile even now, as can his scurrilous description of L'Estrange's polemical skills: 'His Talent is only to Answer Books, just as Mice and Moths do, Nibble the Margins, and leave his Excrement on a Page or two, and so retire to his Hole.'[80] Care was not as funny as Rawlins; rarely does one laugh out loud, although his account of Rawlins's will is very amusing.[81] As things went from bad to worse for him and his side, his light touch failed him. Some readers may agree with the verdict of the nineteenth-century editor of *State Trials*, who found nothing to laugh about in the *Popish Courant* and dismissed Care's 'attempts at wit' as 'but rarely successful,' describing them as 'generally coarse and sometimes brutal.'[82] It is true that Care's humor was often vulgar, achieved by wordplay often overlaid with sexual innuendo, scatological inferences, and anecdotes about the escapades of monks and nuns. But the Restoration 'Mechanick sort,' if not the upper-class educated reader, may well have found the *Courant* to be a genuine 'refreshment.' One needs to remember, as Keith Thomas explained in a pioneering article, 'The Place of Laughter in Tudor and Stuart England,' that what makes people laugh is time and class specific, an index of the society's culture.[83] For Care and the Royalists, laughter was a serious business; mirth was never innocent, and the purpose went beyond laughter. They used jocularity to relax the guard of their readers, to invite them to identify with them, to fix the point in their minds, and to make their target look ridiculous. It took skill to achieve those things.

Care, nonetheless, used his enemies' humor to criticize them for making light of serious questions. Possibly his stated concern reflected his knowledge of and sensitivity to a contemporary ambivalence regarding political humor. When he first launched the *Weekly Pacquet*, he expressed the 'hope' that the *Courant* would 'not prejudice the credit of that Solid Matter that precedes it.' With unaccustomed diffidence, he justified himself by saying, 'Sure we may be allowed a little innocent Mirth when they exercise so much Spleen and Gall.'[84] A brief comment on the era's ambivalence toward humor will clarify the point.

On the one hand, Stuart society, rigid puritans excepted, enjoyed jokes.[85] From the sixteenth century on, mirth was recommended as a powerful physic: 'There is nothing beside the goodness of God, that preserves health so much as honest mirth,' especially when practiced at dinner and at bedtime, wrote the editor of *A compendyous Regyment or dyetary of Helth* in 1542.[86] Certain plants – bugloss and mugwort – were extolled as having the power to provoke merriment.[87] Humor also made life more pleasant. The Reverend Isaac Barrow wrote that one was not obliged always to 'knit the brow and squeeze the brain, to be always sadly dumpish or seriously pensive.'[88] A late Stuart observer concurred, describing humor as truly 'Virtues Friend.'[89] Books with such titles as *London Jests* or *Coffee-House Jests* appeared over the years, demonstrating an ongoing approval of laughter.[90] Moreover, Dryden and other Restoration poets and dramatists, in keeping with a Renaissance literary convention, believed that comedy and satire could improve society by pointing up its vices.[91] Religious leaders agreed; for example, the Reverend Isaac Barrow declared that when one wants 'to correct [men's] lethargic stupidity,... then doth reason freely resign its place to wit.'[92] People of discriminating taste, like John Taylor (the Water Poet), Samuel Pepys, Narcissus Luttrell, Abel Boyer, a newswriter and author, and Archbishop William Sancroft collected witticisms, merry tales or apophthegms. Apart from this innocent attitude toward humor, Restoration 'court wits,' inspired by John Wilmot, earl of Rochester, used a form of humor – sarcasm and 'satirical wit' – as a weapon to criticize society, especially the clergy.[93] A contemporary said that 'sportiveness and drollery' were 'so much the humour of the times' that if one wrote otherwise, his writings would not sell.[94] In other words, Care's contemporaries and others

long before them understood that jocularity was often more
effective than reason in dealing with problems of men and society.
Care and his sparring partners in the press were playing into that
tradition.

On the other hand, there was a convention in Stuart England of
decrying humor when the target was the leaders or the policies of
State and Church. At the turn of the century Sir Francis Bacon
insisted that politics, religion and men of affairs were unacceptable
topics for raillery. Henry Peacham, the author of an early seventeenth-century courtesy book, concurred, writing that 'jests and
scoffs should be far from great personages.'[95] Socially inferior persons should not criticize their betters, especially not in jests. Abel
Boyer wrote at the end of the century that 'different degrees establish'd among Men do often keep Inferiours from speaking their
Thoughts about the *Ridiculum* of those above them.'[96] For Care, or
anyone else, to treat political and religious ideas and leaders in a
humorous fashion could be dangerous. It was also a rather new
departure in polemic, the more so because Care did it every week.
Making jokes at the expense of the establishment was one way that
Care, who had no conventional political power, could exercise a
kind of power. It may be that the negative attitude toward political
humor made him hesitate sometimes and also provided him with a
weapon against his enemies.

IV

Verse and ballads directed to a polemical end were other devices
for adding variety and interest to the serials. Both Care and his
Royalist enemies used them, Care continuing an earlier practice.
One of Care's most effective verses was the 'The Pedigree of
Popery, Or The Genealogy of Antichrist,' which took up the entire
Courant of 8 April 1681. The contest with the Royalist serialists was
in its early stages, and Care was escalating his virulent attacks on
popery. The verse is vicious. Beginning with the lines 'The

Devil begat Sin/Sin begat Ignorance,' the verse proceeds to name the dreadful characteristics of popery: 'Ambition begat Simony/Simony begat the Pope.' Finally Jesuitism begat four monsters, which, in turn, 'beget all kinds of Abominations,' including 'Treason... Masquerade-Popery,... [and] City-burning.'[97] The verses by John Flatman in *Heraclitus Ridens* served Rawlins's polemical ends. For example, 'Jest' presented 'Earnest' with a 'sober Pindaric Ode' evoking the misery of the Civil Wars and implying that the nation stood again on the brink of civil war:

> *Ah Stubborn Isle!*
> *So late from slavish bondage freed,*
> *… … … … … … … … … … … … …*
> *Canst thou so soon forget the Toyl,*
> *Religion and true Loyalty were slain*
> *whilst Rebels did prevail*
> *and Albion look'd like sodoms smoaking Plain.*[98]

Care also turned to fables and stories to lighten his writing and to help illustrate how dreadful popery was. One of the most elaborate and memorable fables dated from 1345, as Care was at pains to point out; it concerned a wolf (symbolizing the Pope and the cardinals), a fox (the clergy) and an ass (the laity). The wolf and the fox confess to each other their unspeakable crimes, and each receives from the other a light penance and absolution. Then the 'silly' ass confesses that to assuage his hunger he had stolen one straw from the pack of a pilgrim who was journeying to Rome. The wolf and the fox turn on the poor ass: they declare his crime the 'most horrid Sacriledge in the World,' condemn him to die and devour him between them. Care, of course, drew out the moral to underscore how the Pope and clergy stretch the law where the laity is concerned, inflict the most extreme punishments and reap every benefit they can.[99]

Myths were used to the same end. One concerned an ancient practice of the monks at St Edmunds-Bury, who promoted the belief that if a barren married woman came with a white bull to the bier of St Edmund she would conceive a child. The tenants of the abbey lands were required to have a white bull at the ready at all times, as deeds still on file in the Augmentation Office proved, Care said. Care, of course, made pointed comments about this practice, saying that the monks promoted the 'Cheat' to win offerings and gifts, that the idea was 'stoln… from the Heathen,' and that the services of a 'lusty young Monk' may well have forwarded the later pregnancies.[100] These and other fables and myths in his text all had the same effect: they caught the reader's attention, drew him along into an imaginative world, and then drove home a memorable point against popery. After all, who can forget, even in the early twenty-first century, the 'silly' ass or the white bull and the points they illustrate?

Analogy, a standby in all writing, was another favored tool. For example, in illustrating a point that he had argued many times before, namely, that divisions between the Church of England and Nonconformists gave papists the opportunity to destroy them both, Care offered a striking analogy to fix the message in the mind of his readers: 'Well!' said his interlocutor 'Jesuit,' 'let Whig and Tory scuffle 'till their Hearts ake, whilst we tour aloft, like the Vulture hovering over the Lion and Wild-boar in their Combatings, as hoping to devour the Carcases of them both.'[101] The animal imagery with its intimation of violence powerfully conveys the point that Care wanted to make.

As he had done in the *Weekly Pacquet*, so in the *Popish Courant* Care employed colloquialisms. For example, saying that he would use 'a more Modish phrase' to inquire about events, he asked, 'How play the circumstances of affairs?'[102] Or he told his readers that 'Look you' was 'the Phrase that nowadays begins all incomparable Speeches.'[103] Or again, we learn from Care that the expostulation 'That's a Celier Sir' was a 'modern and most proper Phrase to signify any Egregious Lye.'[104] Colloquialisms appeared in *Heraclitus Ridens* too. For example, Jest, in ridiculing the notion of moderation, remarked, 'As the saying is: that cuts large thongs out of another mans hide.' Rawlins also referred to Care and another writer as 'riding Whip & spur who shall have the next vacancy in Bedlam.'[105] L'Estrange too used contemporary slang, to the dismay of the author of the entry on him in the *Dictionary of National Biography.* Such devices were helpful in reaching a broad audience.

The serialists also used hyperbolic, even violent language in descriptions, comments and *ad hominem* attacks.[106] Of course, neither extravagant speech nor personal defamation was new. They appeared in Care's early writing and were prominently displayed in his tract *The Character of A Turbulent, Pragmatical Jesuit and Factious Romish Priest* (1686). When Care first engaged in literary controversy, he said defiantly that he would not 'retreat like a snail' before his enemies. A decade later, in 1682, he confessed to a 'natural aversion to Knaves and Fools,' admitting that 'sometimes, if they stand in my way,' he was 'apt to hold them out a Looking-Glass, where, if spying their own sweet features, they grow enrag'd, Who can help it?'[107] Care held out many a looking glass for his Royalist and Anglican enemies to peer into.

Care reserved his most vitriolic language for attacking popery, which he described as a 'loathsome and destructive Monster,' an 'impudent piece of Avaricious Policy design'd chiefly to cheat people of their money and then of their souls, by pretending that the latter may... be saved by a profusion of the former.'[108] Declaring that he would willingly die a martyr to the Protestant cause, he insisted that life would not be worth living if he were 'forc'd to truckle to Popery in Spirituals, and (its natural Concomitant) Tyranny in the Civil State.'[109] Care was not alone in excoriating Catholicism, but he took the lead in using violent language to do so.

The Royalists also had a history of indulging in vituperation. From the beginning of his writing career L'Estrange had written sharply against anyone with whom he disagreed. In *Citt and Bumpkin*, part 2, he had justified name-calling, saying that it was 'speaking to the people in a language that they do both understand and believe.'[110] In the *Observator* he excused his 'warmth' on the grounds that he had been moved by 'a Zeal for the Peace, Welfare, and Safety of my Country' and that, in any case, 'the Phanatiques Themselves made good the Worst Things that ever I said of the party.'[111] Robert Willman believed that in the Exclusion Crisis the Whigs took the lead in invective and name-calling and held it until mid-1681; after then the Royalists were equally adept, responding in full measure or initiating assaults.[112] With the two sides going at each other hammer and tong, the language attained hyperbolic heights that were sustained for months. The purpose, as has been noticed before in another context, was to keep the political temperature at the boiling point and sabotage the message by sabotaging the messenger. The result was to polarize the nation.[113]

These writers repeatedly expressed their loathing for one another. For example, Rawlins called Care an 'ignorant, impudent, Frenchify'd debauch'd scurrilous Buffon.'[114] Reaching for a laugh, *Heraclitus* reported that 'Monkey Care [was] so unlike Mankind, that an Indictment is preferred against his Wife for Bestiality at the Old Baily where he is to prove what Species he is of.'[115] This slanderous diatribe also intimated that Care was suffering from syphilis. In return, Care dubbed Rawlins a 'rallying liar,' called him a 'Ruffian,' ridiculed his 'silly talent' with Jest and Earnest, maligned his 'stupid arguments' as beneath the competence of a schoolboy and made vicious fun of him when *Heraclitus Ridens* closed down.[116] Nathaniel Thompson referred to Care's *Mercury* as 'Anabaptistical' and 'Anti-Christian,' his language as 'Billingsgate,' and Care himself as 'Seditious,' 'Ridiculous,' a 'Scurrilous Monkey,' and a 'Hackney Scribler.'[117] Care dismissed Thompson as a 'Scoundrel Bogtrotter,' a 'Mischievous and Dangerous Varlet' and a 'Prostituted Wretch,' a 'Forger of Lies,' and an 'implement and Hireling of Papists.'[118] He smeared L'Estrange as a 'brazen-faced Liar,' an 'old Blade,' a 'Necromancer,' a 'Soothsayer' and a 'meer Doltish, doating mistaker of common sense.'[119] L'Estrange was furious at having Care throw nasty names at him; he took particular offense, understandably, at 'Miscreant, Olivers Fidler, Madame Cellier's Sweetheart, Towzer, Crackfart.'[120]

Charges of sexual improprieties were hurled back and forth. Care accused L'Estrange of being a 'Puss flogger' and an 'Old Whip Cat.' 'No wonder,' he wrote spitefully, 'if all the good Wives of St Gileses rap so often at his door, and cry... Pray Whip my Cat too.'[121] L'Estrange accused the Whigs of bestiality, bisexuality and incest, calling them 'Boy-Masters' and 'Mare-Masters' and citing specific examples in proof.[122] 'Tory' gleefully answered 'Whig''s question whether Heraclitus was a man or a woman with, 'That's well enough put, let me tell ye. Because the Whigsters (ye know) have occasion for Both Sexes.'[123] Perhaps pressed for time because responsible for answering three enemies, Care endeavored once or twice to dispatch them all in one fell swoop, calling them the three 'Debauchees' – 'Irish Nat, Rayling Rawllins, and Old He Goat, Old Towzer, Leacherous Romish Cur' – and declaring that they were so dreadful that they actually discredited the popish cause.[124] Of course, personal attacks were not new, but what is striking about these exchanges is their viciousness and frequency.

Both sides also used code words and nicknames to demean and belittle their enemies. A couple became widely known, even famous: *Towzer* for L'Estrange and *Monkey* for Care. *Towzer* a name commonly applied to a large dog, such as one used to bait bears or bulls, carried sexual overtones and suggested other demeaning qualities of a dog. L'Estrange appeared as 'Towzer' in many wood-cuts and tracts, and the nickname stuck. Care and the Whigs never let him forget it. In the 17 November 1680 London procession, L'Estrange's detractors in the London mob dubbed him 'the Dog Towzer' and burned him in effigy. Care was dubbed 'Monkey,' which the *Oxford English Dictionary* defines as a term of 'playful contempt' often applied to youngsters. L'Estrange even spoke of Whigs as a 'community of monkeys.'[125]

Other code words that Whigs used were *Protestant* and *True Protestant*. The first signaled opposition to the duke of York's suc-ceeding to the throne. Rawlins underlined the word's usefulness as a 'come-on' when Jest remarked 'Oh, it makes 'em sell: I heard a fellow cry Protestant Pears, and another Hot Protestant Pudding, hot, hot.'[126] Thompson entitled his newspaper the *Loyal Protestant*, suggesting that he expected the word to enhance sales.[127] Whigs called themselves 'True Protestant' and called their opponents 'Protestant Papists' or 'Protestants in Masquerade.' L'Estrange perceived that these words implied that the Church of England was a 'false Protestant,' that is, that it was 'soft' on Catholicism.[128] He tried to turn the language back on the Dissenters by denying that they were 'True Protestants,' declaring them worse than Catholics, and refusing to apply the word *Protestant* to the established Church.[129] Royalists also modified the word *Protestant* to read 'True Bromidgham Protestant,' meaning a 'true counterfeit' Protestant, a formulation that appeared in the preface to Dryden's *Absalom and Achitophel*, printed in November 1681.[130] This counterattack left Care sputtering rather ineffectually that he *was* a 'True Protestant' and proud of it.[131]

The most important and lasting names with which these men smeared each other were *Whig* and *Tory*.[132] The word *Whig* or *Whiggamaire*, had long been used in Scotland to denote a Covenanting rebel, but it was rarely found in England until 1679, when it denoted a small band of Scottish Cameronians, or 'Cargillites,' who held views that were abhorrent in England, such as the lawfulness of regicide. Then it took on a new, radical and deeply pejorative meaning. Thompson, in the *Loyal Protestant* in March 1681, was among the first to use the word *Whig* in that new radical sense, calling Whigs 'Notorious Traytors' who believe in regicide and other 'Villanies.' The word *Whig*, then, became laden with abuse as the press warfare got under way.

The word *Tory*, which had long meant an Irish outlaw, a 'bogtrotter,' also took on a politically pejorative connotation. It will be remembered that in December 1680 Care wrote a highly unflattering description of a Tory, perhaps the first time the word *Tory* appeared in Exclusionist prints.[133] Several months later the word took on a sinister meaning: it signaled that the duke of York and the duke of Ormond were involved with Irish outlaws in a treasonable Irish plot. Whig leaders no doubt gave their press friends appropriate 'hints' to connect Tories with rumors of such a plot. Care used the word *Tory* with that implication in his *Weekly Pacquet* in February 1681. Willman's research showed that Whigs, however, did not immediately exploit the word and that it owed its survival to Tories. L'Estrange was the first to employ 'Whig' and 'Tory' as counterparts when he introduced them as his interlocutors on 2 July 1681 and endowed them with distinct characteristics. This marked the first time that 'English politics were... envisaged as a dialogue between 'Whig' and 'Tory.' Thereafter, the terms *Whig* and *Tory* became part of polemical exchange and remained emblematic of a point of view for years.[134] Dryden highlighted the bitterness and divisiveness they engendered when he explained to the reader in *Absalom and Achitophel* that 'Wit and folly are consequents of Whig and Tory; and every man is a knave or an ass to the contrary side.'[135] Care and the Royalists should be given full credit for introducing these terms into English political partisan discourse.

Despite their sharp *ad hominem* attacks, Care won the grudging admiration of Rawlins and L'Estrange. Rawlins admitted that Care had 'done great things against Popery and did deserve somewhat of the commendation theretofore given him.'[136] L'Estrange paid Care the compliment of having the *Weekly Pacquet* brought to him 'every Fryday morning Piping hot to my breakfast.'[137] An excellent writer himself, L'Estrange admired Care's skills: he queried rhetorically, 'Has he not words at will, and a Story at hand to all purposes?' Although L'Estrange harbored conflicting emotions about Care, he gave him 'his due,' remarking that Care's 'Pen... might deserve to be Employ'd in a Better cause.'[138] (Characteristically, Care promptly rejected the conciliatory gesture, declaring that he felt the 'worse of himself' for the compliment.')[139] L'Estrange's amiable remark holds interest because it shows that long before James II's court wooed Care to join them as a propagandist, Care's enemies admired his writing skills, and that L'Estrange, for one, wished that those skills might be put to better use.

The Royalists triumphed in this press battle. What besides their rhetorical talents explains that fact? They helped their case by relentlessly answering Care and others week after week, blow for blow, tit for tat, making the same points over and over and over again, just as we saw Francis North urging. Court writers were also uniquely clever in turning their enemies' arguments back on them. Each side, but Royalists the more so, borrowed techniques from the other. One may dissect their tactics more closely by examining their response to the three major themes in the serials.

One dominant theme, obsessively pursued by Care, was antipopery, used as a cover for criticizing court, Church and bench, implying that those institutions were riddled with papists. Initially the Royalists moved somewhat cautiously, no doubt recognizing that the Church was vulnerable to the charge that it had become 'soft' on the Roman Catholic Church.[140] They concurred that popery was a menace but insisted that so, too, was Nonconformity. They defended papists on the grounds that they had helped Charles I, whereas Dissenters had brought him to trial and 'murdered' him.[141] They used ridicule. Mocking Care's incessant harping on popery, Rawlins derisively remarked that Care 'makes such a Lerry against popery, that he acts like a dunsical jesuit.'[142] L'Estrange, also seeking to undermine Care's sincerity, derided Care for putting 'himself forth in Two Pages, like a Turning Picture. A Jack-Pudding on the One side and lay-Brother on the other.'[143]

Royalists answered specific points: to Care's claim that Catholics were incapable of being good subjects, Rawlins responded by leveling the accusation at Dissenters, saying that it was they who were incapable of being good subjects.[144] *Heraclitus Ridens* also deflated the myth of the white bull: Jest declared that the story had cured him of belief in miracles, and Ernest rejoined that popish miracles might be over, but 'Fanatick' ones were not; one had only to look at Whig efforts to disprove the Presbyterian plot and to uncover other popish plots.[145]

Furthermore, Royalists offered a counterweight to the Popish Plot: exploiting the uproar over the trials of College and Fitzharris, they charged, as L'Estrange had done earlier, that a Presbyterian plot was afoot and intimated that the Popish Plot did not exist. This charge 'makes Care delirious,' Rawlins noted delightedly, and he went on maliciously to say that Care's zeal to deny it indicated his implication in it.[146] Using another tactic, Nathaniel Thompson asserted that Godfrey was a suicide rather than a victim of murder, a charge that would seriously undermine the Popish Plot. Sutherland thought the charge was a joke.[147] If Thompson *was* kidding, he paid dearly for his fun, for the idea reignited lingering fears of popery, and he was punished. Even so, these steps made it clear that the 'slanting' and 'hinting' and 'trimming' that L'Estrange had practiced in his *History of the Plot* in the autumn of 1679 were gone, replaced by increasingly forthright expressions of doubt about the reality of the plot and the integrity of Titus Oates. In early 1684 L'Estrange said flat out that the plot did not exist; it was a 'sham, like a counterfeit coin.'[148] By that time the contest was long over.

A second major theme in the serials was Dissent and its relationship to the Church of England, a question Care addressed with a fervor nearly equal to his fervor against popery, his attitude hardening over the months. At this time he focused on comprehension, arguing for the inclusion of Dissenters within the Church of England, which could be achieved only if the Church relaxed certain ceremonies and customs. Comprehension, which had been under discussion over the years, had the approval of moderate Anglicans but was adamantly opposed by High Churchmen.[149] Comprehension posed a theoretical problem for the Church that went far beyond the particular ceremony. If the Church agreed to change certain ceremonies to oblige Dissenters, it tacitly admitted that it had wronged them and therefore was guilty of schism. Further, the Church had the authority, in the interests of discipline, uniformity and harmony, to require outward practices, including those regarded as 'indifferent' or adiaphora. In insisting upon such ceremonies, it was in no way stretching the law. On the other hand, certain ceremonies that the Church regarded as 'indifferent' were deeply offensive to Nonconformists; as a matter of conscience they were unable to participate in them. Why, if the Church regarded those ceremonies as 'indifferent,' did they impose them on Dissenters, thereby deliberately creating a situation in which Dissenters must violate their conscience to satisfy an earthly authority? The appeal to 'conscience' created further problems; churchmen regarded dependence on the individual conscience as a dangerous threat to the unity of Christendom. There was no way either side could logically compromise on this issue.

Care was a journalist, not a philosopher, and he did not unfold such difficulties. He passionately objected to the Church's obdurate opposition to changes that would have accommodated Dissenters. In an anticlerical tirade, he railed against 'rigid Church-Ceremony Men,' who were against 'all those whose Conscience is not exactly cast to their Model,'[150] and declared through his interlocutor 'Tory' that their attitude toward Presbyterians was to 'Hang-um, Dam-um, Flea-um, Fry-um.' Care put into Tory's mouth the flat-out confession that 'those Presbyterians I hate mortally, by a natural Antipathy. I had rather be a Papist at any time than a Presbyterian.'[151] Such churchmen were the 'New Fry' in the Church, Care said contemptuously; they were 'prepar'd by Hobbs and the Playhouse, and cared not a farthing for any Religion, provided they may but swagger and domineer, and swear and damn and drink Healths with an Huzza.' Their belief in the Presbyterian plot was symptomatic of their 'secret affection' for Catholicism.[152] He asserted through his interlocutor that he had a 'sincere Veneration' for the Church of England and that he was not comparing it to the Roman Catholic Church; rather, he was comparing the 'fops' within it to 'Dunsical Papists.'[153] Clearly, anticlericalism was a central component in his view of the Church and its position on adiaphora.

Care insisted bitterly that the differences between the Church and the Dissenters concerned matters that the Church admitted were inconsequential; Dissenters accepted all the points of Anglican doctrine and differed only on some ceremonies. Invoking article 19 of the Thirty-nine Articles, which read, 'The visible Church of Christ is a congregation of faithful men, in which the pure Word of God is preached and the Sacraments be duly ministered according to Christ's ordinance in all those things that of necessity are requisite to the same,' Care argued that Dissenters were the 'true visible particular Churches of Christ and consequently part of the true visible national Church of Christ in England.'[154] Care's perspective here is important in exemplifying the 'porosity' of Dissent and Anglicanism.[155] A member of the Church of England, Care was writing in terms that would have been acceptable to Presbyterians at the time. 'A Lover of true Protestants,' as he called himself, he did not want to separate from the Church over certain ceremonies; he was, essentially, a reluctant Dissenter. He wanted the Church to change certain rites and cere-monies that went against Dissenters' consciences so that they might remain within it.

Care looked for support to Latitudinarians, those moderate men in the Church of England, and sometimes attempted to coopt them.[156] Declaring that 'there are abundance... of Grave, Learned, Pious, Sober Divines, [who are] strict and regular sons of the Church of England as by Law establisht,' he maintained that these men believed that a person might be 'a very good Church-man' though he abjured 'Arminius, Socinus, Sybthorp and Manwaring' and that they thought that 'Liberty, and Property, Law, and Allegiance do consist very well together.' In contrast to High Churchmen, these men believed that papists were 'much more Dangerous than Dissenters.' To drive home this point, Care com-pared such men to the 'old thinking serious Elsibeth [sic] Churchmen.'[157]

Care reinforced these points in tracts printed in 1682. In *Some Reasons For Separation From the Communion of the Church of England* he was eloquent on the right of liberty of the religious conscience.[158] In *Utrum horum: Or, The Nine and Thirty Articles Of The Church of England*, he undertook to show by lavish quotations that in their attitude toward the Thirty-nine Articles Presbyterians were much closer to the established Church than were Catholics.[159] He insisted that apart from some rites and ceremonies, Dissenters 'otherwise are Orthodox in Faith, pious towards God, Loyal to the King, and peaceable with their Neighbours.'[160] This was a self-serving idea, but it was consistent with his laying blame for the division in the nation squarely on 'some Church-men.' *Utrum horum* was as sharply anti-clerical as the serials; Care iterated that Anglican clerics 'screw up the Ceremonies higher' on purpose to exclude Nonconformists and then unfairly branded them as 'Whigs, Fanaticks, Enemies to the Church, Disloyal to His Majesty, Disturbers of the Government, and Factious.' Such churchmen were worse than Catholics; they applied penal laws that were really meant for Catholics to Dissenters, believed in a Presbyterian plot and loaded all Dissenters with the guilt of imaginary conspiracies.[161] To assist the circulation of *Utrum horum*, with its sharp indictment, Care advertised it in the *Impartial Protestant Mercury*.[162]

Another tract written in 1682, *A Perfect Guide For Protestant Dissenters. In Case Of Prosecution Upon Any Of The Penal Statutes Made against Them*, presented more complex ideas.[163] Basing his views on the Bible, reason, equal justice and prudent morality, Care's aim, as stated in the preface, was to unite Protestants against the common enemy, popery, to defend them 'from Imputations of Schism, Sedition, and Disloyalty' and rebut the charges of the Royalist writers.[164] Drawing upon his knowledge of the law, Care closely examined the penal statutes, arguing that they were con-trary to the 'Law of God' and inapplicable to Dissenters, since Dissenters were not rebels and no insurrection had occurred (4–5). Penal laws were meant to 'punish Mutiny, Rebellion, and Insurrection against the State and Civil Government,' not a sincere conscience or religious practices of indifferent importance (1–3, 9). Revealing again his increasingly angry anticlericalism, Care railed at 'Persons who call themselves Divines and Teachers of the Doctrine of Charity' for incensing the civil power against Nonconformists 'meerly to establish an unlawful Hierarchie over the Consciences of their Brethren' (3). Tauntingly he declared that the clergy were guilty of Nonconformity in the form of nonresidence and pluralities, which were specifically forbidden by Church law (8). Advancing his argument still further, he dissected the phrase 'according to the Liturgy and Practice of the Church of England,' arguing that it did not oblige Dissenters to use only the Liturgy. Dissenters' prayers did not differ, he said, in 'Matter, Form or end from the English Liturgy of Men... or the Heavenly Liturgy of Christ' (6–7). Commending a contemporary tract, *The Conformists Plea for the Nonconformists*, written by the Reverend Edward Pearse, Care queried whether the penal laws that created 'Arbitrary Distresses and Imprisonments' were not 'contrary to Magna Charta' (11). But in *A Perfect Guide* he did not call upon Dissenters to withdraw from the Anglican Church.

Following still another tack, Care contended in *A Perfect Guide* that power over ecclesiastical matters was vested in the king, a point he would elaborate later as James II's polemicist. Declaring his approval of Charles II's Declaration of Indulgence, Care scolded the Church of England for 'grutch[ing]' Dissenters the exercise of their 'Rights' and underscored that Dissenters acknowledged the king to be the supreme head of both the government and the Church (9). Insisting in the preface upon the 'dangerous consequences' of persecution, Care also took on the 'Pests of the Kingdom, ignorant and greedy Informers,' an issue he had barely touched upon in the serials. It was morally impossible, he argued, to swear that a conventicle was contrary to the Liturgy when no overt act was proved. In those circumstances, an informer judged whether a Dissenter's prayer was agreeable to the Church of England, but it was 10,000 to one that he was incompetent to make that judgment (7). Under the mantle of law, informers 'vex and depauperize the Subject for malice and private ends, never for love of Justice' (7). Their proceedings were not only against Christ's doctrine but also against the interest of the nation; they divided subjects and imperiled trade (11).

He expressed especial bitterness in the spring of 1683, about two months before he succumbed to government pressure and ceased publishing the *Weekly Pacquet*. In answering a tract titled

A Persuasive to Communion with the Church of England he called the Anglican Church 'false,' condemning it for using the same weapons against Dissenters that the Catholic Church had used against it. Contending that the practices of the Church of England transgressed the Word of God, violated early Church custom, and lacked the 'power and form of Godliness,' Care called upon sincere Christians to withdraw from it.[165]

Unfortunately for Care, the Royalists' position on Dissent was exceedingly strong. Early in the press war L'Estrange had taken the initiative with his shrewd and effective tract *Dissenters' Sayings*, a reply to a short, four-page collection of L'Estrange's comments entitled *L'Estrange's Sayings*, published by Langley Curtis about 1 April 1681. *L'Estrange's Sayings* had aimed to demean L'Estrange by quoting his own writings to show him sympathetic to popery, hostile to the common man and fearful of a parliament. L'Estrange was furious. The very next week, *Dissenters' Sayings, part 1*, appeared with the announced goal of painting a 'Picture of [Dissenters] to the life, of their own Drawing,' in other words, from their own writings. Quoting copiously from Dissenters' texts, L'Estrange compiled a thick, forty-six-page tract and followed it with an even longer second part. These two books documented that Presbyterians despised the Church of England, hated the sectaries (and vice versa), demanded toleration but insisted on uniformity as soon as they were in power and held to radical political principles – for example, that the two Houses were above the king and that the king must pass laws presented to him by Parliament – that were subversive of the government.[166] They encouraged domestic tumults by printing seditious pamphlets. Their concern had now shifted from popery to tyranny, so that they were, in effect, guilty of 'downright treason.'[167] L'Estrange's appropriating the approach of the Whigs – that is, doing exactly the same kind of thing in *Dissenters' Sayings* as the Whigs had done in *L'Estrange's Sayings* and even using a similar title so that the reading public would immediately see the connection – was a clever rhetorical strategy. So popular was *Dissenters' Sayings* that it went through three editions. L'Estrange's biographer judged that it 'dealt a severer blow at the Dissenters than any other book,' becoming the *vade mecum* of the clergy and accounting for clerical donations to L'Estrange.[168] *Dissenters' Sayings* was a formidable blow to Care and his side, and L'Estrange never wearied of referring to it in the *Observator*.

Royalist serials built on the advantage they had won with *Dissenters' Sayings*. Rawlins, sarcastically addressing Care as 'Dr. Care' and his 'little Doctorship,' demanded proof that any congregation of Dissenters had the 'pure Word preached, or the Sacraments duly administered' in fulfillment of article 19. Who had told this 'little wrigling Author,' he inquired, what the philosophy of the Church of England was? Care and the Dissenters might disagree with the king over what was necessary and what was inconsequential, but in the end they had to obey him. Pressing his argument, Rawlins denied the notion that Dissenters disagreed with the Church only about ceremonies; in fact, he maintained, they regarded communion with the Church a 'damnable sin,' believed separation from it was necessary to salvation and wanted to erase six specific articles.[169] If they did indeed regard themselves as members of the true Church, they were 'Knaves and Fools to keep up such a stir about ceremonies.' The real issue between the Church and the Dissenters, Rawlins insisted, was not things indifferent; the Dissenters wanted to reduce the bishops to a nullity, cancel laws that restricted them from worshiping as they please and destroy the Church of England, as by law established.[170]

The Royalists also sharply challenged Care's criticisms of the Church of England. To his charge that the Church establishment was 'Janus-faced' – that is, that under the pretense of loyalty to the Church of England it strove to make Protestantism 'contemptible,' thereby to advance popery[171] – L'Estrange and Rawlins rejoined, again using the effective device of turning the argument back on Care, that 'under Pretence of Religion and Allegeance' Dissenters were bent on the destruction of the Church. In 'plain Terms,' said L'Estrange, they aimed to 'destroy... Monarchy and Episcopacy under the Notion of Popery and Tyranny.'[172] Care's intimation that the Church of England aimed to set up a popish successor was met with the claim that Dissenters aimed to set up the sectaries and a republic.[173] L'Estrange answered Care's complaint that the Church wanted to 'hang, fry, and flea' Dissenters with a like account of what had happened when in a fracas in town someone said a gentleman was a Tory: the crowd called out, 'He's a Tory, Kill him, Kill him, He's a Tory.'[174] Furthermore, the charge that the Church and the government contained secret papists masquerading as Protestants was countered by Rawlins's comment that Dissenters and papists 'draw in the same Yoak' and trumped by L'Estrange's allegation that the Dissenters were 'Papists themselves, only under another name.'[175]

Finally, Royalists made a powerful effort to rebut Care by their blistering descriptions of Dissent, which paralleled Care's scurrilous description of popery noted above. L'Estrange wrote: 'The Young Lady of Geneva is every jote as good at a State Gamball as the Course [sic] Courantiers Old Whore of Babylon herself; as Dogmatical in her Sentences; as Cruell and Inexorable in her Executions; as Infallible and Unaccountable in her Claims, as Imperiall in her Constitutions and Decrees. Your Presbytery is a many-Headed Pope and every Mouth worse teeth in't.'[176] Rawlins too returned in full measure the disrespect Care had showered on the established Church. He ridiculed Dissenting preachers and worship services, describing a sermon as delivered with grotesque gestures, the minister 'grinning, howling, groaning, bawling, and whining.'[177] L'Estrange chimed in, saying that Dissenters turned a 'Holy Exercise into a Dialogue of Hickups, and Grimaces between the Minister and the Audience.'[178] Care's Dissenters, Rawlins declared harshly, were the 'Leprosie and Scurvy of the body Politick, both in the Church and the Kingdom.'[179]

Rawlins and L'Estrange also dismissed everything that Care had to say about conscience as it related to religion. 'Liberty of conscience,' Rawlins asserted uncompromisingly, 'was the greatest Cheat in the World;'[180] both he and L'Estrange argued that once in power, Dissenters would refuse liberty of conscience to others, and L'Estrange cited the telling example of their actions in New England to prove his point.[181] But even more powerful than this rejoinder was L'Estrange's insistence that the Dissenters' freedom of conscience was nothing more than a 'Damn'd Contrivance to destroy the King and the Church,' a 'Cover for Sedition.'[182] No-one objected to a private conscience, he wrote; the civil government had nothing to do with a 'Private, Solitary, Temperate, Thinking Religion.' If the Dissenters were truly religious, what difference would arbitrary government, corrupt ministers and so on, make to them? But Dissenters 'cannot relish a bare Freedom of Conscience, unless it be in a Seditious Meeting.' When they got together, 'their Private consciences grow up in a Thrice, to be Publique Ones.' When they created 'Parties against the law' and presented 'Complaints against... the publique Constitution,' their conscience, in effect, became a conspiracy.[183] L'Estrange had his interlocutor 'Trimmer' declare that the 'point at issue is betwixt conformity and Conscience.' Driving home the point, he wrote, 'The Pretext of Conscience Disauthorizes all Laws alike; and supersedes all Duties... it turns Loyalty into Treason; Murder into Sacrifice.'[184] The implications for politics and the constitution of such a situation were dire: if every man invoked his conscience to judge religion, law and the king, the government of England would be changed fundamentally: 'Sovereignty is Then in the Multitude, for wheresoever the last Appeal lies, there's the Supreme Power.' Private opinion regarding religion became a matter of destroying the law, the Church and the monarchy. In his inimitable style, L'Estrange asserted that ''tis religion that makes the Noise,' but ''tis opposing of the Civil Authority... that strikes the Blow.'[185] L'Estrange's remarks strengthen the point made earlier – that religion and constitutional and political issues were inextricably intertwined – and one should not be privileged over the other in our understanding of the Exclusion Crisis.

L'Estrange reinforced these points by reprinting essays that he had written twenty years earlier, notably *Holy Cheat* and *A*

Memento.[186] Both were astonishingly pertinent; the first, it will be recalled, blamed Presbyterians and their teachings for the Civil Wars and the murder of Charles I, and charged that they aimed to 'enslave both King and People under the Masque of Religion.' L'Estrange, ever on the alert for an opportunity to shaft his enemies and draw an analogy between the present circumstances and 1641, amended the preface to include Care and Curtis, comparing them to Prynne, Burton and Bastwick. The second, *A Memento*, blamed the press for the Civil Wars and declared that it was just as guilty as it had been then. This pamphlet also excoriated Presbyterians, calling them 'dangerous' and declaring that 'no Caution can be too early, no Importunity too Earnest, no Restriction too Severe.'[187]

Crisis in law and trial by jury constituted the third major theme in the serials. The context was the ignoramus juries, those Whig-dominated juries that returned an ignoramus verdict in high-profile cases brought against Whigs, such as those of Stephen College in July 1681 and the earl of Shaftesbury in November 1681. The basic issues were not new: the independence of juries had already been established in Bushel's case in 1670,[188] and the major arguments in support of jurors' freedom of conscience in deciding a case had already been presented, most notably by William Penn in 1670 and in other legal cases from 1667 to 1674.[189] But in 1681–82 it was important to the Whigs to justify ignoramus verdicts, for those verdicts confirmed the innocence of persons brought before the juries. It was equally important to the Royalists to charge ignoramus jurors with acting illegally, thereby buttressing the guilt of such persons.

In the *Popish Courant* Care wrote forcefully on behalf of the jury system and eloquently in support of English law. Making similar points to those that appeared in the parliamentary debates in the autumn of 1680, he noted tauntingly that L'Estrange was unconcerned when the jury acquitted Wakeman and asked why he should be troubled at their returning ignoramus now. Malice, ignorance and bias explain why, sneered Care. Launching into a little law lesson in defense of ignoramus juries, Care insisted that jurors were 'the proper and sole Judges' of the credibility of witnesses and that if in conscience they did not believe the matter charged to be true, they could not according to their oath return a true bill.[190] Warming to his theme, Care reminded readers that the king had renewed his commitment to govern by law but that doing so was impossible without juries, 'for the Verdict of a Jury was a most essential point of Law.' Therefore, he concluded, persons who try to 'Over-Awe, Brow-beat, or dare to Hiss at the Verdict of a Jury, are Enemies to his Majesty and the Constitution of our Government, and endeavour as much as in them lies to Subvert the Law, and all the Ancient Methods of Justice.'[191] Nine months later he paid still higher tribute to trial by jury, praising it as an institution 'our Ancestors valued as one of the most precious badges of English Liberty.' If jurors failed to perform the task of judging the credibility of witnesses, he maintained, 'trial by Juries would... [be a] Mockery.'[192] Declaring that 'Law is the Kings Highway and bears... Analogy (at a humble distance) with the Gospel,' he argued that if sheriffs were not legally chosen – he implied that they had not been in the recent London shrieval elections – then there could be 'no Legal Jury, nor any Legal Indictment, and consequently, no Proceedings of Justice.'[193]

So seriously did Care take this issue that he gave it a prominent place in his *English Liberties: Or, The Free-Born Subject's inheritance, containing I. Magna Charta, The Petition of Right, the Habeas Corpus Act...*, a 229–page book on constitutional matters that appeared in 1682, probably in August.[194] George Larkin, the printer, had high expectations for this book: he brought out three issues of the same edition in 1682 and arranged for an exceedingly large print run.[195] Harris noted in the 1700 edition that 5,000 copies were seized when the book first appeared.[196] Probably written over several months for several reasons, *English Liberties* was a kind of legal handbook aimed at instructing the untutored nonelite about the law and rights of Englishmen. As the full title informed the reader, *English Liberties* included the texts of and commentary on Magna

Charta, the petition of right and *Habeas Corpus*, all the laws against Protestants, a disquisition on the antiquity of Parliament and the alleged statutory requirement that it be called each year and a 'discourse of Juries' emphasizing their advantages to Englishmen. The book, whose language about the 'Fundamental rights of Englishmen' was impassioned, advised electors about qualities to look for in choosing members of Parliament, responded to criticism of the ignoramus jury verdict and answered L'Estrange's *Free-Born Subject,* the third edition of which had appeared in 1681. A detailed table of 'Some of the most Material Contents' pointed the reader to whatever topic concerned him or her.[197]

Compiling documents for inclusion in *English Liberties*, drafting commentary on them and dealing with all the topics was a tall order for any writer. Where did Care, who was writing this at the height of the firestorm in the press and must have been extremely busy, get the information and ideas? In addition to his own considerable legal knowledge and previous expressions of his viewpoint (which should not be disparaged), there were pertinent materials available that no doubt helped him. The work of two distinguished legal figures had appeared in 1680 and 1681, respectively: Sir John Hawles's *The English-mans Right. A dialogue Between A Barrister at Law, And A Jury-Man* and Sir John Somers's *The Security of Englishmen's Lives*, which Care specifically recommended.[198] *A Character of Popery and Arbitrary Government*, published in 1681, was a source of ideas and whole paragraphs used verbatim without acknowledgment.[199] The ideas and verbatim language of parliamentary debate also appeared in this essay without acknowledgment.[200] Finally, as Winthrop Hudson pointed out some years ago, although overstating the case, Care, again without acknowledgment, also incorporated into his book ideas and a few sentences verbatim from William Penn's tract *England's Great Interest in the Choice of this new Parliament,* printed in 1679.[201] Hudson also noted that some of the argument and the ordering of the documents paralleled Penn's other writings, for example, *The People's Ancient and Just Liberties Asserted in the Trial of William Penn and William Mead* (1670).[202]

Obviously, Care was less careful in citing his sources in this popular treatise than he was in writing the *Weekly Pacquet*.

Even so, the result is Care's own; using ideas and a handful of quotes, he crafted a treatise that was quite different from any on which he drew. That Penn's *England's Great Interest* figured directly in *English Liberties* and that other of Penn's writings are close to *English Liberties* is worthy of note in light of Penn and Care's relationship during the reign of James II: it shows that the two men knew each other's work in the early 1680s. There is no proof that they were personally acquainted at that time, but it is likely that they were; the point of contact between them could have been the printer George Larkin, with whom Care had often done business and who in 1682 printed Penn's *Some Sober and Weighty Reasons against Prosecuting Protestant Dissenters.*[203] As we shall see, Penn paid Care the ultimate compliment by incorporating a large chunk of *English Liberties* into one of his tracts – without acknowledgment.

Grounding *English Liberties* firmly in the tradition of the ancient constitution,[204] Care praised England's 'fundamental laws [as] coeval with government' and Magna Charta as 'Declaratory of the principal grounds of the Fundamental Laws and Liberties of England' and added nothing new.[205] Describing law as 'the best Birthright the Subject hath,' as an Englishman's 'surest Sa[n]ctuary,' 'strongest Fortress,' and sturdiest 'Buckler' (29), Care explained further that the essence of this birthright was 'to be freed in Person and Estate from Arbitrary Violence and Oppression' (4; see also 30). Continuing, he instructed his readers that an Englishman's birthright shines 'most conspicuously in Parliaments and juries'; in the one the subject has a share in the legislative power, and in the other it joins in the executive part of the law (4–5). Using the attractive metaphor of two 'pillars' supporting English liberty that Henry Powle had uttered in debate in the House of Commons on 23 November 1680,[206] Care, with reference to Parliament and juries, declared that 'these two Grand Pillars of English Liberty' had made the nation 'more free and happy than any other People in the World.' To undermine them, he warned, was to 'strike at the very Constitution' of the government; it was worse than 'letting in the sea or poisoning the springs,' for all posterity would be ruined and enslaved (5).

'Remarkable and advantageous' as the laws that guarded England's liberties were, they are, Care cautioned, 'insignificant Cyphers, if not Honestly put in Execution.' Juries were mainly concerned with the execution of the law and therefore were one of the 'principal bulwarks of England's Liberties' (136). Chapter 29 of Magna Charta, Care opined, 'deserves to be written in Letters of Gold, and... Inscribed in Capitals on all our Courts of Judicature, Town-Halls, and most publick Edifices.' That chapter read: 'No freeman shall be arrested, or detained in prison, or deprived of his freehold, or outlawed,... or in any way molested... unless by the lawful judgment of his peers and by the law of the land.' Care maintained that these guarantees were 'the Elixir of our English Freedoms, the Storehouse of all our Liberties' (22).

Care spent pages describing the ideal juror, stressing the need for 'honest, substantial, Impartial men' (207). Jurors should be drawn from the neighborhood and be of 'worth and repute' to avoid bribery (210). No Dissenter should be barred from serving, if otherwise qualified. Jurors should be able to resolve both law and fact (223). Regretting that jurors were then humble before judges, Care cited the medieval *Mirror of Justices* and other old sources to fortify the point that earlier jurors had much greater standing. Perhaps wearing their hats in court would mark them out and help restore that standing, Care suggested (211). Slyly, he made the point that because of the nature of their tenure, judges were subject to influence, whereas it would be impossible for the honest juror, fulfilling the criteria he set out, to succumb to out-side pressures (208). He rounded out his account with anecdotal evidence drawn from earlier trials to show why jurors, not the judge, must judge the evidence and bring in a verdict consonant with their consciences (217–20).

This book was Care's most powerful. For obvious reasons, it provoked the renewed enmity of the government; a prosecution was instituted in 1682 against Care for maliciously intending to cast odium on the government and create discord between the king and his people with his 'false, scandalous, odious, and malicious libel.' The charge focused on Care's directions regarding choosing a member of Parliament and his qualifications for a member, citing especially the following points: to avoid officeholders, whose tenure was at pleasure, for they might be overawed; to avoid men who themselves or their relations were dependent on the court; and to avoid persons who had been or might be pensioners or received salaries for secret service.[207] A record of the result of the prosecution has not survived, but the charge left no doubt that Care was once more in the government's sights. Further, *English Liberties* also popularized and helped to make enduring not only ideas about the value of Parliament and juries but also the expression that they were 'the two great pillars of the British constitution.' That attractive language might well have remained hidden in the accounts of the parliamentary debate, but Care brought the expression into his *English Liberties*, and that book carried it to the American colonies, where, as we shall see, it reappeared in colonial writings.

L'Estrange rebutted all of Care's points. In his judgment, trial by jury was in deep peril, law was under threat and the nation's governing processes were in jeopardy. Liberty of conscience, the *Observator* declared, had swallowed up the 'Authority of the Government' by claiming precedence over 'all Written or Printed laws.' The problem was that the 'True-Protestant Conscience' was 'Pliant to all profitable Ends and Purposes' in the 'service of a Party' or 'Interest.'[208] In an analogy reminiscent of Care's 'Incomparable Medicament' – the one that got Care into trouble with Scroggs – L'Estrange declared that jury consciences made 'any thing out of Nothing; and turn any thing again into Nothing; they prove True to be False; and False to be True; they Reconcile Distances, and Contradictions.'[209] More seriously, he argued that 'if juries abandon the law, and proceed by new Methods of their own, they have an Arbitrary Power in themselves to pervert Justice.'[210]

Rawlins wrote virtually the same thing about the jury and liberty of conscience. Rebutting Care's parallel with the Wakeman jury, he noted that Wakeman had come to trial, whereas ignoramus verdicts obviously avoided a trial. Rawlins summed up his attitude in a poem called 'The Whigs Save-All':

> *If we're sworn of a Jury*
> *To Try a rank Tory*
> *Though no proof, we'l find him ne'r fear it,*
> *But if by the By*
> *A Whig we must Try*
> *We'l clear him th' Apostles themselves did swear it.*[211]

V

The Royalists' view of the implications of the Dissenters' appeal to liberty of conscience illuminates why they believed the Dissenters posed a danger to the State more serious than the one they posed to the Church of England. These men were animated by constitutional issues as much as by religious ones. L'Estrange said flat out that 'the Question is not Religion, but the State,' declaring that the 'Great quarrel is not so much to the Religion of Geneva, as Sedition by which it was first introduc'd.'[212] Evoking memory of the Civil Wars to show that conscience had been used then as a cover under which to attack the government just as it was now, L'Estrange drew out the point that there was 'nothing like that Holy Fire for the Kindling of a Combustion in a State.'[213] Rawlins expressed the same view when he remarked that 'State Phanaticks' and 'Atheistical Wit-mongers' were just two sides of the same coin.[214] Furthermore, the actions of the Dissenters were grounded in their political principles, Rawlins maintained, and he laid out some of those principles: that sovereignty lay in the people and that the House of Commons expressed that sovereignty; that kings were created by men as trustees of the people. Dissenters called the

House of Commons a Parliament and regarded the king and Lords as ciphers. The effect was to lessen the authority of the king and elevate that of the House of Commons. These and other points were to be found in *Plato Redivivus*, *Oxford Pupil*, and *Jani Anglorum*, all radical tracts, Rawlins noted.[215] L'Estrange sharpened the picture of Whig theory as radical by decrying the doctrine of co-ordination, a teaching that he said would destroy England's monarchy, making it a 'Partnership or Co-equality of Government,' a condition quite contrary to its real nature. L'Estrange also responded head-on to the Whig assertion that 'whoever strikes at Parliament does, by Undermining the Government,... Shake the Pillars of the Throne.' He turned the point around and shoved it down the Whigs' throats, writing that 'whoever limits the role of the Lords and denies its negative over the Commons, or makes the King one of three estates, or the House of Commons representative of the nation, That's the man who shakes the Pillars of the Throne, and the Foundation of the Government.' Insisting that he was not opposed to the 'Power of Parliament' but to the idea that the House of Commons was Parliament, L'Estrange further declared that the king, not Parliament, was the protector of the nation's liberties against arbitrary power.[216] Moreover, Parliament was *not* free because Whiggish efforts to influence the election and the political agenda had destroyed its independence.[217] In these points L'Estrange continued themes advanced in Charles II's *Declaration of Reasons*.

Finally, Rawlins countered Care's scurrilous description of a Tory with an equally libelous depiction of a Whig, again turning the tables on Care and redirecting his idea against him. Ridiculing alleged Whiggish affectations, Rawlins declared that their spokesman at a 'famous True-Protestant Coffee-house' had nodded and leered, pulled 'down the Foretop of his Peruke' and 'stroak'd his chin, according to Rule' before he would answer a question.[218] Rawlins mocked Whigs for using the 'cunning shrug' and talking with their 'head and shoulders,' demonstrating that the gesture was part of the language of exchange and abuse.[219] He said that Whigs 'walk [about] as gravely and gingerly with the Protestant Interest upon [their] shoulders, as a Milkmaid with her Pail upon her head.'[220] This was great satire, sharp, pungent, memorable and arguably more effective than Care's unflattering portrait of a Tory. In sum, for L'Estrange and his friends the Dissenters' understanding of liberty of conscience had wide-ranging implications for the constitution as well as for religion; the concept entirely altered the government in Church and State. It is no wonder that in reflecting on the relationship between Dissent and the establishment Rawlins remarked that the 'wound is incurable and union impossible.'[221]

These, then, are the major themes that stand out in the serials: antipopery, Dissent and the Church of England, law and trial by jury. They are of about the same priority. Little was said about them, or any other issue in the serials, that was fundamentally new; the same points had been made earlier and had been explored at the same time in pamphlets and sermons. The serials played a significant role in fixing the attention of a wide audience on these matters and helped form its view of them.

Thanks to the skills of the participants on both sides, the nature of political rhetoric was changed during the Exclusion Crisis. Although their major devices, such as dialogue, humor, invective, *ad hominem* attacks, name-calling, code words, fables, poems and ballads, were timeworn, they were revitalized and extended in the intense press exchanges. Royalists borrowed techniques from their enemies and were exceedingly clever in turning their enemies' arguments back on them. The rhetorical enticements they practiced kept interest in the issues at boiling point. The Royalists were successful in replacing the near-universal abhorrence and fear of Catholicism and the prevailing distrust of the establishment with fear of Whigs, Dissent and the radical press. They also reaffirmed respect for and confidence in the monarchy as protector of the nation's law, liberty and property and upheld the Church of England as defender of the true Protestant religion, as by law established. It was a considerable achievement.

Still, it must be recognized that the Royalists owed a lot of their success to the persecutory policies the government was pursuing in tandem with the appearance of these printed pieces. Strict execution of the law and severe harassment by government informers brought Care and his press friends to heel and silenced public discussion.

6

Victim

or

Turncoat?

It took many months to bring Care to heel. Finally, on 13 July 1683, equaled if not bested by Royalist writers and harassed by the government, he withdrew his famous *Weekly Pacquet* and *Popish Courant* from the market. To his credit, his *Pacquet* was the longest-lived of the Whig serials. The revelation of the Rye House Plot in June 1683 had strengthend the court's hand, and the so-called Stuart Revenge was in full swing.[1] In these distressing circumstances the fall of the *Pacquet* marked the total collapse of press resistance. Care followed others into some kind of plea bargaining with the court of Charles II in the summer and autumn of 1683. In another move in 1687 he joined the court of the Catholic James II.

Care has the reputation of being nothing more than a time-server, a turncoat, a man who would do anything for money. This was the judgment of unfriendly contemporaries and of nine-teenth-century historians such as Lord Macaulay and Thompson Cooper, author of the entry on Care in the first *Dictionary of*

National Biography. Cooper declared emphatically that Care was 'drawn over... by the Roman catholic party, for bread and money['s] sake and nothing else.' Even Kitchin, who wrote admiringly of Care, remarked that there was 'something mortifying' in Care's surrender, for he had expressed his views 'in such a way as made a change seem out of nature.'[2] Late twentieth-century historians who know a little about Care hold him in low regard mostly for that reason: his anti-Catholicism was so virulent and long-lived as to cancel out any consideration but money. I suggest that his giving up in 1683 should be separated from his switching to James II in 1687 and that in both instances there were several reasons, including, but going beyond, money.

I

The major reason why Care gave up in 1683 was fear, joined with the hope of physical safety; another reason was the prospect of some kind of bargain with the court that may have included financial gain. Following the dissolution of the Oxford Parliament in March 1681, Charles II and his supporters pursued an increasingly savage and comprehensive policy of religious 'cleansing,' which was enthusiastically followed by the Church of England and reinforced in the Royalist serials. In brief, the overall goal of the king's 'new way of ruling' was to draw the instruments of authority at all levels of government into the hands of his friends.[3] The aim was to displace Whigs throughout the government: 'Not one man of them shall be employed either in the Navy or in any branch of the revenue, and even Whitehall will be purged of all the Whiggish party,' wrote one enthusiast.[4] The king declared that he looked on men in the 'Old Loyal Party' as 'the great pillars and supporters of his throne' and that the 'only principles that are safe for the government and comfortable to the conscience' are those of the Church of England and the old Cavaliers.[5] The court secured support in the counties by uprooting unsympathetic justices of the peace and in the cities by *quo warranto* procedures.[6] The shrieval elections in London in June 1682 brought the Tory sheriffs Dudley North and Peter Rich into office, which meant that the court could count on Tory juries to do their bidding; the inauguration of a Tory mayor that autumn further signaled that the city was safe for its interests. London's charter was surrendered in 1683, and thereafter a royal commission governed the city. At about the same time a 'sect of High Tory zealots' who were 'intent on prosecuting Dissent into extinction' had moved into leadership positions in the Church of England.[7] This alliance of king, Church and Tory Party made the monarchy stronger than it had ever been.

Charles further buttressed his position by making certain that the bench was pliant. He had dismissed Scroggs on 11 April 1681 and installed the agreeable Sir Francis Pemberton in his place as Lord Chief Justice. Thereupon ensued some high-profile trials demonstrating the clout of the government: Edward Fitzharris was convicted and then executed in July 1681. Stephen College, the joiner, was brought first before a London jury, which returned an ignoramus in June 1681, and then, in July, before an Oxford jury, which found him guilty; he was executed at the end of August. Shaftesbury, the big prize, was arrested on 2 July 1681 and jailed on a charge of high treason. He escaped trial and punishment thanks to an ignoramus verdict from a London jury on 24 November 1681 and soon afterwards fled to Holland, where he died. These events were of great importance to both sides and received extensive coverage in the serials.

Churchmen defended in powerful terms the harassment of persons who dissented. Mark Goldie has identified three strands in the justification of intolerance of and persecution for Dissent. The first two – the political argument that Dissenters were enemies of the nation, responsible for the late Civil Wars and intent upon sedition; and the ecclesiological idea that *one* Church was desirable and that the establishment might impose adiaphora or 'things indifferent' for the sake of order – legitimated prosecuting Nonconformists as seditious and factious, a danger to State and

Church. The third strand was a theological argument distinguishing between coercion and persecution, conscience and will.[8]
Coercion was directed at compelling apostates, even by force, to
return to obedience to the Church. Citing Luke 14:23,[9] and
drawing upon St Augustine, in particular, and St Thomas Aquinas,
divines argued that while coercion could not change conscience,
it could, by education, discipline and instruction, 'dispose the
mind to reconsider' and thereby change the will.[10] Wrote John
Sharp in 1684, 'It is not our business to persuade any man to
conform against his conscience: but to convince everyman how
dangerous it may be to follow a misinformed conscience.'[11] The
Church also held that punishment to the ends just discussed was
not persecution because it was directed toward a religious end.[12]
Persecution in this reading happened only when a person was punished for adhering to the *true* Church. Persons on the receiving
end of punishment could not be expected to see the subtle differences, but the argument set out by the clergy was rooted in
genuine theological considerations, was circulated in printed sermons and essays, and represented a belief that churchmen, some of
great distinction, had long held.

Royalist writers used their serials to support the establishment
wholeheartedly in its persecution of Dissenters and press critics.
L'Estrange called for rigorously implementing the penal laws
against all recusants, but especially Nonconformists. Regarding
Dissenters with loathing, he justified rigor on the grounds that
Dissenters posed a real and present danger to the government.
Therefore, for 'the sake of Order and of the Publique Peace,' one
should readily sanction a 'strict Provision and Execution of Laws.'[13]
L'Estrange made a simple but powerful case, contending that in the
absence of punishment schism would be seen as 'the Master of the
Law' and the governors would be afraid to execute laws that they
themselves were bound to obey. Citing the experience of Queen
Elizabeth I, he drew the lesson that it was the 'Sovereign Medicine
of Uniformity that set her Right at last, and brought the
Government to rest again.'[14] Rawlins's 'Jest' made virtually the

same point, saying in his witty way that Dissent was 'a mischievous and hardy old Puss' and that old laws, like the Act of 35 Elizabeth I, should have killed her off but had not. 'Earnest' soberly agreed, declaring that the only recourse was to enforce those laws 'thoroughly and with effect' and thereby annihilate the 'Faction.'[15] Again using the device of turning an argument back upon the enemy, Rawlins justified persecuting Dissenters on the grounds that they were 'the Persecutors of the Government.'[16] Further, Royalists were disinclined to entertain the idea of 'moderation,' as Care recommended. Using the same analogies that a member of Parliament had made in the 2 November 1680 debate,[17] Jest responded amusingly about the stupidity of moderation, poking fun at people for 'fighting moderately, riding moderately from danger, and pumping moderately in a leaking ship,' while Earnest solemnly observed that the word *moderately* did not appear in any oaths that a public person was required to take.[18] Jest and Earnest also took on the job of justifying informers who made life miserable for Nonconformists. Earnest announced that informing was 'not only lawful, but a very good and honest work.' He managed to interpret Coke to say that informers were necessary to the operation of the law, and he capped his point by asserting that the informers whom the present government used were ten times more lenient than John Calvin's *Morum censores*.[19]

Its policy reinforced by the press, the government ruthlessly suppressed its enemies. In December 1681 the *London Gazette* carried the court's proclamation, gleefully reported by L'Estrange, that henceforth the penal laws against popish recusants and conventicles would be rigorously enforced.[20] In London more than 4,000 people were punished for attending a conventicle, and many more were punished for not attending Church or for refusing to take the oaths.[21] Fines were enormous, livelihoods ruined, meetinghouses closed or destroyed and jail conditions for Nonconformists who could not or would not pay deplorable.[22] The government did not scruple to use an army of informers, most importantly those organized and led by the disreputable Hilton brothers, John and the younger George, whose despicable efforts to rid London of Dissenters have been reconstructed by Mark Goldie.[23]

Care and his press friends felt the wrath of the court, the Church and Tory loyalists. Care's closest colleague and long-term publisher, Langley Curtis, was summoned more frequently before the authorities than any other press person. He was called in on 9 March 1681 for printing an obnoxious tract, the *Letter to L'Estrange*. He was summoned again on 12 April 1681 for libelous remarks, an interview that resulted in the suspension of the publication of the *True Protestant Mercury* from 16 to 30 April 1681, which Sutherland described as an 'unprecedented break.'[24] So unpopular was Curtis with Tory loyalists that in the spring of 1681 he was threatened in a coffee house and in effect thrown out.[25] His habit was to disappear to escape such attentions, and he was often out of town, as he was in March, April, June, July and August 1681, leaving business affairs in the hands of his capable and feisty wife, Jane. The *Loyal Protestant*, reporting that Langley was before the Privy Council still again in early June, blamed him for brainwashing his wife, who, upon being asked for a copy of the *Observator*, replied that she 'thank'd God she never published any such popish Pamphlets; but she could help him to the *Observator Observed*.'[26] Another friend of Care's, 'Elephant' Smith, closed down his *Protestant Intelligence* on 14 April 1681.[27] Benjamin Harris was hunted down and jailed; he ceased publishing his *Protestant (Domestick) Intelligence* on 15 April 1681. Harris printed a few innocuous pieces thereafter, but on the accession of James II to the throne, he fled to Boston, Massachusetts.[28]

Care was also subjected to arrest, interrogation and harassment, but he was not treated as harshly as were some print people, a fact suggesting his popularity and the reluctance of the court to arouse sympathy for him. On 28 April 1681 he was prosecuted at Hicks Hall for remarks appearing in the first issue of the *Impartial Protestant Mercury*.[29] In his irrepressible way he had once more contemptuously criticized the bench. Writing that the sessions at

Middlesex had given the 'old drudge at speechmaking [a chance] most elegantly to exercise his talents,' he reported that Dissenters and Whigs were 'thrast to atoms' and that some said that 'their Fines and Forfeitures must make up the extraordinary charges of the Government.' It was 'intended,' he asserted, 'that the laws should be briskly put in execution... though possibly [they] might mistake innocent and most useful sheep for Swine that root up the government.' The disposition of the case is unknown, but it is reasonable to conclude that Care was fined; that his writings continued to appear in print suggests that he was not jailed. Indeed, the *Impartial Protestant Mercury* won high praise in July from Samuel Wilson, Shaftesbury's secretary, who wrote in September 1681 that 'Care & Janeway by their Papers continue the Peoples hopes of a Reformation, which does more kindnesse then 1,000 men in Armes.'[30]

The executions of Fitzharris and College, and the arrest of Shaftesbury on a charge of high treason during the summer of 1681 sharpened the Whigs's anxiety and, as Rawlins said, 'Subdued' them.[31] Care himself began to waver at the end of October 1681. His interlocutor pointed to his retreat, asking, 'Is Currantier Tongue-ty'd...? Or Muzzel'd' by the 'Apellation of the Old-Baily Monkey? Or because this Autumn-Season' is inclined to storms, 'does he fear an Hurricane' and 'so creeps by the Shore, just as an Abhorrer skulks in Parliament-time?' Picking up the metaphor of a tempest that 'keeps no bounds,' the other interlocutor responded that one might be driven beyond the Cape of Good Hope, and when the wind rose on such a coast, 'who would not Lower his Sails?'[32] Thus, Care vented his distress without, apparently, taking a further step.

In early 1682 *Heraclitus Ridens* reported confidently that 'Whiggism declines sensibly' and overoptimistically that Care had 'dwindled to nothing.'[33] Rawlins was right that Whiggism had faltered. In April, when the duke of York returned to London with his brother, the city greeted him enthusiastically with bonfires. At the bonfire at the Globe Tavern in Cornhill, Jack Presbyter was

burned to shouts of 'No whig, no whig,' and the plan was for
Whig newspapers, such as Janeway's *Impartial Protestant Mercury* and
Care's *Weekly Pacquet*, to be tossed in after him. But 'by a mistake'
that was not done, and it was said that the burning of the newspapers would be 'reserved till another opportunity.'[34] The incident
holds interest as a measure of the shift in public approval away from
Whigs and toward the court. It also suggests the prominent position Care and his *Weekly Pacquet* still occupied in the public's mind
and how eager some were to see him fall. But Care had not 'dwindled to nothing' yet. As we saw earlier, the Tory Aphra Behn noted
the continuing popularity of the *Weekly Pacquet*, saying that it
'clogs the nation.'[35]

Care and his press friends, however, suffered severe setbacks and
indignities in 1682. In early February, in a move described as 'significant,' Langley Curtis was committed to the marshal's custody
for printing in the *True Protestant Mercury* false and seditious news
about the efforts of the Middlesex grand jury to prevent constables from disturbing conventicles.[36] Almost two months later, on
30 March, he was summoned again before the Privy Council, this
time with Janeway, for printing 'false and seditious' remarks
against the government of Church and State.[37] In early April Care,
Vile and Janeway were called before the Privy Council for 'publishing several treasonable things,' but what specific 'things' and
with what results are unknown.[38] At about the same time, Janeway
was back before the Lord Chief Justice, this time for comments in
number 97 of the *Impartial Protestant Mercury* concerning reports
from the city of York. He won release on sureties to appear at
King's Bench the first day of the next term and promises of good
behavior.[39] At the end of May 1682, Janeway ceased publishing the
Impartial Protestant Mercury, an event Sutherland characterized as a
'turning point' in the government's campaign against the newspapers. Janeway had been hauled before the council in October
1681 for publishing false news, granted bail and then tried in May
1682. A Whig jury found him not guilty, but the government used
a legal technicality to seize the bail and imprison him. Janeway,

realizing that he could not expect much help from fellow press people, plea-bargained his way out of jail, promising to end the *Impartial Protestant Mercury*.[40] It was during this interview with the Privy Council that Janeway revealed that Care and Vile wrote the *Impartial Protestant Mercury*, thereby once more calling Care's name to the attention of the council.[41] Undaunted, Vile, with the help of the radical publisher Richard Baldwin, kept right on pestering the government; he started his own paper, the *London Mercury*, in April and was able to keep it going through the middle of October 1682, when the government resolutely closed down newspapers.[42]

In the absence of Langley Curtis during the summer of 1682, Jane Curtis turned to Care for help in continuing the publication of the *True Protestant Mercury*.[43] Noticing the change in an amusing turn of phrase, L'Estrange announced that the paper was the work of 'Harry and Sybill in a kind of Intellectual Copulation.'[44] The result of the collaboration was trouble for Jane. On 10 June she was indicted for publishing the *True Protestant Mercury* of that date.[45] On 5 July she was summoned before the Privy Council for publishing in language demeaning to the court and the Lord Chief Justice an account of the trial of Aaron Smith, the Whig lawyer for College at his Oxford trial. Three days later she was interrogated again; again she refused to disclose the whereabouts of her husband, who was thought to be busy printing the first part of the very radical tract by the Reverend Samuel Johnson, *Julian the Apostate*.[46]

Care lost much ground with the public. In celebrating the king's birthday on 30 May 1682, the people of Norwich, as we have seen, constructed a huge bonfire of opposition tracts, paraded around the streets with effigies of 'several Factious and Seditious Libellers,' including Care, and then tossed the images into the fire.[47] Care was the only author in this radical company. Responding cleverly to the incident, Care slyly identified the perpetrators with Catholics, remarking that some people 'itch for fire and fagot' and that if they had had the *writ de haeretico comburendo*, they would have 'been glad to have Roasted [him] in bad Earnest.'[48] On that same day, Royalist propagandists taunted the Whigs, and by implication Care, unmercifully. 'Jest,' with 'Earnest' agreeing, indulged in a lengthy sarcastic review of the condition of the 'Cause,' comparing it to a woman who had lost her jointure at the Restoration and had been poor ever since.[49] The next day Thompson weighed in with the news that the 'Brotherhood' had met at a coffee house in 'closed Cabal' to 'consult how to preserve their tottering cause.'[50] Reports of the dire condition of the Whigs continued. In June, Jest noted that Whigs walked around as 'demurely as men in Debt.' They were 'downcast' and 'threaten to flee.' 'The cause is at a standstill.'[51] The crowning blow to the Whigs, as noted above, was the shrieval elections in London during June 1682, which brought Tory sheriffs Dudley North and Peter Rich into office. Henceforth the court could count on Tory juries to do their bidding.

For unknown reasons Care's *Weekly Pacquet* and *Popish Courant* were in serious trouble at the end of July. Perhaps to underline the gravity of the situation, Care used the *Pacquet* rather than the *Courant* to address his readers on the matter. On 28 July 1682 he wrote: 'We hasten – Because sooner than intended, we must, it seems, close these unwelcome and ungratefully received sheets.' Continuing, he inquired self-righteously: 'Who would suspect that in a Protestant Kingdome,... An History of Popery manag'd with an exact fidelity,... should... meet with misconstruction and Contempt.' One can see him shaking his head in disbelief. In his brazen way he also self-servingly excused the *Popish Courant*, describing it as 'some small neither unusefull nor unpleasant digressions for the Reader's Entertainment.' No contemporary would have recognized the hard-hitting *Courant*, with its extreme, often coarse, language, in such a description. In the event, Care was not forced to close down 'these unwelcome... sheets'; apparently the authorities took no steps at all against him.[52]

Within a month a major change occurred in the Royalist serials. Rawlins, after issuing several triumphant announcements that the Whig cause was finished, ceased publishing *Heraclitus Ridens*. The last issue, number 82, came out on 22 August 1682. Rawlins declared that it was boring to carry on a vendetta with adversaries whose conversation was 'dull and insipid' and whose 'Cause is so batter'd, its Friends and Assertors so feeble and out of heart.'[53] There was some wishful thinking in this assessment; Care was not yet 'feeble and out of heart,' and he wrote a brilliant, pointed and funny response to Rawlins in which he revealed the contents of Heraclitus's will. One clause gives his guts to the *Observator* for 'fiddle-strings' to make harmony for Tories. Another directs that his 'Talent of Lying and Slandering' be bestowed upon his 'well-beloved Brother Nat.'[54] Still, the removal of *Heraclitus Ridens* took a lot of steam out of the press warfare.

During that same month a major change also occurred in Care's publishing affairs. Again for reasons that have escaped the record, Care and Langley Curtis parted company: starting with the 25 August 1682 issue, two *Weekly Pacquets* and two *Popish Courants* appeared, one brought out by Care, the other by Curtis. Although Rawlins hinted at a disagreement between Care and Jane Curtis earlier in the month,[55] Care was emphatic that he had initiated the break with Langley Curtis. In an advertisement he announced that as 'the Author, who alone began, and for 195 Weeks (baiting but one) hath carried on this History,' he had 'ease[d] Mr. Curtis (his former Book-seller) of the trouble of publishing it for the Future.' In an attempt to undermine Curtis's rival *Weekly Pacquet*, he announced that 'the true Continuance' of the fifth volume would be printed by A. Maxwell.[56] Three months later Care replaced Maxwell with James Astwood, a radical press man well known to the authorities.[57] In April 1681 he had been brought before the Stationers' Court for printing College's *A Ra-ree Show*. Astwood had refused to pay the fine and declined to name the person who had brought the ballad to him. After College's trial the government had renewed pressure on Astwood to identify that person, and fearful of being charged with complicity in publishing a seditious or treasonous libel, he had succumbed, naming 'Elephant' Smith. Smith was accused and fled. Astwood was also responsible, with other printers, for printing the *Second Part of the Growth of Popery* in the autumn of 1682. For Care to have associated himself with Astwood at this time was provocatively bold.

It is powerful evidence of the popularity of the *Weekly Pacquet* that Curtis immediately began a rival *Weekly Pacquet*. Curtis justified two *Pacquet*s on the grounds that one was insufficient to deal with the Reformation. Curtis engaged William Salmon (1644–1713) to write his *Weekly Pacquet*. A medical practitioner and writer and translator of medical treatises, Salmon had published a compendium of materials about astrology, chemistry and physics in 1671, written many other treatises, and won the admiration of Henry Coley and other students of astrology. He wrote with verve, replicating Care's point of view and apparently striving to ape Care's style. Since Curtis was an established bookseller, he 'probably' held the 'stock-in-trade' of the *Pacquet*s and very likely added Salmon's spurious fifth volume to the remaining copies, selling them as a set. As a consequence Care's own fifth volume is rare, while Curtis's fifth volume is often thought to be Care's.[58] Many readers probably did not know the difference, and it seems likely that sales of Care's true *Weekly Pacquet* decreased as a consequence. Even the usually reliable Kitchin confused the two and reported that Care's *Popish Courant* was dropped in December 1682, whereas it actually continued on with the *Weekly Pacquet* until July 1683.[59]

In the autumn of 1682 the authorities, moving sharply against press people, closed down almost all 'news-books,' both Royalist and Dissenter. A messenger of the press declared that 'neither side shall have cause to think they have had hard measure in being supprest, because all shall fare alike.'[60] On the Royalist side only the *Observator* and the *London Gazette* continued to appear; *Heraclitus Ridens* had already ceased. On 16 November Thompson ceased publishing his *Loyal Protestant* (his efforts to reinstate it in February 1683 failed), and on that same day Thomas Benskin, a Royalist printer, gave up his *Domestick Intelligence*. As for the Whigs, on Wednesday, 25 October 1682, the *True Protestant Mercury*, charged as a seditious libel, ceased publication. Janeway, Harris and Smith had been forced to withdraw their serials earlier, as noted. At the end of 1682 the *Weekly Pacquet* was the only Whig serial left, and it soldiered on.

Difficulties for Care and his associates continued unabated, however. A couple of days before the *True Protestant Mercury* folded, some 'Ruffians' physically assaulted Jane Curtis, forcing their way into her house and dragging her into the street. 'Being strong and undaunted,' she broke loose and ran back to her house, with the men in pursuit. Once inside, the six ruffians blew out the candles, and mistaking a kinswoman for Jane, they dragged her outside too. Care, who no doubt wrote the account of the assault for the last issue of the *True Protestant Mercury*, observed that Jane had suffered the abuse on account of her husband 'because he has been true to the Presbyterian religion.'[61] Within a few days of this indignity, on 27 October, the government arrested Jane for publishing and circulating scandalous libels, a new impression of *Julian the Apostate* and *The Perplext Prince*; one tract was as bad as the other from the government's point of view.[62] Appealing for pity, her counsel painted her as a 'poor distressed woman' and 'begged' for bail, but the court said that Curtis 'had behaved herself so peremptorily they had no reason to believe her again' and refused. After ten days' imprisonment she apologized and promised never to offend again, whereupon she was released on bail.[63]

At about the same time, on 31 October 1682, the London Sessions of the Peace turned its attention to Care, indicting him for remarks about the powers of the lieutenancy in the 20 October issue of his *Weekly Pacquet*.[64] Answering the *Observator* of 16 October, in which L'Estrange insisted that the actions of the lieutenancy were 'no new Encroachment upon [the nation's] Liberties' and that military power was a 'Right, Settled, and Inherent in the Crown,'[65] Care had argued that the law allowed the militia to seize arms only in the case of insurrection or invasion and gave no authority to seize persons. He had maintained that if there were no insurrections the militia could not legally be called

up four times a year, and he had also charged that there was corruption among militia officers.[66] Care did not appear in court and
was said 'not to be found.'[67] In December the London grand jury
returned a '*billa vera*' against him and his *Weekly Pacquet* and also
indicted him and Thomas Vile for writing and printing *Vox Patria:
Or, The Resentments and Indignation of the Free Born Subjects of
England against Popery, Arbitrary Government, the duke of York, etc.* No
further proceedings are recorded.[68]

In 1683 the Church of England turned its fury against Care. On
4 May 1683 the vicar and two church wardens of St Sepulchre's
Church presented Care and thirty-nine other parishioners to the
bishop for not attending church and not participating in the sacrament.[69] Care was found guilty and fined.

The next month, on 12 June 1683, the revelation of the Rye
House Plot by one Josiah Keeling, a London oilman and a 'most
perverse Fanatick,' dramatically hardened the government's attitude toward its critics and justified its taking summary action.[70]
During the next fortnight other informers and men they accused
turned State's evidence, plea-bargained to save their own skins, and
implicated in the conspiracies aristocratic leaders of the Whig
Party, along with less socially elevated conspirators. Among the
latter was the soldier Thomas Walcot, who was the first to mention
Care. In an undated letter to Sir Leoline Jenkins, the secretary of
state, written at about the time of his confession on 8 July 1683,
Walcot sought to recommend himself by declaring that if his
'being with the King' was not known, 'I shall be ten times abler to
serve him than either Mr. Freeman, or Mr. Carr; for they will trust
neither of them.'[71] As Kitchin put it, Walcot's remark implied that
Care was already 'suing for grace with promises of discoveries.'[72]
There is no specific evidence that Care revealed damaging information about other press people, but it is likely that he did. His
willingness to cooperate was no doubt advanced by an event that
occurred in early July, when Messenger of the Press Stephens presented to the London Sessions Care's publisher, Astwood, and
his wife, Bridget; the charge was publishing the *Weekly Pacquet*

without authority. Astwood had been presented in April on the same charge and had pleaded not guilty, a plea the jury sustained. In July, however, he pleaded guilty and was fined three pounds; no action was taken against Bridget.[73] Shortly thereafter, on 13 July 1683, his anxieties no doubt sharpened by this incident and his energies probably flagging because of illness,[74] Care ceased publishing the *Weekly Pacquet*.[75] The date of its fall coincided with two highly important events that were symbolic of the government's rigor against its critics: the suicide – some said murder – of Arthur Capel, earl of Essex, who was in prison on suspicion of involvement in the Rye House Plot, and the trial and conviction of the Whig martyr William Lord Russell for treason against the king in that plot. Whether it was coincidental or calculated, the demise of the *Weekly Pacquet* on that date conveyed subtle but powerful criticism of the court.

Subsequently Care had conversations with the court, and prior to 25 October he made 'application for favour,' as L'Estrange put it.[76] Overflowing with spite and eager for revenge, L'Estrange beseeched Jenkins to allow him to interrogate Care, claiming that he could get more information out of him than anyone else. Arguing that Care had maligned him so deeply that 'he may be obliged to set himself right with me,' L'Estrange explained that in examining Care he could 'ask him such questions as nobody else is privy to.' L'Estrange regarded Care as a great 'catch' for the government and was determined to make him 'sing.' 'I do certainly know that he can make very great discoveries and I will as certainly put him to it.' In further justifying his request, L'Estrange, again showing disdain for press people, declared that to debrief Care was beneath the dignity and position of the secretary.

Alas, evidence of the contents of Care's 'application for favour,' the interview between L'Estrange and Care (if it indeed took place), and the terms reached between Care and the government have not survived. Care probably promised not to write against the government and Church; his pen was silent for the next couple of years except for one learned piece, an eighty-two-page tract published in

1683, entitled *The Darkness of Atheisme Expelled*. This book, which according to the section 'To the Reader' is a translation in the 'main' from a Latin work by Jean Morinus (1591–1659), a French theologian who converted from Protestantism to Roman Catholicism, was printed for Thomas Benskin. The choice of Benskin intimates that Care was not entirely *persona non grata*. More surely, his essay suggests that Care had withdrawn from the polemical fray and that he wrote the piece to display his linguistic and scholarly skills.

Returning to the question why Care gave up in 1683, I believe that the establishment's campaign against Dissent and the press, along with the harassment he personally received, left him feeling threatened and scared. Care caved in out of fear for himself and his family; no doubt he hoped that by so doing he would secure his and their physical and financial security. But I don't think it was money alone that caused him to throw in the towel. It is too bad that we have no evidence of the interview with L'Estrange and no knowledge of the nature of his alleged 'discoveries.' As is often the case in these situations, Care was as much a victim as he was a turncoat.

Care continued to feel the wrath of loyalists, the government and the Church of England. An anonymous loyalist reviled him for abandoning his Whig principles in *Great News From The Old-Bayly, Mr. Car's Recantation… In a Dialogue 'twixt Truman and Amsterdammer*, which appeared in late 1683.[77] Said 'Amsterdammer' with heavy sarcasm, 'Must a little Persecution alter good solid Republican principles? A little Hanging, Drawing, and Quartering and unmerciful butcherly choppings off of Heads terrifie our gigantic Scribler, our Fryday Atlas of Fanaticism?' Indulging in sharp *ad hominem* attacks as the serialists had done, 'Amsterdammer' called Care an ungrateful 'little sneaking Chitterling' who was well paid for his *Weekly Pacquet*. He wondered what the 'puppy Monkey Face' will do to support his 'Rat-like Carkass.' In Care's defense, 'Trueman' declared that Care was now resolved to listen to his conscience, but 'Amsterdammer' dismissed the idea: 'What was it, that Harry's uncontroulable Pen dar'd not to undertake, and now talk of

Conscience?' Such ongoing bitter anger suggests how deeply Care's writings had offended the loyalist public in the preceding years. In the face of such harshness an order his bookseller, Richard Chiswell, received for a copy of volume 5 of the *Weekly Pacquet* in December 1683 from the young Cotton Mather in the colonies must have been especially heartening.[78]

The government and the Church of England continued to harass Care.[79] On 2 January 1685 a warrant was issued from Whitehall to bring Care and his papers before the earl of Sunderland for examination concerning the writing or publishing of several treasonable and dangerous libels.[80] The particular libels were not specified, and no evidence of the outcome has survived. The Church also persisted in its efforts to hurt Care. On an unknown date, internal evidence in his response pointing to the spring of 1684, Care received word that he had been excommunicated from St Sepulchre's Church. In apparently genuine distress, he wrote to an unidentified 'Right Worshipfull' lamenting the news. Vigorously defending himself, he declared that although he had been a resident in the parish, as 'several worthy Inhabitants' on oath had testified (a reference to witnesses at his trial), had 'frequented the Church and publique prayers' at that time, and still paid rent on a 'little house' there, he had not lived in or near that parish 'for above a year & an half.' Asserting that under those circumstances neither 'the Canons of the Church or any Law' could oblige him to receive the 'Blessed Eucharist' at St Sepulchre's Church last Easter, he maintained that he had been maliciously misrepresented by people whose 'Interest and Business' was 'to Blacken' him. Care denied that he was a 'Phanatick' or of 'factious Humour' and said that he was a 'Loyal Subject and peaceable Protestant (at just defianse both to popery and phanatisism).' Avowing that he 'truly' had that 'Reverense for the power of ye Keys rightly handled, and ye Order of our Church (I mean that of England by Law establisht) that I would not (if possible to bee avoided) fall under ye Indignation of her Censure,' he assured his correspondent that he was 'so farr from obstinate Refusal, that I scruple not the Reseiving yt sacred Ordinanse at ye hands of ye publique Minister, and in yt humble Reverent posture too, wch ye Liturgy enjoins.' He invoked the name of the Reverend Dr William Bell, vicar at St Sepulchre's from 1 October 1662 until his death on 19 July 1683, writing that were Dr Bell alive, he 'would have satisfied you That I am of no such factious Humour' as some represented. Care expressed hope of an answer and gave the address of an attorney-at-law in 'Blackfryers' who would see that he received it.[81] If a reply came, no record has survived.

This letter is of uncommon importance. One may argue that a skilled polemicist like Care would have understood the language of confession and been able to shape a defense to his best advantage, and one may suspect as much from him. But the letter is marked by such apparent sincerity and anguish of spirit that it may well be that for all his criticism of the Church of England, Care was devoted to the ideal of what he wished that Church to be. Like John Locke, with whom he shared a number of views, Care wanted to remain within the Church – a reformed Church, to be sure. At this time he fit the mold of a Presbyterian. This letter adds a singularly intimate perspective on Care's anticlericalism and provides a further explanation of his willingness to support James II's policy of toleration.

7

Dissent's Defender

and

RELIGIOUS LIBERTY

Henry Care did not immediately join the court when
James II ascended the throne upon his brother's death
on 6 February 1685. It was not until sometime in 1687
that Care entered the king's service and began to play a leading
role in the hitherto neglected campaign in the press to win the
nation over to the king's new policies. Ironically, Care surpassed
L'Estrange in service to James, for L'Estrange was unable to support the royal policy of toleration. In the press contest with
Anglicans and Tories, Care wrote a new, semiofficial weekly newspaper, *Publick Occurrences Truely Stated*, and also published a number
of pamphlets. Again, his voice was before the public more than
that of any other identifiable polemicist, this time on the court
side. Addressing himself particularly to Dissenters who were reluctant to join the Catholic king, Care offered a richly textured argument to justify James's policy of toleration for Catholics and
Dissenters. He was among those who wrote about the liberty of
religious conscience, the inviolability of the individual conscience,

the relationship between Church and State and the moral impera-
tive of keeping the two separate. His views, which were in print in
1687 and 1688, closely parallel those of John Locke, whose *Letter
on Toleration* was not published until 1690.

I

Care was invited to join the court because of the failure of the
king's initial tactics; had they succeeded, we would hear nothing of
Care as James's polemicist. For the first eighteen months or so of
his reign James followed a complicated and 'naive' strategy that
reveals how seriously he misread his subjects' religious and political
convictions.[1] Despite evidence to the contrary, he was confident of
the ultimate support of Church of England men and their Tory
allies; during his brother's reign they had enthusiastically supported
monarchy, upheld the principle of nonresistance and expressed
loathing of Dissenters. James reasoned that once churchmen were
assured of their benefices, and Tory gentlemen of their abbey lands,
they would endorse his policy, secure in the knowledge that he
would favor them as well as his fellow Roman Catholics. Ignoring
the deeply ingrained national anti-Catholic prejudice, which Care
had inflamed just three or four years earlier, James brought immediate relief to his Catholic subjects. Using his prerogative power, he
suspended laws against them and released recusant prisoners who
could demonstrate their (or their nearest relative's) loyalty to the
crown in the Civil Wars.[2] Four or five months later Monmouth's
Rebellion gave him the pretext to appoint Catholics as officers in
the army and keep them there. Further, exploiting the Conventicle
Act and other penal laws, the court, joined by Tory magistrates,
Anglican priests and government informers, ruthlessly persecuted
Dissenters.[3] Care himself felt the government's rigor: in November
1685 for reasons unknown the government renewed its animus
against him and confiscated his *English Liberties* as a 'seditious
book,' announcing that it would be suppressed.[4] Many thousands

of Dissenters in London, Middlesex and at a local level all around the nation suffered fines, confiscations and imprisonment. So severe was the treatment that they feared that the government intended their total extinction.[5]

James had no success in winning over Anglicans and Tories. Antipopery prejudice and fear of losing property, place and status in a Catholic State overwhelmed their long-term commitment to the throne and to the principle of nonresistance. When it became obvious that they would not cooperate, the king reversed course and attempted to build an extraordinary alliance made up of court, Catholics, Dissenters and, perforce, 'apostate Tories.'[6] He strengthened his hand by several moves. Briefly, in June 1686 James sought a court ruling to confirm his authority to dispense with the law: *Godden v. Hales* was brought before compliant judges who affirmed the validity of the dispensing power. This ruling was controversial then and remains so in modern scholarship,[7] but it gave the king confidence that he was acting within the law when he appointed Catholics to various posts and issued his Declaration of Indulgence in April 1687.[8] Further, in July 1686 the court created an Ecclesiastical Commission, whose purpose was to curb the preaching and other activities of the Church of England and whose work signaled further the king's determination to win over the Dissenters.[9] At the same time, the court began seriously to woo Dissenters: James granted individual petitions and dispensations (for a payment) to whole congregations, released some prisoners and appointed Nonconformists to office. Within the year he took the matter much further: on 4 April 1687 he issued, on the authority of his royal prerogative, a comprehensive Declaration of Indulgence. In it the king, conveniently forgetting his previous attitude and actions, declared that he had long believed 'that conscience ought not to be constrained, nor people forced in matters of mere religion.'[10] He also suspended the operation of the penal laws, thus ensuring the right of Dissenters to worship freely with certain provisions, abrogated the oaths of supremacy and allegiance and the Test Acts, or Tests, and pardoned all persons who had violated the law because of non-conformity in religion.

Finally, in tandem with all these steps, the king and his ministers embarked on a multipronged propaganda campaign. Although propaganda is not always associated with James,[11] the fact is that he recognized that neither his prerogative powers, coercion nor the law was sufficient to assure the success of his policy. No sooner was he on the throne than strenuous efforts were made to restrict printed matter and shape public opinion. The king drew Roger L'Estrange into his service: he showered him with marks of favor, bestowed on him a knighthood, endorsed his successful election to Parliament and in May 1685 authorized him to enforce regulations respecting treasonable, seditious and scandalous publications.[12] L'Estrange took no prominent part in James's Parliament, but it is a guess that on the last day of the first session, 2 July 1685, he had a hand in assuring that the old Licensing/Printing Act would be revived. Although Lord Macaulay felt that the revival made little difference, for unlicensed printing had been strictly forbidden since the Rye House Plot, the act gave James legal authority to restrict the press.[13] L'Estrange had come full circle and was for the moment performing for James II the same offices he had undertaken for Charles II.

Strenuous efforts were made to control the press. For example, between February 1685 and November 1687 the government issued thirty-four warrants to suppress certain pamphlets,[14] offered a reward of £1,000 to discover the author of an offending tract,[15] seized unlicensed works and punished those responsible. Famously, the Reverend Samuel Johnson was arrested, degraded and whipped for his *Humble and hearty Address*.[16] One historian has remarked that the severity and success of James's press campaign are revealed by the absence of criticism at the time of the Bloody Assizes; not until after the revolution of 1688–89 did printed protests appear.[17]

Steps were also taken to shape people's opinions in favor of the court. The government appointed Henry Hills, a Catholic convert, as printer to the household and chapel and granted him the right to print books for Catholic services without penalty, despite certain laws;[18] granted permission to Obadiah Walker to set up a Catholic press in Oxford; and sent James Watson to Edinburgh to do like service there.[19] To have such outlets for their writings was a great boon to Catholics; J.R. Jones believed that it was 'easily the most valuable of the new freedoms' that James bestowed on them.[20] To show the positive side of Catholicism and to set out Catholic doctrine in easily understandable terms, Jacques Bossuet's *Exposition* was translated, and John Gother's *Papist Misrepresented and Represented*, among many others, was printed in 1685.[21] Catholic books were advertised in the *London Gazette*, and numerous devotional manuals appeared; they and other books about Catholicism were distributed free.[22] Anti-Catholic books were not allowed to appear in the term catalogues. An attempt was made to suppress accounts of Louis XIV's persecution of Huguenots.[23] To underscore the Catholicism of Charles II, Father Huddleston's account of the king's death and Charles's own reasons for converting were published.[24] In the fall of 1687, during the campaign to remodel local government, the court instructed local correspondents to place 'books and papers... in coffee houses and houses of publick entertainment' in an effort to persuade the public of the merit of royal policies.[25] 'Some Horse loads of Pamphlets... were distributed into several Counties of England.'[26] A contemporary complained that 'papists bring papers into coffeehouses and plead their cause out of them, as out of so many Briefs.'[27] Another remarked in the spring of 1688 that 'neither art, money, nor pains are omitted' in the campaign to influence public opinion.[28]

Among those 'pains' was the hiring of 'many... Scribler[s] to plague the Nation with fulsome Declamations against the Penal Laws and Tests.'[29] Care was not among the first of the hired 'Scriblers,' for the court's initial steps were not aimed at Dissenters. But in late 1686 or early 1687, when their strategy had changed, James II and his court turned to Care, despite the obvious animus in their previous relationship. How was it possible for these two erstwhile bitter enemies to become reconciled? Why did the king, who had personally felt the sting of Care's pen, allow men about him to seek Care's help and why did Care agree?

James and his advisers needed a person identified in the public mind with Dissenters and Whigs, an individual whose arguments could be expected to carry weight with that community. They needed a writer equal in skill to L'Estrange who would whole-heartedly endorse James's policy of religious toleration, as L'Estrange was unwilling to do. The court's propaganda effort was weakened at about that time because L'Estrange had closed down his *Observator* on 9 March 1687, reportedly at James's request.[30] Care's reputation as a superb writer, a man possessed of a quick and agile mind stored with a wealth of knowledge about religion, law and history, recommended him. Ironically, his previous reputation as a violent antipapist, a 'Lover of true Protestants' and the 'Secretarius' of the opposition also recommended him, for his support of religious toleration for Catholics and Dissenters would be all the more persuasive. Furthermore, his 1682 tract *Some Reasons For Separation From the Communion of the Church of England. And The Unreasonableness of Persecution Upon that Account*, with its eloquent defense of liberty of the religious conscience and its bitter denunciation of the Church of England for its persecutory policies, may have underscored in the mind of court advisers Care's probable usefulness to the government. Care's antipopery was so positive, extensive and well documented, and it was argued with such passion and resolve, that Care's willingness to defend James II was a great feather in the cap of the new monarch. Care could appeal to the Dissenting community.

It is a guess that L'Estrange, who earlier had regretted that Care's talents were not used in a better cause, suggested Care. Men in high places knew him or certainly knew of him: Care had been in the presence of the authorities many times. One may guess again that Sunderland, who licensed Care's first publication for James, supported the appointment. Perhaps Sir William Williams, who had defended Care at his trial in 1680 and was appointed solicitor general in December 1687, also had a hand in it. Perhaps Penn, whom Care probably knew and with whom he would work closely, was persuasive in luring Care to James's side, as one scholar has suggested.[31] In any case, Care was a big catch for the Catholic court.

Why did Care accept the assignment, and were there conditions? First, there is no evidence that James's government had so frightened and intimidated Care that he went over to the court out of fear, as was the case when he gave up in 1683, although he must have worried about his physical safety and economic well-being should he decline the offer to write for the court. Second, his move was 'not all for belly's sake,'[32] as his enemies and all previous historians would have it. Care rejected out of hand what he called the 'stale Witticism' that he 'Writes for Bread.' Flashing confidence and pride in his abilities, and with his usual rapier touch, he asserted that if he 'were never to Print a Line more, he might get as Comfortable a Living by the Profession (no way Dishonourable) he was bred to, as this Gentleman [a cleric] would do, without his Benefice.'[33] Despite this disclaimer, money must have been part of the inducement. Care had kept a very low profile since 1683, publishing only two tracts, *The Darkness of Atheisme* (1683) and *The Character and Qualifications of an Honest Loyal Merchant* (1686), the latter on a subject far removed from the issues that really mattered to him. He may even have had trouble getting his writing published: he said that he had written *The Tutor To True English* 'in a tedious time of inforc'd Leisure and Retirement,' but, significantly, the tract was not licensed until 21 July 1687.[34] How he survived financially is unknown; perhaps he was able to return to the 'Profession he was bred to' and get work as a clerk with a lawyer. No doubt the idea of again writing regularly under pressure on matters of great importance and of deep interest to him and being paid to do it had powerful appeal. That he was paid well is intimated by the £100 bounty given to his wife after his death.[35]

Third, there is no indication that he was asked to convert to Roman Catholicism or that he did so. No contemporary leveled

either charge against him. He was always identified as the partisan
of Dissenters, and he addressed himself primarily to them. But capping proof comes from a tract he published entitled *A Modest
Enquiry. Whether St Peter Were ever at Rome and Bishop of that Church?
Wherein… Some Considerations taken notice of, that render the Negative
highly Probable.* The date of the imprimatur, 16 April 1687, makes
this pamphlet exceedingly interesting, all the more so because
Care wrote it earlier: in the manuscript versions he refers to 'this
present year 1686' and to spending a 'few vacant Hours in rum-
maging' the subject. He took pains with it; it is the only pamphlet
to survive written out in his hand. The title of the manuscript version, which begins 'A Blow at the root, or modest enquiry,' suggests
the devastating implications to the Catholic religion of what follows.[36] The manuscript also intimates that the pages are part of a
larger project: chapter numbers appear, and he promises that 'in
another Chapter' he 'may possibly' do so-and-so. So it is reasonable
to think that he was aware of the significance of the date of publication, that is, about a fortnight after the promulgation of James's
Declaration of Indulgence on 4 April.

The purpose of the *Modest Enquiry* was to answer the question
whether St Peter was ever in Rome and bishop there by examining the historical record. This had been the topic of the very first
issue of the *Weekly Pacquet*, in which Care had addressed the question and answered it in the negative. He said much the same thing
at greater length in 1687. Insisting that his 'sole aim' was a 'free
impartial sifting out of Truth, not the advancement of any self-
interested Opinion,' he wrote that he wanted to discover the
proofs that substantiated the Catholic assumption, argued by their
great spokesmen, Bellarmine and Baronius, that St Peter had been
in Rome and there built his church. This question, he said, was
'Historical' in nature; the facts could be summed up by a lay
person, 'without incurring ye Censure of presumption.' He was
moved to do so because so many books and pamphlets written by
Catholics, including Gother's *Papist Misrepresented and Represented*,
had presented the positive case, as if it were beyond dispute. He

acknowledged that Valance, a 'Learned Lutheran,' had written a book on the subject, but since he did not possess the book and no other Protestant had addressed the topic, he had decided to do so. He argued that if he proved the contrary, Catholic thinkers would accept that conclusion, not wanting to support a point of faith with a falsehood. Care pointed out that this thesis was the foundation stone on which the Roman Church had built its 'loftiest superstructures.' Using his legal expertise and his wide knowledge of Church history, Care dissected the proofs, which, he pointed out, were all 'humane testimony,' taking pains to reveal their inconsistencies and errors. At the end of this lengthy disquisition he concluded that the claim had been erected on 'Bogg and Quicksand.'

It was a bold gesture for anyone, much more so the exposed Henry Care, to publish such a negative assessment of the foundation stone of Roman Catholicism so soon after the king issued his Declaration of Indulgence. Surely the tract signaled his independence and testified that he had *not* abandoned his views about the errors of Catholicism. Notwithstanding its appearance, James II's court wanted Care badly enough to bring him on to their side and keep him there.

A fourth consideration explaining Care's switch was his belief that by joining with James he could help his fellow Dissenters and advance the cause of religious liberty by persuading them to support the new king. Like James, Care insisted that he had always believed in religious liberty, writing, 'Ever since I was capable of understanding any thing of Religion, I have thought Liberty of Conscience to be the Birth right of Mankind by a Charter Divine.'[37] Unlike James, Care had some basis for this claim in his earlier writing, but in the early 1680s he did not extend liberty of conscience to Catholics. Nevertheless, he should not be scorned as a hypocrite: his own intellectual development and the persecution he and Nonconformists suffered could well have given rise to a sincere belief in religious liberty for every individual, including Catholics, as a birthright.

A fifth reason was no doubt the opportunity to revenge the treatment he and the Dissenting community had suffered at the hands of the Church of England. Naturally, he did not admit that he was set on revenge. On the contrary, in characteristic fashion Care placed his writing in the service of a principle, saying that it 'was mainly design'd against the Spirit of Persecution,' which he described as the 'Badge of Antichristianism.' 'The contrary Freedom, to be perpetually Establisht, is all that I would Advance,' he declared.[38] Finally, he insistently justified his move as a 'Duty' he owed his prince and his country, avowing in the first issue of *Publick Occurrences* that 'National Service [was his] End.'[39] Two months later he declared even though he had won the ill will of angry men, 'God is my Witness, my chief Aim, is that England may be happy upon a Moral, Just and National Foot.'[40] He returned to the thought again, saying that he would be a 'Cincinnatus,' thereby evoking the image of a man who serves his country selflessly and retires to his plow at the end of his service.[41] In language reminiscent of Machiavelli, Care averred that a man 'is both Safe and Happy, and Rich and Honourable enough, that endeavours with Integrity to serve his Country.'[42] In sum, Care accepted the post for multiple reasons, including a need of money, a desire to help fellow Dissenters and advance the principle of religious toleration, a newly found belief in religious liberty for all, revenge and a sense of responsibility to serve his country. For all these considerations, he allowed himself to be seduced and became, as a modern historian has put it, the 'hardest working horse' in the royal 'journalistic stable.'[43]

II

The controversy in the press in 1687 and 1688 over James II's policy generated a unique political geometry: it was not just Anglican churchmen and Tories ranged against Dissenters but rather Anglicans and Tories ranged against the crown, Catholics and Dissenters, with Dissenters holding the wild card; they were wooed by both sides.[44] The exchange was more extensive than has been recognized, numbering more than 450 items.[45] On the one hand, at least thirteen major Church figures wrote on behalf of the Anglicans and Tories. They included, under the leadership of William Sherlock, John Tillotson, dean of Canterbury and arch-bishop of Canterbury after the revolution, Thomas Tenison, another archbishop of Canterbury after the revolution, Edward Stillingfleet, dean of Saint Paul's and bishop of Worcester after the revolution, and above all, according to Bishop Gilbert Burnet, William Wake, who would become archbishop of Canterbury in 1716, described in 1687 as 'the young David... raised up to conquer the giants, which defy our church.'[46] The most famous disputant was George Savile, the first marquis of Halifax, the author of the anonymous *Letter to a Dissenter.*

On the other hand, many people, with varying degrees of enthusiasm and from different perspectives, wrote apologia for James. L'Estrange, the royal censor, was the most prominent long-term friend of the king among them. The Quaker William Penn was also one of James's foremost supporters. Catholic spokesmen like John Gother and John Sergeant were also tireless in pre-senting Catholic doctrine in its most attractive guise. The poet laureate, John Dryden, served his master by publishing *The Hind and the Panther* a few weeks after his Declaration of Indulgence in April 1687. Regarded today as Dryden's most complex and orig-inal poem, *The Hind and the Panther* found its audience among the intellectual and cultivated.[47] The Reverend Samuel Parker, bishop of Oxford, whom James finally appointed president of Magdalen College, was another of the king's friends who took up his pen. John Northleigh, an Anglican physician, and Independent ministers, such as Stephen Lobb and Vincent Alsop, may also be added to the list of persons who wrote for the king. The breadth of support is seen in the appearance of tracts by women, notably the well-educated Quaker Anne Docwra, who justified the king's use of the suspending power,[48] and the printer, author and eccentric, Elinor James, who defended the Church of England and called the Dissenters 'Disturbers of Government' but at the same time endorsed the king's policies on the grounds that James II, whom she boldly advised to return to the Church of England, deserved obedience.[49] Most prolific of all was Henry Care. Over about eighteen months he published at least nine tracts and the new, semiofficial weekly newspaper *Publick Occurrences*, which appeared from 21 February 1688 until his death in August.

Contemporary observers assessed these two sides differently: according to Burnet, some maintained that '*both* sides' were rather evenly matched and that each showed itself to 'best advantage.'[50] Burnet himself took a different view: he felt that the two sides were 'very unequally yoked' and that those who supported the position of the Church of England wrote with 'judgment... clearness... learning and vivacity' and were 'among the best writers that have yet appeared on the protestant side.' He noted that they wrote against popery (the Dissenters did not) and that usually 'once a week some new book or sermon came out' from the churchmen.[51]

Burnet's appraisal of the relative strength of the two sides is, I believe, accurate, but he gave too much credit to the writing talents of the Anglican/Tories and failed to notice that both sides were weakened by their previous attitudes and actions. The appeal of Anglican/Tories to the Dissenting community to trust them was vitiated by the record of their previous role in Parliament and the press during the Exclusion era just four or five years before, their immediate past record of persecuting Dissenters, and their well-known, longstanding dislike of Nonconformity. The strength of James's polemicists was equally diluted by their previous reputation and religious orientation. L'Estrange, who had earlier been the darling of Tories and Anglicans, suffered ridicule as an apostate, especially when he wrote viciously against the Church of England in *Reply to the Reasons of the Oxford Clergy against Addressing*, printed in 1687, because some Anglicans had supported the duke of Monmouth.[52] L'Estrange's voice was further weakened by his refusal to endorse the king's policy of toleration and by the court's order that he cease publication of the *Observator*. His answer to Halifax's *Letter to a Dissenter* was regarded as only lukewarm, as discussed below.

Penn's effectiveness was attenuated by the general national hostility toward Quakers. The Catholicism of Gother and Sergeant did not recommend their writings. Care also suffered the charge of apostasy, and like L'Estrange, but for different reasons, he became the butt of satirical comment. Dryden's poem did not strengthen the king's case. Dryden had shown his animosity to Dissenters in the preface to his *Religio Laici*, published in 1682, and in the text of *The Hind and the Panther*; it was difficult to reach a group he clearly despised. In the event, he wrote so ambivalently in the highly ambiguous *Hind and the Panther* that he weakened rather than fortified James's position.[53] Parker's previously expressed loathing of Dissenters and contempt of common people, amply displayed in powerful tracts written over the years from 1667, was not a plus for James's effort to win over Dissenters.[54] His earlier writings would have vitiated anything he had to say. In my view, it was not that Anglican/Tory polemicists wrote so much better than those in James's camp, as Burnet would have it – after all, James was defended by L'Estrange and Care and Dryden and Penn, all excellent writers – but that their argument stood a better chance of winning favor with the public because it played into the deep vein of national anti-Catholicism.

There is delicious irony here. These new enemies of James II made antipopery their most powerful weapon against his policy of toleration, just as Care and others had made it their most powerful weapon against the Church and Tories during the Exclusion Crisis. Further irony inheres in the fact that Care, who had promoted antipopery with such a vengeance, now had to endure its being turned back upon him, weakening the position he was championing on behalf of the king's cause.

III

Operating from the center of the press controversy, Care wrote largely in response to arguments advanced by the contrary side, as the occasion required and perhaps as he was assigned. Thus, he answered *A Letter to a Dissenter*, replied to *Fagel's Letter* at Penn's request, defended James's Ecclesiastical Commission, abstracted and explained the penal laws, and justified the king's dispensing power. Particularly in *Publick Occurrences* he exposed the persecutory policy and actions of the Church of England. The message of his tracts and newspaper was identical in several respects to that of Penn's three works under the title *Letter From a Gentleman in the Country* and *Som Free Reflections* and, with respect to liberty of religion and anticlericalism, to *Good advice to the Church of England, Roman Catholick, and Protestant dissenter.*[55] Contemporaries associated the two men with each other, one addressing to both of them a tract ridiculing their views on religious liberty.[56] Care's pamphlets, as well as *Publick Occurrences*, are written with verve, displaying vast learning in religion and law, as would be expected from his pen. What makes them different from his earlier pamphlets is the absence of rollicking humor and vicious *ad hominem* attacks; perhaps such rhetorical devices were considered inappropriate in written defenses of the king's religious and constitutional policies.

In keeping with an apparent decision to divide up the audience, Care addressed primarily Dissenters, as did William Penn. Care identified himself as a 'sincere Professor of, and Well-wisher to the Protestant Religion.'[57] Contemporaries thought that to be his mission.[58] As he had done earlier, Care sought to reinforce Latitudinarians, as did Penn.[59] Occasionally he expressed hope that the Church of England would relent, and he often addressed himself to the 'impartial reader.' He had little to say directly to Catholics or about Catholicism, although he of course defended Catholics' religious and civil rights. But Care's role in the king's propaganda campaign was large and important, a measure of his perceived importance to the court.

One of Care's most significant services to the court was to respond to the most famous and effective statement of Anglican and Tory polemic, the anonymous *Letter to a Dissenter, upon Occasion of His Majesties Late Gracious Declaration of Indulgence,* which contemporaries almost immediately guessed was the work of Halifax. Probably written in August 1687 and published in early September, *A Letter to a Dissenter* was enormously popular.[60] Care admitted that it was 'wrote with a great deal of Art, full of pert Sallies of Wit,... plausible Expression of Kindness, and a Stile altogether accommodated to amuse and inveigle.'[61] It was ordered suppressed, but it went through six editions within six weeks, with two more editions in French translation; it was reduced to a single sheet 'for conveniency of Postage,' and 20,000 copies were circulated.[62] It provoked approximately twenty-four answers.[63]

A Letter to a Dissenter sought not only to discredit James's Declaration of Indulgence but also to persuade Dissenters to trust the Church of England and to convince future members of Parliament (Parliament was expected to meet in November) not to repeal the penal laws or Test Acts. To that end, as the editor of Halifax's works pointed out, *A Letter to a Dissenter* includes over-generalizations, wishful thinking and outright lies.[64] The essence of the argument was that James's use of the dispensing power was illegal and his promise of toleration for Dissenters illusory. The king's aim was to divide the Dissenting community, embarrass those who had joined him and persuade the rest not to be enticed. The Dissenters' 'new friends' (James II) made them not 'their Choice, but their Refuge.'[65] The king's real intention was to empower his Catholic subjects by giving them religious and civil rights and freedoms even as he destroyed the rights and liberties of all Protestants. As a devout Catholic he could not grant liberty of religion: the Catholic Church 'not only dislike[s] the allowing, but by its Principles it cannot do it' (251). In a memorable statement Halifax declared, 'You are therefore to be hugged now, onely that you may be the better squeezed at another time' (252). Catholics would take over major public offices and dominate Parliament; once entrenched in power, they would destroy all who did not convert to Catholicism. Dissenters should not fall into that trap but should cast their lot with the Church of England.

Halifax implicitly recognized that the Dissenting community was already divided between those who wanted religious toleration or religious liberty for themselves but not for Catholics and those who would grant religious freedom to all. To bring along all Dissenters, Halifax admitted that the Church of England had earlier preserved memory of the 'rough usage' it had suffered during the Civil Wars and Cromwellian regime and had succumbed to revenge at the time of the Restoration. But now the church had changed (258). 'All the former Haughtiness towards you is for ever extinguished;... it hath turned the Spirit of Persecution into a Spirit of Peace, Charity, and Condescension' (259). Dissenters should trust the Church; it would grant them, but not Roman Catholics, toleration. Adding a threat, directed particularly at those who would give Catholics religious and civil rights as well as freedom, Halifax intimated that Dissenters had no viable choice but to ally themselves with the Church. If the Church should comply with the king, they would be thrown 'back into [a] state of Suffering' (259). If the king succeeded in this policy of abolishing the penal laws and Tests, then Dissenters 'after the squeaziness of starting at a Surplice... must be forced to swallow Transubstantiation' (262). These points, reflecting a deep-seated anti-Catholicism recently intensified by the Popish Plot hysteria, carried weight with the Dissenting community and weakened its support for James. Halifax's *Letter to a Dissenter* posed a severe challenge to James's court and propagandists.

L'Estrange and Care were among the many who responded to *A Letter to a Dissenter*. L'Estrange's twelve-page *Answer To A Letter To A Dissenter* was advertised in the 29 September–3 October 1687 issue of the *London Gazette*.[66] It was not a success. Written without enthusiasm, with comments about how 'unpleasant' the task was and the tiredness of the author,[67] L'Estrange's pamphlet offered what a contemporary described as 'heavy Answers.'[68] It provoked 'no small talke,'[69] with people complaining that in the course of answering *A Letter to a Dissenter* point by point L'Estrange had, in effect, reprinted it and furthered its circulation. An anonymous author of an undated manuscript tract addressed to Care chastised L'Estrange sarcastically, remarking that he no longer believed his conversion: there was 'so little Weight or Sense' in L'Estrange's response to Halifax that the author thought he 'is still of his former Opinion.'[70] L'Estrange's *Answer* so outraged another man that he embarrassed the author in a coffee house by looking 'almost rudely' upon him. When L'Estrange asked him what was wrong, the fellow said that he took L'Estrange to be the 'Observator,' implied that he was guilty of apostasy and declared that he had heard that L'Estrange was the author of the *Letter to a Dissenter*. 'You are mistaken,' rejoined L'Estrange, 'I answered it.' 'Nay,' replied the other, '*You* are mistaken, you published it, but you did not answer it.'[71] With a friend perceived in such terms as these, James hardly needed enemies.

Care's much stronger response to *A Letter to a Dissenter*, a lengthy tract entitled *Animadversions On A Late Paper, Entituled, A Letter to a Dissenter*, came out a week later, in early October. His radical perspective was that of Dissenters who had joined James, and his goal was to persuade others not to listen to the siren call of the Church of England. In a bid for sympathy Care recalled the terrible suffering of Dissenters, so intolerable that many had fled, choosing to 'expose themselves to all the Hazards abroad' rather than remain at home.[72] To demonstrate the insincerity of the Church of England's offer to Dissenters, Care took up a point that James reportedly had made the 'common subject' of conversation: the Church's cruelty to the Dissenters.[73] Churchmen were not just 'Instruments' but 'Authors' of the outrageous treatment Dissenters had borne. 'Have we not seen them animating Informers' and pulling down meetinghouses? he queried.[74] They continue to do so, Care declared, offering proof in an incident that he reported had occurred since the Declaration of Indulgence.[75] Boldly, Care called upon the Anglican Church to answer just one question: did it believe in persecution? If it did, then it should say how far it would go in persecuting Dissenters. Would it go to the length of burning them? queried Care, slyly evoking memory of the Marian fires. If it did not, it should publicly declare that position and 'make... Repentance as notorious as the Scandal [of its previous actions].'[76]

Softening his approach, Care pointed out that there were men in the Church who were not stained by the persecuting spirit. In tracts and sermons these Latitudinarians had urged healing the break between the Church and Dissent, and had suffered for it.[77] Their names, such as that of Samuel Bolde, for example, should be honored.[78] This was not the first time that Care had sought to ally himself with Latitudinarians, but the approach had added urgency in the politics of 1687–88. This minority among the clergy, part of the 'Trimmers' whom L'Estrange found so tiresome, was a target of opportunity for Care and James's court.

Care turned on its head the plea to Dissenters to trust Anglicans to grant toleration to all but Catholics. In an earnest bid to Dissenters not to be misled by this entreaty, Care warned that it was the promises of the Church of England that were not to be trusted. As he put it, one would have to 'wear a Muckinder,' that is, to be a child, not to see through the Church's offer.[79] It was the Church of England, not the king, that Dissenters should mistrust. It was the Church of England, not the king, that had made a sudden shift in attitude and policy. James II had *always* believed in religious toleration, Care insisted (although he must have known this to be false), just as his Declarations of Indulgence maintained.[80]

Care's *Animadversions On A Late Paper* also invoked, significantly, the principle of liberty of conscience in support of James's policy of toleration and extended it for the first time to all persons, including Catholics. Going beyond his position of four or five years earlier, Care asserted that liberty of individual conscience was the 'Birth-right of Mankind by a Charter Divine' and that to worship without soiling one's conscience was 'a natural Birth right.'[81]

Thus, he placed religious freedom on a different basis from that in the king's declaration. The fundamental right to worship as one pleased according to one's conscience had nothing to do with law or the prerogative of the king to dispense with law. Such a right was beyond toleration, for it did not acknowledge an established Church or the idea of an 'indulgence' from it. Care conceived of religion as a 'natural right' of all mankind, not just Englishmen; it was rooted in natural law, in God's law, and it applied to everyone, including Roman Catholics.

This powerful statement about liberty of conscience was amplified in Care's other writings. Religious belief, Care explained, was of a 'Transcendent Nature, wherein every man (on Peril of his Soul) must endeavor to satisfie his Conscience, and stand or fall in the great day of Trial, to his own Master; who alone is the Judge thereof.'[82] Reiterating, he declared again that liberty of conscience was 'every mans natural Birth-right.' The civil authority had no power whatsoever over the individual conscience, and neither did institutionalized spiritual authority, the Church of England. Natural law, reason and Christian principle required, Care insisted, 'that no man for his meer Religious Opinions (not violating the Civil Peace or Morality) ought to be subjected to any Temporal Penalty, or Incapacity whatsoever.'[83] According to natural law and God's law, conscience was inviolable: no human law could restrain it. 'The Divine Laws which respect the essential parts of the worship of God are in themselves invariable, and not to be changed by any human authority.' England's penal laws and Test Acts are 'not only Unjust, but Impious; they profane the Holy Sacrament, by exposing it to Secular Ends and Designs.'[84] The penal laws violated God's laws and the law of nature. They were *void* on the grounds of principle.

To this line of argument Care added another major point in his response to *A Letter Writ by Mijn Heer Fagel, Pensioner of Holland, to Mr. James Stewart*. Standing somewhat apart from the tracts written by Englishmen and said to be 'more influential' than the others,[85] this pamphlet was dated 4 November 1687 at Amsterdam and printed in great quantities for an English audience about mid-January 1688 under the title *Their Highness The Prince and Princess of Orange's Opinion about a General Liberty of Conscience.*[86] It provided an accounting, approved by Prince William and Princess Mary of Orange, of their views on King James's policy. Stating that William and Mary were emphatically opposed to religious persecution, the *Letter* represented them as favoring toleration for Catholics and Dissenters, and repeal of the penal laws but not of the Test Acts. Their Highnesses would deny Catholics any 'share in the government or in Offices of Trust,' including a role in Parliament.[87] This meant that they would not disturb the Anglican monopoly of office.

The pamphlet seriously damaged James, for on the one hand it reassured Catholics and Dissenters that they would not suffer persecution when William and Mary inherited the crown (as they were expected to do, for at that time James and his wife, Mary of Modena, were still childless), and on the other hand it reassured Anglicans that they would not lose their monopoly of office. Moreover, it showed that one of James's favorite arguments – that the Dutch enjoyed economic prosperity *because* they practiced religious toleration – was problematical.[88] In fact, William's attitude toward the situation in England conformed to Dutch reality: no religious persecution but exclusion from office of persons who were not members of the State Church. Fagel's letter presented a formidable challenge to James's supporters.

Care dedicated his response, *Animadversions upon Mijn Heer Fagels Letter Concerning Our Penal Laws And Tests*, to William Penn, 'my worthy Friend,' who Care said had asked him to 'consider' Fagel's *Letter.*[89] The most theoretical statement to come from his pen, this lengthy pamphlet dissected Fagel's letter point by point and offered a disquisition on law and the origins of civil government and religion. Care's view of the nature of government and its relationship to religion was unexceptional: 'Civil government,' he opined,' is Ordained of God for the good of Mankind; dominion is founded in Nature.' Religion is also of 'Divine Ordination.'[90] What is exceptional about Care's argument is the sharp division he made between civil government and religion. Care maintained that each of these spheres was 'distinct from the other, in their foundation, continuance, and use.' They 'thrive best when they retain themselves within their distinct Sphears and Order, without encroaching one upon the other.' Applying the point, Care asserted that the State could not compel anyone's religious beliefs; nor could the Church censure its members any further than to expel them from their religious communion, without in any way affecting their secular standing.[91] Although the two spheres must be kept separate, Care maintained that the magistrate had the authority to make laws for the safety of his subjects, which might include mandating freedom of religion for all subjects. Those subjects, in turn, were obliged to obey. The English king, whose royal prerogative inhered in English common law, had the power to dispense with laws to achieve the end of liberty of worship for all his subjects, and the political and public service of all subjects for the benefits of the crown.[92] Further, subjects must accept what the king had done for the greater good of the whole. Care made still another interesting point when he asserted that religion and religious bodies needed the social and political stability that a government might assure: the 'Christian Religion cannot be preserved in any society, where Natural and Civil Government is destroyed.' But civil society was not equally dependent on religion; it might last even after religion was 'rejected' or destroyed.[93]

To conceptualize liberty as a 'Birth-right' of all mankind, to separate religion and State into two spheres, as Care did, independently of others, was remarkable. John Locke made these selfsame points. One may follow them in his *Letter on Toleration*, in which he wrote that the whole jurisdiction of the magistrate reached only to such civil concerns as impartial execution of equal laws, security of possession and punishment for violation of laws of public justice and equity. Faith, he said, was a personal, individual conviction of the mind and could not be compelled. He defined a Church as a society of members 'voluntarily' uniting in public worship of God.

Laws regulating the Church belonged only to the members. Excommunication could not deprive a person of any civil goods he possessed, for those things belonged to the civil government. No person was to suffer prejudice in enjoying civil rights because of his religious beliefs.[94]

The foundation of Care's belief in liberty of conscience, then, rested on the principle of natural rights and on the theory of the separation of Church and State. His argument was extraordinary for his time. Care advanced the same basic points that John Locke made in greater detail and at greater length. Locke was a great philosopher, Care a journalist of great intelligence and learning. Locke, of course, far exceeded Care, but the latter wrote briefly about the same principles. It should be acknowledged that Care had those principles before the public in printed form before Locke. Thus Care, rather than John Locke, was among the first, if not *the* first, to develop in print during the Restoration a justification for religious liberty on the grounds of natural right and the separation of Church and State.[95]

Care and Locke differed in three specific respects: First, Care did not suggest that religious persecution might justify resistance, as Locke does;[96] Care was intent upon arguing that toleration produced harmony, while persecution might cause rebellion. Second, Care defended the king's right to dispense with laws in the interest of the good of the whole society, whereas Locke did not grant the king the power to dispense. And third, Care went beyond Locke in his willingness to grant liberty of conscience to Catholics, logically applying his principle that it was a 'Birth-right of mankind.'[97] It is worth noting that Locke thought well enough of Care's tracts to have two of them in his library, and it is not impossible that they had some influence on him and his *Letter on Toleration*.[98]

Further to defend James's policy of religious toleration, Care offered other reasons of varying degrees of sophistication, including the perfidy of religious persecution, the legality of the king's creation of the Ecclesiastical Commission, the lawfulness of the royal dispensing power, the king's moral integrity, the moral bankruptcy and corruption of the Anglican Church, the moral responsibility and religious self-interest of Dissenters, and economic self-interest. To show how ancient and evil was religious persecution, Care wrote his most understated and one of his most effective tracts, a thirty-page pamphlet entitled *Liberty of Conscience Asserted. Or A Looking-Glass For Persecutors*, published by himself and printed in 1687 by his old friend Richard Janeway.[99] Insisting that he wrote out of 'Duty to improve this Opportunity' for toleration and not to stir up animosities, Care unfolded a seemingly innocent history of religious persecution, including the reasons for it, the methods used and the consequences to the perpetrators. Drawing upon his wide knowledge of the Bible and using biblical texts alone, Care piled up example after example to show that people who disagreed with Jesus and his followers persecuted them, for example, libeling them as enemies of kings and governors, calling them 'Rebels, Traytors, Seditious, Factious,' and enacting 'Laws and Decrees Civil and Ecclesiastical' to ensnare and destroy them.[100] The reasons why they did this included pride, ignorance of God, jealousy, fear of losing authority and rule, blind zeal for traditions and ceremonies to which they were accustomed, desire to please those in power, and profit from their present religion. Care drove home the last point with his story of the silversmiths who crafted silver shrines for the goddess Diana, whom they professed to adore. Care showed that they stirred the people up against the apostle Paul 'not [out of] their zeal for Diana so much as for their Profit,' which they expected to lose if Christianity triumphed.[101] Care concluded the essay with a warning of punishment to come in this world and the next to all those who were guilty of religious persecution. Although he did not draw a parallel to the contemporary scene, it was plainly there for readers to make themselves.

Care justified James's creation of the Ecclesiastical Commission in three tracts: *Vindication of the Proceedings of His Majesties Ecclesiastical Commissioners*, with an imprimatur of 21 December 1687; *Legality of the Court*, approved by Sunderland on 25 February 1687/88, which ran through the same points; and *An Answer to a*

Paper importing a Petition Of The Archbishop of Canterbury, published in the spring of 1688, after the second Declaration of
Indulgence. The reference was to James's creating an Ecclesiastical
Commission in July 1686 to act as his surrogate in visiting
and disciplining ecclesiastical bodies, including universities. The
most important person injured by the commission was Henry
Compton, the bishop of London, who was suspended for failing to
discipline a rector, John Sharp, for preaching sermons hostile to
Catholicism. The most important institution to be hurt was
Magdalen College, Oxford, where a president of whom the college's fellows disapproved was installed, some Catholics were
admitted as fellows, and the college's fellows were severely punished.[102] These incidents had become the 'common talk' of
London, and Care sought to provide a 'Just and Naked' account to
show the 'World' 'What Manner of Men Our Censorious Clergy
and their Creatures are.'[103]

Arguing in a logical and careful way, Care readily established
that the commission James had established claimed only the
powers of ecclesiastical jurisdiction that laws in 1641 and at the
Restoration had specifically granted to the king. Meeting an
Anglican argument head-on, Care insisted that James II's use of the
dispensing power to set aside the penal laws and Test Acts was legal.
Appealing to men 'learned in the law' and himself showing wide
knowledge of the law, Care used law and history as proof that an
English king possessed the power to dispense with or suspend
ecclesiastical laws in the interests of the State's welfare and that the
king's legal authority over ecclesiastical matters was absolute. That
authority superseded canons, acts of Parliament and 'anything that
is but *Malum prohibitum*.'[104] Citing legal cases, early statutes from
the reigns of Elizabeth I and Charles II, rulings of judges, the
principles of common law, and Anglican Church law and pro-
nouncements from the time of the Reformation on, including one
by Archbishop Bancroft, 'the Church of England's darling,' Care
demonstrated that the English king's ecclesiastical supremacy was
one of his 'richest Jewels.'[105] He dismissed as 'vain and ludicrous' the

argument of the fellows that the obligation of their oath bound their conscience and prevented them from obeying the king.[106] They had pleaded their duty to a college statute (which had been dispensed) and to the rights of the university, placing such things above the interests of the crown. He also chastised churchmen for disavowing royal dispensing power as a 'contradistinction to the Non-resisting Doctrine' and declared that Dissenters 'went not half so far' in disobedience when they absented themselves from the sacrament.[107] Care made as strong a case as could be made for James's actions.

Care put his legal knowledge in the service of the king again when he published *Draconica*, probably in late 1687. As the lengthy title explained, this pamphlet was *An Abstract Of All the Penal-Laws Touching Matters of Religion; And; the Several Oaths and Tests thereby Enjoyned*.[108] His underlying point was that the purpose of the recusancy laws had shifted over time from a religious to a partisan political one. Noting that the penal laws were debated throughout the nation, even though not one person in ten really knew their 'extent' and 'grievous Unequal Penalties and Destructive Effects,' Care, addressing 'all Honest Unbiass'd Englishmen,' set forth the laws and, teacher that he was, drew out their implications.[109] Underscoring the unfairness of the twenty-three or twenty-four laws that made up the penal code – one had to be a lawyer before one could be a Christian, he observed (13) – Care showed that these laws stripped away from the recusant all the natural privileges of 'freeborn Englishmen.' The people they punished were not seditious or rebellious but rather persons of conscience who refused to worship according to certain ceremonies that were regarded as 'indifferent' by the Church of England itself (13). These laws, Care declared, were 'not only Unjust, but Impious, profaning the Holy Sacrament, by exposing it to Secular Ends and Designs' (15). And with warmth he asserted, 'Persecution for Conscience is an unwarrantable Tyranny over the just Priviledges and Liberty of a Christian'; to compel belief compelled the individual to renounce his Reason, his 'most essential part' (14). In extravagant language

Care charged that Dissenters had suffered in 'kind (though not degree) as those put to death' (13; see also 16).

Furthermore, Care used the backdrop of his canvas of penal laws to defend Roman Catholics and extend to them more explicitly than in any other pamphlet the principle of religious liberty. He insisted that it was grossly unfair of the Church of England to promise toleration to Dissenters but deny it to Catholics. Catholics were not traitors. Their allegiance to the Pope was limited to spiritual matters only; for that they should not be stripped of rights and privileges due all Englishmen (16–18). He pointed out that early parliamentary acts had restrained papal authority in England and that an act for liberty of conscience could do so too. He reported that James had 'frankly offered' to support such a law 'in all Discourses on this Subject' (17). Care appealed to the history of a Catholic ruler recounted by a Protestant historian to show that a Catholic king might promote freedom of conscience, just as might be expected from James (18). According to equity, the Christian golden rule, human reason and the law of the land, a policy of toleration should include Catholics. In another essay Care noted that a litany of the Church of England acknowledged as much and said that churchmen sinned if they did not believe what they said.[110] With its generally measured tone, logical reasoning, carefully presented argument and useful compilation of penal laws, *Draconica* seemed to meet a need. A second and third edition were printed in 1688, and one of them was translated into German and Dutch. Bishop Burnet, no admirer of Care, had a copy of the second edition in his library.[111]

IV

Care was preoccupied in the spring of 1688 with writing the new newspaper *Publick Occurrences*, which began on 21 February 1688 and came out every week thereafter until the week before his death in August.[112] Described by the historian of the

Restoration newspaper as a 'genuine government newspaper,'[113] *Publick Occurrences* appeared 'With Allowance.' Whose idea it was to publish a newspaper as a propaganda organ is unknown – perhaps Care's or L'Estrange's or Penn's – but the paper plainly had the blessing of the court. Perhaps it had to do with the commission of enquiry discussed below. In any case, that the court authorized Care to write it is a testament to the confidence and trust the court placed in him. The avowed purpose was to rebut the maligning of the government with 'punctual Truth' – a 'Duty' Care said he owed his prince and country.[114] The central theme was bitter criticism of the Church of England for its past and present attitudes and actions toward Dissent and liberty of conscience. Care pursued this point so vigorously that a contemporary, who showed his interest in what Care had to say by frequent marginalia,[115] scrawled across the first issue 'By Henry Care. agt. ye Church of England.'[116] Criticizing, taunting, threatening and cajoling High Churchmen, and also appealing to Latitudinarians, Care did his best to embarrass the Church and also to show that the king's policy of religious toleration was in its interests as well as in those of the nation.

Care was intent upon revealing evidence of past and present persecution of Dissenters by Tories and Anglicans. To this end he drew upon revelations compiled by the 300-member commission of enquiry the king had appointed at the end of 1687 to discover persons who had exploited the Conventicle Act of 1670 and the Act of 35 Elizabeth I to harass recusants (of all kinds) and profit from the financial penalties the laws imposed on them. The purpose of the commission was to name persons who had levied fines and punishments, and to find out where the money had gone. Mark Goldie hypothesized that Penn argued that the results could help dissuade Dissenters from joining with the Church of England and persuade them to enlist with the court.[117] *Publick Occurrences* was a medium for that purpose. The first issue called attention to the commission of enquiry, and subsequent issues contained horror stories of the Dissenters' sufferings. A most affecting tale concerned a sick Dissenter whose bed was removed

Publick Occurrences

Truely Stated.

with Allowance.

By Henry Care, as of the Church of England.

Tuesday February 21th 1687.

THe *Title speaks both the Occasion and Scope of this Paper: He must wink hard, that does not see to what disadvantages the Government is daily Exposed by false Reports; Every thing liable to Misconstruction, Trumpetted through the Kingdom, and dressed up in all the ill Colours that Malice, or Mis-imploy'd Witt, can invent, to amuse and infest People with Jealousies; whilst what tends to its Honour, and giving a right notion of our Superiours proceedings, is industriously stifled. To prevent or detect such bad Practices, is a duty that every honest man owes both to his Prince and his Countrey (for their Interests are Inseparable.) Without consulting the Stars, both the Difficulties and Calumnies attending such an undertaking may be foreseen. But an Honest Intention being the Motive, and a National Service the End, may I hope procure a favourable Reception with unprejudic'd Persons; Since nothing but punctual Truth (as far as it can be discovered) shall here be Advanc'd, nor any thing but groundless Tales, extravagant Actions, and mischievous designs Exposed. And all this without Reflections on any, farther than by their own ill Conduct they shall justly have deserved and rendred it necessary.*

London Feb. 20. The Commissions granted by His Majesty for Inquiring what has been taken away from Dissenters, on the Score of Religion, within Ten Years past, are Issued or ready to be Issued into most parts of the Kingdom; The Commissioners here have Sat several days, and Multitudes appear before them with Complaints. In earnest, next to the *Indulgence* it self, which put a Period to those Outrages, nothing could be either more Gracious or more Assuring then this Procedure; for as thereby Right (so far as can be) will be done to the Oppressed; So the mighty devastations made by our dearly *Beloved Penal Laws,* will partly appear; Together with the true Complexion of such who *Spoiled their Neighbours for Gods Sake,* and defrauded their King out of *Pure Loyalty.* Nor can the Precedent but be of excel-

lent use, if ever (which God forbid) Violence should gain the like Ascendent in any Party whatever hereafter. In the mean time, 'tis pleasant to Observe, what variety of little underhand Arts are used to divert the People injured, from making their Applications to these Commissioners. —— The *Covetous* are told, they shall get nothing by it, though 'tis well known, Three Fourths of what shall appear to be Embezill'd, is to be returned to the Parties; the other fourth part being but a very reasonable deduction for the Charges. —— The *Timerous* are Hector'd That they were better be quiet; for if the Church-men once again get Power, Such as now Complain shall be markt out for greater Severities—— Some *Easie Good Men* are wheadled to forbear by Suggestions, That 'tis a sort of Revenge contrary to a Christians Spirit; Who ought to take the spoiling of his Goods Joyfully, and not return Evil for Evil.—— A rare *Plea* for *Fellons* and *Murtherers;* As if because God says *Vengeance is mine;* he had discharged Mankind from the duties of Justice. But this seems too gross a fallacy to pass with any but such as have made a private Composition; which I dare foretell them will be strictly inquired into, and such Trickers forc'd (as in Justice they ought) to Refund. A Fourth discouragement is by Proclaiming in some News Letters (which only serve to kindle Faction) That there are great defects in the Commission it self, which if true, as 'tis false, were yet Impertinent. For tho the Commissioners in Acting, should find some new Powers requisite, 'Tis not to be doubted but his Majesty would readily grant what shall be necessary for the designed End.

3. His Majesty proceeds in his Method of Regulating Corporations and Counties, that such Persons may be in Authority, as are for an *Equal Liberty of Conscience;* being that Great and Noble End he has proposed and resolved to make this Kingdom happy by.

4. *Francis Smith,* a Bookseller formerly at the *Elephant* and *Castle* in *Cornhil,* having

A been

by overzealous officials and who died as a result. Another story reported that a Dissenter's house was left 'as dissolate as if a Regiment of Tartars had Quarter'd there.'[118] Inspection of jails where Dissenters were incarcerated revealed exorbitant charges and dreadful conditions (no. 5 [20 March 1687/88]). This persecution was not a thing of the past; there were examples of 'fresh rigors,' which Care recounted, among them the story of Church wardens entering Dissenters' houses and taking 'what they think will be most missed' (no. 3 [6 March 1687/88]).

Care also derided the Church for its obdurate refusal to agree to removal of the Test Acts. Describing the Tests as 'unrighteous Laws,' comparable to the 'Statutes of Omri' (no. 11 [1 May 1688]),[119] Care, in keeping with the principle of the separation of Church and State, emphasized in *Publick Occurrences* that the Tests inflicted a civil incapacity where no civil crime had been committed; in other words, they 'punish religious misapprehensions with Temporal Forfeitures' and 'prophane the Sacrament by making it an Inlet to Secular Employments' (no. 9 [17 April]). The laws were also poor political policy – a 'violation upon the Constitution itself' (ibid.) – because they deprived the king of the services of all his subjects. 'Civil Tenure [should] be recovered to the Government' (no. 12 [8 May]). Why should the Church cling to such laws as if they were the 'Bulwarks' of religion, comparable to the 'Banks for Holland?' (no. 8 [10 April]). Because the Church was selfish and grasping. The offices and preferments in its possession were 'too sweet morsels to be disgorged' to assure religious liberty for all, a principle in which the Church did not believe.[120] Continuing the indictment, Care declared in *Publick Occurrences* that if the Church leaders were honest, they would admit that they had 'engrossed to [their] own Party, all the Preferments of the Nation, with Power to Crush all other Perswasions,' and had made those who dissented 'tremble' before their harsh persecution. Moreover, they 'Colour the matter artificially with Zealous Pretexts for Religion and Property' (no. 15 [29 May]), opposing the removal of the Tests on the grounds that the king's dispensing power was illegal. Rebutting the point, Care maintained that it was just a 'Pretence'; it was not the 'Mode but the Matter, the very Liberty it Self, that is the Eye-sore' (ibid.). In exasperation Care thundered in one of the last issues of *Publick Occurrences* that 'none but a Mad-man can pretend *his* Conscience Obliges him to *burden all others*' (no. 20 [3 July]).

Care hurled another sharp and hurtful accusation against the Church, charging that it was guilty of rebellion. Taunting it for abandoning its traditional principle of nonresistance, Care argued that in disobeying James's commands it had committed the sin of resistance. It was a turncoat, just as it had accused Dissenters who supported James of being. Cleverly turning against the Church of England the charge of sedition that it had relished leveling against Dissenters, Care described it as 'Uneasy, Jealous, Factious, and avowedly Dissobedient,' like those they 'branded as Natural Enemies to Monarchy' (no. 15 [29 May]). Care warned Anglicans not to give 'foolish People' the 'least Example of Disobedience,' lest they incite rebellion.[121] He explained in *Publick Occurrences* that the Tests made those who were excluded feel 'injur'd.' This kept up a 'perpetual Nursery for Rebellion' (no. 12 [8 May]). With equal cleverness Care summoned memory of the Church's opposition to Exclusion and declared that the 'Maxims on which [Exclusionists] then, and you now proceed, seem to me nothing different.' The Tests were an advance effort to 'justle out the rightful heir,' and that 'Precedent will hold.' Support of the Tests meant logically that no advocate 'can justify you from being (if not Intentionally, yet Vertually) exclusioners' (no. 14 [22 May]). These were deep insults.

Introducing a hint of threat, Care cautioned that the Church's actions might bring upon them the 'greatest odium and contempt imaginable.'[122] Its obduracy set a bad example for Dissenters 'if ever the Tables turn,' Care warned ominously in *Publick Occurrences*. Nonconformists had conscience to plead, 'but you none; Since it can never be a Plea of Conscience to give no ease or room to another Mans' (no. 13 [15 May]). He also pointed out to clergymen that the king would promote those who assisted him and would regard others as his enemies (no. 4 [13 March]). Addressing

Churchmen earnestly, Care asked them to remember 'that nothing else supports you, but that you have been for the Crown.' This reputation would not last when the king saw that they supported the crown only 'because the Crown was always for you' (no. 13 [15 May]). Comments such as these – and many others – added up to a very harsh indictment. One can understand why the scrawler mentioned previously should have written in the margin of the twelfth issue of *Publick Occurrences* that 'this is called ye Jesuites Pisse pot thrown by Henry Care in ye Church of England men's faces.'[123]

In fact, however, Care interlarded his harsh words with a softer approach. Following the terms of the king's Declaration of Indulgence, he assured the Church that the king's policy deprived it of none of its advantages – except that of forcing conformity on others.[124] Confident, as before, of a Bible-literate readership for *Publick Occurrences*, Care again called upon men to stop the cries of 'Great is Diana of the Ephesians' (no. 6 [27 March]). In other words, the Church was not endangered by the king's policy. He even tried cajoling the Church to 'come into this Glorious Liberty' of toleration, reassuring it that it would be even stronger: its friends would treble, as would its 'Interest and Honours.' In conciliatory gestures Care wrote that he had 'enough charity to think that the Church of England has charity enough to accept so good a thing' (no. 13 [15 May]). Recognizing the strength of the Church's charge of hypocrisy against him, Care asked for 'justice and patience,' saying that despite the 'Incredible Venom' aimed at 'this poor Paper,' what he wanted for the Church was its 'real honor and safety' (no. 5 [20 March]).

In a move he had made before, Care also appealed to Latitudinarians. Hoping to draw these temperate men to the king's side, he acknowledged that there was a 'Sober, Moderate and (God be thanked) numerous Party... amongst the Clergy that abhor persecution and favor the establishment of a general liberty.' These men regarded their brethren with a 'just Abhorrence' (no. 22 [17 July]).[125] Addressing in particular the London clergy, he made it clear that he meant no reflection on them, for 'amongst [them],' he said, 'there are divers, in whose worthy Persons, I honour a Learning above the common Standard of This Age and a Piety and Moderation becoming the Best' (no. 12 [8 May]). He warmly recounted stories of clerics who had preached in favor of toleration in issues 6, 8 and 12 (27 March, 10 April, 8 May 1688).

Care constructed other, less sophisticated defenses for King James and his policies. One tack was to show what a fine fellow the king was. James treated all his subjects dispassionately, according to law, not religion; for example, he ordered that a Roman Catholic woman found guilty of murdering her husband be burned, as law required, whereas enemies said the king would spare a fellow religionist (no. 3 [6 March]). The king displayed 'innate clemency and goodness' in pardoning a man who had been involved in the Monmouth Rebellion and in releasing another from prison (nos 16, 23 [5 June, 24 July]). He appointed people not on religious grounds but based on merit, advancing a Dissenter over an unqualified Catholic (no. 1 [21 February]). The king welcomed French Huguenots and placed an *English* Bible and a copy of the *Book of Common Prayer*, 'covered with Crimson Velvet and strongly Embossed,' in the newly redecorated Guard Chamber in London (no. 5 [20 March]). Concerned about the social deterioration in London, which the Church of England had failed to stem, James promoted moral reform in the city: as Care explained, the king was a friend of liberty of conscience, not of licentiousness (no. 1 [21 February]). Touching up the king's image was important, for there had been little in James's prior public attitudes, language or policies to inspire confidence among Dissenters or, more latterly, among Anglicans. The implication of these tributes was that the word of such an evenhanded, generous, attentive man as the king could be trusted and also that he was a much better person than the churchmen.

Another strategy denied rumors circulated by the Church of England and Tories aimed at undermining public faith in the court. This gossip included that the Irish army had landed, that the French fleet had joined the English fleet, that Penn had converted to Roman Catholicism, that all Bibles were to be banned, and that Westminster Abbey and St Paul's were to be converted to use as Catholic churches (nos 3, 6, 19, 21 [6, 27 March, 26 June, 10 July]). Care's denial of these vicious rumors had the effect of showing how mean-spirited – and also threatened – James's enemies were.

Addressing Dissenters directly, Care argued that they had a moral responsibility as Christians to help the king to realize his policy of toleration. If they preferred a 'parliamentary way,' so did James. Accordingly, Nonconformists should elect to Parliament sympathetic persons who would take steps to translate James's policy into law, a law the king conceived of as 'founded on the Natural Principle of Christianity, Moral Equity, and Reason' (no. 4 [13 March]). Reminding Dissenters of the Church's harsh treatment of them by reciting a violent incident that had occurred in Mildenhall, Suffolk, Care asserted that they should not trust to the goodwill of the Church (no. 7 [3 April]). At this time church-men put on a false 'Sweetening Mask,' but their promises were 'mere Banter'; they had said in print that liberty of conscience was against their principles. Their offer was a 'trick to Seduce the Dissenters from their Interest and their Duty.' Dissenters who believed them 'must be Credulous to Dotage' (no. 21 [10 July]). The remark recalled one he had made in *Draconica*, when, in chas-tising uncooperative Dissenters as 'peevish and ungrateful,' Care had declared that those who refused to join the court were 'either fool[s] or atheist[s],' who 'must be intoxicated beyond the Reclaim of Hellebore,' that is, crazy, if they failed to work for the removal of the penal laws and Test Acts.[126] It was absurd to think that the king would allow liberty of religion to all but Roman Catholics, which, of course, would include himself. Besides, a par-tial indulgence violated the principle of a 'universal Maxim [based] on the immutable Laws of God and Nature.' Dissenters who refused to take advantage of James's generosity failed in moral responsibility for themselves and the nation; if they missed this opportunity, then they did not 'deserve' the liberty to worship freely (no. 21 [10 July]).

The point of least interest to Care was the economic advantages that toleration would bring, the argument that dominated James II's two Declarations of Indulgence, said to be 'new' in Restoration England.[127] Care did maintain that in the wake of religious toleration would come many material advantages: an increase in trade, growth in population, and higher wages and revenue. He pointed out that Dissenters were prominently involved in trade and industry and that their disaffection or emigration would harm the well-being of society.[128] It was no coincidence that his tract *The Character and Qualifications of an Honest Loyal Merchant*, printed in 1686, was repeatedly advertised in *Publick Occurrences*.[129] But he bent his mind to other arguments.

V

Care constructed an exceedingly strong and comprehensive defense of James II and his policy of toleration, as set out in the king's Declarations of Indulgence. He did it for multiple reasons, most importantly to advance the prospects of the Dissenting community. Ironically, his message probably carried less weight with Dissenters than it did with his enemies, Tories and Anglicans. It seems apparent, in the event, that Care's radicalism in grounding his theory of religious liberty in natural rights and extending that liberty even to Catholics and his Royalism in upholding the dispensing power for the king did not appeal to reluctant Dissenters who had imbibed from Care's earlier writings an abiding suspicion and fear of Catholicism. His earlier writings undercut his present message. Care's enemies labeled him a radical. Wrote Burnet, 'It were a great injustice to charge all the Dissenters with the impertinences that have appeared in many addresses of late, or to take our measures of them [from] the impudent strains of... a Care.'[130] Of course, it can never be known with any exactitude how successful Care's writings were in attracting more Dissenters to James II's side than previously thought. Care was overtaken by death in August 1688, and by the end of the year James had lost his crown.

It can be said for certain that Care's opponents regarded him as a threat and undertook to sabotage him even as the cause for which he was writing was faltering. Scorning and ridiculing his apostasy was one tactic. The most effective printed piece, *Heraclitus Ridens Redivivus: or, A Dialogue Between Harry and Roger*, threw brickbats at both L'Estrange and Care. 'Roger' opens the exchange with a confession that his *Answer to the Letter to a Dissenter* was regarded as the weakest of all the replies and explains that the problem was that his 'wit lay so much the other way.' He says that his printing *A Letter to a Dissenter* made the 'world think him a disperser of the libel.' 'Harry' responds that L'Estrange's *Answer* allayed the Dissenters' enmity, to which L'Estrange rejoins that he would have spoken more fully for toleration, 'except for self-contradictions.' Self-contradictions indeed! Not to worry, counsels 'Harry': he should appeal to the change of circumstances; what was abominable in one reign is law and gospel in another. 'Roger' now baits 'Harry,' remarking that the *Weekly Pacquet* and *Publick Occurrences* are 'as opposition as Fire & Water.' Is that not shameful? he queries. At this, another interlocutor, a Dissenter, is introduced. Ironically, and significantly, he is very severe with Care, saying that he is made of either 'Knavery or Forgetfulness,' but he thinks Knavery is the chief ingredient. He concludes his insults with the charge that Care has been 'always false and shifting.' This subtle and venomous piece is worth recounting at length for what it reveals of the loathing and fear that Care had aroused.

The most effective manuscript poem against Care was the anonymous 'On the Late Toleration.'[131] Marveling at the 'wondrous change' that had brought the 'Two great Antagonists Roger Le-strange and Henry Care... together,' the author compared them derisively to Herod and Pilate and mocked them for joining in

> *Hostill wars*
> *Against the Truth; bespattring with ye Pen*
> *The sober Steady Church of England Men.*

Continuing in words that testify to the important role Care's *Weekly Pacquet of Advice from Rome* and L'Estrange's *Observator* had played, he directed his reader to

> *Look! now Rome's famous pacquet of advice*
> *And the great Observator cog the dice*
> *Are sweetly Reconcil'd sharply contend*
> *with Industry and skill to put an end*
> *To Englands well Established government*
> *This! This! no doubt 'Tis both their full intent.*[132]

The hatred coming specifically from Church of England men was vehemently expressed; it is a measure of how formidable an adversary they considered Care to be. They aimed 'Incredible Venom' at *Publick Occurrences*, 'Rav[ing]' against it.[133] They maligned Care himself, calling him a 'thousand ill Names.' The infamous Captain Hilton, 'generalissimo of the Arabian Troops called Informers,' as Care characterized him, tore up copies of *Publick Occurrences* that he had found in a coffee house.[134] Friends of the Church sent Care 'many Scores of Reviling and Threatening Letters,' one of which, addressed at the end of May to his printer George Larkin, threatened Care and Larkin with physical injury — a slit nose — if Care did not stop reviling the Church of England.[135] The physical threat also carried a personal insult, for to deform the face implied a charge of homosexuality.[136] When it was rumored in early August 1688 that Care was dead, his friend Settle reported that the 'Faction' was overjoyed. At about this time another threatening letter reached Larkin, this one excoriating Care for writing 'so Scurrilously of the C-of-E' and saying that Care was in danger of 'forfeiting his----for the lavishment of his Pen.'[137] As he approached death, Care was still in the eye of the press storm.

Conclusion

Care died at his house in Blackfriars on 8 August 1688 between 2 a.m. and 3 a.m. The cause of death, his doctors judged, was 'an ill Habit of Body, first Contracted by a Sedentary Life,' from which 'complicated Distempers' developed that 'ended in a Dropsy.'[1] This diagnosis probably means that Care died of kidney failure or perhaps liver disease caused by overwork and drink; Daniel Defoe, writing some fifteen years later, regretted Care's 'unhappy love of his bottle.'[2] Care probably had been ill for a while, but the first indication was the absence of his essay in the 31 July issue of *Publick Occurrences*. A week later that publication mentioned his illness, and his death was announced in the 14 August issue. His body lay at his house until 10 August, when it was buried in Saint Anne's Parish on property belonging to Blackfriars Church.[3] A paper entitled *An Elegy upon the most Ingennious Mr. Henry Care; who Departed this Life on the Eighth day of August 1688, and in the Two and Fortieth Year of his Age* was 'nailed to his coffin' and, as might be expected, advertised in *Publick*

Occurrences; it cost a penny.[4] Care's wealth is unknown (no will survives), but his property taxes (noted in ch. 2), income from his several tracts in print, and the bounty of £100 given to his widow indicate that he prospered. A London tradesman would have had to work more than six years to earn as much as the bounty alone.

Care remained controversial in the immediate aftermath of his demise. His enemies vilified him for assailing the Anglican Church and writing in defense of religious liberty. Slanderous rumors circulated: that Care's right hand had rotted off before he died, a judgment for writing against the Church of England; that his body had been in a house that caught fire on 8 August, a judgment on the place for harboring an enemy of the Church.[5] 'An Epitaph on Henry Care, 1688,' containing an especially nasty metaphor of a snake, demeaned Care for his apostasy:

> *A true Dissenter here does lye indeed;*
> *He ne'er with any, or himself agreed;*
> *But rather than want subject to his spite,*
> *Snake-like, he'd turn and his own Tail would bite.*
> *. . . . .*
> *Thus purg'd from good, and thus prepar'd by evil,*
> *He Fac'd to Rome, then march'd off to the Devil.*[6]

Another poem, entitled *Harry Care's Last Will and Testament*, portrayed Care on his deathbed, making his will 'in dying accents.' He mentions his wife, daughter, the 'Kinder Folks that propt my Pains' and the females among the 'Numerous Crowd' that survives, concluding:

> *I've nothing more to give to all the rest,*
> *But leave Ten Thousand curses on the Tests;*
> *And who do its Abolishing withstand,*
> *I leave upon them an Eternal Brand.*
> *And for the Penal Laws, they like as well,*

I'le write for their Repeal when I'm in Hell;

… … … … … … … … … … … … … … … … … …

I Hells black Tyrant will both sooth and praise,
And even in Sulphrous Styx Sedition raise.[7]

Such scurrility is a measure of his perceived influence and the
strong feelings that he and his writings aroused.

On the other hand, Care found admirers after death. His *Last
Will and Testament* was reprinted in 1690 in a collection of poems
by the 'Most Eminent Wits of the Nation.'[8] His friend Elkanah
Settle praised 'his Known worth and great Abilities,' which had
'deservedly rendered him one of the most Celebrated Writers of
this Age.' Settle went further, justifying Care's attitude toward the
Church of England in devastating remarks about that Church.
Insisting that Care had venerated 'all moderate Men of the
Church,' he declared that Care had only exposed the 'Diabolical
Persecuting Action of some that, usurping the Title of Church of
England, were a Reproach and Scandal, not only to that Church,
but to the Nation.' He quoted at length Care's words from
Draconica in which he vindicated himself, thereby spreading them
even further. Satisfied that the criticism of Care was undeserved
and that his paper was useful in vindicating the 'great Justice and
Equity' of toleration by a 'Law as firm as Magna Charta,' Settle
announced that he would continue its publication.[9] Apparently he
faced some competition, for rumor had it that Mr Vernon, secretary to the late duke of Monmouth, would take over the paper.[10] It
was an undeniably great tribute to the value placed on Care's paper
that it should be carried on. With George Larkin as publisher, it
lasted until 2 October, appearing on Tuesdays.

Settle relentlessly reiterated the same points that Care had made
about the Church. For example, he ridiculed the Church's promise
to help Dissenters only if the Tests were preserved, and he insisted
that the Church was opposed to toleration because of greed. In a
nice turn of phrase, Settle wrote that interest procured the Tests and
religion concealed the true cause.[11] The 'hot and angry' Anglican

clerics were hypocrites, he wrote; indeed they were 'greater Dissenters from the True Principles of that Church, than any of those People that are generally so called' (no. 29 [4 September]). Settle also dealt with the constitutional issue, asserting that the king possessed the power to dispense, especially in ecclesiastical matters, and taunting the Church with the accusation that 'in the past they granted the King prerogatives... far greater' than he was now using (no. 28 [28 August]). As the political situation deteriorated, Settle put the best face possible on events, saying that James's declaration barring Catholics from serving in Parliament had given the Church everything it could want and had confounded such noxious tracts as the *Anatomy of an Equivalent* and *Mijn Heer Fagel's Letter*. He also attacked William's *Declaration of Reasons* as the 'blackest of libels,' revealing its author's (Settle suspects John Wildman) 'wonderful Confidence of the English Credulity and Stupidity' (nos 32, 34 [25 September, 2 October]) and he declared that many seamen and watermen were daily offering their services, the contrary notwithstanding (no. 31 [18 September]). The issues of Settle's *Publick Occurrences* in the Bodleian Library contain much marginalia, indicating interest but also showing skepticism: at a sentence saying that Roman Catholics would not take over all positions appear the words 'its too soon yet,' and at the story of the seamen offering their services is the comment 'A lye' (nos 30, 31 [11, 18 September]). Settle's *Publick Occurrences* disappeared with the 2 October issue, without warning or later comment.

Settle, however, continued to try to exploit Care's reputation and put his former writings to work on behalf of the new political situation created by the arrival in England of the prince of Orange with an army and the flight of James II to France. Practicing his own political expediency, Settle then introduced a continuation of the *Weekly Pacquet of Advice from Rome* on 5 January 1688/89. This volume 6 lasted for two more issues, dated 1 February and 8 February. Aping Care, Settle said that his *Weekly Pacquet* would appear on Fridays, 'being the usual Day for it formerly.' He explained that the second number had been delayed out of deference to the order appearing in the 7–10 January issue of the *London Gazette*, which some people had used to prohibit it. But others, high placed in affairs, had read and approved it, so it had come out with a 'Virtual though not a Formal License.'[12]

Declaring in the first issue that the former *Pacquet*s had been 'deservedly well Esteemed of, for their Serviceableness to the Protestant Interest,' Settle explained that they were needed now more than ever; Roman Catholicism was 'worse than thought.' Disparaging himself with the remark that the present author was inferior to the former, 'whose Golden Pen rendered him deservedly famous,' Settle declared that he shared Care's zeal against popery to the point of suffering for it. His aim was to expose papists and Protestants who 'weakly, or wickedly joyn Hands with them' to divide the nation and oppose Prince William of Orange. His audience, like Care's, was persons who had neither the time, the money nor the learning to read the treatises of like purpose. Settle extended an olive branch to the Church of England, which he applauded for its part in inviting the prince to the rescue, and, in a reversal of Care's previous position, commended it for violating the 'Nonsensical and Slavish Doctrine of Non-Resistance.' But, he said, there was still a party in the Church that looked 'Rome-ward,' preferred papists to Presbyterians, and was part of the 'Tantivy Tribe,' which murmured against William of Orange. That party contributed as much to the 'Enslaving of the Nation by the Authority of their Gown and Cirsingles, as the Corrupt Judges by their Scarlet and Ermine.'[13] Settle devoted some pages to the cruelty of papists and their efforts to prevent a Protestant from succeeding to the throne, citing Philip of Spain; he thanked God that 'None of the Race of that Serpentine Viperous Brood [of Philip and Mary was] left to sit upon the English Throne.' Settle's grasp of historical detail was not as secure as Care's. He promised, however, that in addition to the *Weekly Pacquet*, a history of Louis XIV's persecution of the Huguenots would be ready 'in a few days.'[14] Nothing came of that, and volume 6 ended with the 8 February issue.

The revival of the *Weekly Pacquet* holds interest for another reason beyond documenting Care's reach. It took Curtis, Care's former publisher, only two days to fly into action; in an advertisement in the *Orange Gazette*, one of the short-lived newspapers that sprang up, he declared that he was the 'Onely Proprietor' of the previous five volumes of *Weekly Pacquet*s, announced that he intended 'within a short time' to bring out a sixth volume, and denounced George Larkin for his 'imprudent and unjust Intrusion' in publishing a 'Continuation of the said Advice.'[15] Although there was as yet no copyright law in English press law, Curtis was doing his best to claim copyright in the *Weekly Pacquet*. The promoters of the sixth volume sputtered a response in the second issue of the *Weekly Pacquet*, which appeared on 1 February. First, they lashed out at Curtis for advertising that only he had the first five volumes on offer, saying that his fifth volume was 'spurious, and Written by a Quack Doctor.' 'The true and genuine Fifth Volume,' they maintained, was 'only to be had of Mrs. Care, whose Husband was the Author and Beginner of the other four volumes.' Second, they disputed Curtis's claim to a right in the stock, arguing that since Care was 'the Author and Beginner of the other four volumes,' and since he had been 'Deceased near six months ago, the author and printer concerned in this [present venture], are as free to continue it, as the first Author was to begin it, without justly incurring any such scandalous Reflections as that paper impudently and unjustly calls upon them.'[16] The matter faded, overtaken by political events, and nothing more was heard of the *Weekly Pacquet* for the time being, but the story offers insight into the problems of the absence of copyright.

In the meantime, in the autumn of 1688 a tract printed for Thomas Cockerill appeared under a lengthy and revealing title: *The Last Legacy of Henry Care, Gent. Lately Deceased. Containing A Brief Sum of Christian Doctrine, By Way of Question and Answer Particularly relating to Several of the most Important Points controverted between Us, and the Romanists.*[17] No author is indicated, but judging from the title and the stated purpose, audience, language and message, I believe that Care himself put together these pages using the popular dialogue mode and that someone else, perhaps Elkanah Settle, published them after his death.[18] The authorship, however, is immaterial to the point that Henry Care's *Last Legacy* was a reaffirmation of his commitment to Protestant Christianity and an emphatic rejection of Catholic dogma and practices. The purpose and audience were quintessential Care: 'These plain Papers,' addressed to the 'meaner sort of People,' who had neither the time, the money nor the 'capacities' to read more 'Sublime and Scholastical Disputes,' aimed to 'strengthen weak Souls' so that they would not be 'shaken from their Holy Faith.'[19] The author identified his sources as 'chiefly' the Bible and the 'testimonies of the Ancients' and made it clear that the authority of the Scriptures did not depend on the authority of the Church.[20] Whoever wrote this dialogue was deeply familiar with the history of Christianity, both Roman and Protestant. As the title page promised, the 'most Important Points controverted between Us, and the Romanists' were canvassed, including among many other points, prayers for the dead, transubstantiation and the question whether St Peter had ever been bishop of Rome, all to the end of showing the 'Usurpation and Corruptions of the Church of Rome.' Protestants had not brought in a new religion or erected a new Church; rather, they had restored the 'true Ancient Religion of Christ.' The answer to the question 'Where was your Religion before Luther?' was simple: it was 'in Christ and the apostles' and in 'all those that held the true, Ancient Catholic Doctrine.'[21] In short, these seventy-nine pages were bent on persuading the reader to hold fast to the 'Reformed Religion' and on presenting that message as Care's 'last legacy.' No comment on this tract has survived, but when it appeared in the autumn of 1688 it must have been seen as a further blow to James II's cause, written by or on behalf of his major pro-pagandist. No mention was made of the principle of religious liberty nor of any form of toleration.

Care's legacy extended into the eighteenth and nineteenth centuries. Daniel Defoe wrote appreciatively of Care, freely admitting, as was charged against him, that his *Review* was a 'Mimic' of Care's *Weekly Pacquet of Advice from Rome*. Defoe declared that in Care's 'Design, and the length of his happy performance' there was 'such a spirit, such learning, such strength of reason, and such a sublime fancy' that he could not 'esteem himself worthy to carry his books after him.' Continuing this paean of high praise, Defoe announced that he would 'always value [his] Undertaking so much the more as it resembles [Care's] and wishes, for the sake of the reader as well as himself, he could near him in the performance.'[22] Implying that he knew Care personally, Defoe acknowledged his 'imperfections' and regretted that the 'fury of the Times,' poverty, and drink had 'reduced him too low for a man of his capacity.' Defending Care against his detractors, he declared that if they 'think the work mean and the performance dull (which the present scarcity and value of these Collections plainly contradict), it remains for these gentle-men to tell us where the meannesses are.' It is a worthy legacy that 'Pacquetier' and 'Courantier' should have served as the avowed model for Defoe's *Review* and remarkable that the connection has not been noticed before.

The *Weekly Pacquet* continued to attract interest for another reason. Sometime after 1728 an unknown person, perhaps a Mr Alderman Bertham, who gave the sheets to Dr Zachary Grey, drafted an essay entitled 'Mahometism and Popery compared: In Several Articles of importance By the Late Ingenious, Mr. Henry Care, Author of The Weekly Pacquet of Advice from Rome. To which is prefix'd A short Account of Mahomet's Life.' The basic text is essays on Islam drawn from volume 3 of Care's *Weekly Pacquet*, numbers 73 and 74. The texts are heavily edited, with passages rearranged, sentences omitted and so on, and copious references added, the latest dated 1728. That a person interested in the subject of Islam should have turned to Care's essays written fifty years ear-lier speaks to Care's ongoing reputation for learning and accuracy.

Care's *Weekly Pacquet* and *Popish Courant* helped to embed a vein of Catholic prejudice still more deeply in England's national consciousness. In 1735 and 1736 there appeared a two-volume adaptation of the *Weekly Pacquet* by 'several gents' entitled *The History of Popery*. Introducing their *History* with an essay brimming over with anti-Catholic sentiment drawn directly from Care's introduction to volume 2 of the *Weekly Pacquet*, these 'gents' praised the *Weekly Pacquet* as 'Rational and Historical, Plain and Scriptural,' and applauded it for furnishing the 'uneducated and stupid' with weapons against Catholic sophistry. These men confessed that they had changed some things respecting the style and content to make the volumes appealing to their present audience; otherwise, they said, they had followed Care closely, even to publishing sheets in weekly installments to bring the message to the lower classes. It is a fine tribute to Care's *Weekly Pacquet* that of all the histories of popery that might have served as a guide and model, it was the one these eighteenth-century gents chose.

For the next 100 years interest in Henry Care faded from the record. In 1839 some of his writings – the *Weekly Pacquet*, *Publick Occurrences*, *Poor Robins Intelligence*, as well as *Poor Robin's publick and private Occurrences and Remarks* – were included in C.H.Timperley's *Dictionary*.[23] Twenty years later, in 1851, an anonymous contributor to *Notes and Queries* showed that *A Modest Enquiry* was still being read. The correspondent wanted to discover the author of this excellent tract. He recommended *A Modest Enquiry* as 'logical, clear and satisfactory,' full of 'much theological learning,' and altogether convincing in its argument that St Peter was never in Rome. Coming right to the point and showing his anti-Catholic prejudice, he declared that all other Catholic claims were 'founded alone upon this fact, and must stand or fall with it.'[24] He went on to suggest that *A Modest Enquiry* would be 'well worth reprinting in a cheap and popular form.' Nothing came of his suggestion, and no answer to his query appeared in *Notes and Queries*, but his interest shows that Care's antipopery writing still retained the power to impress a reader after 165 years or so.

Care's life and writing attracted the attention of only a few historians. Except for the Whig-inclined Laurence Echard, eighteenth-century historians ignored Care. Echard mentioned Care's trial and excoriated him and other Nonconformists for shifting to James II's side, blaming them, especially Care, for weakening the Church of England 'to the great Benefit of the Papists' and thereby furthering James's aim to divide Anglicans and Dissenters.[25] Save for Lord Macaulay, nineteenth-century historians also overlooked Care. Macaulay, however, included him among Dissenters who had supported James II and dismissed the lot as 'a few busy men whose judgment was defective or were biassed by interest.' He dismissed Care as a particularly egregious turncoat who had been 'as loud in adulation [of James II] as he had formerly been in calumny and insult.'[26] Given this low level of interest in Care, it comes as a surprise that he was mentioned in the *Dictionary of National Biography*, published in 1886. The brief entry was written by Thompson Cooper, who left no doubt of his disapproval of the subject. Kitchin's admiring comments noted in the introduction to this book, written at the beginning of the twentieth century, were unprecedented and still stand almost alone.

How should Henry Care be judged at the end of the twentieth century, now that different kinds of historiographical interests and questions have brought him out of oblivion? How do Restoration print culture, law, religion and ideology look from a Care perspective? Care, although not at the first rank of importance, was a man whose contributions and influence were of considerable significance. First, he was a remarkable polemicist, journalist and writer whose personality, character and experiences brought fresh insights into Restoration print culture. Care began life without social standing, formal education, money or connections. Highly intelligent, witty, widely read, inclined to things of the mind, learned in history, law and religion, a quick study, possessed of a 'Golden Pen' and sincerely religious, Care was also ambitious, impatient, needy, dirty-minded, vengeful, and guilty of lying, plagiarizing and libeling his enemies. These characteristics helped him to get a start, win notice and develop a writing career. Until 1678 Care wrote, while employed by a lawyer or lawyers, out of ambition, poverty and love of writing, adapting his subject matter to the market and choosing nonpolitical topics. The twists and turns he took illuminate what such a person might do to win notice and establish a toehold as a published author. The subjects he chose – women, letter writing, the French court, religion, health, jokes – offer an index to what was thought marketable and, therefore, profitable. From early in his career he included common folk in his audience. Studying Care and his early writings helps to penetrate the anonymity of lower-middle-class life in London from the point of view of an aspiring author.

Care was an expert at exploiting the journalistic opportunities in events: at two times in his life, during the Exclusion Crisis and when he was employed by James II, he made a living by writing. He was a polemicist but also the author of books on many topics, including religious esoterica, the 'honest merchant,' and orthography and arithmetic for the untutored, the last named enjoying two reissues, a new edition in 1699 and its reprint in 1971. Care targeted the nonelite, thereby enlarging the public political arena. He gave the individual an opportunity for quasi-political participation in affairs. Although not unique as a 'professional writer,' Care was rare for his time, inviting comparison to Nedham, Behn and Defoe.

Care stands out among propagandists in utilizing the polemical possibilities in popular history. Author of a history that was rare in its audience (the common man) and its format (weekly install-ments), Care was the most important popular historian in early modern England. He used his history of religion to instruct a mar-ginally literate audience and also as a cover for criticizing the government, the bench and the Church. A measure of the ongo-ing appeal of his *Weekly Pacquet* is that it served as a model in 1736 for a similar history and that it was translated into German in 1766 and 1769.

Care's pen enabled him to make a name for himself, achieve financial reward, improve his social standing and accomplish what he wanted most of all – acceptance by press people and men engaged with the major issues of the time. Throughout his life he tried to associate with persons of greater note than himself: the 'court wits,' Robert Loveday, William Kiffin, Henry Coley, radical publishers and printers, Whigs in Parliament, Elkanah Settle and William Penn. He sought upward mobility by dedicating his pamphlets to the queen of England and the duke of Monmouth and by giving himself the title 'Gent.' It must have delighted him when others applied that title to him. He no doubt also took satisfaction in being mentioned by name in parliamentary debate and in his tract *Draconica*'s being translated into German and Dutch in 1688. In some respects his temperament and attitude were like those of his archrival, Sir Roger L'Estrange. 'Roger' and 'Harry' make a fascinating pair, both revealing so much about the print world in which they played such a prominent part.

Care took a leadership role in making the press a force of unsurpassed importance in the two most important political and religious battles of his time, Exclusion and James II's campaign to win support for religious toleration. The activities of the press men and women changed the character of these two events, turning both into crises. First, Care's voice was before the public more than anyone else's, for the opposition from late 1678 to mid-1683, when he was known as the 'Secretarius' of the Whigs in the press, and on behalf of James II's court from sometime in 1687 to mid-1688. He was well aware of the potency of the printed word: he wrote of the power printing exercised in the Protestant Reformation, describing printing as 'inferior to no Art in the World' and the press as 'An Invention that... yields to none of the Miracles of Life.'[27] Together with others, he exploited that great invention for political and religious ends.

The polemicists on both sides of the debate restyled political rhetoric during the Exclusion Crisis, using such devices as dialogue, humor, invective and *ad hominen* attack, and addressing primarily a lower- to middle-class audience. He and his Royalist sparring partners should be credited with preserving colloquialisms that otherwise might be lost and with introducing into this discourse the code words *Whig* and *Tory* and making them part of long-term political discourse. Printed matter, especially the weekly serials – Care's *Weekly Pacquet* and *Popish Courant* from 1678 to mid-1683 and the Royalists' *Observator, Heraclitus Ridens* and *Loyal Protestant* from 1681 to mid-1682 – targeted the nonelite and poured into the minds of common readers, as well as those farther up the social scale, the major ideas and arguments on both sides. These serials drove the controversies in the press, thereby influencing the attitudes and policies of the court, the Church and the bench, and pushing all three into harsh and oppressive ways. The monarchy's reaction to blistering press criticism, in which Care was a leader, was twofold: to adopt a new policy of using the press that it despised and to intensify a policy of repression in an effort to control printed matter. That the press wielded such power, forcing the establishment to rethink how its authority was mediated, is noteworthy. The press was already acting as the fourth estate.

Second, a 'Care perspective' brings into somewhat different focus Restoration legal history and the politics related to law. Care and his press friends were harassed, brought to trial, found guilty of violating print laws and punished. Yet, following his trial Care escaped severe penalties, a sign of the government's reluctance to treat him harshly in 1680 because of the popularity of his writings and another gauge of the power of the press. Dealing with Care and the issues associated with him induced the government to recognize that to some degree public consent was necessary if it was to realize its goals. On the other hand, the authorities' treatment of the press and print people inspired the fear that law, legal processes and Parliament were being sacrificed by judges and law courts. The sense of a crisis of authority led to the attempt to impeach Scroggs, the Lord Chief Justice of the Court of King's Bench. Scroggs's handling of press people and his role in press trials figured directly in four of the eight articles of impeachment and indirectly in two others. In the history of English print culture the press's role in the attempted impeachment was a landmark event. More broadly, the sense of a crisis of authority, often expressed in parliamentary debate, was central to the effort to bring down government ministers and legal officers. The anxiety over the displacement of law and Parliament was an important component in the Exclusion Crisis; recognition of its role deepens our understanding of that complicated event.

Third, Care's religious views and experiences, although offering the narrow perspective of one man, still illuminate Restoration religion. He expressed anti-Catholicism more persistently and virulently than anyone else from 1678 through mid-1683, promoting a hysteria that he deliberately used as a smoke screen for attacking the establishment. Almost equally bitter was Care's anticlericalism, which he directed at High Churchmen, who dominated the Church of England in the early 1680s. He and Penn were notable in painting these Church leaders as intolerant, vengeful, mean-spirited, inflexible in their distaste for Dissenters and uncompromising in harassing Nonconformists. The Church of England, however, was no more monolithic than was the Dissenting community: a group of moderates, the Latitudinarians, inclined toward a policy of comprehension that would soften the discipline so that Nonconformists might remain comfortably within the church. Care was at pains during the Exclusion Crisis to win these men over to a policy of comprehension and later to draw them over to James II's side in support of the king's policy of toleration and to persuade them of the merits of liberty of religion. Care's attitudes were not rigorously consistent. He expressed a Presbyterian view when he argued for a policy of comprehension. He sounded like an Independent when he promoted religious liberty for Nonconformists outside the Church of England. But this 'Lover of true Protestants' did not himself want to leave the Anglican Church; he wanted it to alter and to practice 'toleration' so that he could remain. The relationship between the Anglican Church and Dissent was a complex one that Care's experiences and response illuminate.

Fourth, Care was an intellectual – Kitchin called him the 'brain' of the opposition in the press[28] – as well as a propagandist, and he deserves recognition for the ideas he advanced. Of surpassing importance are Care's radical view of religious liberty as a 'Birthright of Mankind' and his idea of the separation of church and

State, concepts he put forward in his *Publick Occurrences* and in many tracts written in 1687–88. Until Richard Ashcraft noted Care's response to *A Letter Writ by Mijn Heer Fagel*, no historian had said anything in print about his views on religious liberty and the separation of Church and State. Care's ideas, like those of William Penn and John Locke, which they profoundly resemble, were ahead of their time.[29] That fact should not, however, diminish his role in articulating them and in putting them in print before John Locke. Indeed, Care's fame should be magnified. Unfortunately for his reputation, however, his writings about these matters were lost in the collapse of James II's government and in the triumph of the Church of England. The writings of a loser were of no interest and were swept aside in England. Even more regrettably, they did not travel to the American colonies, where they would have supported Roger Williams and surely would have been welcomed otherwise. One may be confident that had they turned up in the colonies, the world would have heard of Henry Care before now.

Just as important as his views on religious liberty was Care's *English Liberties*. This book, in one version or another, was reprinted more often than any of his other writings in both England and the colonies – eight times in England – to serve various purposes.[30] The reprints in 1691 and 1692, one scholar has argued, were an attempt to 'provide the type of theoretical justification for the new regime that was sought by the publication of Locke's *Two Treatises of Government*.'[31] In effect, *English Liberties* complemented Locke's work by providing constitutional documents, English precedents, and compelling language on the rights and liberties of Englishmen and thus might be seen as more useful than Locke's highly theoretical essay. The 1692 announcement underlined that *English Liberties* contained the 'terms of Liberty of Conscience confirmed by Act of Parliament in the second year of King William and Queen Mary.'[32]

Further, in 1700 Care's old friend Benjamin Harris brought out a new version of *English Liberties* in which the laws against

Protestants were removed and two sections added, one on justices of the peace, the other on the duties of the coroner and the constable. These 'Useful Additions' were compiled by a 'Well-Wisher to his Country,' who was identified in the 1719 edition as William Nelson (b. 1653), of the Middle Temple. In the 'Epistle Dedicatory,' directed to the 'Honourable House of Commons,' Harris made clear that the book continued to have a political purpose: to condemn past indignities and punishments suffered by critics of the government, to make available in a small book (large volumes of laws were readily accessible but less useful, he explained) the 'Laws, Rights and Priviledges' that every English 'Man and Woman' is heir to at birth and to praise the present government. A fourth and fifth edition appeared in 1719 and 1721, again edited by Nelson. It is an ironic compliment to Care, who had no formal legal training, that a man from the Middle Temple who was formally trained in the law should have been responsible for the 1700, 1719 and 1721 editions. Successive generations clearly found *English Liberties* useful as a handbook that made Magna Charta and other documents readily available and as a 'help to justices as well as a guide to constables.' It was recommended to all 'true lovers of the liberty and welfare of their native country.'[33] In 1766 Edward and Charles Dilly, well-regarded London publishers, brought out a new edition entitled *British Liberties; or, The Freeborn Subject's Inheritance, Containing the Laws that Form the Basis of those Liberties with Observations thereon.* In an introduction emphasizing the security that the fundamental laws of the British constitution afforded the rights and liberties of the people, the editors credited Care with the 'design, method, and much of that part of the work which relates to positive law' and linked his essay with the work of Coke, Locke and Sidney.[34] Care was flying in very elevated circles.

English Liberties was in several libraries in England in the eighteenth century, testament to its ongoing importance. Lord Anglesey's collection of 'all remarkable [tracts] relating to Government' contained a copy.[35] The library at Sion College received a copy in 1711 from Elinor James, widow of the printer Thomas James.[36] *English*

Liberties was given to Brasenose College, Oxford, in 1770 as part of the collection of Francis Yarborough, a principal from 1745 to 1770, and a fellow earlier in the century.[37] John Evelyn included it in his collection of books, as we saw in another connection.[38] The book was also in the library of John Edward Molesworth (1790–1877), vicar of Rochdale, the great-grandson of Robert, the first Viscount Molesworth.[39] Given its demonstrated popularity, *English Liberties* was surely in many more early libraries than can be documented; at that time libraries did not record the date when they acquired books. Today every major library in the British Isles and the United States holds at least one copy of *English Liberties.*

English Liberties had a much longer and more significant reach in the American colonies than in England. Along with many other English and Scottish works from Care's era and beyond studied especially by Caroline Robbins in her *Eighteenth-Century English Commonwealthman*,[40] it played an important role in spreading concepts about English law, history, government, liberties and especially juries. Devotion to the principle of trial by jury, which took hold among colonists and has been called the 'genuinely crucial right,' central to the preservation of other rights and liberties,[41] was advanced by Care's book. The essential message of *English Liberties* was available throughout the colonial era. William Penn silently lifted a sizable portion of *English Liberties*, pages 2–40, into his *Excellent Privilege of Liberty and Property Being The Birth-Right Of the Free-born Subjects of England*, which was printed in Philadelphia in 1687.[42] *English Liberties* was reprinted in the colonies by James Franklin in Boston in 1721 and by John Carter in Providence, Rhode Island, in 1774. It was not a question of lack of availability – English editions were available – but a question of interest and the promise of sales that moved colonial printers to bring out their own editions of Care's book. Its inclusion in private and public colonial libraries is evidence of the book's popularity.[43] For example, the Burlington, New Jersey Library Company held a copy, as did a private subject, Daniel Dulany, a well-to-do, well-read, well-educated Marylander.[44] The Library Company of

Philadelphia, founded in 1731 by Benjamin Franklin, acquired the 1719 edition of *English Liberties* in 1764 and another edition by 1770. Franklin also placed the book in his private collection, and it was given as part of that collection to the Library of Congress, where the copy remains. Other copies are known to have been in Philadelphia in the colonial period.[45] Thomas Jefferson added two copies of *English Liberties* to his library and arranged that it be included in the library of the University of Virginia.[46] The book was advertised in New York, Williamsburg and Philadelphia, in the latter by Benjamin Franklin.[47]

Care's vocabulary and ideas appeared in the writings of the founding thinkers of the United States of America – Samuel Adams, John Adams, John Dickinson and Alexander Hamilton. In their speeches and writings appears exactly the same language that Henry Care used in *English Liberties* when he praised the 'two Grand Pillars of the British Constitution,' identifying those pillars as Parliament and trial by jury.[48] Care had lifted these words from a parliamentary debate and preserved them for future use. John Adams responded to the rhetoric in an expansive way, writing, 'In these two powers [Parliament and juries] consist wholly the liberty and security of the people. They have no other fortification against wanton, cruel power;... no other defence against fines, imprisonments, whipping-posts, gibbets, bastinadoes and racks.'[49] As colonists did in other areas, they took English concepts, the lineage they had inherited, and expanded them.[50] For example, Americans started with Care's statement that the 'two Grand Pillars' of an Englishman's birthright shone 'most conspicuously in Parliament and juries' and reasoned from it that since the Constitution was 'founded in the Common Rights of Mankind,' and since the 'Rights of Nature' were 'happily interwoven' in its 'ancient fabrick,' the right to parliament and juries was 'properly the birthright of free men everywhere.'[51] One may note that all of the claims to rights made since the eighteenth century include the basic provisions of trial by jury and due process of law, which Care and others in Stuart England tried to protect.

Throughout the eighteenth century, colonists found in Care's *English Liberties* support for their views about the Saxons, Magna Charta as a reaffirmation of old laws guaranteeing the rights of all freemen and ways to protect themselves against oppression.[52] Indeed, one scholar suggested some thirty years ago that *English Liberties* 'had more to do with preparing the minds of American colonists for the American Revolution than the larger but less accessible works of Coke, Sidney and Locke.'[53] Recently, J.C.D. Clark came independently to that point in his revisionist study of the 'language of liberty' in the Anglo-American world. Arguing that the Commonwealthmen played a less important role than previously thought in the transmission of ideas to the colonies, he pointed (in a footnote) to other English works, among them Care's *English Liberties*, that 'clearly did engage closely with colonial concerns.'[54] The point might well be expanded, for Care's *English Liberties* deserves more than a footnote.

Finally, how should one respond to the fact that Care has been reviled as a turncoat and to the charge that he was driven by money and switched his religion for mercenary reasons alone? Care was as much a victim of the Stuarts' harsh policies as a traitor to the Whig cause in 1683. He had held out longer than any other opposition writer before he finally gave in. Care was not alone then in caving in to the repressive policies of the court. Nor was he alone in 1687, when more Dissenters than used to be thought went over to James's side in hopes of religious toleration. The difference in Care's case is that his name was so visibly and closely identified with hysterical antipopery. It is arguable that he was as much an opportunist working on behalf of the Dissenting community as he was a turncoat. Contrary to received opinion, he did not convert to Catholicism, as did some others who joined the camp of James II. He championed liberty of religion for Catholics, but he continued, rather astonishingly, to undermine the foundations of Catholicism by publishing a tract that presented many arguments to show that St Peter had never been in Rome. Moreover, there was consistency in his attitude toward the

Anglican Church and toward Dissent, and a deepening and broadening in his view of religious liberty, so he cannot be said to have been a turncoat in those critically important respects. Changes in the views of much greater minds than his, for example, Locke's, are readily accepted. Care's changes should not occasion so much venom on the part of historians. Personal experience and intellectual maturity may well have led to a genuine change in some of his ideas in 1687.

Care's name and writing career, however, are not unblemished. It is not for giving in to Charles II's government or switching to James II that he should be censured. Rather, he should be censured for manipulating the hysteria of the Popish Plot, fanning that hysteria in the Exclusion Crisis, and using it as a cover to advance political ends and win financial profit. In his own way, that is, by using his pen, Care behaved like Shaftesbury in cynically exploiting the fear the Popish Plot engendered.[55] There can be no doubt that Care's *Weekly Pacquet*, appearing week after week in London and the counties, contributed significantly to an anti-Catholic prejudice in the national consciousness, a residue of which remains. His writings against Catholics brought him approving notice in eighteenth- and nineteenth-century England, whereas his views on liberty of religion were forgotten.

The second consideration that properly blackens his name is that his *Weekly Pacquet* and many other writings contributed substantially to polarizing Protestants, and creating deep and abiding hostility between Dissenters and Anglicans. As Bishop Gilbert Burnet remarked in 1689, the divisions between the two groups arose not so much from doctrinal differences (which he regarded as 'inconsiderable') but from 'the secret dislike that we bear to one another.'[56] Care had a lot to do with generating that dislike.

Henry Care has been pushed to the margins of history by his enemies, who felt threatened by his sharp pen; by later historians, who with one exception (Kitchin) accepted uncritically the judgment of his contemporary detractors; and by the power of the 'Whig' view of history, which inclined to ignore or slight persons on the losing side of events. A different perspective emerges, however, when one studies Care and the contributions he made objectively and carefully: each one deserves recognition. He was a translator, a composer of the largest collection of model letters for women to that date, the most important popular historian of his era, a polemicist who was at the center of press warfare in 1679–83 and again in 1687–88 and who, with others, restyled public political discourse. Beyond these considerable achievements, Care was a compiler of legal handbooks, a framer of an advanced theory of religious liberty who made the same points as John Locke and put them into print before Locke did, and a promoter of a 'jury ideology,' which extolled the virtues of trial by jury, parliamentary government and the rule of law in ways that influenced thinking in the American colonies that some scholars now believe was paramount. These accomplishments go beyond those commonly expected of a polemicist and journalist; they show Care to have been a man of ideas who contributed to intellectual discourse in both England and the colonies, as well as to print culture, law and religion. Taken together, they are a worthy legacy of the man whom friend and foe alike called 'the Ingenious Mr. Henry Care.'

Notes

Short titles are given for tracts and pamphlets in the notes. Full titles appear in the bibliography.

INTRODUCTION

1. House of Commons, *Journals of the House of Commons*, 56 vols (1803–20), 8: 425.
2. See Janet Todd, *The Secret Life of Aphra Behn* (New Brunswick, N.J.: Rutgers Univ. Press, 1997); and idem, ed., *Aphra Behn Studies* (Cambridge: Cambridge Univ. Press, 1996).
3. See major articles on Boyer by Graham C. Gibbs, most recently, 'Abel Boyer and Jonathan Swift: A "French dog" bites back,' *Proceedings of the Huguenot Society*, 27 (1999): 211–231. See also Rex A. Barrell, ed., *The Correspondence of Abel Boyer, Huguenot refugee, 1667–1729* (Lewiston, N.Y.: E. Mellen Press, 1992).
4. Daniel Defoe, 'A Supplemental Journal to the Advice from the Scandal Club; For the Month of September, 1704,' in *The Works of Daniel Defoe*, 20 vols (1840–41), Vol. VII, p.618. See Paula R. Backscheider, *Daniel Defoe: His Life* (Baltimore: Johns Hopkins Univ. Press, 1989).
5. Sir George Kitchin, *Sir Roger L'Estrange: A Contribution to the History of the Press in the Seventeenth Century* (London: Kegan Paul, Trench, Trubner & Co., 1913). See also Violet Jordain, ed., *Sir Roger L'Estrange. Selections from the* Observator *(1681–1687)*. The Augustan Reprint

Society. Publication n. 141. William Andrew Clark Memorial Library (Los Angeles, Ca.: Univ. of California Press, 1970). B.J. Rahn, ed., *Sir Roger L'Estrange Citt And Bumpkin (1680)*. The Augustan Reprint Society, no.117 (Berkeley and Los Angeles: Univ. of California Press for the William Andrew Clark Memoiral Library, 1965).

6. For example, J.R. Jones, 'The Green Ribbon Club,' Durham Univ. Journal, Vol. IL (1956), p.18, n. 9.

7. For example, F.C. Turner, *James II* (New York: Macmillan, 1948). Also, John Miller: *James II* [Yale edn, rev. edn] (New Haven, CT: Yale Univ. Press, 2000) and *idem, Popery and Politics in England, 1660–1688* (Cambridge: Cambridge Univ. Press, 1973), and John Callow, *The Making of King James II: the formative years of a fallen king* (Stroud, Gloucestershire: Sutton, 2000). For the Secretary of State, see J.P. Kenyon, *Robert Spencer, Earl of Sunderland* (New York: Longmans, Green, 1958).

8. For example, Mark Goldie, 'John Locke's Circle and James II,' *The Historical Journal*, Vol. XXXV (1992), pp.557–586; *idem*, 'James II and the Dissenters' Revenge: the Commission of Enquiry of 1688,' *Historical Research. The Bulletin of the Institute of Historical Research*, 66, no.159 (February 1993), pp.53–88. Gordon Schochet, 'Between Lambeth and Leviathan: Samuel Parker on the Church of England and political order,' *Political Discourse in Early Modern Britain*, eds Nicholas Phillipson and Quentin Skinner (Cambridge: Cambridge Univ. Press, 1993), pp.189–208.

9. William Cobbett, *Cobbett's Complete Collection of State Trials and Proceedings For High Treason And Other Crimes And Misdemeanors from the Earliest Period To The Present Time*, ed. Thomas Howell *et al.* 33 vols (London, 180–26), 7: Col. 1118.

10. J.A.I. Champion, *The Pillars of Priestcraft Shaken, The Church of England and its enemies 1660–1730* (Cambridge: Cambridge Univ. Press, 1992). Also Bernard Capp, *Astrology and the Popular Press: English Almanacs 1500–1800* (Cambridge: Cambridge Univ. Press, 1981). Margaret Spufford, *Small Books and Pleasant Histories* (Cambridge: Cambridge Univ. Press, 1981).

11. John Miller, 'The Potential for "Absolutism" in Later Stuart England,' *History* 69 (1984): 187–207.

12. G.H. Jones, *Convergent Forces. Immediate Causes of the Revolution of 1688 in England* (Ames, Iowa: Iowa State Univ. Press, 1990), p.80.

13. Kitchin, *Sir Roger L'Estrange*, p.272.

CHAPTER 1: EARLY LIFE AND WRITINGS

1. See *An Elegy upon the most Ingenious [sic] Mr. Henry Care; who Departed this Life on the Eighth day of August 1688. and in the Two and Fortieth Year of his Age* (1688).

2. *Loyal Protestant*, no.161 (30 May 1682).

3. Anthony A. Wood, *Athenae Oxonienses: An Exact History Of All The Writers And Bishops Who Have Had Their Education In The University of Oxford. By Anthony Wood, M.A. of Merton College.* ed. Philip Bliss. 4 vols 1813–20. Reprint, Hildesheim: Georg Olms Verlagsbuchhandlung, 1969, 2:469.

4. [Johan Gibbon], *Flagellum mercurii Anti-Ducalis: Or, The Author of the disingenuous Touch of the Times Brought to the Whipping-Post, to prevent his coming to the Gallows* (n.p., n.d. [1679], 1)

5. Bodl., Ms. Rawlinson A 289, fol. 127.

6. Daniel Defoe, *Supplementary Journal to the Advice from the Scandal Club for the Month of September, 1704,* reprinted in *An English Garner,* ed. Edward Arber, 8 vols (1877–96) 7: 618.

7. Guildhall Library MS 3162, 'St. Sepulchre – names of communicants 1680–1682,' 1685. Care is listed as a communicant in Old Bailey Precinct in 1680 as an unmarried man (fol. 15r), as a man with a wife (unnamed) in 1681 (fol. 29r), and with a wife and one maidservant in 1682 (fol. 47v).

8. *Harry Care's Last Will and Testament* (1688). This two-page satire mentions a daughter. Unique copy at Chetham's Library, Manchester.

9. Guildhall Library, MS 4510/1: Bridget Care was buried in St Ann's Parish, Blackfriars on 22 October 1699.

10. Surviving records locate him in Sepulchre's Parish in 1678, 1680, 1681 and 1682, in the Great Old Bailey in 1679, 1681 and 1682, and in Blackfriars in 1687 and 1688 where he died.

11. John Stowe, *A Survey of London,* 2 vols, ed. Charles L. Kingsford (1908, Reprinted from 1603 text), Vol. II, pp.21–22, 33.

12. Roger North, *Examen: Or, An Enquiry Into The Credit and Veracity Of A Pretended Complete History;...* (1740), p.572.

13. K.H.D. Haley, *The First Earl of Shaftesbury* (Oxford, Clarendon Press, 1968), pp.410–411.

14. Yet, Care himself declared that he met Shaftesbury only once: *Weekly Pacquet of Advice...,* Vol.V, no.9, 20 October 1682, p.71.

15. Tim Harris, *London Crowds in the Reign of Charles II: Propaganda and*

Politics from the Restoration until the Exclusion Crisis (Cambridge, Cambridge Univ. Press, 1987), pp.66–67. More generally, Gary De Krey, *A Fractured Society The Politics of London in the First Age of Party 1688–1715* (Oxford, Clarendon Press, 1985), Chaps 3 and 4.

16. Haley, *The First Earl of Shaftesbury*, p.411.

17. A visit to the church, still standing today, helps to vivify the scene where Care worshipped.

18. *A most Safe and Effectual CURE for the RICKETS, And means to Preserve Children from the same* (n.p., n.d. [1675]. The date is established from internal evidence).

19. *Essex's Excellency: Or The Gallantry of The Freeholders of that County.* Kishlansky, *Parliamentary Selection*, pp.183, 187.

20. See Kitchin, pp.300–302; L'Estrange and Thompson also had their correspondents on the scene. Care mentions that Thompson's 'correspondents' covered an event in Agmondesham: *Impartial Protestant Mercury*, no.78, 17–20 Jan. 1681/82.

21. *Anti-Roman Pacquet: or, Memoirs of Popes and Popery* 3, no.21 (26 November 1680): 162; Weekly Pacquet 4, no.2 (30 December 1681): 13.

22. Nathaniel Thompson, *The Loyal Protestant*, no.165, 8 June 1682. *Weekly Pacquet of Advice*, Vol. IV, no.26, 16 June 1682. Others burned in effigy were 'Curtis, Janeway, Baldwin, Smith and Vile,' all publishers and/or printers or booksellers. No record of the incident survives in the Norfolk Record Office: letter to the author from Miss Jean M. Kennedy, County Archivist, 30 April 1993.

23. Henry Care, *The Darkness of Atheism Expelled by the Light of Nature,… With an Appendix touching the most proper Method of Preaching the Gospel among the Heathens.* (1683). In an unpublished manuscript Care referred to the 'simple Indians' who sold their freedom for Spanish toys. BL, Sloane Mss 2285, f. 142. In *Poor Robin's Intelligence*, 11 April 1676, Care mentioned Barbados, New England and Virginia. He also referred to 'America' in a poem dated April 17, 1676 commending *Clavis Astrologiae Elimata; Or A Key To the whole Art of Astrology New Fil'd and Polished* (n.p., n.d.). He reported news of the colonies in newspapers for which he wrote: *Impartial Protestant Mercury* and *True Protestant Mercury.*

24. In December 1683 young Cotton Matthew made the request of his bookseller, Richard Chiswell. See Carolyn Nelson, 'American readership of early British serials,' *Serials And Their Readers 1620–1914,*

eds Robin Myers and Michael Harris (Winchester: St Paul's Bibliographies. New Castle, Delaware: Oak Knoll Press, 1993), p.34.

25. A work by Jean Morin (1591–1659) became *The Darkness of Atheism Expelled* 'Englished by H.C.'

26. P.W. Thomas, *Sir John Berkenhead (1717–1679) A Royalist Career in Politics and Polemics* (Oxford: Clarendon Press, 1969), p.13.

27. *The Weekly Pacquet*, Vol. III, no.60 (29 July 1681): 477.

28. *Ibid.*, no.1, (24 December 1681): 'Preface.'

29. Basil Duke Henning, ed., *History of Parliament: The House of Commons, 1660–1690*, 3 vols. (London: Secker & Warburg for the History of Parliament Trust, 1983), I: 44–47.

30. Bodl., MS Rawlinson A. 289, ff. 127–128: Henry Care to 'Right Worshipfull,' undated [1684?].

31. *A Touch of the Times. or. Two Letters Casually Intercepted. The First. From the Author of a late Pamphlet Intituled Day-Fatality: To the supposed Author of the Weekly Packet of Advice from Rome. 1679. The Second. The Answer thereunto.* The first letter is signed Johan Gibbon and dated 15 Sept. 1679. The second letter is signed Hen. Care. and dated 17 Sept. 1679. The quote is from the first letter, p.1. Care's name is not in the surviving lists of attorneys, but legal scholars say that the lists are unreliable.

32. C.W. Brooks, *Pettyfoggers and Vipers of the Commonwealth The 'Lower Branch' of the Legal Profession in Early Modern England* (Cambridge: Cambridge Univ. Press, 1986), pp.18–20, 152, 162, and *passim*.

33. *Great News from the Old-Bayly* (1683). Wood, *Athenae Oxoniensis*, 2: 469.

34. *Practical Physick: Or Five Distinct Treatises Of the most Predominant Diseases Of these Times. In English, by H. Care, Student in Physick, and Astrology* (1676), To the Reader.

35. *The Weekly Pacquet*, Vol. 5, no.4 (8 September 1682): 32.

36. *Publick Occurrences*, no.18 (19 June 1688).

37. *The Weekly Pacquet*, 3, To the Reader (24 December 1681).

38. The three men were James Copin, a Public Notary and Proctor in the Ecclesiastical Court; John Mallose, an Attorney in the Court of Common Pleas, and John Hill, an Attorney in the Court of King's Bench: *The Courant* 3, no.70 [7 Oct. 1681], 560.

39. *English Liberties: Or, The Free-Born Subject's Inheritance...* (1682), 20.

40. Bodl., Rawl. C. 732, fol. 128. [1684?].

41. Care, *Darkness of Atheism*, Advertisement. Francis Kirkman, *The Thracian Wonder. A Comical History* (1661), last leaf also mentions

lending libraries. I thank Steven Zwicker, who discusses lending libraries in a forthcoming study, for the reference to Kirkman.

42. Lambeth Palace Library, Sion MS ARC I. 40.2 E29, 'Album Admissorum ad Studentum in Bibliotheca. MDCXXIX,' Student Admissions to the Library 1632–1693, fol. 52v.

43. William Reading, *The History of the Ancient and present State of Sion College nr. Cripplegate, London and of the London Clergy's library there* (1724), p.37.

44. Lambeth Palace Library, Sion Ms ARC E40.2E12, Catalogue of the Governors of Sion College, 1632–1740, ff. 7r–10r *passim*. Also, Lambeth Palace Library, Sion MS ARC I.40.2. E.6.4., Sion College Book of Benefactors 1629–1888

45. Robert Stephens, a.k.a. Robin Hog: *Courant*, no.37 [4 May 1683]: 296.

46. Kitchin, *Sir Roger L'Estrange*, 272.

47. *Observator* I, nos. 46 (24 August 1681) and 204 (13 Sept. 1682); *Great News from the Old-Bayly.*

48. *Heraclitus Ridens: Or, A Discourse between Jest and Earnest, where many a true Word is spoken in opposition to all Libellers against the Government*, no.80 (8 August 1682).

49. These physical characteristics may remind some readers of the eighteenth-century polemicist, John Wilkes.

50. Elkanah Settle, *Public Occurrences*, no.26 (14 August 1688).

51. *The Female Secretary*, Preface. The picture which I identify as Care in Roger L'Estrange's tract, *The Committee; Or Popery in Masquerade* (1680), is a representation, not a likeness. Interestingly, in *The Observator* (no.57, 28 Sept. 1681) L'Estrange refers to Care's picture at the bottom of his last pacquet, but no such picture appears.

52. Defoe remarked that Care's love of the bottle was a weakness (Defoe, *Supplementary Journal*, 618.

53. *The Female Secretary*, p.145.

54. B.L., Sloane MS 2285, fol. 163.

55. B.L., Sloane MS 2285, fols. 141–141v

56. *Poor Robin's Intelligence*, 13 June 1677.

57. The official title was: *The Act for preventing the frequent Abuses in printing seditious, treasonable and unlicensed Bookes and Pamphets and for regulating of Printing and Printing Presses* in *Statutes of the Realm*, ed. A. Luders et al., 11 vols. [1810–28], 5:428–33.

58. Cyprian Blagden, *The Stationers' Company: A History, 1403–1959* (Stanford: Stanford Univ. Press, 1960).

59. Kitchin, *Sir Roger L'Estrange*, 128.

60. Although much resented and bitterly criticized, this power was not officially condemned until 1766 (James Sutherland, *The Restoration Newspaper and Its Development* (Cambridge: Cambridge University Press, 1986): 3).

61. Kitchen considers this pamphlet to be the 'most informative and perhaps forceful document of the seventeenth-century press which we possess.' *Sir Roger L'Estrange*, 130.

62. The king's grant creating the office is conveniently found in the preface to Henry Plomer, *Dictionary of the Booksellers and Printers Who Were at Work in England, Scotland & Ireland from 1641 to 1667* reprint, (Oxford: Oxford Univ. Press for the Bibliographical Society, 1968).

63. Edward Arber, *Term Catalogues, 1668–1709*, 3 vols (London: privately printed, 1903), l: xii; Kitchin, *Sir Roger L'Estrange*, 171–72; N.H. Keeble, *The Literary Culture of Nonconformity in Later Seventeenth-Century England* (Athens: Univ. of Georgia Press, 1987), 105–08.

64. See, Louis B. Wright, *Middle Class Culture in Elizabethan England* (Chapel Hill, N.C.: Univ. of North Carolina Press, 1935), Chap. 13, 'The Popular Controversy over Women.' Katherine Usher Henderson, and Barbara F. McManus, eds, *Half Humankind. Contexts and Texts of the Controversy about Women in England, 1540–1640* (Urbana and Chicago: Univ. of Illinois Press, 1985); Suzanne W. Hull, *Chaste Silent & Obedient. English Books For Women 1475–1640* (San Marino: Huntington Library, 1982), pp. 106–26; For the Restoration era, see Robert H. Michel, 'English Attitudes towards Women, 1640–1700,' *Canadian Journal of History* Vol. XIII (1978), pp. 35–60, and Jerome Nadelhaft, 'The Englishwoman's Sexual Civil War: Feminist Attitudes Towards Men, Women, and Marriage 1650–1740,' *Journal of the History of Ideas* Vol. XLIII (1982), pp. 555–579. For the continent, see L. McDowell Richardson, *Forerunners of Feminism in French Literature of the Renaissance* (Johnson reprints, reprint of 1929 edn, 1973).

65. David Cressy, *Literacy and the Social Order Reading and writing in Tudor and Stuart England* (Cambridge: Cambridge Univ. Press, 1980), p. 147.

66. This calculation is based on Hilda Smith and Susan Cardinale, compilers, *Women and the Literature of the Seventeenth Century. An Annotated Bibliography based on Wing's Short-title Catalogue* (New York and London: Greenwood Press, 1990).

67. Henry Care, 'The Translator's Preface,' *Female Pre-eminence,...* (1670), A 3.

68. *Ibid.*, A 5.

69. *Ibid.*, A 2.

70. *History of Babylonish Cabal* (1682), Preface.

71. Care, *Female Pre-eminence*, 'The Epistle Dedicatory.' Agrippa had dedicated his book to Princess Margaret of Austria, who later had become the Empress.

72. Care, *Female Pre-eminence*, A4 verso.

73. See Katherine Gee Hornbeak, *The Complete Letter-Writer in English 1568–1800* (Smith College Studies in Modern Languages, Northampton, Mass.: 1934), Vol. XV, Nos. 3–4, p.2. Collections of letters and letter manuals in Latin, Italian and French were available to guide English epistolary efforts.

74. *Ibid.*, 1, 17.

75. Howell's *Letters* came out in installments in 1645, 1647, 1650 and 1655. The quotation is from the *DNB*. Annabel Patterson dissected the nature of the letters, arguing that the 1645 edition provides a version of Royalist history, shaped to avoid the wrath of the censor. *Censorship and Interpretation. The Conditions of Writing and Reading in Early Modern England* (Madison, Wisconsin: Univ. of Wisconsin Press, 1984), pp.210–218.

76. *Catalogue of The most vendible Books in England, Orderly and Alphabetically Digested, Under the Heads of Divinity, History, Physick and Chyrurgergy, Law, Arithmetick, Geometry, Astronomy...* (1657), Sig. T 4. See Louis B. Wright, 'Handbook Learning of the Renaissance Middle Class,' in *Studies in Philology* Vol. XXVIII (January 1931), no.1, pp.69–71 and n. 24.

77. Care, *The Female Secretary*, The Preface (unpaginated) and 137, 138.

78. Two contemporary comments on the state of female education are: [Edward Chamberlayne], *An Academy Or Colledge: Wherein Young Ladies and Gentlewomen May... be duly instructed in the true Protestant Religion, and in all Vertuous Qualities...* (1671) and Bathusa Makin, *An Essay to Revive the Antient Education of Gentlewomen, in Religion, Manners, Arts and Tongues* (1673).

79. Care, *The Female Secretary*, 72–73.

80. *Ibid.*, 136–146. Such instructions were rare: of the letter manuals printed between 1660–1670 only one, *The Academy of Complements*, includes a similar section.

81. Care, *Female Preeminence*, A 1.

82. See Kirkman, *The Thracian Wonder*, Preface: 'I intend to increase my

Store as I sell; And I hope you will by your frequent buying, encourage Your servant Francis Kirkman.'

83. Mark Goldie, 'The Revolution of 1689 and the Structure of Political Argument An Essay and an Annotated Bibliography of Pamphlets on the Allegiance Controversy,' *Bulletin of Research in the Humanities* (1980) 481.

84. Other books about the war recounted the battles. Only Sir William Temple's *Observations upon the United Provinces of the Netherlands* focused on politics and society.

85. Henry Care, *The Grandeur and Glory of France...* (1673), 72, 109, 112, 114, 115, 118.

86. A search by computer reveals that only six tracts printed between 1660 and 1700 identify the author as a 'gentleman,' or 'a gent', or 'a young gentleman.'

87. Allan Richard Botica, 'Audience, Playhouse and Play in Restoration Theatre, 1660–1710,' (Unpub. PhD. diss., Oxford Univ., 1985), p.45 supplies a list. Fourteen out of approximately 375 compilers of almanacs claimed the status of gentleman without legal warrant: see Bernard Capp, *Astrology and the Popular Press English Almanacs, 1500–1800* (Ithaca, N.Y., Cornell Univ. Press, 1979), p.293, and pp.294–340.

88. Francis Kirkman, *The Unlucky Citizen, Experimentally Described in the Various Misfortunes of an Unlucky Londoner* (1673), pp.181–82, quoted in Mihoko Suzuki, 'The Case of Mary Carleton: Representing the Female Subject, 1663–73,' *Tulsa Studies in Women's Literature* Vol. XII (1993), p.77.

89. *The Last Legacy of Henry Care, Gent. Lately Deceased...* (1688). Robert Watt, *Bibliotheca Britannic; or A General Index to British and Foreign Literature* 2 vols (1824).

90. Henry Care, *The Jewish Calendar Explained...*, title-page and 41. For subsequent quotations, 8, 12–13, 29–30.

91. *Dictionary of National Biography*, s.v. 'Kiffin, William.'

92. *Catalogue of The most vendible Books in England*; Clavell, *A Catalogue Of All The Books Printed in England*, e.g., 22–23, and nos 12, 15, 16, 18. Of the 3,550 books printed in England between 1666 and 1680, 135 dealt with physic. (see C.H. Timperley, *Dictionary of Printers and Printing, with the Progress of Literature...* (1839), 561). At least nine books on medicine were registered by the Stationers' Company in 1675 and 1676, the years when Care's medical tracts were printed.

93. A unique copy of this broadside is in the British Library at C 12. f. 9 (22).

94. Daniel Sennert (1572–1637) was noted for his practical treatment of maladies and his confutation of Aristotelian medicine. See *Nouvelle Biographie Generale*, ed. M. LeDr Hoefer (Paris, 1844).

95. Capp, *English Almanacs 1500–1800*, Biographical list: pp.295, 302, 307, 309, 311, 313, 334, 337 shows that eight out of approximately 375 compilers of almanacs used that label.

96. Derek Parker, *Familiar To All. William Lilly and Astrology in the Seventeenth Century* (London: Jonathan Cape, 1975) and Patrick Curry, *Prophecy and Power. Astrology in Early Modern England* (Princeton, N.J.: Princeton Univ. Press, 1989).

97. It was Coley whom Care had defended against a critic, using unguarded terms of disparagement. See above.

98. Sutherland, *Restoration Newspaper*, 86.

99. The entire run is available in the English newspaper file at the Bodleian Library.

100. *Dictionary of National Biography*, s.v. 'Winstanley, William.'

101. Rawlins, *Heraclitus Ridens*, no.64 (18 April 1682) and no.81 (15 August 1682).

102. Corporation of London Records Office, Misc. MSS 112.5

103. *Poor Robin's Intelligence*, 4 April 1676, 18 April 1677, 25 July 1677.

104. Rawlins, *Heraclitus Ridens*, no.64 (18 April 1682) The identification of Russell as prince of Whigland is confirmed by *Ibid.*, no.76 (11 July 1682), cited in Zook, *Radical Whigs and Conspiratorial Politics*, 57. Care's connection with Russell is also alluded to in *Great News from the Old-Bayley*.

105. Sutherland, *Restoration Newspaper*, 199–200, quoting Thompson, *Loyal Protestant*, no.178 (8 July 1682). Michael Treadwell, 'London Trade Publishers 1675–1750,' *The Library*, Sixth Series, Vol. IV, no.2 (1982), p.128. Plomer, *A Dictionary Of The Printers And Booksellers Who Were At Work In England... 1641–1667*, 96.

106. Henry Care, *The Plain Englishman's Historian* (1679), 'To the Reader.'

107. *Catalogus Librorum Theologicorum, Philologicorum, Mathematicorum, etc.*, ed. David Stockes *et al.* (1685). I thank Jackson Boswell for this reference.

108. Bathsua Makin, *An Essay To Revive the Antient Education Of Gentlewomen* (1673), 4.

109. Smith and Cardinale, *Women and the Literature of the Seventeenth Century*, xvii, 278, 292. See also *A Present for the Ladies: Being an*

Historical Account of Several Illustrious Persons of the Female Sex (1693) by Nahum Tate (said to have 'derived' from Care's translation), and William Walsh's *A Dialogue concerning Women, being a Defence of the Sex* (1691), which offered arguments similar to those of Agrippa.

CHAPTER 2: *THE WEEKLY PACQUET OF ADVICE FROM ROME*

1. Henry Care, *A Word in Season...* (1679).
2. The *Weekly Pacquet* on 2 July 1680, in the week of Care's trial.
3. J.P. Kenyon, *The Popish Plot* (London: William Heinemann, 1972), ch. 3 and p.79.
4. *Ibid.*, 97; Haley, *First Earl of Shaftesbury*, ch. 21, esp. 457.
5. David Ogg, *England in the Reign of Charles II*, 3rd edn, 2 vols (Oxford: Clarendon Press, 1962), 2:559–61.
6. Kenyon, *Popish Plot*, 42–43.
7. See Pocock, 'Wicked and Turbulent Though It Was.'
8. Steven C. A. Pincus, 'From Butterboxes to Wooden Shoes: The Shift in English Popular Sentiment from Anti-Dutch to Anti-French in the 1670s,' *Historical Journal* 38 (1995): 333–62.
9. Lois G. Schwoerer, *'No Standing Armies!': The Antiarmy Ideology in Seventeenth-Century England* (Baltimore: Johns Hopkins Univ. Press, 1974), 115–30.
10. De Krey, *Fractured Society*, 13 and n. 7.
11. Ogg, *England in the Reign of Charles II*, 2: 483–84.
12. Kitchin, *Sir Roger L'Estrange*, 167, 225 and n. 1.
13. This rare tract is reproduced in William Cobbett, *Cobbett's Parliamentary History of England: From The Norman Conquest, In 1066, to The Year 1803*, ed. T.C. Hansard, 36 vols (1806–20), 4: appendix pp.xxii–xxxiv; and in *Aungervyle Society Reprints*, 1st ser. (1881–82), 1–24. The reward was offered to no avail.
14. Sir Roger L'Estrange, *The Parallel, or An Account of the Growth of Knavery* (1678), 'To the Reader,' 2, 4, 5, 12.
15. Sir Roger L'Estrange, *The Reformed Catholique or The True Protestant* (1678), 2–5, 8–9, 13–15, 20, 26, 35.
16. Sir Roger L'Estrange, *Tyranny and Popery, Lording it over... King and People* (1678), 49, 77, 79, 91.
17. The date and the word 'Licensed' appear on the title page. The date is written on the tract in Bodl., Ashmole MS 1223.

18. *Journal of the House of Lords*, 13:629–30.

19. Kenyon, *Popish Plot*, 78.

20. The piece was signed 'H.C.,' and Wing, *Short-title Catalogue*, assigns it to Care. It was licensed on 30 October 1678.

21. Henry Care, *The Character of A Turbulent, Pragmatical Jesuit and Factious Romish Priest*, 4. Care liked the phrase 'Stars dart their influence' and used it again in *Weekly Pacquet* 2, 'The Preface To the Unbyas'd Protestant Readers' (11 July 1679): A 2.

22. Care, *Character of A Turbulent, Pragmatical Jesuit*, 6.

23. Kenyon, *Popish Plot*, 115–25, provides a detailed account.

24. The Jesuit priests were Thomas Whitbread, William Ireland, John Fenwick, Thomas Pickering and John Grove.

25. For the tracts see *A Compleat Catalogue Of All The Stitch'd Books and Single Sheets Printed since the First Discovery of The Popish Plot (September 1678) to January 1679–80* (1680). Two notable sermons are *A Sermon Preached by Joseph Bedle, Vicar of Great Bursted in Essex...*, on 5 November 1678, and Edward Stillingfleet's sermon of 27 November, which sold out by nightfall of the first day it appeared (Knights, *Politics and Opinion*, 183).

26. *Weekly Pacquet* 1, no. 1 (3 December 1678): 2. Each issue consisted of eight pages: six pages were devoted to a scholarly history, and two contained ribald comments on contemporary affairs.

27. From 3 December 1678 to 30 May 1679 each issue of the *Weekly Pacquet* carried the words 'Licensed' and 'Printed for LC' (Langley Curtis). The *Pacquet* did not appear in the Stationers' Company register until 1682, when each issue of volume 5 was registered. The licensing of the *Weekly Pacquet* later became an embarrassment to the court, and Care's defense used it at his trial in July 1680. Care's charge against L'Estrange appeared in the *True Protestant Mercury*, no. 154 (24–28 June 1682).

28. *Courant* 5, no. 2 (1 September 1682), 16.

29. Settle, *Weekly Pacquet* 6, no. 2 (1 February 1688/89): 16. Settle, a poet and a friend of Care's, revived the *Weekly Pacquet* at the time of the Glorious Revolution.

30. Care, *Plain Englishman's Historian*, 'To the Reader,' in Care, *Grandeur and Glory of France*, 119.

31. Champion, *Pillars of Priestcraft Shaken*, 39–40, 225–26.

32. *Weekly Pacquet* 1, 'To the Reader' (3 December 1678).

33. Daniel R. Woolf, 'Narrative Historical Writing in Restoration

England,' in *The Restoration Mind*, ed. W. Gerald Marshall (Newark: Univ. of Delaware Press, Associated Univ. Presses, 1997), 211. Wing's *Short-title Catalogue* lists approximately sixty-seven histories printed between 1660 and 1690.

34. Woolf, 'Narrative Historical Writing in Restoration England,' 221.

35. Harris, *London Crowds*, 107; for a list of contemporary newspapers, see 232–33.

36. Some writers have stated that Care dropped the *Popish Courant* in December 1682 (e.g., Kitchin, *Sir Roger L'Estrange*, 297 n. 2), but that is an error born of confusing Care's volume 5 with the volume 5 printed by Curtis.

37. For example, [Marchamont Nedham], *A Pacquet of Advices and Animadversions,…* (1676); *idem, A Second Pacquet of Advices and animadversions…* (1677); *idem, The Pacquet Boat of Advice…* (1678); and *A Weekly Packet from Germany* (1678).

38. *Weekly Pacquet* 1, 'To the Reader' (3 December 1678), A2 verso; 3, 'Preface' (24 December 1681).

39. *Ibid.* 1, no.1 (3 December 1678): 3. A penny was the usual cost of a single sheet. See Keeble, *Literary Culture of Nonconformity*, 133–34, for prices of Nonconformist texts.

40. *Weekly Pacquet* 1, no.1 (3 December 1678): 2–3.

41. Rare single unbound sheets of the *Weekly Pacquet* are in the Public Record Office (at PRO, SP 30/G) and at the Folger Shakespeare Library. In 1704 Daniel Defoe commented on the 'present scarcity and value' of the *Weekly Pacquet* ('The Prototype and Plan of the Review,' in *Works of Daniel Defoe*, 7: 618).

42. [Henry Care?], *Clodpate's Ghost: Or A Dialogue Between Justice Clodpate, and his [quondam] clerk Honest Tom Ticklefoot; Wherein Is Faithfully Related all the News from Purgatory, about Ireland, Langhorn, etc.* (25 August 1679), 12; also quoted in Knights, *Politics and Opinion*, 169.

43. Carolyn Nelson and Matthew Seccombe, eds *Periodical Publications, 1641–1700: A Survey with Illustrations*, Periodical Papers of the Bibliographical Society (London: Bibliographical Society, 1986), 15.

44. *Weekly Pacquet* 1, no.1 (3 December 1678): 3; see also *ibid.* 2, 'Preface' (11 July 1679).

45. Watt, 'Publisher, Pedlar, Pot-Poet.' The first and sometimes two or three subsequent issues of new newspapers were sent to 'all coffee houses in London' (Sutherland, *Restoration Newspaper*, 222; see also Knights, *Politics and Opinion*, 170–76).

46. *Weekly Pacquet* 1, no.1 (3 December 1678): 1.

47. *Ibid.*, no.2 (10 December 1678): 9; *Popish Courant* 1, no.4 (24 December 1678): 32. Care does not identify the competition. Changing the day of publication was not unusual; Benjamin Harris did the same thing and for the same reasons (*Domestick Intelligence*, no.4 [17 July 1679]).

48. See, e.g., *Weekly Pacquet* 1, no.16 (21 March 1678/79): 127; 2, no.47 (28 May 1680): 374; 4, 'Preface' (n.d.); 5, no.1 (25 August 1682): 1. Care made the same pitch to 'dear Protestant Countrymen' in his *History Of The Damnable Popish Plot...* (1680), 357.

49. *Weekly Pacquet* 1, nos 1 (3 December 1678): 2; 15 (14 March 1678/79): 117; and 26 (30 May 1679): 201; 2, 'Preface' (n.d.): A2.

50. *Ibid.* 5, no.1 (25 August 1682): 1; see also *ibid.*, 1, no.16, 21 March 1678/79, 127.

51. *Ibid.* 4, no.4 (20 January 1681/82): 38.

52. *Ibid.* 1, no.20 (18 April 1679): 153. See also *ibid.*, nos 8 (24 January 1678/79): 59 and 14 (7 March 1678/79): 106.

53. Cressy, *Literacy and the Social Order*, 72–73 and chs 3, 6, 7. Margaret Spufford insists that all statistics underestimate the ability to read (see 'First Steps in Literacy: The Reading and Writing Experiences of the Humblest Seventeenth-Century Autobiographers,' *Social History* 4 [1979]: 407–35. See also Keith Thomas, 'The Meaning of Literacy in Early Modern England,' in *The Written Word: Literacy in Transition*, ed. Gerd Baumann [Oxford: Oxford Univ. Press, 1986], 103; and Tessa Watt, *Cheap Print and Popular Piety, 1550–1640* [Cambridge: Cambridge Univ. Press, 1991], which focuses on earlier years).

54. *Weekly Pacquet* 1, 'The Introduction' (3 December 1678): 2–3; no.23 (9 May 1679): 177; 2, 'Preface' (n.d.): A 2.

55. Roger Finlay, *Population and Metropolis: The Demography of London, 1580–1650* (Cambridge: Cambridge Univ. Press, 1981), 51, 63, 66–68.

56. S.R. Smith, 'The Social and Geographical Origins of the London Apprentices, 1630–60,' *Guildhall Miscellany* 4, no.4 (1973): 195–206. See also Harris, *London Crowds*, 17–18.

57. E.A. Wrigley and R.S. Schofield, *The Population History of England, 1541–1871: A Reconstruction* (Cambridge: Cambridge Univ. Press, 1989), 640.

58. For the following figures, see Cressy, *Literacy and the Social Order*, 124, 125, 134–36; and Keeble, *Literary Culture of Nonconformity*, 136–39.

59. Harris, *London Crowds*, 14–15, 17, 20–21, 28–29.

60. *Ibid.*, 41–49 and esp. ch. 7.

61. See Peter Burke, *Popular Culture in Early Modern Europe* (London: Temple Smith, 1978), 23–24, 28–31, 58–63.

62. *Weekly Pacquet* 2, 'Preface' (n.d.): A 2 verso; no.15 (17 October 1679): 117.

63. Sir Roger L'Estrange, *Citt and Bumpkin. The Second Part* (1680), 9. See also *idem, The History of the Plot: Or a Brief and Historical Account of the Charge and Defence of Edward Coleman et al.* (1679), 'To the Reader.'

64. *Weekly Pacquet* 2, no.21 (28 November 1679): 166.

65. R.W. Scribner, *For the Sake of Simple Folk: Popular Propaganda for the German Reformation* (Cambridge: Cambridge Univ. Press, 1981), 7–10. Scribner focused on the woodcut broadsheet.

66. The use and translation of Latin words into English occurs throughout the *Weekly Pacquet*; for Greek words, see, e.g., 1, nos 16 (21 March 1678/79): 123 and 28 (13 June 1679): 221; 3, no.61 (5 August 1681): 482.

67. *Ibid.* 1, no.18 (4 April 1679): 137.

68. *Ibid.* 4, no.4 (20 January 1681/82): 34; 1, no.7 (17 January 1678/79): 53.

69. *Ibid.* 1, no.26 (30 May 1679): 201, 203.

70. *Popish Courant* 1, no.16 (21 March 1678/79): 127.

71. *Weekly Pacquet* 1, nos. 19 (11 April 1679): 146 and 20 (18 April 1679): 153.

72. *Ibid.*, no.15 (14 March 1678/79): 113.

73. *Ibid.* 3, no.68 (23 September 1681): 537–38.

74. *Ibid.* 1, no.14 (7 March 1678/79): 105; 2, no.9 (5 September 1679): 65. *Anti-Roman Pacquet* 3, no.6 (13 August 1680): 41.

75. *Weekly Pacquet* 3, no.33 (21 January 1680/81): 257.

76. *Ibid.* 1, no.3 (17 December 1678): 22.

77. *Ibid.*, no.20 (18 April 1679): 155.

78. *Ibid* id., no.15 (14 March 1678/79): 115.

79. *Ibid.* 3, no.61 (5 August 1681): 482.

80. *Ibid.*, no.73 (28 October 1681): 578. L'Estrange used the same phrase to describe Dissenters' approach to the Bible in *An Answer to the Appeal from the Country to the City* (1681), 14.

81. *Weekly Pacquet* 4, no.5 (20 January 1682/83): 34. A 'Muckinder' was a bib, but the word also means 'handkerchief' or 'table napkin' *(Oxford English Dictionary).*

82. *Weekly Pacquet* 2, no.15 (14 March 1678/79): 113.

83. *Popish Courant* 1, no.8 (24 January 1678/79): 63.

84. *Popish Currant* (variant title) 3, no.29 (24 December 1680): 232. Another effective verse was the 'The Pedigree of Popery, Or The Genealogy of Antichrist.' Starting with 'The Devil begat Sin/Sin begat Ignorance,' it describes the dreadful characteristics of popery up to the generation of the Pope himself: 'Ambition begat Simony/Simony begat the Pope.' Finally, 'Jesuitism begat four monsters,' which, in turn, 'begat... all kind of Abominations,' including recognizably contemporary things: 'Treason,... Perjury, Masquerade-Popery,... [and] City-burning' (*Courant* 3, no.44 [8 April 1681]: 351–52).

85. *Popes Harbinger, By way of Diversion* 3, no.12 (24 September 1680): 95 (hereafter *Popes Harbinger*).

86. *Ibid.*, no.13 (1 October 1680): 103.

87. *Popes Harbinger*, no.3 (23 July 1680): 23–24.

88. *Ibid.*, no.21 (26 November 1680): 167–68.

89. *Weekly Pacquet* 1, no.17 (28 March 1678/79): 129–30.

90. *Popish Courant* 1, no.8 (24 January 1678/79): 64.

91. *Weekly Pacquet* 3, no.49 (13 May 1681): 386.

92. *Ibid.* 2, no.9 (5 September 1679): 65–70.

93. *Ibid.* 1, no.28 (13 June 1679): 217–22; *Anti-Roman Pacquet* 3, no.21 (26 November 1680): 162.

94. *Weekly Pacquet* 3, no.68 (23 September 1681): 537.

95. *Ibid.* 2, no.27 (9 January 1679/80): 209–10.

96. *Ibid.* 3, no.74 (4 November 1681): 586.

97. *Ibid.* 1, no.26 (30 May 1679): 205.

98. *Ibid.*, no.25 (23 May 1679): 194.

99. *Ibid.*, no.16 (21 March 1678/79): 121–26.

100. Champion, *Pillars of Priestcraft Shaken*, 26–32.

101. *Weekly Pacquet* 3, no.72 (14 October 1681): 569, 570; *Popes Harbinger* 2, no.3 (23 July 1681): 24.

102. *Weekly Pacquet* 2, 'Preface' (n.d.): A2 verso.

103. See, e.g., *ibid.* 3, nos 3 (18 June 1680): 18–22 and 70 (7 October 1681): 556–57.

104. *Ibid.* 1, no.22 (2 May 1679): 173.

105. *Ibid.*, 'To the Reader' (3 December 1678), A2 verso.

106. *Ibid.* 5, no.1 (25 August 1682): 3.

107. *Ibid.*

108. *Ibid.* 1, 'To the Reader' (3 December 1678).

109. *Ibid.* 4, no.4 (20 January 1681/82): 34; 3, nos 1 (4 June 1680): 3–4 and 33 (21 January 1680/81): 259; 5, no.5 (22 September 1682): 36–37.

110. He called it the 'Divine Code,' 'the Magna Charta of Salvation' (*Popish Courant* 2, no.20 [21 November 1679]: 160; *Weekly Pacquet* 2, nos 22 [5 December 1679]: 171 and 23 [12 December 1679]: 177–82).

111. *Weekly Pacquet* 1, no.2 (10 December 1678): 13.

112. *Popes Harbinger* 3, no.16 (22 October 1680): 127. Bacon's chaplain was Dr William Rawley (1588–1667), to whom Bacon left some of his manuscripts (see A.W. Green, *Sir Francis Bacon* [New York: Twayne, 1966], 81, 101, 105).

113. *Courant* 3, no.70 (7 October 1681): 560.

114. *Popish Courant* 3, no.37 (18 February 1680/81): 296.

115. *Anti-Roman Pacquet* 3, no.21 (26 November 1680): 162. By *publick Library* Care meant the university library, as distinguished from college libraries.

116. *Weekly Pacquet* 5, no.5 (22 September 1682): 39.

117. Ibid. 4, no.2 (30 December 1681): 13. Corpus Christi College was often referred to as Benet College until the nineteenth century (see Christopher Brooke and Roger Highfield, *Oxford and Cambridge* [Cambridge: Cambridge Univ. Press, 1988], 100).

118. *Weekly Pacquet* 3, 'To the Reader' (24 December 1681).

119. *Ibid.*

120. Narcissus Luttrell, *Narcissus Luttrell's Popish Plot Catalogues,* intro. F.C. Francis (Oxford: Basil Blackwell for the Luttrell Society, 1956), opp.22.

121. *Calendar of State Papers, Domestic Series, October 1, 1683–April 30, 1684, preserved in Her Majesty's Public Record Office,* ed. F.H. Blackburne Daniell, M.A. and Francis Bickley (London: His Majesty's Stationery Office, 1938), 51, 53, 54; John Dunton, *The Life and Errors of John Dunton Late Citizen of London* (1705), 282, 283. I thank Melinda Zook for this reference. For the names of several newswriters, see Knights, *Politics and Opinion,* 174–78.

122. *Weekly Pacquet* 3, 'Preface' (24 December 1681).

123. *Ibid.* 1, 'To the Reader' (3 December 1678): A2 verso; 2, 'To the Reader' (n.d.): A2.

124. *Ibid.* 3, no.1 (24 December 1681); *Popes Harbinger* 3, no.10 (10 September 1680): 80. For the contemporary idea of the 'perfect historian,' see *The Complet History of England with the Lives of all the Kings and Queens thereof,* 3 vols (1706), preface. Care did not come close to qualifying.

125. *Weekly Pacquet* 3, no.1 (24 December 1681).

126. *Ibid.* 4, 'Preface' (n.d.): A2 verso.

127. L'Estrange remarked upon Care's capacity to read Greek (*Observator* 1, no.234 [1 November 1682]).

128. *Weekly Pacquet* 3, no.61 (5 August 1681): 482.

129. *Ibid.*, no.60 (29 July 1681): 475, 477.

130. *Ibid.*, 'To the Reader' (24 December 1681). L'Estrange wrote that Care was indebted to Chemnitius and R. Boulter's translation, but he did not accuse him of plagiarism (see *Observator* 1, no.67 [2 November 1681]).

131. *Popish Courant* 1, no.19 (11 April 1679): 151.

132. *Popes Harbinger*, 3, no.3 (23 July 1680): 24.

133. For example, see Care's use of William Crashaw, *A Mittimus To The Iubile at Rome: Or, The Rates Of The Popes Custome-House* (1625), 30–32, in *Popes Harbinger* 3, no.2 (16 July 1680): 16; and see the use of John Copley's *Doctrinal And Morall Observations Concerning Religion* (1612) in *Popish Courant* 2, no.36 (12 March 1679/80): 287–88.

134. Alexis de Salo, *An Admirable Method To Love, Serve and Honor the B. Virgin Mary* (1639), in *Courant* 3, no.69 (30 September 1681): 551–52. See also Andrew Willet, *Synopsis Papismi...* (1592), in *Weekly Pacquet* 3, no.61 (5 August 1681): 485.

135. *Weekly Pacquet* 4, 'Preface' (n.d.).

136. *Ibid.* 3, 'To the Reader' (24 December 1681).

137. Wood, *Athenae Oxonienses*, 2: 468–69.

138. *Weekly Pacquet* 3, no.80 (16 December 1681): 638.

139. *Ibid.*, no.61 (5 August 1681): 485; 1, The Introduction (3 December 1678): 2.

140. Thomas Staveley, *The Romish Horseleech: Or, An Impartial Account Of The Intolerable Charge Of Popery To This Nation...* (1674).

141. William Hughes, *The Man of Sin: Or a Discourse of Popery...* (1677).

142. *Courant* 3, no.73 (28 October 1681): 584.

143. Champion, *Pillars of Priestcraft Shaken*, 77–83.

144. Foxe's *Acts and Monuments* appeared eighteen times between 1554 and 1684 in those various forms. The ninth full edition came out in 1684. Care enthusiastically announced a proposal to reprint Foxe (*Weekly Pacquet* 5, no.44 [22 June 1683]: 352).

145. Champion, *Pillars of Priestcraft Shaken*, 45–51.

146. *Ibid.*, 26.

147. See, e.g., Sir Roger Twysden, *An Historical Vindication of the Church of England* (1675).

148. Barbara Shapiro, *Probability and Certainty in Seventeenth-Century England* (Princeton: Princeton Univ. Press, 1984).

149. Champion, *Pillars of Priestcraft Shaken*, 32–44.

150. Nelson and Seccombe, *Periodical Publications*, 15.

151. *Weekly Pacquet* 3, 'Preface' (24 December 1681), unpaginated.

152. Aphra Behn, *Prologue to Romulus* (1682), preface. I am grateful to Melinda Zook and Mark Goldie, who, within days of each other, sent me this reference.

153. Care himself speaks of tracts that were 'scatter[ed]... up and down ' (Care, *History Of The Damnable Popish Plot*, 267, 312). L'Estrange mentions a tract that was 'stuck t'other night upon Sam's Coffee-House door' (*Observator* 1, no.85 [4 January 1681/82]). For ways of disseminating political news and views, see Knights, *Politics and Opinion*, 171–75.

154. Peter Fraser, *The Intelligence of the Secretaries of State* (Cambridge: Cambridge Univ. Press, 1956), 128.

155. Watt, 'Publisher, Pedlar, Pot-Poet,' 71–72; idem, *Cheap Print and Popular Piety*.

156. *Loyal Protestant*, no.165 (8 June 1682). The incident is not mentioned in John T. Evans, *Seventeenth-Century Norwich Politics, Religion, and Government, 1620–1690* (Oxford: Clarendon Press, 1979). Chapter 7 deals with the intense partisan rivalry in the city.

157. For the public library in Cambridge, see above, n. 115.

158. See Bodl., Ashmole MS 1059, catalog, 74 [recto 174], lot 162; Knights, *Politics and Opinion*, 172 n. 138 mentions the catalog. I thank Eric Nelson, George Washington University's Shapiro Oxford fellow, for checking it for me.

159. BL, MS Library catalog [1687?], JE EL 3, 54v (no.710), 76r (no.110); *Catalogus Bibliothecae Evelyniae*, JE EL 11, 49: Care, *Utrum horum*. The index is incomplete; possibly other works by Care will be identified in the future.

160. BL, '*Bibliotheca Nobilissimi Principis Johannes Ducis de Novo-Castro*, etc., being a large collection of books contained in the libraries of... late Dukes of Newcastle... which will be sold... 2nd March 1718–19,' 55, lot 608 and 58, lot 713.

161. These *Pacquet*s were given by John Lawson, M.D., in 1705. See the catalog at Lambeth Palace Library, Sion MS AB.XI.5, 'Sion College Library Catalogue.' The library contained a total of seven tracts by Care.

162. Young Cotton Mather placed the order with Richard Chiswell in December 1683 (Nelson, 'American Readership of Early British Serials,' 34).

163. *Weekly Pacquet* 3, 'Preface' (24 December 1681), unpaginated.

164. Knights, *Politics and Opinion*, 168 and nn. 101, 102. See also Goldie, 'Revolution of 1689 and the Structure of Political Argument,' 481; and L. A. Maidwell, *A Scheme for a Public Academy: Some Reasons for its Institution* (1700?) 3, where the figure is given as 1,000 to 1,500. I thank Steven Zwicker for calling this latter reference to my attention.

165. Shesgreen, *Criers and Hawkers of London*, xii.

166. *Orange Gazette*, no.4 (7–10 January 1688/89); *Weekly Pacquet* 6, no.2 (1 February 1688/89): 16. Settle made no mention of the other four volumes or of single sheets.

167. Kitchin, *Sir Roger L'Estrange*, 233–34.

CHAPTER 3: THE ACQUITTAL OF GEORGE WAKEMAN

1. Knights, *Politics and Opinion*, Chap. 2 for the politics of exclusion in spring 1679.

2. *Cobbett's State Trials and Proceedings*, 7: cols. 1–510 for the trials. The only acquittal, on February 8, 1679, was Samuel Atkind, Samuel Pepys's clerk, against whom Bedloe testified.

3. PRO, Adm. 77, Greenwich Hospital Original Newsletters, no.1 (12 February 1678/79); cf. *Calendar of State Papers Domestic Series, January 1st 1679, to August 31st, 1680*, ed. F.H. Blackburne Daniell (London: His Majesty's Stationery Office, 1915), 81, hereafter *C.S.P.D., 1679–80*.

4. Quoted in *Dictionary of National Biography*, s.v. 'Scroggs, William.'

5. *Popish Courant* 1, no.30 (27 June 1679): 240. Also *ibid.*, no.31 (4 July 1679): 247–48. He revisited the theme in *The History Of The Damnable Popish Plot*, 267.

6. Kitchin, *Sir Roger L'Estrange*, 323 links Care with John Phillips, Milton's nephew, as collaborators in writing 'numerous Plot Narratives, etc,' but he offers no proof and I have found none.

7. Almost as well known as Oates, Bedloe was a disreputable character who, in pursuit of a government award for information about Godfrey's murderers had earlier fingered more than one innocent:

See Haley, *First Earl of Shaftesbury*, 477–79.

8. Kitchin, *Sir Roger L'Estrange*, 225–28, for tracts on London fires.

9. Sir Roger L'Estrange, *Lestrange's Narrative Of The Plot. Set Forth for the Edification Of His Majesties Liege-People* (1680), 17–18; *Observator* 1, nos 46 (4 August 1681), 50 (7 Sept. 1681), 369 (4 July 1683).

10. *Observator* 1, no.369 (4 July 1683).

11. *Ibid.*, no.344 (24 May 1683).

12. See Bedloe, *A narrative and Impartial Discovery of the Horrid Popish Plot…* (1679), e.g. 8, 10–13.

13. Without identifying a sum, Kitchin remarked that the profit was substantial (*Sir Roger L'Estrange*, 238 and n.2).

14. The *London Gazette*, no.1426 (17–21 July 1679); *Domestick Intelligence*, 22 July 1679; *Faithful Mercury, Imparting News Domestick and Forei[g]n*, 22 July 1679; *The English Intelligencer*, no.2 (24 July 1679).

15. *Popish Courant* 1, no.8 (24 Jan. 1678/79), 64 (first p.64).

16. *Popish Courant* 2, no.4 (1 Aug. 1679): 32.

17. Luttrell, *Brief Historical Relation*, I:18.

18. See, e.g., Historical Manuscript Commission Reports, *Seventh Report*, app. 1, 495; and Folger Shakespeare Library, 'The Newdigate Newsletters, Addressed to Sir Richard Newwidgate, lst Bart., and to 2nd Bart, 1673/74–1715' L.c. 818, 2 August 1679.

19. Possibly Scroggs and the other justices were summoned to a Privy Council meeting to discuss the problem of the queen's involvement. Scroggs may have received some instruction from Sir Francis North as they were returning by carriage to London from Hampton Court (see A.F. Havighurst, 'The Judiciary and Politics in the Reign of Charles II,' *The Law Quarterly Review* [London] 66 (1950): 235 and n.33; J.P. Kenyon, 'The Acquittal of Sir George Wakeman:18 July 1679,' *Historical Journal*, 14 (1971): 698.

20. Knights, *Politics and Opinion*, 210, quoting Historical Manuscript Commission, *Calendar of the Manuscripts of the Marquess of Ormonde, K.P., Preserved at Kilkenny Castle*, n.s., vol. 5 (Hereford: His Majestry's Stationery Office, 1908), 158.

21. Luttrell, *Brief Historical Relations*, I: 18. It was said that the visit was a tactical move by Catholics to ruin Scroggs; although pleased with his handling of the Wakeman trial, they could not forgive his treatment of Catholics in previous trials (Bishop Gilbert Burnet, *History of His Own Time: With Notes by the Earls of Dartmouth and Hardwicke, Speaker Onslow, and Dean Swift*, 6 vols [1833], 2: 227–28.

22. Luttrell, *Brief Historical Relation*, 1:17. *Domestick Intelligence*, no.8 (31 July 1679).

23. Knights, *Politics and Opinion*, 222.

24. Folger Shakespeare Library, 'The Newdigate Newsletters,' L.c. 818 (2 August 1679).

25. *London Gazette*, no.1426 (17–21 July 1679). The *English Intelligence*, no.2 (24 July 1679), picked up the story.

26. *Domestick Intelligence*, no.5 (22 July 1679).

27. PRO, PC 2/68, 179, 190.

28. Haley, *First Earl of Shaftesbury*, 407.

29. *Ibid.*, 543.

30. George Hickes told Arthur Charlett that 'folkes suspected' Care was the author: Bodl., Ballard MS 12, fol. 22, 8 August [1679?]. For comments on the election, see Kishlansky, *Parliamentary Selection*, 183, 187.

31. See Care, *Essex's Excellency*, A, A 1, B verso, B 2 verso, for quotations.

32. Also known as *Essex's Insolency* from comment on page 7 in the text. Printed 28 August 1679.

33. Bodl., Ballard MS 12, f. 22, 8 August [1679?].

34. *Faithful and Impartial*, 6, 7, 8.

35. *Some Observations upon the late Trial*, second p.8 [misnumbered]. Reprinted in St Tr., VII, 687–94. 'Clodpate' was a caricature of Scroggs. This unflattering name also appeared in a manuscript satire: BL, Add. Ms. 34,362, f. 95b. It was followed by an anonymous printed sheet, *Clodpate's Ghost: Or A Dialogue Between Justice Clodpate, and his [quondam] clerk Honest Tom Ticklefoot; Wherein Is Faithfully Related all the News from Purgatory, about Ireland, Langhorn, etc.* (From Green-Goose-Fair, 25 August 1679). Francis Smith was the publisher. In its use of humor, rhyme, reference to a deadly cordial and to *Poor Robin's Pharmacopeia*, *Clodpate's Ghost* sounds much like Care.

36. *C.J.*, IX, 690.

37. Other printed tracts included: *The Tickler Tickled: Or The Observator Upon the Late Tryals of Sir George Wakeman, etc. Observed: By Margery Mason Spinster* (1679); *Justice in Masquerade. A Poem* (n.d. [1680]); and *The Bellowings Of A Wild-Bull: Or, Scroggs's Roaring Lamentation For Being Impeached of High-Treason* (n.p., n.d. [1681]). Two unpublished lampoons, similar in nature, are in BL, Add. Ms. 34,362, ff. 95, 95b; a third is in the Pepys Papers at Magdalene College, 2881/89.

38. Luttrell, *Brief Historical Relation*, 1: 19–20. *Memoirs Of The Verney Family During The Seventeenth Century Compiled From The Papers and*

Illustrated By The Portraits At Claydon House By Frances Parthenope Verney and Margaret M. Verney, 2nd edn, 2 vols (1907), II, 321.

39. Frederick George Stephens, *Catalogue of Political and Personal Satires Preserved in the Department of Prints and Drawings in the British Museum*, I (1878): 1320–1689, entries 1071–1114.

40. Siebert, *Freedom of the Press*, 297, 298; Hamburger, 'Development of the Law of Seditious Libel,' 683, n. 68.

41. Knights, *Politics and Opinion*, 207.

42. Timothy Crist, 'Government Control of the Press After the Expiration of the Printing Act in 1679,' *Publishing History*, 5 (1979), 49.

43. Knights, *Politics and Opinion*, 207. Danby arranged for the release of the two tracts favoring him (Anchitell Grey, *Debates of the House of Commons, from the year 1667 to the year 1694*, 10 vols [1763]) 7: 32, 49.

44. Thomas Hobbes, quoted in Walker, 'Censorship of the Press,' 223. In chapter 18 of his *Leviathan*, Hobbes insisted that governing the press was 'annexed to the Soveraignty.' He wrote that 'It belongeth... to him that hath the Soveraign Power, to be Judge, or constitute all Judges of Opinions and Doctrines, as a thing necessary to Peace, thereby to prevent Discord and Civill Warre.' See C.B. Macpherson, ed., *Thomas Hobbes: Leviathan* (Harmondsworth, Penguin Books, 1978), 233.

45. Charles Blount, *A Just Vindication of Learning: Or, An Humble Address To the High Court of Parliament In behalf of the Liberty of the Press* (1679), 3–4, 6, 9–12, 16, 18. Blount anticipated some of the arguments that appeared in the 1690s, when his own tract was reissued under a slightly different title.

46. William Lawrence, *Marriage by the Morall Law of God Vindicated* (1680), 164–67.

47. Douglas R. Lacey, *Dissent and Parliamentary Politics in England, 1661–1689: A Study in the Perpetuation and Tempering of Parliamentarianism* (New Brunswick, N.J.: Rutgers Univ. Press, 1969), 133.

48. The exact date of the expiry is given variously. See Knights, *Politics and Opinion*, 156, n. 15.

49. PRO, PC 2/68, 60.

50. *Ibid.*, 236, 256. Blagden, *The Stationers' Company*, 165.

51. PRO, PC 2/68, 314.

52. Crist, 'Francis Smith,' 108–09.

53. In January 1679 he had taken the opposite position: see Kitchin, *Sir Roger L'Estrange*, 217.

54. PRO, PC 2/68, 76, 94; Longleat, Coventry MSS, L'Estrange to Henry Coventry, 10 June 1679, fols. 64–71. I used the microfilm held by the Institute of Historical Research.

55. Crist, 'Francis Smith,' 185–87. PRO, PC 2/68, 94; Blagden, *The Stationers' Company,* 163–64 and 163 n. 1.

56. Significantly the 1684 Charter was not replaced until 1933. Blagden, *The Stationers' Company*, 174, 278.

57. PRO, PC 2/68, 203, 204, 212, 229, 242. Hamburger, 'The Development of the Law of Seditious Libel,' 684, n. 71, interprets a clause such as 'if there shall be occasion' to mean that the Council was not sanguine about its authority to proceed against press people. The Council had the authority under common law to proceed once a tract was published; it seems more likely that the clause referred to a politically appropriate occasion.

58. PRO, SP 30/G. The issues of the *Weekly Pacquet* for 12 and 26 September 1679 were included.

59. *Observator* 3, 'To Posterity' and 'The Reasons of This Undertaking,' 39; Kitchin, *Sir Roger L'Estrange*, 240–41.

60. L'Estrange, *History of the Plot*, 'To the Reader.'

61. *Ibid.*, 73.

62. Kitchin, *Sir Roger L'Estrange*, 246, n. 1. Kitchin offers no proof that Care was approached.

63. *An Appeal From The Country To The City, For the Preservation of His Majesties Person, Liberty, Property, And The Protestant Religion. Salus Populi, Suprema Lex. Laopolis* (1679) has been assigned to Shaftesbury, John Ayloffe, Robert Ferguson and, now reliably, to Charles Blount. See *Domestick Intelligence*, no.30 (17 Oct 1679), for the date. One of Shaftesbury's friends was arrested at about this time for distributing 'damned libels' against the government: see Haley, *First Earl of Shaftesbury*, 553, n 3.

64. Blount, *Appeal From The Country To The City*, 1–6.

65. *Ibid.*, 17, 25–26.

66. PRO, PC 2/68, 229.

67. *Domestick Intelligence*, no.30 (17 October 1679). The two women were Mary Thompson, wife of Nathaniell, who was said to have first printed the *Appeal*, and Abigail (not Anne) Brewster, widow of the printer Thomas; the two clerks were Charles Ray and Robert Murray (see Treadwell, 'London Trade Publishers,' 110, n. 19 for Brewster's name). Thompson, who was later associated with the

Tory/Anglican party; was said to have been 'unpredictable' (see Sutherland, *Restoration Newspaper*, 188. Muddiman, *King's Jouranlist*, 218, n. 1, identified the two clerks. Murray was said to be a 'breaksetter or printer' and a 'clerk in the Penny Letter Office' (see Morrice, 'Ent'ring Book,' I, 211; and *C.S.P.D., 1679–1680*, 469, 488, 492).

68. L'Estrange, *An Answer to the Appeal*, 1, 14–16, 23, 25, 32–33 for quotations.

69. PRO, PC 2/67, PC 2/68, 154, 179, 207, 212, 229, 231, 243, 289, 292, 311, 478, 528.

70. PRO, PC 2/68, 389. But see *Journals of the House of Commons*, 9: 688–89. *Domestick Intelligence*, nos 30 and 33 (17 and 28 October 1679); and *Weekly Pacquet* 3, 'Preface' (24 Dec. 1681). It is worth noting that Shaftesbury was dismissed the day before Care and Curtis appeared.

71. [Gibbon], *Flagellum mercurii Anti–Ducalis*, 3.

72. *Popish Courant* 2, no. 10 (12 Sept. 1679): 80.

73. *Ibid.*, 2, no. 11 (19 Sept. 1679): 88.

74. PRO, SP 30/G.

75. *Popish Courant* 2, no. 14 (10 Oct. 1679), 112.

76. PRO, PC 2/68, 236.

77. J.S. Cockburn, *A History of English Assizes 1558–1714* (Cambridge: Cambridge Univ. Press, 1972), 250.

78. Sir Matthew Hale, *The History of the Common Law of England*, ed. Charles M. Gray (Chicago: Univ. of Chicago Press, 1971), 44–46. For the judges' role in law-making, see J.H. Baker, *An Introduction to English Legal History* (London: Butterworths, 1979), 172–174.

79. PRO, PC/28, 256, 263. The ruling was printed in the *London Gazette* on 6 November, (no. 1457) (see also Robert Steele, ed., *A Bibliography of Royal Proclamations of the Tudor and Stuart Sovereigns and of Others Published Under Authority, 1485–1714*, 2 vols [Oxford: Clarendon Press, 1910], 1: no. 3699. It offered forty pounds to the person who identified the authors or printers of seditious tracts and a pardon to hawkers who fingered their supplier and to booksellers and printers who revealed the author. Persons who did not assist the government in wiping out libels would be liable as 'Contemners' of royal authority.

80. Historical Manuscript Commission Reports, *Seventh Report*, app. 1, 494.

81. For an account of his appointment to King's Bench, see Charles Hatton to Christopher First Viscount Hatton, in *Correspondence of the*

family of Hatton, being Chiefly letters addressed to Christopher First Viscount Hatton 1601–1704, ed. E.M.Thompson, Camden, n.s., 2 vols (London, 1878), 1: 163–64.

82. See *Dictionary of National Biography*, s.v. Scroggs, William, for the comment. In the speech Scroggs expressed abhorrence of corruption and popular favor, saying that he sought 'Reputation and a Good Name' by doing his 'Duty' and not otherwise. *A Speech Made by Sir William Scrogg,… At his Admission To… the Court of Common Pleas* [1676], 5–7.

83. *The Lord Chief Justice Scroggs: His Speech To the Lord Chancellour* [1678].

84. One Richard Radley had accused Scroggs of taking bribes (see Crist, 'Francis Smith,' 115. See also below; and Luttrell, *Brief Historical Relation*, 1: 26). An information contains charges against someone that are presented to a court without using the formal procedure of grand jury and indictment.

85. All Souls College Library, MS 171 ,77v: Narcissus Luttrell, cited in Crist, 'Francis Smith,' 116.

86. *The Lord Chief Justice Scroggs: His Speech In The Kings-Bench… Together With what was Declared at the same Time… by Mr. Justice Jones, and Mr. Justice Dolbin* (23 October 1679), 1, 7.

87. *Domestic Intelligence*, no.33 (28 October 1679); *Weekly Pacquet* 3, 'Preface' (24 Dec. 1681).

88. *Journals of the House of Commons*, 9: 688–89.

89. Folger Shakespeare Library, 'Newdigate Newsletters,' L.c. 854, 27 October 1679

90. Cambridge University, Magdelene College, Pepys Library, PL 2,875/465–91, 'The Journall of ye Green-Ribbon-Clubb at ye King's Head Taverne over against ye Temple in Fleet Street viz. from 1678 to 1681,' 474.

91. 31 Car. 2, c.2 (1679), *Statutes of the Realm*, 5:935–38.

92. *The Practick Part of the Law: Shewing the Office of an Attorney, In the Courts of Kings-Bench, Common Pleas, and Pleas in the Exchequer* (1681), 54, 296–97, 336–53; Wrigley and Schofield, *Population History of England 1541–1871*, app. 9.

93. Sir Richard Bulstrode, *Memoirs and Reflections upon the Reign and Government of King Charles the Ist. and K. Charles the IId* (1721), 299.

94. *Weekly Pacquet* 2, no.17 (31 October 1679): 134.

95. *Domestick Intelligence*, no.65 (February 1679/80); *Weekly Pacquet* 3, 'Preface' (24 Dec. 1681).

96. The original Information is in PRO, KB 10/1, part 4. The Information is printed in Latin in W.H. Hart, comp., *Index Expurgatorius Anglicanus: or A Descriptive Catalogue of the Principal Books Printed or Published in England, which have been suppressed, or burnt by the common hangman, or censured, or for which the Authors, Printers, or Publishers have been prosecuted* (London, reprint, Burt Franklin, 1969), 213–214. An abbreviated version appears in English in *Cobbett's State Trials and Proceedings*, 7: cols 1111–1113, and in the *The Triall of Henry Carr, Gent. At The Guild-Hall of the City of London, the 2d Day of July, 1680...Also the Tryal of Elizabeth Cellier, At The Kings-Bench-Bar, July the 11th 1680* (1681).

97. *Domestic Intelligence*, no.65 (17 February 1679/80); *Cobbett's State Trials and Proceedings*, 7: cols 1114. I have been unable to identify Benedict Brown.

98. Crist, 'Francis Smith,' Ch. I, *passim. A Biographical Dictionary of British Radicals in the Seventeenth Century*, ed. Richard L. Greaves and Robert Zaller, 3 vols (Brighton: Harvester, 1982), 2: 184–85.

99. *Cobbett's State Trials and Proceedings*, 7: col. 933.

100. *Journals of the House of Commons*, 9:690.

101. 'An Account of the injurious Proceedings of Sir George Jeffreys, knt. late Recorder of London, against Francis Smith, Bookseller,... Together with an Abstract of very many former Losses, and public sufferings sustained by him both in his Person and Estate,' in *Cobbett's State Trials and Proceedings*, 7: cols 937–960, quotation at col. 955.

102. *Journals of the House of Commons,* 9:690. The writ of *Habeas Corpus* and other writs cost Smith thirty-six pounds ('Account of the injurious Proceedings of Sir George Jeffreys,' col. 956).

103. *Journals of the House of Commons*, 9: 690.

104. Ibid.; *Domestick Intelligence*, no.54 (9 January 1679/80). Crist, 'Francis Smith,' 132, n. 1, thinks that Smith gave this information to Harris to publish.

105. *Journals of the House of Commons*, 9: 690.

106. It cost his father twelve pounds in fees to win his release (see Crist, 'Francis Smith,' 132).

107. The fullest contemporary account is PRO, ADM 77, Greenwich Hospital Newsletters, no.39. See also Charles Hatton to L. Hatton, 11 December 1679, in Thompson, *Corrrespondence of the family of Hatton*, 1: 207–210; and Haley, *First Earl of Shaftesbury*, 559–60.

108. BL, Add. MSS 28. 053, fol. 114. The paper is undated.

109. Haley, *First Earl of Shaftesbury*, 543.

110. Mark Knights, 'London's "Monster" Petition of 1680,' *Historical Journal* 36 (1993): 39–67.

111. *Ibid.*, 44, 46. Steele, *Bibliography of Royal Proclamations*, 1: no.3703.

112. See Knights, 'London's "Monster" Petition of 1680,' 45–46, 48–64 for a prosopographic analysis.

113. Mark Knights, 'Petitioning and the Political Theorists: John Locke, Algernon Sidney and London's "Monster" Petition of 1680,' *Past and Present*, no.138 (February 1993), 104. I thank Knights for sending me a copy of the sheet on which Care's name appeared. The signature is Care's.

114. *Domestick Intelligence*, no.53 (6 January 1679–80).

115. *Articles of High Misdemeanours... against Sir William Scrogs... Together with his Lordships Answer thereunto* [1680]. This tract was in print by 17 January (Morrice, 'Ent'ring Book,' 1: 277).

116. The news of this outrageous remark traveled far enough for Charles Hatton to note it (Thompson, *Correspondence of the family of Hatton* 1: 220).

117. *Ibid.*, 2 September 1678 (1:192).

118. Bodl., MSS. Carte 39, Ormonde Correspondence, 113. PRO, PC 2/58, 355, 359; *C.S.P.D., 1679–80*, 376; PRO, ADM 77, Greenwich Hospital Newsletters, no.42.

119. *Innocence Unveil'd: Or, A Poem On the Acquittal of the Lord Chief Justice Scroggs* (1680).

120. L'Estrange, *Further Discovery of the Plot*, 5. *History Of The Damnable Popish Plot*, priced at three shillings, was identified as written by the 'authors of the Pacquet of Advice from Rome' and advertized in the *Weekly Pacquet* 2, nos. 29 (23 January 1680): 232 and 30 (30 January 1680): 236. It is listed in the Term Catalogue, 1: 382, 425.

121. Kitchin, *Sir Roger L'Estrange*, 246.

122. Care, *History Of The Damnable Popish Plot*, 'To both Houses of Parliament,' A 4, A 4 verso.

123. *Ibid.*, A 5 verso (recto). No doubt to ingratiate himself further, Care ladled high praise on Sir William Waller, saying that to him 'the Nation and the Protestant Religion in general, under God, in an high measure, owes its preservation' (335).

124. It was in the bookstalls sometime between 26 January and 18 February 1680 (see Beverly Rahn, *Sir Roger L'Estrange: Citt and Bumpkin* (1680). Augustan Reprint Society, 117 (Berkeley and Los Angeles: Univ. of California Press for the William Andrew Clark

Memorial Library, 1965)), iv–v.

125. *Ibid.*, viii. Rahn regarded *Citt and Bumpkin* as the 'best written pamphlet on petitioning.' L'Estrange had used dialogue in pieces printed during the Civil War.

126. L'Estrange, *Citt and Bumpkin*, 3; see also 8 and, for example, 13–14, 29, 34.

127. *Ibid.*, 26, 34.

128. Rahn, *Sir Roger L'Estrange*, xi, xii.

129. PRO, PC 2/68, 369. Cited in Crist, 'Francis Smith,' 137.

130. H.C. Foxwell [Foxcroft], ed., 'Some Unpublished Letters of Gilbert Burnet,' *The Camden Miscellany, Volume The Eleventh* , Camden, 3rd ser., 13 (London: Royal Historical Society, 1907), 7.

131. *Cobbett's State Trials and Proceedings*, 8: col. 182; the speaker was Henry Sidney. See also Grey, *Debates of the House of Commons*, 8: 60 where the speaker was Henry Powle.

132. Hamburger, 'The Development of the Law of Seditious Libel,' 685–86. The general contents of the ruling were revealed in Scroggs's speech in Smith's trial discussed below.

CHAPTER 4: CARE'S TRIAL AND SIR WILLIAM SCROGGS'S IMPEACHMENT

1. Earl of Anglesey, quoted in Scott, *Algernon Sidney and the Restoration Crisis*, 47.

2. See above, ch. 4.

3. Through her attorney, Curtis admitted the record, so the court did not proceed to trial but called Curtis to stand before it (*Cobbett's State Trials and Proceedings*, 7: cols 959–60).

4. *Ibid.*, col. 925.

5. *Ibid.*, cols. 931–32.

6. Only one person dared to speak out against Harris, and he was threatened by the crowd (Muddiman, *King's Journalist*, 218. *C.S.P.D., 1679–80*, 397).

7. *Cobbett's State Trials and Proceedings*, 7: col. 1126.

8. *Ibid.*, col. 928.

9. *Ibid.*, cols 929–30.

10. See above, ch. 1.

11. Holdsworth, *History of English Law*, 8: 340.

12. *Cobbett's State Trials and Proceedings*, 7: cols 931–32.

13. *Ibid.*, cols 929–30. Sutherland, *Restoration Newspaper*, 189.

14. Scroggs refused Harris's request to address the jury, denied his plea to be imprisoned in Newgate rather than in King's Bench prison, and recommended that he be publicly whipped. Justice Jones sentenced Harris to stand in the pillory for an hour, to pay a fine of £500, and to post sureties for good behavior for three years. Justice Pemberton intervened, opposing the whipping (*Cobbett's State Trials and Proceedings*, 7: cols 931–32; *London Gazette*, no.1486 [16 February 1679/80]; *C.S.P.D., 1679–80*, 392).

15. *Cobbett's State Trials and Proceedings*, 7: cols 937–38. Sutherland, *Restoration Newspaper*, 200, makes this suggestion.

16. *Cobbett's State Trials and Proceedings*, 7: col. 960. For Jane Curtis, see Bell, 'Women and the Opposition Press after the Restoration,' 39–60.

17. *A Short, but Just Account Of The Tryal Of Benjamin Harris...* (1679 [1680]).

18. Sutherland, *Restoration Newspaper*, 191. The Stationers' Company weighed in with further punishment, removing Harris from the livery for having 'undergon the punishment of law for Some offences by him committed' (Crist, 'Francis Smith,' 123).

19. PRO, PC 2/68, 477, quoted in Hamburger, 'Development of the Law of Seditious Libel,' 686–87.

20. Foxwell [Foxcroft], 'Some Unpublished Letters of Gilbert Burnet the Historian,' 10.

21. Havighurst, 'Judiciary and Politics in the Reign of Charles II,' 237.

22. Gilbert Burnet, quoted in John Lord Campbell, *The Lives of the Chief Justices of England from the Norman Conquest till the death of Lord Tenterden*, 3rd edn, 4 vols (1874), 2: 284. See also Edward Foss, *Biographica Juridica: A Biographical Dictionary of the Judges of England from the conquest to the present time, 1066–1870* (1870), 507–8. The understanding that Pemberton was 'too much opposite the court interest' was widespread enough for Luttrell to report it (Luttrell, *Brief Historical Relation*, 1:36).

23. Atkyns was replaced by Sir Thomas Raymond (1627–83), a baron of the Court of Exchequer; Pemberton by Bointon of York (not noticed in the *Dictionary of National Biography*) (Foxwell [Foxcroft], 'Some Unpublished Letters of Gilbert Burnet the Historian,' 7; Luttrell, *Brief Historical Relation*, 1: 35).

24. PRO, PC 2/68, 496.

25. Hamburger, 'Development of the Law of Seditious Libel,' 687.

26. Steele, *Bibliography of Royal Proclamations*, vol. 1:450 (no.3714). A copy of the original proclamation is at the Folger Shakespeare Library.

27. *Cobbett's State Trials and Proceedings*, 8: col. 193. See also *Journals of the House of Commons*, 9:691.

28. John Smith's *Currant Intelligence*, R. Harford's *Mercurius Anglicus*, and Nathaniel Thompson's *True Domestick Intelligence* all ceased publication (see Crist, 'Francis Smith,' 138 n. 2).

29. *Weekly Pacquet* 3, 'Preface' (24 December 1681). The information is reprinted in Hart, *Index Expurgatorius Anglicanus*, 213–14. See also *C.S.P.D., 1679–80*, 536.

30. North, *Examen*, 564–65.

31. *Weekly Pacquet* 3, 'Preface' (24 December 1681).

32. *Cobbett's State Trials and Proceedings*, 7: col. 1118.

33. North, *Examen*, 565.

34. *Ibid.*, 564–65.

35. L'Estrange, *Narrative Of The Plot*, 4; L'Estrange, *Further Discovery of the Plot*, 24.

36. L'Estrange, *Narrative of the Plot*, 25.

37. Sir Roger L'Estrange, *Discovery upon Discovery* (1680), 19. There is no evidence that the government paid him for these tracts.

38. See the list in Kitchin, *Sir Roger L'Estrange*, 414. The four reprints were *Tyranny and Popery*, *The Reformed Catholique*, *The Freeborn Subject* and *The Case Put, Concerning the Succession Of His Royal Highness The Duke of York*.

39. *A Brief Answer To Mr. L'Estrange His Appeal* (1680), 6.

40. *Popish Courant* 2, no. 39 (2 April 1680): 312.

41. L'Estrange, *Discovery upon Discovery*, 17. Care's remark was noted in E.P. [Edward Phillips?], *Citt and Bumpkin answered*, 'Epistle Dedicatory.'

42. L'Estrange, *Further Discovery of the Plot*, 2, 5–6.

43. See Antony Griffiths, *The Print in Stuart Britain, 1603–1689* (London: British Museum, 1998), 287, for a brief discussion of the date, the authorship, and some annotations by Narcissus Luttrell, who preserved the print in his collection.

44. The *Oxford English Dictionary* defines *babby* as 'same as baby.'

45. *Tope*, 'drink to excess'; *vapour*, 'to talk and/or act boastfully, blusteringly, braggingly'; *dry bob*, 'a blow that does not break the skin. Fig. a sharp rebuke, a bitter jest' (*ibid.*).

46. *Observator* 1, no. 57 (28 September 1681).

47. Griffiths confirmed the attribution to Luttrell in a conversation with Isabel Kenrick in September 2000.

48. Griffiths, *Print in Stuart Britain*, 287.

49. E.P. [Edward Phillips?], *Citt and Bumpkin answered*, 'Epistle Dedicatory.'

50. *Cobbett's State Trials and Proceedings*, 7: col. 1115. See also Historical Manuscript Commission Reports, *Seventh Report*, app. 1, 479.

51. 'The Report of the Committee of the House of Commons appointed to examine the Proceedings of the Judges,' in *Cobbett's State Trials and Proceedings*, 8: col. 187. See also *Weekly Pacquet* 3, 'Preface' (24 December 1681).

52. *Weekly Pacquet* 3, 'Preface' (24 December 1681); 'The Report of the Committee of the House of Commons, appointed to examine the Proceedings of the Judges,' in *Cobbett's State Trials and Proceedings*, 8: cols 186–87.

53. Care and Curtis appeared before the grand jury on 1 July, the date and place of the trial were announced, and Curtis was again commanded never to print the *Weekly Pacquet* (Folger Shakespeare Library, 'Newdigate Newsletters,' L.c. 954, 1 July 1680).

54. Gary De Krey suggested the likely political inclination of the twelve jurors in 1680 as follows: Henry Averie (T), Leonard Bates (T), Nicholas Bendy (T in 1680), Nicholas Caplin (T), Richard Cawthorne (T), Emmanuel Conyers (T), Randal/Randolph Dod (T), Thomas Gilby (T), John Odensel/Odingsells (not identified, or NI), James Rood (NI), William Yap (NI), Arthur Young (W) (letter to the author, 15 January 1993).

55. This was Richard Radley, mentioned in ch. 4, n. 75. See also Morrice, 'Ent'ring Book,' 1:263.

56. Haley, *First Earl of Shaftesbury*, 579–80. An anonymous pamphlet demeaning York in twenty-one particulars had prepared the way. See also a paper signed by Whig leaders entitled 'Reasons why the Duke of York may most strongly be reputed to be a Papist,' paper with signatures in PRO, PRO 30/24/6 B. 420.

57. North, *Examen*, 564.

58. Hart, *Index Expurgatorius Anglicanus*, 213–14.

59. Quotations in this paragraph and the next are from *Cobbett's State Trials and Proceedings*, 7: cols 1114–15.

60. By *boy* was meant a young servant, not a son. As noted in ch. 2, Care was unmarried in 1680.

61. Historical Manuscript Commission Reports, *Seventh Report*, app. 1, 479.

62. *Cobbett's State Trials and Proceedings*, 7: col. 1122. The following men were called in sequence: a Mr Sutton, a Mr Ambler, and a Mr Ayliffe. None can be positively identified. There were seven men with the surname Sutton in the London livery in the 1680s; Ambler may have been the William Ambler who was suspected in Monmouth's Rebellion; Ayliffe was possibly the John Ayloffe who was associated with the Green Ribbon Club and was a member of a Whig radical club that met at King's Head. (Gary De Krey to the author, 15 January 1993). Ayloffe, like Care, signed the 'Monster' Petition (see Knights, 'London's 'Monster' Petition of 1680,' 54).

63. *Cobbett's State Trials and Proceedings,* 7: col. 1125. Winnington reportedly rejoined that anyone who found Care guilty had a 'Popish' conscience (Historical Manuscript Commission Reports, *Seventh Report*, app. 1, 479).

64. *C.S.P.D., 1679–80*, 536; *Cobbett's State Trials and Proceedings*, 7: col. 1130.

65. Folger Shakespeare Library, 'Newdigate Newsletters,' L.c. 957 (5 July 1680), 998 (22 October 1680).

66. Morrice, 'Ent'ring Book,' 1:263 (misnumbered).

67. Oxford University, All Souls College Library, MS 171, 119v, cited in Crist, 'Francis Smith,' 139 n. 4.

68. *New Anti-Roman Pacquet: Or, Memoirs Of Popes and Popery Since the Tenth Century*, no.1 (9 July 1680): 1.

69. Bodl., Eng. MSS, Misc. c. 4., Papers of George Hickes, 17–19. I thank Mark Knights for this reference.

70. *Popes Harbinger* 3, no.16 (22 October 1680): 128.

71. Folger Shakespeare Library, 'Newdigate Newsletters,' L.c. 998, 22 October 1680.

72. *Weekly Pacquet* 3, 'Preface' (24 December 1681).

73. *C.S.P.D., 1679–80*, 596.

74. *Weekly Pacquet* 3, 'Preface' (24 December 1681). Neither the *Journals of the House of Commons* nor Grey, *Debates of the House of Commons*, contains evidence that the House *ordered* a lifting of the ban against the *Weekly Pacquet*.

75. See *An Exact Collection Of the most Considerable Debates in the Honourable House of Commons...* (1681), 15–16, for Winnington's speech.

76. *Popes Harbinger* 3, no.20 (19 November 1680): 160.

77. *Popish Currant* 3, no.27 (10 December 1680): 215–16.

78. Sir John Somers, *Somers Tracts* (1750), pt. 2, 3: 282–84, as noted in Ogg, *England in the Reign of Charles II*, 2:609–10. Ogg did not notice the

connection with Care's description. The tract does not appear in the 1809–15 edition of *Somers Tracts.*

79. Robert Willman, 'The Origins of "Whig" and "Tory" in English Political Language,' *Historical Journal* 17 (1974): 260, does not mention this passage but writes that '"Tory" did not appear in Exclusionist prints until their Royalist counterparts... had already begun to use it,' that is, in the spring of 1681.

80. *Popish Currant* 3, no.29 (24 December 1680): 232.

81. *Triall of Henry Carr... the 2d Day of July, 1680.*

82. *Journals of the House of Lords*, 13: 626.

83. See Schwoerer, 'Attempted Impeachment of Sir William Scroggs,' from which I have drawn ideas and language.

84. *Journals of the House of Commons*, 9: 688–91.

85. J.G.A. Pocock, *The Ancient Constitution and the Feudal Law: A Study of English Historical Thought in the Seventeenth Century, A Reissue with a Retrospect* (Cambridge: Cambridge Univ. Press, 1987).

86. The move was reinforced by the recent appearance of accounts of those earlier trials. *An impartial Account Of The... Trial... Of Thomas late Earl of Strafford...* (1679); *The Trial Of Thomas Earl of Strafford...* (1680); P. Heylyn, *Cyprianus Anglicus: Or, The History Of The Life and Death, Of... William... Lord Archbishop of Canterbury...* (1671).

87. Grey, *Debates of the House of Commons*, 8: 237.

88. Conrad Russell, 'The Theory of Treason in the Trial of Strafford,' *English Historical Review* 80 (1965): esp. 34, 38 (quotation), 39, 42.

89. *Cobbett's State Trials and Proceedings*, 8: col. 183; see also col. 182. Care 'borrowed' Powle's language later on in writing *English Liberties; or, The Free-Born Subject's inheritance.*

90. Grey, *Debates of the House of Commons*, 8: 206. Powle iterated the point in parliamentary debate on 4 January 1680/81 (*ibid.*, 250).

91. See *Journals of the House of Commons*, 9: 688–91, for this and the following paragraphs.

CHAPTER 5: RESTYLING POLITICAL RHETORIC IN THE EXCLUSION CRISIS

1. Theodore F. M. Newton, 'The Mask of Heraclitus,' *Harvard Studies and Notes in Philology and Literature* 16 (1934): 145–60, established the authorship of *Heraclitus Ridens.*

2. Scott, *Algernon Sidney and the Restoration Crisis*, 11, 14, 43, 47–49,

emphatically denies the existence of parties, a controversial proposition that I cannot accept.

3. *Ibid.*, 64–72, maintains that exclusion did not drive parliamentary moves.

4. J.R. Jones, *Charles II: Royal Politician* (London: Allen & Unwin, 1987), ch. 7. See also Ronald Hutton, *Charles II: King of England, Scotland, and Ireland* (Oxford: Clarendon Press, 1989), 392–407.

5. The full title was *Touching the Causes and Reasons That moved Him to Dissolve the Two Last Parliaments.* Several drafts were considered by the king and the Privy Council. Charles insisted on a moderate statement that would unite his subjects (see Knights, *Politics and Opinion,* 316–25).

6. The *Declaration of Reasons* is found conveniently in Andrew Browning, ed., *English Historical Documents, 1660–1714* (London: Eyre & Spittiswoode, 1966), 185–88.

7. See Knights, *Politics and Opinion,* 325–29, for the responses.

8. Victor Stater, *Noble Government: The Stuart Lord Lieutenancy and the Transformation of English Politics* (Athens: Univ. of Georgia Press, 1994), 189.

9. See Crist, 'Francis Smith,' 183–88. Neither Jones nor Hutton discusses the king's effort to control the Stationers' Company in 1681.

10. Mark Goldie, 'The Theory of Religious Intolerance in Restoration England,' in *From Persecution to Toleration: The Glorious Revolution and Religion in England,* ed. Ole Peter Grell, Jonathan I. Israel and Nicholas Tyacke (Oxford: Clarendon Press, 1991), ch. 13. For informers, see Goldie, 'Hilton Gang and the Purge of London.'

11. Knights, *Politics and Opinion,* 164.

12. Roger North, *The Lives of The Right Hon. Francis North, Baron Guilford; The Hon. Sir Dudley North; and The Hon. and Rev. Dr. John North By The Hon. Roger North, Together With The Autobiography Of The Author,* ed. A. Jessop, 3 vols (1826), 1: 199–200.

13. BL, Add. MSS 32,520, fol. 185: Roger North, quoted in Knights, *Politics and Opinion,* 171.

14. North, *Lives,* 1:199.

15. L'Estrange, however, did not return from Holland until the third week in February (*True Protestant Mercury,* no.17 [19–23 February 1681]).

16. *Observator* 1, 'To the Reader' (preface to the bound issues, published in 1684).

17. North, *Lives,* 1: 200.

18. Volume 1 contained 470 issues and ran from 13 April 1681 to 9 January 1683/84; volume 2, 215 issues dated 10 January 1683/84 to 7 February 1684/85; volume 3, 146 issues dated 11 February 1684/85 to 9 March 1686/87. It also included 'To Posterity'; 'A Brief History of the Times'; and 'Reasons for this Undertaking.'

19. Kitchin, *Sir Roger L'Estrange*, vi, viii.

20. *C.S.P.D., 1682*, 32.

21. Sutherland, *Restoration Newspaper*, 193–97; Leona Rostenberg, 'The Catholic Reaction: Nathaniel Thompson, "Protector of the Faith,"' in *Literary, Political, Scientific, Religious, and Legal Publishing*, 2: 315–43; Goldie, 'Hilton Gang and the Purge of London,' 49.

22. *C.S.P.D., May 1684 to February 1685*, 187.

23. Knights, *Politics and Opinion*, 160–61.

24. Newton, 'Mask of Heraclitus,' 156. See also *Loyal Protestant*, no.56 (17 September 1681).

25. *True Protestant Mercury*, no.1 (28 December 1680).

26. *Ibid*.

27. *Observator* 1, 'To the Reader.' His derisive remarks conform to the low regard with which the profession was held in Restoration England.

28. L'Estrange said it was indecorous for 'an Old Fellow that now Writes Sixty Eight to run about, Masquerading and Dialoguing' (*Observator* 1, no.15 [21 May 1681]; see also 'To the Reader').

29. Burnet, *History of His Own Time*, 2:211.

30. L'Estrange suffered a 'sharp fit of gout' in January 1682 and was 'very much indisposed with fits' in March 1683 (*C.S.P.D., 1682*, 31; Luttrell, *Brief Historical Relation*, 1:252). There was a five-day interval between two issues of the *Observator* (3 and 8 March 1683), but thereafter the one- or two-day schedule was resumed.

31. *Observator* 3 (1687): 40.

32. Newton, 'Mask of Heraclitus,' 157.

33. Care advised Thompson and L'Estrange to find better correspondents (*Impartial Protestant Mercury*, no.78 [17–20 January 1681/82]; *True Protestant Mercury*, no.177 [13–16 September 1682]).

34. *Observator* 1, no.323 (20 April 1683); *C.S.P.D., 1682*, 141–42.

35. *C.S.P.D., 1682*, 142.

36. *Observator* 1, 'To The Reader.'

37. See, e.g., *Popish Courant* 2, no.41 (16 April 1680), and 3, nos 29 (24 December 1680) and 44 (8 April 1681); and *Popes Harbinger* 3, nos 3 (23 July 1680), 9 (3 September 1680), 16 (22 October 1680).

38. See Newton, 'Mask of Heraclitus,' 152, for comment on Flatman.

39. *Heraclitus Ridens,* e.g., nos 2, 3, 7, 9, 10, 48, 53, 75, 80. Issue no.53 (31 January 1682) is a 'lost and found' for 'a Great Senseless Thing,... with a Swarthy, malicious Look, black Mouth and slandering Tongue.' Anyone with news of this creature was advised to 'send word to Harry Care and he shall write his next Courant in his Commendation.' This unflattering caricature of Care underscores his importance in the press war.

40. For example, 'Whether private men taking upon themselves to teach and advise Kings, does not look as if they thought themselves Kings, or that they Intend to be so as soon as they can?' (*ibid.,* no.19 [7 June 1681]).

41. See *Several Weighty Quaeries Concerning Heraclitus and the Observator, In A Dialogue Betwixt the Corn-Cutter and Mr. Scruple* (1681), for subsequent quotations.

42. *C.S.P.D., 1682,* 446.

43. *Courant* 3, no.46 (22 April 1681): 368.

44. Burnet, *History of His Own Time,* 2: 284–85.

45. See Crist, 'Francis Smith,' 188, 208–22 *passim.*

46. Kitchin, *Sir Roger L'Estrange,* 275.

47. *Ibid.,* 323.

48. See Crist, 'Francis Smith,' 207–8 for a different view of the significance of the label 'Squire.' Care applied that label to his enemies (see *Courant* 3, no.78 [2 December 1681]).

49. *Observator* 1, no.55 (21 September 1681); see also nos 15, 27, 34, 37, 41, 47, 50, 57. Rawlins also showcased Care with the publishers (*Heraclitus Ridens,* nos 1, 6, 15, 17, 19, 34). Thompson too joined Care with a bunch of publishers: 'People... were daily impos'd upon by Curtis, Smith, Harris, Care, Vile, Baldwin, Janeway, etc' (*A choice Collection of 180 Loyal Songs* [1685], preface).

50. *Observator* 1, no.323 (20 April 1683).

51. For example, *The Protestant Cuckold: a new ballad...* (1681) contained a refrain with the words 'Help Care, Vile, Smith, and Curtis.' And *The Lecherous Anabaptist; or, The dipper dipt. A new Protestant ballad, to the tune of Packington's pound* (1681), disparaging Smith, declared, 'He writes twice a week News Domestick & Forrain/As Seditious as Care, Ben. Harris, or Curtis.' Fitzharris's case was truly stated in *A Letter to Mr. C., L.C., F.S. and B.H.* (1681), the initials referring to Care, Curtis, Smith and Harris. The title of *A Faithful Souldier; Or The*

Speech Of A Private Souldier Concerning his Arrears... Dedicated to Parson Peter's Seconds, Smith, Care, Harris, Curtis, and to all the Crew (1681) also linked Care with the publishers.

52. See *Observator* 1, no.51 (8 September 1681).

53. The same formula was used for one other entry, that for Langley Curtis.

54. Sutherland, *Restoration Newspaper* 114, 210–11.

55. *Ibid.*, 210–11. Care was helped by Jasper Hancock, a writer of newsletters, in addition to Vile, who translated the foreign news.

56. *Heraclitus Ridens*, no.27 (2 August 1681). According to the *Dictionary of National Biography*, Care was ill in July 1683, but I cannot confirm this.

57. *Heraclitus Ridens*, no.45 (6 December 1681).

58. This was not the only time during the Restoration when violence and wickedness prevailed (see Pocock, 'Wicked and Turbulent Though It Was').

59. North, *Lives*, 1: 200. Another contemporary historian, Laurence Echard, also credited L'Estrange and Rawlins with 'stem[ming] the Tide of a popular Current' against the government (*The History of England: From the First Entrance of Julius Caesar and the Romans...* [1720], 1009).

60. Knights, *Politics and Opinion*, 347, states that 'mid 1681 marked a turning point' in the defeat of the opposition press. That date downplays the struggle and ignores Care's intransigence.

61. Sir Roger L'Estrange, *The Case Put, Concerning the Succession of His Royal Highness The Duke of York* (1679; reprint, 1680), 7, 8.

62. *Observator* 1, 'To the Reader.' L'Estrange's admission that the 'Faction had the Ascendant of the Government and [that] the Multitude bore down All before them like a Torrent' (*ibid.*) must have rent his soul.

63. *Heraclitus Ridens*, no.16 (17 May 1681); see also no.64 (18 April 1682).

64. *Observator* 1, no.31 (7 July 1681); see also nos 38 (30 July 1681) and 81 (17 December 1681).

65. *Heraclitus Ridens*, nos 10, 19, 36, 47, 48 (4 April, 7 June, 4 October, 20, 27 December 1681).

66. Venting anger and frustration, Care toyed with the idea of not responding to the *Observator* (*True Protestant Mercury*, nos 109 [5–9 May 1682] and 154 [24–28 June 1682]).

67. *Popish Courant* 3, no.46 (22 April 1681).

68. Susan Wiseman, *Drama and Politics in the English Civil War* (Cambridge: Cambridge Univ. Press, 1998), 10.

69. *Ibid.*, 35–36.

70. *Heraclitus Ridens*, no.67 (9 May 1682).

71. *Observator* 1, no.236 (6 November 1682).

72. *Ibid.*, no.40 (6 August 1681).

73. Habermas, *Structural Transformation of the Public Sphere*, 27, 29–30, 38–42.

74. Freist, *Governed by Opinion*, 248–53.

75. *Popish Courant* 3, no.37 (18 February 1681). See also *ibid.*, 2, no.37 (19 March 1680); *True Protestant Mercury*, no.6 (12 May 1681); and *Impartial Protestant Mercury*, no.159 (12–15 July 1682).

76. *Heraclitus Ridens*, no.2 (8 February 1681).

77. *Observator* 1, 'To the Reader.'

78. *Popish Courant* 3, no.2 (11 June 1680) 16; *Courant* 3, no.59 (22 July 1681): 472.

79. *True Protestant Mercury*, no.32 (13–16 April 1681); see also nos 45, 52, 58, 60.

80. *Courant* 3, no.77 (25 November 1681).

81. *Popish Courant* 5, no.1 (25 August 1682).

82. *Cobbett's State Trials and Proceedings*, 7: 113.

83. Keith Thomas, 'The Place of Laughter in Tudor and Stuart England,' *Times Literary Supplement*, 21 January 1977, 77–81.

84. *Weekly Pacquet* 1, no.1 (3 December 1678).

85. Thomas, 'Place of Laughter in Tudor and Stuart England,' 80–81.

86. *A compendyous Regyment or dyetary of Helth,* quoted in John Wardroper, *Jest upon Jest: A Selection from the Jestbooks and Collections of Merry Tales Published from the Reign of Richard III to George III* (London: Routledge & Kegan Paul, 1970), 5–6.

87. *The Grete Herball* (1529).

88. Reverend Isaac Barrow, 'Sermon 16: "Against Foolish Talking and Jesting,"' in *The Theological Works of Dr. Isaac Barrow*, ed. Rev. Alexander Napier, 9 vols (1859), 2: 8.

89. Sir Carr Scroope, quoted in John Harold Wilson, *The Court Wits of the Restoration* (Princeton: Princeton Univ. Press, 1948), 113.

90. Wardroper, *Jest upon Jest*, ix–x, 10–14, 19. The tradition of jest books dated back to 1526, when the first English jest book, *A Hundred Merry Tales*, was printed.

91. Stuart M. Taves, *The Amiable Humorist: A Study of the Comic Theory and Criticism of the Eighteenth and Early Nineteenth Centuries* (Chicago: Univ. of Chicago Press, 1960), 42, 44–46.

92. Barrow, 'Sermon 16,' 9, 11, 14.

93. The most famous example was John Eachard, *The Grounds and Occasions of the Contempt of the Clergy and Religion Enquired Into...* (1670) (see Spurr, *Restoration Church,* 220–21).

94. Spurr, *Restoration Church,* 227.

95. Thomas, 'Place of Laughter in Tudor and Stuart England,' 79.

96. Abel Boyer, *The Wise and Ingenious Companion, French and English; or, A Collection of the wit, of the illustrious person, both ancient and modern* (1700), introduction.

97. *Courant* 3, no.44 (8 April 1681): 351–52.

98. *Heraclitus Ridens,* no.7 (15 March 1681).

99. *Weekly Pacquet* 3, no.71 (14 October 1681): 563–64.

100. *Popish Courant* 3, no.70 (7 October 1681): 558–69 [recto].

101. *Courant* 4, no.17 (14 April 1682): 135.

102. *Ibid.* 3, no.75 (11 November 1681): 599.

103. *Popish Courant* 2, no.11 (19 September 1679): 87.

104. *Popes Harbinger* 3, no.10 (10 September 1680): 79.

105. *Heraclitus Ridens,* nos 49 (3 January 1681/82) and 19 (7 June 1681).

106. Willman, 'Origins of "Whig" and "Tory,"' 254, argues that the use of invective developed outside of Parliament when it was not in session.

107. *Weekly Pacquet* 5, no.1 (25 August 1682): 2.

108. *Ibid.* 3, 'Preface' (24 December 1681); *Popish Courant* 3, no.73 (28 October 1681): 584.

109. *Weekly Pacquet* 3, 'Preface' (24 December 1681).

110. L'Estrange, quoted in Knights, *Politics and Opinion,* 109–10.

111. *Observator* 1, 'To the Reader.'

112. Willman, 'Origins of "Whig" and "Tory,"' 254. Cf. *Heraclitus Ridens,* no.67 (9 May 1682), complaining that it was 'the way of the Party still... constantly to put the worse Names and Characters upon all they don't like.'

113. Harris, *London Crowds, passim.*

114. *Heraclitus Ridens,* no.38 (18 October 1681).

115. *Ibid.,* no.56 (17 September 1681).

116. *True Protestant Mercury,* no.159 (12–15 July 1682).

117. *Loyal Protestant,* nos 107 (24 January 1681/82), 151 (6 May 1682), and 152 (9 May 1682); no.107 (24 January 1681/82); no.133 (25 March 1682); no.128 (14 March 1681/82).

118. *Impartial Protestant Mercury,* no.104 (18–21 April 1682); no.13 (3–7 June 1681); no.89 (24–28 February 1681/82); no.140 (6–10 May 1682).

119. *Popish Courant* 3, no.65 (2 September 1681): 519; *True Protestant*

Mercury, nos 164 (29 July–2 August 1682), 155 (28 June–1 July 1682), 158 (8–12 July 1682).

120. Observator 1, no.76 (30 November 1681).

121. True Protestant Mercury, no.155 (28 June–1 July 1682); Courant 3, no.77 (25 November 1681): 615–16.

122. Observator, no.43 (17 August 1681).

123. Ibid., no.57 (28 September 1681).

124. True Protestant Mercury, nos 138 (29 April–3 May 1681), 155 (28 June–1 July 1682).

125. Observator 1, no.29 (2 July 1681).

126. Heraclitus Ridens, no.2 (8 February 1681).

127. Sutherland, Restoration Newspaper, 17.

128. Sir Roger L'Estrange, Dissenters Sayings. The Second Part... (August 1681), 'Epistle Dedicatory,' 7; L'Estrange, Observator 1, no.294 (24 February 1682).

129. Observator 1, no.70 (12 November 1681); see also ibid., no.55 (21 September 1681).

130. Willman, 'Origins of "Whig" and "Tory,"' 255.

131. Popish Courant 3, no.37 (18 February 1681).

132. This paragraph and the next draw upon Willman, 'Origins of "Whig" and "Tory,"' esp. 253, 258–59, 260.

133. See above.

134. Willman, 'Origins of "Whig" and "Tory,"' 261–62. Willman errs (262) in saying that L'Estrange kept 'Whig' and 'Tory' for the next two years.

135. John Dryden, Absalom and Achitophel A Poem, in The Poems of John Dryden, ed. James Kinsley, 4 vols (Oxford: Clarendon Press, 1958), 'To the Reader,' 1: 215.

136. Heraclitus Ridens, no.45 (6 December 1681).

137. Observator 1, no.97 (8 February 1681/82).

138. Ibid., no.204 (13 September 1682).

139. Popish Courant 5, no.4 (15 September 1682): 32.

140. Spurr, Restoration Church, 121–22.

141. Heraclitus Ridens, no.9 (29 March 1681).

142. Ibid., no.38 (18 October 1681).

143. Observator 1, no.55 (21 September 1681). A 'Jack-Pudding' was a buffoon, a fool (Oxford English Dictionary).

144. Heraclitus Ridens, no.64 (18 April 1682).

145. Ibid., no.40 (1 November 1681).

146. *Ibid.*, nos 27 (2 August 1681) and 33 (13 September 1681).

147. See Sutherland, *Restoration Newspaper,* 195–96. Thompson printed *A Letter to Mr. Miles Prance* (1682) and *A Second Letter* (1682) and iterated the point in the *Loyal Protestant,* nos 125 (7 March 1682) and 127 (11 March 1682).

148. *Observator* 2, no. 19 (21 February 1683/84).

149. For this paragraph, see Spurr, *Restoration Church,* 126–28; Gordon J. Schochet, 'John Locke and Religious Toleration,' in *The Revolution of 1688–89: Changing Perspectives,* ed. Lois G. Schwoerer (Cambridge: Cambridge Univ. Press, 1992), 149.

150. *Popish Courant* 3, no. 40 (11 March 1680/81): 320.

151. *Ibid.*, no. 60 (29 July 1681): 479–80.

152. *Ibid.*, no. 59 (22 July 1681): 471–72.

153. *Ibid.*, no. 68 (23 September 1681): 543–44.

154. *Ibid.*

155. See Mark Goldie and John Spurr, 'Politics and the Restoration Parish: Edward Fowler and the Struggle for St Giles Cripplegate,' *English Historical Review* 109 (1994): 572–96, quotation on 595.

156. John Spurr, '"Latitudinarianism" and the Restoration Church,' *Historical Journal* 31 (1988): 61–82; W. M. Spellman, *The Latitudinarians and the Church of England, 1660–1700* (Athens: Univ. of Georgia Press, 1993).

157. *Courant* 5, no. 6 (29 September 1681): 47–48.

158. *Some Reasons For Separation From the Communion of the Church of England. And The Unreasonableness of Persecution Upon that Account. Soberly Debated, in a Dialogue between a Conformist, and a Nonconformist (Baptist)* (1682) has been assigned to both Hercules Collins and Care.

159. The title continued: *At large recited: And compared with the Doctrines of those commonly called Presbyterians on the one side: And the Tenets of the Church of Rome On the other. Both faithfully quoted from their own most approved Authors by Hen. Care.* It was signed 'Old Bayly, Febr. 6th, 1681/82.'

160. Care, *Utrum horum,* 'To the Reader,' A 2 verso–A 3.

161. *Ibid.*, 'To the Reader.'

162. The ad appeared in *Impartial Protestant Mercury,* no. 93 (10–14 March 1681/82).

163. *A Perfect Guide For Protestant Dissenters. In Case Of Prosecution Upon Any Of The Penal Statutes Made against Them. Together With The Statutes of 35 Eliz. and 22 Car 2. at large. To which is added. A Post-script about*

Ecclesiastical Courts. and Prosecution in Them (1682) was printed for the publisher Richard Baldwin.

164. *Ibid.*, 12.

165. *Popish Courant* 5, nos 36 (27 April 1683) and 37 (4 May 1683): 281–88.

166. See, e.g., L'Estrange, *Dissenters' Sayings*, pt. 1: 20, 32.

167. *Ibid.*, 45. See also *Dissenters Sayings. The Second Part*, 7, 13, 29, 50, 77–79.

168. Kitchin, *Sir Roger L'Estrange*, 266–67. L'Estrange described *Dissenters Sayings. The Second Part* as 'Rubbing up of... some of their own Old Apothegms' (*Observator* 1, no.66 [29 October 1681]).

169. *Heraclitus Ridens*, no.38 (18 October 1681). Rawlins specified articles 19, 20, 26, 27, 34, 35. L'Estrange made essentially the same point in the *Observator* 1, no.31 (7 July 1681).

170. *Heraclitus Ridens*, no.38 (18 October 1681).

171. *Popish Courant* 3, no.34 (28 January 1680/81): 271–72; *Impartial Protestant Mercury*, no.33 (12–16 August 1681).

172. *Observator* 1, no.76 (30 November 1681); *Heraclitus Ridens*, no.13 (26 April 1681).

173. *Heraclitus Ridens*, no.9 (29 March 1681).

174. *Observator* 1, no.76 (30 November 1681).

175. *Heraclitus Ridens*, no.21 (21 June 1681); *Observator* 1, no.31 (7 July 1681).

176. *Observator* 1, no.70 (12 November 1681).

177. *Heraclitus Ridens*, no.72 (13 June 1682).

178. *Observator* 1, no.85 (31 December 1681).

179. *Heraclitus Ridens*, no.38 (18 October 1681).

180. *Ibid.*, no.22 (28 June 1681).

181. *Ibid.*, *Observator* 1, no.66 (29 October 1681).

182. *Observator* 1, nos 395 (30 August 1683) and 293 (21 February 1682).

183. *Ibid.*, nos 82 (21 December 1681), 49 (3 September 1681), 395 (30 August 1683), and 294 (24 February 1682).

184. *Ibid.*, no.293 (21 February 1682).

185. *Ibid.*, no.395 (30 August 1683).

186. L'Estrange also reissued the *Relaps'd Apostate...* in 1681.

187. L'Estrange, *A Memento*, 161.

188. In 1670 Edward Bushel was imprisoned for refusing to follow the direction of the bench to render a guilty verdict in a case involving William Penn. The ruling in Bushel's case made punishing jurors for giving a verdict contrary to the judge's instruction illegal.

189. De Krey, 'Rethinking the Restoration.'

190. *Courant* 3, no.78 (2 December 1681): 624.

191. *Ibid.*

192. *Ibid.* 5, no.3 (8 September 1682): 23–24.

193. *Ibid.*, no.4 (15 September 1682): 32.

194. The lengthy title introduces the contents. Wing, *Short-term Catalogue*, 1:411, gives the date as '1682(?),' but internal and other evidence shows incontrovertibly that the date is 1682. Ashcraft, *Revolutionary Politics*, 204–5 n. 98, also argues for a 1682 date.

195. One of the issues was for Benjamin Harris, one was for John How, and the third was 'to be sold by most booksellers' (see Winthrop S. Hudson, 'William Penn's *English Liberties:* Tract for Several Times,' *William and Mary Quarterly*, 3rd ser., 26 [1969], 578 n. 1).

196. *Ibid.*, 583. See 'Epistle Dedicatory,' in the 1700 edition of Care's *English Liberties.*

197. Hudson, 'William Penn's *English Liberties*,' 579, 584, implies that the table was introduced first in the 1700 edition; however, it appeared in the original edition.

198. Sir John Hawles, *The English-mans Right. A dialogue Between A Barrister at Law, And A Jury-Man...* (1680); Sir John Somers, *The Security of English Men's Lives; or, The Trust, Power and duty of the Grand Jurys of England* (1681), in part a defense of the grand jury's ignoramus verdict in the indictment of Lord Shaftesbury. Other legal handbooks were also available: *A Guide to English juries, settling forth their antiquity, power, and duty* (1682) and two by Joseph Keble, of Gray's Inn, *An Explanation of the laws against recusants, etc.* (1681) and *The Statutes at Large, in Paragraphs and Sections from Magna Charta until this time* (1676; reprint, 1681), the latter advertised in *Loyal Protestant*, no.159 (25 May 1682).

199. Ashcraft, *Revolutionary Politics*, 229 n. 8, assigns this tract to Care, but I cannot accept the attribution. The author refers to his 'Estate and Family,' fails to translate Latin phrases, and writes in a style unlike Care's. It is likely, however, that Care appropriated a handful of sentences; compare *ibid.*, 5–6, with Care, *English Liberties*, 98–99.

200. In the 23 November 1680 debate, Henry Powle said, 'The two great pillars of the government, are parliament and juries; it is this gives us the title of free born Englishmen; for my notion of free Englishmen is this, that they are ruled by laws of their own making, and tried by men of the same condition with themselves' (quoted in *Cobbett's*

State Trials and Proceedings, 8:183). Anchitell Grey did not include the comment in his notes on the debate.

201. Hudson, 'William Penn's *English Liberties*,' 580, writes that 'a major portion of the discussion of Parliament in *English Liberties* (pages 95–110) is lifted verbatim from Penn's tract.' The ideas are similar, but the verbatim indebtedness is limited to some sentences on pages 3 and 4. Hudson's hypothesis that *English Liberties* was written by Penn has been amply discredited (see Edwin B. Bronner and David Fraser, eds, *William Penn's Published Writings, 1660–1726: An Interpretive Bibliography*, vol. 5 of *The Papers of William Penn*, ed. Richard Dunn and Mary Dunn [Philadelphia: Univ. of Pennsylvania Press, 1986], 333 n. 2. See also Ashcraft, *Revolutionary Politics*, 204–5 n. 98).

202. Hudson, 'William Penn's *English Liberties*,' 581.

203. *Ibid.*, 582 n. 8.

204. Zook noted Care's radical defense of the ancient constitution, describing it as 'influential' (*Radical Whigs and Conspiratorial Politics*, 80–82).

205. Care, *English Liberties*, 3, 19. Unless noted otherwise, quotations in this paragraph and the next two are from this source.

206. Henry Powle, quoted in *Cobbett's State Trials and Proceedings*, 8:183.

207. Hart, *Index Expurgatorious Anglicanus*, 241–42.

208. *Observator* 1, no. 106 (2 March 1681); see also no. 32 (9 July 1681).

209. *Ibid.*, no. 33 (13 July 1681).

210. *Ibid.*, no. 76 (30 November 1681).

211. *Heraclitus Ridens*, no. 42 (15 November 1681).

212. *Observator* 1, nos 75 (26 November 1681) and 85 (31 December 1681). Rawlins echoed the point when he remarked, apropos of mayoralty elections, that 'the present contention is for Power' (see *Heraclitus Ridens*, no. 77 [16 July 1682]).

213. *Observator* 1, no. 293 (21 February 1682).

214. *Heraclitus Ridens*, no. 77 (16 July 1682).

215. *Ibid.*, nos 18 (31 May), 19 (7 June), and 29 (16 August 1681).

216. *Observator* 1, no. 31 (7 July 1681).

217. *Ibid.*, nos 5 (25 April 1681) and 41 (10 August 1681), both cited in Knights, *Politics and Opinion*, 308.

218. *Heraclitus Ridens*, no. 75 (4 July 1682).

219. *Ibid.*, nos 76 (11 July 1682) and 77 (15 July 1682).

220. *Ibid.*, no. 75 (4 July 1682).

221. *Ibid.*, no. 29 (16 August 1681).

CHAPTER 6: VICTIM OR TURNCOAT?

1. See Ogg, *England in the Reign of Charles II*, vol. 2, ch. 17.
2. Kitchin, *Sir Roger L'Estrange*, 323–24.
3. See Hutton, *Charles II*, ch. 15.
4. The enthusiast is quoted in Keith Feiling, *History of the Tory Party* (Oxford: Clarendon Press, 1924), 200.
5. Miller, *Popery and Politics*, 189.
6. Hutton, *Charles II*, 405–6.
7. Spurr, *Restoration Church*, 82.
8. Goldie, 'Theory of Religious Intolerance in Restoration England,' esp. 332–34. See also Gordon J. Schochet, 'Samuel Parker, Religious Diversity, and the Ideology of Persecution,' in *The Margins of Orthodoxy: Heterodox Writing and Cultural Response, 1660–1750*, ed. Roger D. Lund (Cambridge: Cambridge Univ. Press, 1995), 119–48.
9. Luke 14:23 reads: 'And the lord said unto the servant, Go out into the highways and hedges, and compel them to come in, that my house may be filled.'
10. Goldie, 'Theory of Religious Intolerance in Restoration England,' 347–50. Force implies education and instruction. The goal is to change the will, not the conscience. Simon Patrick, *Friendly Debate between a Conformist and a Nonconformist* (1669), underlined Proverbs 15:32, 'He that heareth reproof getteth understanding.'
11. Goldie, 'Theory of Religious Intolerance in Restoration England,' 355–56.
12. *Ibid.*, 359–62.
13. *Observator* 1, nos 82 (21 December 1681) and 293 (21 February 1682).
14. *Ibid.*, nos 85 (31 December 1681) and 82 (21 December 1681).
15. *Heraclitus Ridens*, no.77 (18 July 1682).
16. *Ibid.*, no.72 (13 June 1682).
17. *Exact Collection Of the most Considerable Debates in the Honourable House of Commons...* (1681), 31–32.
18. *Heraclitus Ridens*, no.49 (3 January 1681/82).
19. *Ibid.*, no.57 (28 February 1682).
20. *Observator* 1, no.82 (21 December 1681).
21. See Harris, *London Crowds*, 64–67 and nn.
22. Recusancy fines for the years 1681–85 came to a total of £24,330, compared with £3,403 for 1676–80 (Goldie, 'James II and the Dissenters' Revenge,' 57 n. 13).

23. Goldie, 'Hilton Gang and the Purge of London.' The Hiltons inaugurated a newspaper, the *Conventicle Courant*, which lasted from July 1682 to mid-February 1683, its pages full of accounts of the 'proceedings for suppressing unlawful meetings.' Its title was probably a deliberate play on Care's *Popish Courant*, and even if it was not deliberate, it would have evoked Care's publication in the minds of readers, additional evidence of the prominent position Care had attained in the press.

24. Sutherland, *Restoration Newspaper*, 200–201.

25. *Loyal Protestant*, no.7 (29 March 1681).

26. *Ibid.*, no.28 (11 June 1681).

27. Corporation of London Records Office, London Sessions File SF 290: Sessions Book SM 52.

28. Sutherland, *Restoration Newspaper*, 191–92.

29. See Hart, *Index Expurgatorious Anglicanus*, 240–41, for the terms of the charge.

30. BL, Stowe MSS 186, fol. 48r, cited in Richard L. Greaves, *Secrets of the Kingdom: British Radicals from the Popish Plot to the Revolution of 1688–1689* (Stanford: Stanford Univ. Press, 1992), 49.

31. *Heraclitus Ridens*, no.31 (31 August 1681).

32. *Popish Courant* 3, no.73 (28 October 1681): 583–84.

33. *Heraclitus Ridens*, nos 51 (17 January 1682), 53 (31 January 1682).

34. Quoted in Harris, *London Crowds*, 170–71.

35. See above, n. 3; and Behn, *Prologue to Romulus*, preface.

36. *C.S.P.D., 1682*, 68. See also Kitchin, *Sir Roger L'Estrange*, 296–97.

37. *C.S.P.D., 1682*, 146–47.

38. *Loyal Protestant*, no.138 (6 April 1682).

39. *Impartial Protestant Mercury*, no.100 (4–7 April 1682).

40. See Sutherland, *Restoration Newspaper*, 202, for the quotation and note of Janeway's plea bargaining.

41. *C.S.P.D., 1682*, 199.

42. Sutherland, *Restoration Newspaper*, 202–3. Leona Rostenberg, 'English 'Rights and Liberties': Richard and Anne Baldwin, Whig Patriot Publishers,' in *Literary, Political, Scientific, Religious, and Legal Publishing*, 2: 369–416.

43. *Heraclitus Ridens*, no.166 (10 June 1682).

44. *Loyal Protestant*, nos. 1 (9 March 1680/81), 7 (29 March 1681), 27 (7 June 1681), 28 (28 June 1681); Sutherland, *Restoration Newspaper*, 200–201.

45. Sutherland, *Restoration Newspaper*, 246 n. 42.

46. *Ibid.*, 201.

47. See above, ch. 2.

48. *Popish Courant* 4, no.26 (16 June 1682): 207–8.

49. *Heraclitus Ridens*, no.70 (30 May 1682).

50. *Loyal Protestant*, no.162 (1 June 1682); see also no.163 (2 June 1682).

51. *Heraclitus Ridens*, nos 72 (13 June), 73 (20 June), 76 (11 July), 77 (25 July 1682).

52. *Weekly Pacquet* 4, no.32 (28 July 1682): 249.

53. *Heraclitus Ridens*, nos 79 (1 August), 80 (8 August), 82 (22 August 1682).

54. *Popish Courant* 5, no.1 (25 August 1682): 8.

55. *Heraclitus Ridens*, no.80 (8 August 1682).

56. *Popish Courant* 5, no.2 (1 September 1682): 16.

57. Astwood took over starting with number 14 of the *Weekly Pacquet*. Astwood was an established printer with two presses in St Christopher's Alley off Threadneedle Street (see Crist, 'Francis Smith,' 189–90, 259–66).

58. *Dictionary of National Biography*, s.v. 'Care, Henry.'

59. Kitchin, *Sir Roger L'Estrange*, 297 n. 2. The copy of Curtis's spurious fifth volume, written by William Salmon, bears the title *The Fifth Volume Of The Pacquets Of Advice from Rome: Or, The History of Popery, And the Reformation: begining with the Preaching of Martin Luther and the Pope-dome of Leo X and continued till the begining of the English Reformation, in the Reign of Henry VIII. The manner how the Reformation was begun and carried on, A Character of the Roman Clergy. A brief Disquisition of Heresie, and the Punishment due to Hereticks. The lives of some of the first and Principal Reformers, with other things of material Consequence.* The Folger Shakespeare Library lists it as Care's. The only copy of Care's true, complete fifth volume is in the Bodleian Library.

60. Sutherland, *Restoration Newspaper*, 19–20.

61. *True Protestant Mercury*, no.185 (25 October 1682).

62. *Calendar of State Papers, Domestic Series, January 1 to June 30, 1683*, ed. F.H. Blackburne Daniell (London: His Majesty's Stationery Office, 1933), 37–38, hereafter *C.S.P.D., January–June 1683*.

63. *Loyal Protestant*, no.230 (7 November 1682).

64. Corporation of London Records Office, London Sessions File, SF 301, October 1682.

65. *Observator* 1, no.224 (16 October 1682).

66. *Courant*, vol. 5, no.9 (20 October 1682): 71.

67. Nathaniel Thompson speculated that Care had 'gone to look after his Companion the Mayor of Goatham [Langley Curtis]' and remarked that his absence had thrown the 'Brethren' into 'Mourning for the loss of [their Champion]' (*Loyal Protestant*, no.227 [31 October 1682]).

68. *C.S.P.D., 1682*, 564; Corporation of London Records Office, London Sessions File, SF 302, December 1682.

69. Guildhall Library, MS 9060, Archdeaconry of London, Assignation Book in Respect of Proceedings taken against Dissenters, 1680, fol. 97, 4 May 1683.

70. This paragraph draws upon my article 'The Trial of Lord William Russell (1683): Judicial Murder?' *Journal of Legal History* 9 (September 1988): 142–68. The existence of the Rye House Plot can no longer be denied (see Ashcraft, *Revolutionary Politics*; and Zook, *Radical Whigs and Conspiratorial Politics*).

71. *Cobbett's State Trials and Proceedings*, 9: 449. See also Zook, *Radical Whigs and Conspiratorial Politics*, 103–4, 106, 111.

72. Kitchin, *Sir Roger L'Estrange*, 323.

73. Corporation of London Records Office, London Sessions File, SF 307, July 1683.

74. The *Dictionary of National Biography* notes that Care was ill at this time, but I am unable to confirm this.

75. Five and a half years later, Elkanah Settle remarked without explanation that Care's reason for discontinuing the *Weekly Pacquet* was known (*Weekly Pacquet* 6, no.1 [5 January 1688/89]: 2).

76. *C.S.P.D., January–June 1683*, 434. L'Estrange's remark is quoted in full in Kitchin, *Sir Roger L'Estrange*, 324.

77. Another piece, *Juvenalis Redivivus, Or, The First Satyr of Juvenal taught to speak plain English* (1683), 22, linked Care with the radicals Thomas Hunt and Robert Ferguson.

78. See Nelson, 'American Readership of Early British Serials,' 34.

79. Kitchin, *Sir Roger L'Estrange*, 324–25 and n. 1, thought that 'some sort of peace was probably arranged' in 1685, but he gave no evidence.

80. *C.S.P.D., May 1684 to February 1685*, 272.

81. Care was reported in October 1682 as 'not to be found' (see above). As noted in the text, Care remarked that he had not lived in or near St Sepulchre's Parish nor even in London for more than eighteen

months, which would place the excommunication at about May 1684 (Bodl., Rawlinson MS A 289, fols 127–28, Henry Care to 'Right Worshipfull,' [1864?]).

CHAPTER 7: DISSENT'S DEFENDER AND RELIGIOUS LIBERTY

1. See Miller, *Popery and Politics*, ch. 10, for the following points. The quotation is from p.201.

2. *Ibid.*, 203–6. 'Certificates of loyalty' favored Catholics, who were more likely than Dissenters to have supported the king in the Civil Wars. Miller thinks that if toleration had succeeded in 1685, 'loyal' and 'disloyal' Dissenters would have been distinguished.

3. *Ibid.*, ch. 11 and 205.

4. *Calendar of State Papers, Domestic Series, For the Reign of James II, 1685–1689*, ed. Edward Kenneth Timings, 3 vols (London: Her Majesty's Stationery Office, 1960–72), 1: no.1885, hereafter *C.S.P.D., James II.*

5. Marshall, 'Protestant Dissent in England in the Reign of James II,' presents copious examples of the suffering of Dissenters (see ch. 1, esp. 107, 109, 126, 134–35, 136–40, 152–55).

6. Feiling, *History of the Tory Party*, 217; Miller, *Popery and Politics*, 219.

7. For modern historiography and contemporary disagreement noted therein, see, e.g., Paul Birdsall, '"Non Obstante": A Study in the Dispensing Power of English Kings,' in *Essays in History and Political Theory in Honor of Charles Howard McIlwain*, ed. Carl F. Wittke (Cambridge: Harvard Univ. Press, 1936), 37–76; Harris, 'The People, the Law, and the Constitution in Scotland and England,' 39–42; Holdsworth, *History of English Law*, 6: 223–25; Howard Nenner, *By Colour of Law* (Chicago: Univ. of Chicago Press, 1977), 92, 100–101; and Schwoerer, *Declaration of Rights, 1689*, 59–64.

8. Miller, *James II*, 156–57.

9. Goldie, 'James II and the Dissenters' Revenge.'

10. Miller, *Popery and Politics*, 211–13. For the Declaration of Indulgence, see J.P. Kenyon, ed., *Stuart Constitution: Documents and Commentary* (Cambridge: Cambridge Univ. Press, 1966), 410–12, quotation on 410.

11. W.A. Speck, *Reluctant Revolutionaries: Englishmen and the Revolution of 1688* (Oxford: Oxford Univ. Press, 1988), 135; J.R. Jones, *The Revolution of 1688 in England* (London: Weidenfeld & Nicolson, 1972). But see Spurr, *Restoration Church*, 90–94; and Schwoerer, *Declaration of Rights, 1689*, ch. 5.

12. *Dictionary of National Biography*, s.v. 'L'Estrange, Sir Roger.' Rumor had it that L'Estrange would be elevated to the peerage; although unfounded, it underscored the favor he was enjoying at that time.

13. Thomas Babington Macaulay, *History of England from the Accession of James II*, ed. C.H. Firth, 6 vols. (London: Macmillan, 1913–15), 2: 574.

14. *C.S.P.D., James II*, vols 1 and 2 *passim*.

15. See Nottingham University Library, Portland MSS, PwA 2143, for notice of the reward. See also Steele, *Bibliography of Royal Proclamations*, 1: nos 3859, 3798; and *C.S.P.D., James II*, 3: no.760.

16. Zook, *Radical Whigs and Conspiratorial Politics*, 143–44.

17. Ogg, *England in the Reigns of James II and William III*, 153.

18. *C.S.P.D., James II*, vol. 2, no.58; see also no.1084.

19. Kitchin, *Sir Roger L'Estrange*, 365.

20. Jones, *Revolution of 1688*, 87.

21. Miller, *Popery and Politics*, 256; Spurr, *Restoration Church*, 90.

22. Miller, *Popery and Politics*, 257; Jones, *Revolution of 1688*, 88.

23. Miller, *Popery and Politics*, 256.

24. Jones, *Revolution of 1688*, 88; Miller, *Popery and Politics*, 244; Copies of Two Papers written by the late King Charles II and one by the Duchess of York (1688).

25. George F. Duckett, *Penal Laws and Test Act: Questions Touching Their Repeal Propounded in 1687–88 by James II...* (1882), 196; see also 195, 222–23.

26. *Letter to the Author of the Dutch Design Anatomized* (1688), 3.

27. Bodl., Tanner MS 17, fols 1–2, undated.

28. Nottingham University Library, Portland MSS, PwA 2159.

29. *Letter to the Author of the Dutch Design Anatomized*, 3.

30. *Dictionary of National Biography*, s.v. 'L'Estrange, Sir Roger,' citing Luttrell, *Brief Historical Relation*, 1: 392–96.

31. Hudson, 'William Penn's *English Liberties*,' 582 n. 8.

32. Kitchin, *Sir Roger L'Estrange*, 324 n. 1, an apt paraphrase of Care's justification in his *Draconica: Or, An Abstract Of All the Penal-Laws Touching Matters of Religion...*, 2nd edn. (1688), 40. The remark does not appear in the first edition.

33. *Publick Occurrences*, no.18 (19 June 1688).

34. Henry Care, *The Tutor To True English: Or, Brief and Plain Directions, Whereby all that can Read and Write, May Attain to Orthography, (Or the Exact Writing of English)...* (1687).

35. John Yonge Akerman, ed., *Moneys Received and Paid for Secret Services of Charles II and James II*, Camden, 2nd ser., vol. 52 (1851), 199; Guildhall Library, MS 7768/5.

36. The manuscript copy is at the Cambridge University Library, at Ee.4.36 (E). The pagination is imperfect.

37. Care, *Draconica*, 2nd edn, 40. For William Penn, see Gary De Krey, 'The First Restoration Crisis: Conscience and Coercion in London, 1667–73,' *Albion* 25 (1993): 572.

38. Care, *Draconica*, 2nd edn, 40.

39. *Publick Occurrences,* no. 1 (21 February 1688).

40. Ibid., no. 9 (17 April 1688).

41. Care, *Animadversions On A Late Paper*, 39.

42. Care, *Draconica*, 2nd edn, 40; 3rd edn, 21.

43. Jones, *Convergent Forces*, 80.

44. Catholic apologia in this exchange need to be investigated.

45. Francis Peck, comp., *A Complete Catalogue Of All The Discourses Written, Both for and against Popery, In the Time of King James II. Containing in the Whole, An Account of Four hundred and Fifty seven Books and Pamphlets, a great Number of them not mentioned in the three former Catalogues* (1735).

46. Burnet, *History of His Own Time*, 3: 105; the quotation is from Spurr, *Restoration Church*, 90–91.

47. Steven N. Zwicker, 'The Paradoxes of Tender Conscience,' *English Literary History* 63 (1996): 851–69.

48. Anne Docwra, *Spiritual Community, Vindicated amongst people of different persuasions in some things* (1687).

49. For Elinor James's writings, see, e.g., *An Injur'd Prince Vindicated, or, a Scurrilous, and Detracting Pamphlet Answered* [1688?]; *Mrs. James's Defence of the Church of England* (1687); and *Mrs. James's vindication of the Church of England, in an Answer to a Pamphlet entitled a New Test of the Church of England's Loyalty* (1687).

50. Burnet, *History of His Own Time*, 3: 104 n. c.

51. Ibid., 104, 106. Care commented that the clergy labored 'strenuously' and 'daily' brought out 'seditious pamphlets' (*The Legality of the Court Held By His Majesties Ecclesiastical Commissioners, Defended...* [1687 / 88], 31).

52. Kitchin, *Sir Roger L'Estrange,* 365.

53. Zwicker, 'Paradoxes of Tender Conscience,' *passim.*

54. Schochet, 'Samuel Parker, Religious Diversity, and the Ideology of Persecution.'

55. Care dedicated to Penn his *Animadversions On A Late Paper.*

56. *Some Queries concerning Liberty of Conscience, directed to William Penn and Henry Care* [1688]. Wing suggests the date.

57. Care, *Animadversions On A Late Paper*, 8.

58. *Heraclitus Ridens Redivivus*, 3.

59. William Penn, *Som Free Reflections Upon Occasion of the Public Discourse about Liberty of Conscience. And the Consequences thereof in this present Conjuncture...* (1687), 8.

60. Halifax, *Works of George Savile Marquis of Halifax*, 1:76.

61. Care, *Animadversions On A Late Paper*, 8.

62. *Ibid.*, 7; Halifax, *Works of George Savile Marquis of Halifax*, 1: 81–82.

63. Halifax, *Works of George Savile Marquis of Halifax*, 1: 84.

64. *Ibid.*, 76–78.

65. *Ibid.*, 251. *A Letter to a Dissenter* appears in *ibid.*, 250–64, from which the following quotations are drawn.

66. *Ibid.*, 81–82.

67. L'Estrange, *An Answer To A Letter To A Dissenter...* (1687), 3, 11, 12.

68. Bodl., Rawlinson MS C 732, 'A Letter to Mr. Care. Upon his Animadversions on a Letter to a Dissenter' [1687], fol. 1. Kitchin calls L'Estrange's reply 'feeble' (*Sir Roger L'Estrange*, 325 n. 1).

69. Halifax, *Works of George Savile Marquis of Halifax*, 1: 82.

70. Bodl., Rawlinson MS C 732.

71. Historical Manuscript Commission Reports, *Seventh Report*, app. 1, 505b.

72. Care, *Animadversions On A Late Paper*, 3.

73. Burnet, *History of His Own Time,* 3: 103, 105.

74. Care, *Animadversions On A Late Paper*, 31.

75. *Ibid.*, 33.

76. *Ibid.*, 34.

77. For example, under pressure Daniel Whitby retracted his *The Protestant Reconciler* (1682). Samuel Bolde published his sermon against persecution in 1682 but then withdrew it. Edward Pearse's *The Conformists Plea for the Nonconformists...* (1681) likewise riled the authorities (Mark Goldie, 'Politics and the Restoration Parish: Edward Fowler and the Struggle for St Giles Cripplegate,' *English Historical Review* 109 [1994]: 574–75. See also Spurr, *Restoration Church*, 83–84).

78. Care, *Animadversions On A Late Paper,* 32. On Bolde, see Spurr, *Restoration Church*, 83, 153–54.

79. Care, *Animadversions On a Late Paper*, 31. He had used this disparaging phrase earlier (see above, ch. 3).

80. *Ibid.*, 4.

81. *Ibid.*, 4, 36–37.

82. *Publick Occurrences*, no.10 (24 April 1688).

83. *Ibid.*, no.20 (3 July 1688).

84. Care, *Draconica*, 14–15.

85. Speck, *Reluctant Revolutionaries*, 184. The circumstances under which this tract was written are set out in John Carswell, *The Descent on England: A Study of the English Revolution of 1688 and Its European Background* (London: Cresset Press, 1969), 83–84, 96–98, 102–4, 107–10.

86. *A Letter Writ by Mijn Heer Fagel, Pensioner of Holland, to Mr. James Stewart To which is prefixt an Account in Dutch of the Letter Translated… into English* (1688), 2. Fagel's explanatory preface is dated 10 April 1688.

87. *Ibid.*, 4.

88. Carswell, *Descent on England*, 110.

89. *Animadversions upon Mijn Heer Fagels Letter Concerning Our Penal Laws And Tests* (1688), dedicated 'To William Penn Esq.' Richard Ashcraft first attributed this tract to Care, but without explanation (see *Revolutionary Politics*, 487). There is little doubt that Care was the author. The dedication to Penn, the statement that Penn had asked him to consider Fagel's letter, the description of his religious views, the evident legal learning and the careful reasoning all point to Care.

90. Care, *Animadversions upon Mijn Heer Fagels Letter*, 5, 22.

91. *Ibid.*, 24.

92. *Ibid.*, 15.

93. *Ibid.*, 22.

94. John Locke, *A Letter Concerning Toleration,* in *Locke on Politics, Religion, and Education*, ed. Alan Cranston (London: Collier-Macmillan, 1965), 108, 110, 113, 114.

95. See Schochet, 'John Locke and Religious Toleration,' 147–64, for a different view.

96. Gordon J. Schochet, 'Toleration, Revolution, and Judgment in the Development of Locke's Political Thought,' *Political Science* 40 (July 1988): 84–96.

97. Ashcraft, *Revolutionary Politics*, 501.

98. John Harrison and Peter Laslett, *The Library of John Locke* (Oxford: Bibliographical Society, Oxford Univ. Press, 1965), 101. The two tracts were *Legality of the Court* and *A Vindication of the Proceedings of His Majesties Ecclesiastical Commissioners. Against the Bishop of London, and the Fellows of Magdalen-College* (1688).

99. *Liberty of Conscience Asserted. Or A Looking-Glass For Persecutors...* (1687).

100. *Ibid.*, 3, 4, 5, 10.

101. *Ibid.*, 18, 20, 23, 24, 26.

102. See Schwoerer, *Declaration of Rights, 1689*, 65–66; and Ogg, *England in the Reigns of James II and William III*, 175–80.

103. Care, *Vindication of the Proceedings*, 2.

104. *Ibid.*, 47, 48.

105. See the following, all by Care: *ibid.*, esp. 38–41, 44, 46–48, 61; *Legality of the Court*, 7, 9, 11–15, 17–19, 29; *Draconica*, 10; *An Answer to a Paper, importing a Petition Of The Archbishop of Canterbury. And Six other Bishops...* (1688), 20–26; and Care, *Animadversions On A Late Paper*, 28, 29. The quotations are from *Legality of the Court*, 7, and *Vindication of the Proceedings*, 61. Care argued correctly that article 17 of the Elizabethan Act of Supremacy vested in the king visitorial power and that at the Restoration a law affirmed the king's supremacy over all ecclesiastical affairs and persons.

106. Care, *Vindication of the Proceedings*, 58.

107. *Ibid.*, 70.

108. In writing *Draconica* Care may have used William Cawley, *The laws of Q. Elizabeth, K. James and K. Charles the first. Concerning Jesuits, seminary priests... explained* (1680); Keble, *Explanation of the laws against recusants, etc.*; and *idem, Statutes at Large, in Paragraphs and Sections*.

109. Care, *Draconica*, intro.

110. Care, *An Answer to a Paper*, 20.

111. Burnet's copy is in the Folger Shakespeare Library at C511.

112. Elkanah Settle continued the paper for a time (see the conclusion, below).

113. Sutherland, *Restoration Newspaper*, 22.

114. *Publick Occurrences*, no. 1 (21 February 1687/88).

115. Marginalia appear in *ibid.*, nos 8, 12, 14 (twice), 16, 22 (10 April, 8, 22 May, 5 June, 17 July 1688).

116. See the copy at the Bodleian Library.

117. Goldie, 'James II and the Dissenters' Revenge,' hypothesis on 60.

118. *Publick Occurrences*, no. 3 (6 March 1687/88). Unless otherwise noted, the quotations in the next several paragraphs are from this newspaper.

119. The reference was to the court of a great mogul.

120. Care, *Animadversions On A Late Paper*, 34.

121. Care, *Answer to a Paper*, 9–10, 14.

122. Care, *Legality of the Court*, 15.

123. See the copy of *Publick Occurrences*, no.12 (8 May 1688), in the Bodleian Library.

124. Care, *Animadversions On A Late Paper*, 4–5.

125. See also *Publick Occurrences*, no.6 (27 March 1687/88).

126. Care, *Draconica*, 12, 15.

127. Mary Maples Dunn, *William Penn Politics and Conscience* (Princeton: Princeton Univ. Press, 1967), 64.

128. Care, *Animadversions On A Late Paper*, 20; Care, *An Answer To a Paper, importing a Petition Of The Archbishop of Canterbury*, 4, 18.

129. See *Publick Occurrences*, nos 9, 15, 16, 21 (17 April, 29 May, 5 June, 10 July 1688).

130. Bishop Gilbert Burnet, *Apology for the Church of England* (1688), 3.

131. Other material demeaned Care. A broadside entitled *The Advice* referred to Care as 'that jack of all Religions' and intimated that he resided in Hell. A poem, 'To the King's most Excellent Majesty,' reviewed James's policies regarding corporations and parliament and remarked sarcastically that 'your new Friends stand every where,/Of which we recommend one pair,/Honest Will Pen, and Harry Care' (*A Collection of the newest and Most Ingenious Poems* [1687], 3).

132. Bodl., Firth MSS, b. 20, fol. 135r. A slightly different version appears on fol. 136r. The Bodleian gives the date as 1687.

133. *Publick Occurrences*, nos 7 (3 April) and 18 (19 June 1688).

134. *Ibid.*, no.7 (3 April 1688).

135. *Ibid.*, no.15 (29 May 1688).

136. Freist, *Governed by Opinion*, 256 and n. 45.

137. Settle, *Publick Occurrences*, no.25 (7 August 1688).

CONCLUSION

1. Luttrell, *Brief Historical Relation*, 1: 453; Settle, *Publick Occurrences*, no.26 (14 August 1688).

2. Defoe, 'Prototype and Plan of the Review,' 7: 618.

3. It is impossible now to identify the exact site of Care's grave.

4. For the paper, see Guildhall Library, MS 4510/1. The *Dictionary of*

National Biography states that an 'inscription' was 'nailed' to Care's coffin. The paper was advertised in Settle, *Publick Occurrences*, no.26 (14 August 1688).

5. Settle, *Publick Occurrences*, no.26 (14 August 1688).

6. See *A Third Collection of the newest and Most Ingenious Poems, Satyrs, Songs, etc. against Popery and Tyranny, relating to the Times* (1689), 7–8.

7. *Harry Care's Last Will and Testament* [1688]. A unique original copy is located at Chetham's Library, Manchester.

8. See *The Muses Farewel To Popery & Slavery, Or, A Collection Of Miscellany Poems, Satyrs, Songs…* (1690), 51–53.

9. Settle, *Publick Occurrences*, no.26 (14 August 1688).

10. Historical Manuscript Commission Reports, *Seventh Report*, app. 1, 483a.

11. Settle, *Publick Occurrences*, nos 28 (28 August) and 30 (11 September 1688).

12. Settle, *Weekly Pacquet* 6, no.2 (1 February 1689): 16; *London Gazette*, no.2417 (7–10 January 1689). The order instructed the master of the Stationers' Company and others to search out all 'false, scandalous, and seditious books, papers of news, and pamphlets' and to bring the persons responsible for them to justice (see Morrice, 'Ent'ring Book,' 2: 427).

13. Settle, *Weekly Pacquet* 6, no.1 (5 January 1688/89): 1–4.

14. *Ibid.* 6, no.3 (8 February 1688/89): 17–18, 24.

15. *Orange Gazette*, no.4 (7–10 January 1688/89).

16. Settle, *Weekly Pacquet* 6, no.2 (1 February 1688/89): 16.

17. The tract is dated 1688; it appeared in the *Term Catalogue* in the spring of 1689.

18. The tract is listed in Wing, *Short-title Catalogue*, under Care's name.

19. *The Last Legacy of Henry Care, Gent.*, 'To the Reader.'

20. *Ibid.*, 'To the Reader' and 10–11.

21. *Ibid.*, 77–78.

22. Defoe, 'Prototype and Plan of the Review,' 7: 618.

23. Timperley, *Dictionary of Printers and Printing*, 552, 556, 570, 571, 573.

24. M. 'Who was the Author of 'The Modest Enquiry,' etc.' *Notes and Queries* 3, no.75 (5 April 1851): 264.

25. Echard, *History of England*, 1085.

26. Macaulay, *History of England*, 2: 872–73. The first Lord Acton included in his papers extracts from three of Care's tracts, including *Draconica* and *Animadversions On A Late Paper* (see Cambridge

University Library, Transcripts and Extracts. 'A Collection of mis-cellaneous historical notes, transcripts & extracts made by & for the 1st Lord Acton,' Add. MSS 4877 [B], fols 28, 276. See also 'Roman Catholicism in England: Extracts concerning,' Add. MSS 4857 [C], fol. 234).

27. *Weekly Pacquet* 5, no. 1 (25 August 1682): 4–6, quotation on 4.

28. Kitchin, *Sir Roger L'Estrange*, 272.

29. There is no evidence that Care, Penn, or Locke knew of the advanced proposals for religious liberty propounded in the 1640s.

30. *English Liberties*, originally published in 1682, was reprinted in England in 1688, 1691, 1692, 1700, 1703, 1719, 1721 and 1766; in America in 1721 and 1774.

31. Hudson, 'William Penn's *English Liberties*,' 584 and n. 13.

32. *Ibid.*

33. This recommendation appeared in the prefaces of the 1719, 1721 and 1774 editions.

34. Hudson, 'William Penn's *English Liberties*,' 585.

35. Bodl., Ashmole MS 1059, catalog, 75, lot 84 (section on common and statute law).

36. See the catalog at Sion College. James also gave the library a copy of Care's *Practical Physick*. A printer, writer and political activist on behalf of James II and printers, James was regarded as eccentric by her contemporaries. Today she is beginning to be noticed (see Lois G. Schwoerer, 'Women's Public Political Voice in England: 1640–1740,' in *Women Writers and the Early Modern British Political Tradition*, ed. Hilda L. Smith [Cambridge: Cambridge Univ. Press, 1998], 66–72; and McDowell, *Women of Grub Street, passim*).

37. Mrs Elizabeth Boardman, archivist, All Souls College, Oxford, letter to author, 19 August 1997. The Codrington Library at All Souls College holds the 1719 edition, but there is no record of the date of acquisition.

38. See above, ch. 8.

39. See the bookplate in the copy of *English Liberties* at the Folger Shakespeare Library.

40. See Caroline Robbins, *The Eighteenth-Century English Commonwealthman: Studies in the Transmission, Development, and Circumstance of English Liberal Thought from the Restoration of Charles II until the War with the Thirteen Colonies* (Cambridge: Harvard Univ. Press, 1959).

41. Forrest McDonald, *Novus Ordo Seclorum: The Intellectual Origins of the Constitution* (Lawrence: Univ. Press of Kansas, 1985), 40.

42. The lengthy title continued, *Containing I. Magna Charta, with a learned Comment upon it… V. The Charter of Liberties granted by… William Penn to the Free-men and Inhabitants of the Province of Pennsilvania… in America.* A facsimile was reprinted in 1897. Winthrop Hudson, in 'William Penn's *English Liberties*,' was the first to note Penn's indebtedness to *English Liberties.* As mentioned above, in chapter 6, Penn scholars and others reject Hudson's hypothesis that Penn was the author of *English Liberties.*

43. H. Trevor Colbourn, *The Lamp of Experience: Whig History and the Intellectual Origins of the American Revolution* (Chapel Hill: Univ. of North Carolina Press, 1965), 14.

44. *Ibid.*, 135, 205.

45. See Edwin Wolf, *Book Culture of a Colonial American City* (Oxford: Oxford Univ. Press, 1988), 119–20. See also Colbourn, *Lamp of Experience*, 206–8.

46. E. Millicent Sowerby, ed., *A Catalogue of the Library of Thomas Jefferson*, 5 vols (Washington, D.C.: Library of Congress, 1952–59), 118–19; Colbourn, *Lamp of Experience*, 159, 218, 221.

47. An advertisement appeared on pp. 55–56 of Franklin's reprint of *Every Man his own Doctor: or, The poor planter's physician…* (1673; reprint, 1734).

48. Clinton Laurence Rossiter, *Seedtime of the Republic: The Origin of the American Tradition of Political Liberty* (New York: Harcourt, Brace & Co., 1953), 388–89.

49. John Adams, quoted in Rossiter, *Seedtime of the Republic*, 388–89.

50. See Lois G. Schwoerer, 'British Lineages and American Choices,' in *The Bill of Rights: Government Proscribed*, ed. Ronald Hoffman and Peter J. Albert (Charlottesville: Univ. Press of Virginia for the United States Capitol Historical Society, 1997), 1–41.

51. Rossiter, *Seedtime of the Republic*, 388.

52. Colbourn, *Lamp of Experience*, 29, 37.

53. Hudson, 'William Penn's *English Liberties*,' 585.

54. J.C.D. Clark, *The Language of Liberty, 1660–1832: Political Discourse and Social Dynamics in the Anglo-American World* (Cambridge: Cambridge Univ. Press, 1994), 27 n. 101.

55. Haley, *First Earl of Shaftesbury*, 744–45.

56. Bishop Gilbert Burnet, *An Exhortation To Peace and Union, In A Sermon Preached at St Lawrence-Jury* (1689), 15.

Selected Bibliography

MANUSCRIPT SOURCES

Bodleian Library: Add. MSS 34,362, fol. 95b; Ashmole MSS 1059, 1223; Ballard MSS 12; MSS Carte 39; Eng. MSS, Misc. c. 4, Papers of George Hickes; Firth MSS, b. 20; Hearne Diaries; Rawlinson MS A 289, Henry Care to 'Right Worshipfull,' [1684?]; Rawlinson MS C 732, 'A Letter to Mr. Care. Upon his Animadversions on a Letter to a Dissenter' [1687]; Rawlinson MS D 924, fol. 391, speech of James II, n.d.; Tanner MS 17, 'Some Queries For Mr. Care to Chew, Relating to His Ignoramus Juries,' dated 14 December 1681.

British Library: Sloane MSS 2285; MS Library catalog [1687?], JE EL 3; Catalogus Bibliothecae Evelyniae, JE EL 11; 128.i.1 (2), 'Bibliotheca Nobilissimi Principis Johannes Ducis de Novo-Castro, etc., being a large collection of books contained in the libraries of the most Noble William and Henry Cavendish, and John Hollis. [*sic*], late Dukes of Newcastle... which will be sold by Nath. Noel, 2nd March 1718–19' [London, 1719].

Cambridge University, Magdalene College, Pepys Library: PL 2,875/456–91, 'The Journall of ye Green-Ribbon-Clubb, at ye King's Head Taverne over against ye Temple in Fleet Street viz. from 1678 to 1681'; Pepys Papers, 2881/89.

Cambridge University Library: Add. MSS 4857 (C), Lord Acton's Collection; Add. MSS 4877 (B), Lord Acton's Further Collection; Ee.4.36 (E), MSS in Henry Care's hand.

Corporation of London Records Office: London Sessions File SF 290: Sessions
   Book SM 52; SF 301, SF 302, SF 307; Misc. MSS 112.5, St Sepulchre's
   Parish, 1678.
Dr Williams's Library: Roger Morrice, 'Ent'ring Book, Being an Historical
   Register of Occurrences From April, Anno, 1677 to April 1691.' 4 vols.
Folger Shakespeare Library: L.c. 1–3950, 'The Newdigate Newsletters,
   Addressed to Sir Richard Newdigate, 1st Bart., and to 2nd Bart.,
   1673/74–1715.'
Guildhall Library: MSS 3162, St Sepulchre – names of communicants,
   1680–82, 1685; 4510/1; 7768/5, 9060.
Lambeth Palace Library: Sion MS AB.XI.5, 'Sion College Library
   Catalogue'; Sion MS ARC E40.2, 'Catalogue of the Governors of
   Sion College, 1632–1740'; Sion MS ARC I.40.2.E.6.4, 'Sion College
   Book of Benefactors, 1629–1888'; Sion MS ARC L40.2.E29, 'Album
   Admissorum ad Studentum in Bibliotheca MDCXXIX.'
Library of Congress, Manuscript Division: 0452B, London Newsletter
   Collection.
Longleat: Coventry MSS.
Public Record Office: Admiralty 77, Greenwich Hospital Original
   Newsletters; KB 10/1; PC 2/67; PC 2/68; PRO 30/24/6 B. 420; SP
   30/G.

PRINTED CATALOGS, LETTERS, MEMOIRS, AND
PARLIAMENTARY MATERIALS

*Articles of High Misdemeanours, Humbly offered and Presented to the
   Consideration of His Most Sacred Majesty, and his Most Honourable Privy
   Councel, against Sir William Scrogs Lord Chief Justice of the Kings Bench,
   Exhibited by Dr. Oats, and Captain Bedlow. Together with his Lordships
   Answer thereunto.* [1680].
A Biographical Dictionary of British Radicals in the Seventeenth Century. Ed.
   Richard L. Greaves and Robert Zaller. 3 vols. Brighton: Harvester,
   1982.
Boyer, Abel. *The Wise and Ingenious Companion, French and English; or, A
   Collection of the wit, of the illustrious persons, both ancient and modern.*
   1700.
Bulstrode, Sir Richard. *Memoirs and Reflections upon the Reign and
   Government of King Charles the Ist. and K. Charles the IId.* 1721.

Burnet, Bishop Gilbert. *History of His Own Time: With Notes By The Earls of Dartmouth and Hardwicke, Speaker Onslow, And Dean Swift* 6 vols. 1833.

Calendar of State Papers, Domestic Series, Of The Reign Of Charles II. 1661–1662, preserved in the State Department of Her Majesty's Public Record Office. Ed. Mary Anne Everett Green. 1861.

Calendar of State Papers, Domestic Series, Of The Reign Of Charles II. 1663–1664, preserved in the State Department of Her Majesty's Public Record Office. Ed. Mary Anne Everett Green. 1862. Reprinted with the permission of the Controller of Her Britannic Majesty's Stationery Office, Nendeln, Liechtenstein: Kraus Reprint, 1968.

Calendar of State Papers, Domestic Series, Of The Reign Of Charles II. 1664–1665, preserved in the State Department of Her Majesty's Public Record Office. Ed. Mary Anne Everett Green. 1863. Reprinted with permission of the Controller of Her Britannic Majesty's Stationery Office, Nendeln, Liechtenstein: Kraus Reprint, 1968.

Calendar of State Papers, Domestic Series, 1660–1670, preserved in the State Paper Department of Her Majesty's Public Record Office. Ed. Mary Anne Everett Green. 1895. Addenda.

Calendar of State Papers, Domestic Series, January 1st, 1679, to August 31st, 1680. Ed. F.H. Blackburne Daniell. London: His Majesty's Stationery Office, 1915.

Calendar of State Papers, Domestic Series, September 1st, 1680, to December 31st, 1681. Ed. F.H. Blackburne Daniell. London: His Majesty's Stationery Office, 1921.

Calendar of State Papers, Domestic Series, January 1st to December 31st, 1682. Ed. F.H. Blackburne Daniell. London: His Majesty's Stationery Office, 1932.

Calendar of State Papers, Domestic Series, January 1 to June 30, 1683. Ed. F.H. Blackburne Daniell. London: His Majesty's Stationery Office, 1933.

Calendar of State Papers, Domestic Series, October 1, 1683–April 30, 1684, preserved in Her Majesty's Public Record Office. Ed. F.H. Blackburne Daniell, M.A. and Francis Bickley. London: His Majesty's Stationery Office, 1938.

Calendar of State Papers, Domestic Series, For the Reign of James II, 1685–1689. Ed. Edward Kenneth Timings. 3 vols London: Her Majesty's Stationery Office, 1960–72.

Catalogus Librorum Theologicorum, Philologicorum, Mathematicorum, etc. Ed. David Stockes *et al.* 1685.

Clarke, Rev. J.S., ed. *The Life of James the Second King of England. etc. collected Out of Memoirs Writ Of His Own Hand.* 2 vols 1816.

Clavel, Robert, comp. *A Catalogue Of All The Books Printed In England Since The Dreadful Fire of London, in 1666. To the End of Michaelmas Term, 1672. Collected by Robert Clavel.* 1673.

Cobbett, William. *Cobbett's Complete Collection of State Trials and Proceedings For High Treason And Other Crimes And Misdemeanors from the Earliest Period To The Present Time.* Ed. Thomas Howell *et al.* 33 vols 1809–26.

————. *Cobbett's Parliamentary History of England: From The Norman Conquest, In 1066, to The Year 1803.* Ed. T.C. Hansard. 36 vols 1806–20. New York: Johnson Reprint Co., 1966.

A Compleat Catalogue Of All The Stitch'd Books and Single Sheets Printed since the First Discovery of The Popish Plot, (September 1678.) to January 1679/80. To which is Added a Catalogue of all His Majesties Proclamations, Speeches, and Declarations, with the Orders of the King and Council, and what Acts of Parliament have been Published since the Plot. 1680.

A Complete Collection of Papers, In Twelve Parts: Relating to the Great Revolutions In England and Scotland, From the Time of the Seven Bishops Petitioning K. James II. against the Dispensing Power, June 8, 1688, to the Coronation of King William and Queen Mary, April 11. 1689. 1689.

Dalrymple, John. *Memoirs of Great Britain and Ireland.* 2 vols 1771–73.

Dunton, John. *The Life and Errors of John Dunton Late Citizen of London.* 1705.

Echard, Laurence. *The History of England: From the First Entrance of Julius Caesar and the Romans, To the Conclusion of the Reign of King James the Second, and the Establishment of King William and Queen Mary upon the Throne, in the Year 1688.* 1720.

Ellis, G.A., ed. *The Ellis Correspondence, 1686–1688.* 2 vols 1831.

Evelyn, Sir John. *The Diary of John Evelyn.* Ed. E.S. De Beer. 6 vols Oxford: Clarendon Press, 1955.

An Exact Collection Of the most Considerable Debates in the Honourable House of Commons, At The Parliament Held At Westminster The One and twentieth of October, 1680. 1681.

Foxcroft, H.C., ed. *The Life and Letters of Sir George Savile, Bart. First Marquis of Halifax.* 2 vols 1898.

Foxwell [Foxcroft], H.C., ed. 'Some Unpublished Letters of Gilbert Burnet the Historian.' In *The Camden Miscellany, Volume The Eleventh.* Camden, 3rd ser., 13. London: Royal Historical Society, 1907.

Gee, Edward, comp. *Catalogue Of all the Discourses Published Against Popery, During the Reign of King James II. By the Members of the Church of England, And by the Non-conformists. With the names of the Authors of them.* 1689.

Grey, Anchitell. *Debates of the House of Commons, from the year 1667 to the year 1694.* 10 vols 1763.

Hale, Sir Matthew. *The History of the Common Law of England.* Ed. Charles M. Gray. Chicago: Univ. of Chicago Press, 1971.

Henning, Basil Duke, ed. *History of Parliament: The House of Commons, 1660–1690.* 3 vols London: Secker & Warburg for the History of Parliament Trust, 1983.

Historical Manuscripts Commission. *Calendar of the Manuscripts of the Marquess of Ormonde, K.P., Preserved at Kilkenny Castle.* New series, vol. 5. Hereford: His Majesty's Stationery Office, 1908.

————. *Seventh Report of the Royal Commission on Historical Manuscripts.* Parts 1 and 2. London: Her Majesty's Stationery Office, 1879.

————. *Eleventh Report, Appendix, Part II. The Manuscripts of the House of Lords, 1678–1688.* London: Her Majesty's Stationery Office, 1887.

————. *Twelfth Report, Appendix, Part VI. The Manuscripts of the House of Lords, 1689–1690.* London: Her Majesty's Stationery Office, 1889.

————. *Thirteenth Report, Appendix, Part V. The Manuscripts of the House of Lords, 1690–1691.* London: Her Majesty's Stationery Office, 1892.

————. *Fourteenth Report, Appendix, Part VI. The Manuscripts of the House of Lords, 1692–1693.* London: Her Majesty's Stationery Office, 1894.

House of Commons. *Journals of the House of Commons.* 56 vols London, 1803–20.

House of Lords. *Journals of the House of Lords.* 1660–89.

An Impartial Account Of The Tryal Of Francis Smith, Upon an Information Brought against him For printing and Publishing a late Book commonly known by the Name of Tom Ticklefoot, etc. As Also Of the Tryal of Jane Curtis, Upon an Information brought against her for Publishing and putting to Sale a Scandalous Libel, called A Satyr Against Injustice Or Scroggs upon Scroggs. 1680.

Kenyon, J.P., ed. *Stuart Constitution: Documents and Commentary.* Cambridge: Cambridge Univ. Press, 1966.

Locke, John. *The Correspondence of John Locke.* Ed. E. S. De Beer. 8 vols Oxford: Oxford Univ. Press, 1976–89.

Lord, George de F., ed. *Poems on Affairs of State: Augustan Satirical Verse, 1660–1714.* 7 vols New Haven: Yale Univ. Press, 1963–75.

Luttrell, Narcissus. *A Brief Historical Relation of State Affairs: from September 1678 to April 1714.* 6 vols 1857.

————. *Narcissus Luttrell's Popish Plot Catalogues.* Intro. F. C. Francis. Oxford: Basil Blackwell for the Luttrell Society, 1956.

Memoirs Of The Verney Family During The Seventeenth Century Compiled From The Papers and Illustrated By The Portraits At Claydon House By Frances Parthenope Verney and Margaret M. Verney. 2nd edn 2 vols London: Longmans, Green, 1907.

The Muses Farewel To Popery & Slavery, Or, A Collection Of Miscellany Poems, Satyrs, Songs, etc. Made by the Most Eminent Wits of the Nation, as the Shams, Intreagues, and Plots of Priests and Jesuits gave occasion. Second Edition, with Large Additions, most of them never before printed. 1690.

North, Roger. *Examen: Or, An Enquiry Into The Credit and Veracity of a Pretended Complete History; shewing The perverse and wicked Design of it and the Many Falsities and Abuses of Truth contained in it.* 1740.

————. *The Lives of The Right Hon. Francis North, Baron Guilford; The Hon. Sir Dudley North; and The Hon and Rev. Dr. John North By The Hon. Roger North, Together With The Autobiography Of The Author.* Ed. A. Jessop. 3 vols 1826.

Reading, William. *The History of the Ancient and present State of Sion College nr. Cripplegate, London and of the London Clergy's Library there by William Reading, MA, Library Keeper.* 1724.

The Resolutions Of The House Of Commons, For The Impeachment Of Sir William Scroggs Knt. Chief Justice of the Court of King's Bench;... Upon the Report of the Committee of the Commons Appointed to Examine the Proceedings of the Judges in Westminster Hall. 1680.

Scott, Sir Walter. *A Collection of Scarce and Valuable Tracts... Selected from... Pub-lic as well as Private Libraries, Particularly That of the Late Lord Somers.* 13 vols 1809–15.

Scroggs, Sir William. *The Answer Of Sir William Scroggs, Kt. Lord Chief Justice of the King's Bench, To The Articles of Dr. Titus Oates, and Mr. William Bedlow.* 1680.

Sowerby, E. Millicent, ed. *A Catalogue of the Library of Thomas Jefferson.* 5 vols Washington, D.C.: Library of Congress, 1952–59.

Statutes of the Realm. Ed. A. Luders *et al.* 11 vols. 1810–28.

A Third Collection of the newest and Most Ingenious Poems, Satyrs, Songs, etc. against Popery and Tyranny, relating to the Times. 1689.

Thompson, E.M., ed. *Correspondence of the Family of Hatton, being Chiefly letters addressed to Christopher First Viscount Hatton, 1601–1704.* Camden, n.s., 2 vols London, 1878.

Thompson, Nathaniel, comp. *A choice Collection of 180 Loyal Songs.* 1685.

Thoyras, Paul de Rapin. *The History of England, as well Ecclesiastical as Civil.* Trans. N.Tindall. 15 vols 1728–31.Vols 13–15 cover Restoration England.

Timperley, C.H. *A Dictionary of Printers and Printing, with the Progress of Literature, ancient and modern, Bibliographical illustration.* 1839.

The Triall of Henry Carr, Gent. At The Guild-Hall of the City of London, the 2d Day of July, 1680… . Also the Tryal of Elizabeth Cellier, At The Kings-Bench-Bar, July the 11th 1680. 1681.

Wood, Anthony A. *Athenae Oxonienses: An Exact History Of All The Writers And Bishops Who Have Had Their Education In The University of Oxford. By Anthony Wood, M.A. of Merton College.* Ed. Philip Bliss. 4 vols 1813–20. Reprint, Hildesheim: Georg Olms Verlagsbuchhandlung, 1969.

NEWSPAPERS AND JOURNALS BY HENRY CARE

Poor Robins Intelligence, 28 March 1676–2 October 1677, 23 October 1677–6 November 1677. Unnumbered sheets at Bodleian Library.

Poor Robins Intelligence, newly revived; published for the accommodations of all ingenious persons, nos. 1–3 (4–16 September 1679); continued as *Poor Robins Intelligence revived,* nos. 4–29 (24 September 1679–10 March 1680), 31–32 (24 March–1 April 1680).

Poor Robins Public and Private Occurances. And Remarks written for the Sake of Merriment, and harmless Recreation, 12 May–[2] June, 13 June–4 July 1688.

Publick Occurrences Truely Stated, nos. 1–23 (21 February–24 July 1688) by Care; no.24 (31 July 1688) probably by Elkanah Settle; nos. 25–34 (7 August–2 October 1688) by Elkanah Settle.

Snotty Nose Gazette: or, Coughing Intelligence, 24 November 1679.

The True Protestant Mercury, Or Occurrences Foreign and Domestick, nos 1–188 (28 December 1680–25 October 1682). Written largely by Care. Published by Langley Curtis and, in his absence, Jane Curtis.

The Weekly Discoverer Strip'd Naked: Or, Jest and Earnest Expos'd to Publick View in his Proper Colours, nos 1–5 (16 February–16 March 1681).

The Weekly Pacquet of Advice from Rome: Or, The History of Popery. A Deduction of the Usurpations of the Bishops of Rome, and The Errors and Superstitions By them from time to time brought into the Church. In the Process of which, The Papists Arguments are Answered, their Fallacies Detected, their Cruelties Registred, their Treasons and Seditious Principles Observed, and the whole Body of Papistry Anatomized. Perform'd by a Single Sheet, Coming out every Friday, but with a continual Connexion. To each being added, The Popish Courant Or, Some occasional Joco-serious Reflections of Romish Fopperies. Printed by Langley Curtis. Contains vols 1–4 (1679–82).

The Weekly Pacquet Of Advice from Rome: Or, The History of Popery. The Fifth volume. Friday, August the 25th, 1682. Printed by A. Maxwell for Care, 1682. Apparently the only complete copy is at the Bodleian Library.

[Spurious] *Fifth Volume Of The Pacquets Of Advice from Rome: Or, The History of Popery, And the Reformation: beginning with the Preaching of Martin Luther and the Pope-dome of Leo X and continued till the begining of the English Reformation, in the Reign of Henry VIII. The manner how the Reformation was begun and carried on, A Character of the Roman Clergy. A brief Disquisition of Heresie, and the Punishment due to Hereticks. The lives of some of the first and Principal Reformers, with other things of material Consequence.* Printed by Langley Curtis. Written by William Salmon. 1682–83.

OTHER NEWSPAPERS AND JOURNALS

Domestick Intelligence; Or, News both from City and Country, nos 1–55 (9 July 1679–13 January 1681). Published by Benjamin Harris. Continued as *Protestant (Domestick) Intelligence.*

Heraclitus Ridens: Or, A Discourse between Jest and Earnest, where many a true Word is spoken in opposition to all Libellers against the Government, 1 February 1681–22 August 1682.

The Impartial Protestant Mercury, Or Occurrences. Foreign and Domestick, 27 April 1681–30 May 1682. Written by Care and Thomas Vile. Published by Richard Janeway.

The London Gazette, 1660–89.

The Loyal Protestant and True Domestick Intelligence: Or, News both from City and Country, March 1681–March 1683. By Nathaniel Thompson.

The Observator, In Dialogue, 13 April 1681–2 March 1687. By Roger L'Estrange. 3 vols. in 2. 1684.

Orange Gazette, nos 1–18 (31 December 1688–9 March 1689).

A Supplementary Journal to the Advice from the Scandal Club for the Month of September, 1704. By Daniel Defoe. Reprinted in *An English Garner,* ed. Edward Arber, 8 vols (1877–96), 7: 618.

The True Domestick Intelligence: Or, News both from City and Country, June 1679–May 1680. By Nathaniel Thompson.

The Weekly Discoverer Strip'd Naked; Or, Jest and Earnest Expos'd to Publick View in his Proper Colours, nos 1–5 (16 February–16 March 1681). Published by B. Harris.

TRACTS BY HENRY CARE

Animadversions On A Late Paper. Entituled. A Letter to a Dissenter upon occasion of his Majesties late Gracious Declaration of Indulgence. 10 October 1687.

Animadversions upon Mijn Heer Fagels Letter Concerning Our Penal Laws And Tests. 1688.

An Answer To a Paper importing a Petition Of The Archbishop of Canterbury. And Six other Bishops. To His Majesty, Touching their not Distributing and Publishing The Late Declaration For Liberty of Conscience. 1688.

The Character and Qualifications of an Honest Loyal Merchant. 1686.

The Character Of A Turbulent, Pragmatical Jesuit And Factious Romish Priest. 1678.

The Darkness of Atheisme Expelled by the Light of Nature, Or, The Existence of a Deity: And His Creation and Government Of The World. Demonstrated from Reason, and the Light of Nature only. With an Appendix touching the most proper Method of Preaching the Gospel among the Heathens. Englished by H.C. 1683.

Discourse Concerning the Illegality of the late Ecclesiastical Commission In answer to Edward Stillingfleet. 1689.

Discourse for Taking Off the Tests and Penal Laws. 19 September 1687.

Draconica: Or, An Abstract Of All the Penal-Laws Touching Matters of Religion; And; the Several Oaths and Tests thereby Enjoyned, Now so much Controverted. With Brief Observations Thereupon. Published for more General Information and Satisfaction. 1687. 2nd edn 1688. Translated into German and Dutch.

An Elegie Sacred to the Memory of Sir Edmund-bury Godfrey Knight; Whose Body was lately found Barbarously Murthered, and since Honourably Interr'd, the 31th of October, 1678. 1678.

English Liberties: Or, The Free-Born Subject's inheritance, containing I. Magna Charta, The Petition of Right, the Habeas Corpus Act; and divers other most useful statutes: With Large Comments upon each of them. II. The Proceedings in Appeals of Murther; The Work and Power of Parliaments. The Qualifications necessary for such as should be chosen to that great Trust. Plain Directions for all Persons concerned in Ecclesiastical Courts; and how to prevent or take off the Writ De Excommunicato Capiendo. As also the Oath and Duty of Grand and Petty Juries. III. All the laws against Conventicles and Protestant Dissenters, with notes, and Directions both to Constables and others concern'd, thereupon; And an Abstract of all the Laws against Papists. 1682. Later editions in 1688, 1691, 1692, 1700, 1703, 1719, 1721, 1766.

Essex's Excellency: Or The Gallantry of The Freeholders of that County. Being a short Account of the Brave British Behaviour of those Worthy Freeholders, in the Choice of their Knights to serve in the next Parliament. Together with The Truly Noble Lord Gray His Speech at the Close of their Choice. Published by an Eye-Witness of their most Noble Courage for the Example of their Neighbouring Counties. 1679.

Female Pre-eminence; Or The Dignity and Excellency of that Sex, above the Male. An Ingenious Discourse: Written Originally in Latine, by Henry Cornelius Agrippa, Knight, Doctor of Physick, Doctor of both Laws, and Privy-Counsellor to the Emperor Charles the Fifth. Done into English with Additional Advantages by H.C. 1670.

The Female Secretary: Or, Choice new Letters. Wherein each degree of Women may be accomodated with Variety of Presidents [i.e., precedents] for the expressing themselves aptly and handsomly on any Occasion proper to their Sex. With Plain. yet more Exact and Pertinent Rules and Instructions for the Inditing and Directing Letters in general, than any Extant. By Henry Care. Translator of Female-Pre-Eminence. 1671.

The Grandeur And Glory Of France. Drawn In the Triumphant Portraitures of Her present Victorious Monarch. And most Illustrious Nobility. Galliae Speculum. Or, A New Survey Of the French Court and Camp. Illustrated with the particular Characters of His Most Christian Maiesty now Raigning, His Consort Royal, The Dauphin, Princes of the Blood, Grand Ministers of State, chief Martial, Officers and Forces, by Sea and Land. With several choice Remarques on the Policies and Present Affairs of that Puissant Monarchy. By H.C. Gent. 1673.

The History Of The Damnable Popish Plot, In its various Branches & Progress. Published for the satisfaction of the present and future Ages, By The Authors Of *The Weekly Pacquet of Advice from Rome.* 1680.

The Jewish Calendar Explained; Or, Observations On The Ancient Hebrew Account, of the Year. Months. and Festivals used by the Patriarchs. and mentioned in the Holy Scripture. Wherein is shown the Order, Names, and Significations of their Months. The Reasons for first Instituting their several Feasts, as Passover. Tabernacles, &c. With the exact days whereon they were celebrated; and what they were to shadow forth under the Gospel. Published for assisting weak Capacities better to understand what they read in Holy Writ, more than two hundred difficult places of which, are here explained. By Hen. Care. 1674.

The King's Right of Indulgence in Spiritual Matters. with the equity thereof, Asserted. By A Person of Honour. and Eminent Minister of State lately Deceased. Edited by Henry Care. 1688.

The Legality of the Court Held By His Majesties Ecclesiastical Commissioners, Defended. Their Proceedings No Argument Against the Taking Off Penal Laws & Tests. 25 February 1687/88.

A Letter to the Author of the Vindication of the Ecclesiastical Commissioners, concerning the Legality of that Court. Published under the name Philonomous Anglicus. [1688].

Liberty of Conscience Asserted. Or A Looking-Glass For Persecutors; Being a plain Deduction from Scripture History of the Original Grounds & Pretences For Persecution. The Methods taken to put the same in Execution: Together with the sad Consequences thereof: Or the Reward that attends Persecuting-Spirits. 1687.

A Modest Enquiry. Whether St Peter Were ever at Rome. and Bishop of that Church? Wherein I, The Arguments of Cardinal Bellarmine and others, for the Affirmative, are Considered. Some Considerations taken notice of, that render the Negative highly Probable. 1687.

A most Safe and Effectual Cure for the Rickets, And means to Preserve Children from the same. [1676?].

Observations on a paper intituled The declaration of the Lord Petre upon his death, touching the plot in a letter to His Most Sacred Majesty: being a full answer thereunto. 1684.

A Perfect Guide For Protestant Dissenters. In Case Of Prosecution Upon Any Of The Penal Statutes Made against Them. Together With The Statutes of 35 Eliz. and 22 Car 2. at large. To which is added. A Post-script about Ecclesiastical Courts. and Prosecution in Them. 1682.

The Plain Englishman's Historian: Or, A Compendious Chronicle of England, From its first being Inhabited to this present Year 1679. But, more especially containing the chief Remarques of all our Kings and Queens since the

Conquest, their Lives and Reigns, Policies, Wars, Laws, Successes, and Troubles. With the most Notable Accidents, as Deaths, Tempests, Monstrous Births, and other Prodigies that happened in each of their times respectively. 1679.

Practical Physick: Or, Five Distinct Treatises Of the most Predominant Diseases Of these Times. The First of the Scurvy, The Second of the Dropsie. The Third of Feavers and Agues of all sort. The Fourth of the French Pox. And The Fifth of the Gout. Wherein The Nature, Causes, Symptomes, various methods of Cure, and waies of preventing every of the said Diseases. are severally handled, and plainly discovered to the meanest capacity. Written in Latine by the Famous Dr. D. Sennertus late pukblick Professor of Physick in the University of Wittenburgh. In English by H. Care, Student in Physick and Astrology. 1676.

Rich redivivus. or. Mr. Jeremiah Richs Short-Hand Improved In a more Briefe & Easy Method then Hath been Set forth by Any heretofore. Now made Publique for General Advantage By Nathaniel Stringer. A Quondam Scholar To the Said Mr Rich. 1686.

Sober And Seasonable Queries Humbly Offered to all Good Protestants in England in Order To A Choice Of The New Parliament. The Second Edition With Considerable Additions by another Author. 1679.

Some Reasons For Separation From the Communion of the Church of England. And The Unreasonableness of Persecution Upon that Account. Soberly Debated, in a Dialogue between a Conformist, and a Nonconformist (Baptist). 1682.

A Touch of the Times, Or, Two Letters Casually Intercepted. The First. From the Author of a late Pamphlet Intituled Day-Fatality: To the supposed Author of the Weekly Packet of Advice from Rome. 1679. The Second. The Answer thereunto. 15, 17 September 1679.

Towser the Second a Bull-Dog. or a short Reply to Absalon and Achitophel. 1681.

The Tutor To True English: Or, Brief and Plain Directions, Whereby all that can Read and Write, May Attain to Orthography, (Or the Exact Writing of English) As Readily as if bred Scholars. Very much Conducing likewise to the due Sounding and perfect Reading all sorts of Words used in the English Tongue. With an Introduction to Arithmetic: More Easie than any yet Extant. And several other Observations of General Use; Especially, for the Youth of either Sex, and Forreigners. 1687.

Utrum horum: Or, The Nine and Thirty Articles Of The Church of England, At large recited: And compared with the Doctrines of those commonly called

Presbyterians On the one side; And the Tenets of the Church of Rome On the other. Both faithfully quoted from their own most approved Authors by Hen. Care. 6 February 1682.

A Vindication of the Proceedings of His Majesties Ecclesiastical Commissioners. Against the Bishop of London, and the Fellows of Magdalen-College. 1688.

A Word in Season: Being A Parallel between the intended Bloody Massacre of the People of the Jews, in the Reign of King Ahasuerus; and the Hellish Powder-Plot against the Protestants, in the Reign of King James. Together With an Account of some of the Wicked Principles and Practices of the Church of Rome, Demonstrated in their Barbarous and Cruel Murders and Massacres of the Protestants in the Netherlands, France, Ireland, Piedmont, the Albigenses, &c. Also Shewing That the present Church of Rome is an Apostate Church, and so discovered to be that Mystery Babylon, Mother of Harlots, and Abominations of the Earth, mentioned in the Revelations. By H.C. a Lover of true Protestants. 1679.

OTHER TRACTS AND BOOKS

Advice to Protestants. 1687.

Alsop, Vincent. *The humble address of the Presbyterians, presented to the King by Mr. Hurst, Mr. Chester, Mr. Slater, etc… with his Majesties gracious answer.* 1687.

————. *The Mischief of Impositions: or, an Antidote Against a Late Discourse Partly Preached at Guild-Hall Chappel, May 2. 1680. Called The Mischief of Separation.* 1680.

Bacon, Sir Francis. 'Of Seditions and Troubles.' In *The Works of Francis Bacon,* ed. James Spedding *et al.,* 6: 406–12. 14 vols 1857–74.

Bedloe, William. *A Narrative and Impartial Discovery of the Horrid Popish Plot: Carried on for the Burning and Destroying the Cities of London and Westminster, With their Suburbs, etc. Setting Forth The several Consults, Orders and Resolutions of the Jesuites etc Concerning the same. And Divers Depositions and Informations, Relating thereunto. Never before Printed.* 1679.

Behn, Aphra. *Prologue to Romulus.* 1682.

The Bellowings Of A Wild-Bull: Or, Scroggs's Roaring Lamentation For Being Impeached of High-Treason. 1680.

Blount, Charles [Junius Brutus]. *An Appeal From The Country To The City, For the Preservation of His Majesties Person, Liberty, Property, And The Protestant Religion. Salus Populi, Suprema Lex. Laopolis.* 1679.

Blount, Charles. *A Just Vindication of Learning: Or, An Humble Address To the High Court of Parliament In behalf of the Liberty of the Press.* 1679.

Bohun, Edmund. *An Apologie for the Church of England against the Clamours of the Men of No Conscience.* 1685.

Bolde, Samuel. *A Plea for Moderation Towards Dissenters: Occasioned by The Grand-Juries Presenting the Sermon Against Persecution, at the last Assizes holden at Sherburn in Dorset-shire.* 1682.

Boyle, Robert. *Reasons why A Protestant Should not Turn Papist: or, Protestant Prejudices Against the Roman Catholic Religion.* 1687.

Cade, William. *The Foundation of Popery shaken, or The Bishop of Rome's supremacy opposed in a Sermon on Matth. 16. 18, 19.* 1678.

Care, George [G.C.]. *Liberty of Conscience Asserted and Vindicated. By a Learned Country-Gentleman. Humbly offered to the Consideration of the Lords and Commons in this present Parliament.* 1689.

————. *A Reply To The Answer Of The Man of No Name, To His Grace the Duke of Buckingham's Paper of Religion, and Liberty of Conscience. By G.C. an Affectionate Friend, and true Servant of his Grace the Duke of Buckingham's.* 1685.

C[heyney], J[ohn]. *The Conforming Non-conformist And The Non-conforming Conformists Pleading The Cause of either Side against violent Opposers, and modestly answering to the many Exceptions made by Mr. Baxter against Conformity, in his late Book, intituled, The Con-formists Plea for Peace.* 1680.

Clodpate's Ghost: Or A Dialogue Between Justice Clodpate, and his [quondam] clerk Honest Tom Ticklefoot; Wherein Is Faithfully Related all the News from Purgatory, about Ireland, Langhorn, etc. 25 August 1679.

A Collection of the newest and Most Ingenious Poems. [1687].

Crashaw, William. *A Mittimus To The Iubile at Rome: Or, The Rates Of The Popes Custome-House.* 1625.

Defoe, Daniel. *A Letter to a Dissenter, from his Friend at the Hague, Concerning the Penal Laws and the Test; shewing that the Popular Plea for Liberty of Conscience is not concerned in that Question.* 1688.

A Dialogue Between A Monkey in the Old Bayly And An Ape in High Holbourn. 1681.

A dialogue between Father P...rs and William P...n. [1687?].

A discourse For Taking Off The Tests And Penal Laws About Religion. 1687.

A Discourse Shewing That Protestants are on the Safer Side, notwithstanding the uncharitable Judgment of their Adversaries; And That Their Religion is the Surest Way to Heaven. 25 February 1687.

Dryden, John. *Absalom and Achitophel A Poem*. In *The Poems of John Dryden*. Ed. James Kinsley. 4 vols Oxford: Clarendon Press, 1958.

E.P. [Edward Phillips?]. *Citt and Bumpkin answered*. 1680.

A Faithful and Impartial Account of the Behaviour of a Party of the Essex Free-Holders, at their late Election of Parliament-Men (At Chelmsford) for that County. Occasioned by a most false and scandalous Pamphlet, Intituled The Essex Excellency. In a Letter to a Friend. 28 August 1679.

A Friendly Debate Upon the next Elections Of Parliament And the Settlement of Liberty of Conscience. In a Dialogue between a City and Country Elector. 1687.

[Gibbon, John]. *Flagellum mercurii Anti-Ducalis: Or, The Author of the disingenuous Touch of the Times Brought to the Whipping-Post, to prevent his coming to the Gallows*. [1679].

————. *Touch of the Times, Or, Two Letters Casually Intercepted. The First, From the Author of a late Pamphlet Intitutled, Day-Fatality: To the supposed Author of the Weekly Packet of Advice from Rome. The Second, the Answer thereunto*. 1679.

Gother, John. *An Agreement Between The Church of England And Church of Rome, Evinced from the Concertation of some of Her Sons With their Brethren the Dissenters*. 1687.

————. *A Discourse Of The Use of Images: In Relation to the Church of England and the Church of Rome*. 1687.

————. *Papists Protesting Against Protestant Popery. In Answer to a Discourse Entituled, A Papist not Mis-represented by Protestants. Being A Vindication Of the Papist Mis-represented and Represented, And the Reflections upon the Answer*. 1687.

Great News from the Old-Bayly. Mr. Car's Recantation: or the true Protestant Renegade. the Courantier turn'd Tory. In a dialogue 'twixt Trueman and Amsterdammer. 1683.

Halifax, George Savile, marquis of. *A Letter to a Dissenter* (1687). In *The Works of George Savile Marquis of Halifax*, ed. Mark N. Brown, 1: 250–64. 3 vols Oxford: Clarendon Press, 1989.

————. *The Works of George Savile Marquis of Halifax*. Ed. Mark N. Brown. 3 vols Oxford: Clarendon Press, 1989.

Harry Care's Last Will and Testament. [1688].

Hawles, Sir John. *The English-mans Right. A dialogue Between A Barrister at Law, And A Jury-Man; Plainly setting forth, I. The Antiquity II. The excellent designed use. III. The Office and just Priviledges of Juries. By the law of England*. 1680.

Heraclitus Ridens Redivivus: or, A Dialogue Between Harry and Roger. [1688].

Hughes, William. *The Man of Sin: Or a Discourse of Popery Wherein The Numerous and Monstrous Abominations, in Doctrine and Practice, of the Romish Church are by their own Hands exposed so to open Light, that the very Blind may see them, and Antichrist in Capital Letters engraven on them: particularly in the infinite Drove of their Adored, but Lying Wonders and Miracles. By no Roman, but a Reformed Catholic.* 1677.

Innocence Unveil'd: Or, A Poem On the Acquittal of the Lord Chief Justice Scroggs. 1680.

A Just and Modest Vindication of the proceedings of the Two last Parliaments. 1681.

Justice in Masquerade. A Poem. [1680].

Juvenalis Redivivus, Or, The First Satyr of Juvenal taught to speak plain English. 1683.

The Last Legacy of Henry Care, Gent. Lately Deceased. Containing A Brief Sum of Christian Doctrine, By Way of Question and Answer. Particularly relating to Several of the most Important Points controverted Between Us, and the Romanists Decided by Express Testimonies of the Holy Scripture, and evident Reason. 1688.

Lawrence, William. *Marriage by the Morall Law of God Vindicated.* 1680.

The Lecherous Anabaptist: or, The dipper dipped. A new Protestant ballad, to the tune of Packington's pound. 1681.

L'Estrange, Sir Roger. *An Answer To A Letter To A Dissenter, Upon Occasion of His Majesties Late Gracious Declaration of Indulgence.* 1687.

———. *An Answer to the Appeal from the Country to the City.* 1679. Reprint, 1681.

———. *The Case Put, Concerning the Succession Of His Royal Highness The Duke of York.* 1679. Reprint, 1680.

———. *Citt and Bumpkin, in a Dialogue over A Pot of Ale, concerning Matters of Religion and Government.* 1680 (4 printings). Reprint, 1681.

———. *Citt and Bumpkin. The Second Part.* 1680.

———. *The Committee; Or Popery in Masquerade.* 1680.

———. *Considerations and Proposals In Order to the Regulation of the Press: Together With Diverse Instances of Treasonous, and Seditious Pamphlets, Proving the Necessity Thereof.* 1663.

———. *Discovery Upon Discovery.* 1680.

———. *The Dissenter's Sayings, In Requital for L'Estrange's Sayings. Published in Their Own Words, for the Information of the People.* 1681. Reprint, 1685.

————. *Dissenters Sayings. The Second Part. Published in their own Words, for the Information Of the People.* 1681.

————. *The Free-born Subject. Or, The Englishmen's Birthright Asserted against all Tyrannical Usurpations Either In Church or State.* 1679. Reprint, 1681.

————. *A Further Discovery of the Plot.* 1680. Reprint, 1680.

————. *The History of the Plot: Or a Brief and Historical Account of the Charge and Defence of Edward Coleman et al.* 1679.

————. *Interest Mistaken or The Holy Cheat: Proving, From the Undeniable Practices and Positions of the Presbyterians, That The Design of that Party, is to en-Slave both King and People Under the Masque of Religion.* 1662. Reprint, 1682.

————. *L'Estrange His Apology, with A Short View, of some Late and Remarkable Transactions, Leading to the happy Settlement of these Nations under the Government of Our Lawfull and Gracious Sovereign Charles II. whom God Preserve.* 10 June 1660.

————. *Lestrange's Narrative Of The Plot. Set Forth for the Edification Of His Majesties Liege-People.* 1680.

————. *A Memento: Directed To all Those that Truly Reverence the Memory of King Charles the Martyr.* 1662. Second edition published with changes under the title *A Memento. Treating, Of The Rise, Progress, and Remedies of Seditions.* 1682.

————. *A Modest Plea Both for the Caveat And The Author of It.* 1661.

————. *The Parallel, Or An Account Of The Growth Of Knavery Under the Pretext of Arbitrary Government and Popery.* 1679. Reprint, 1681.

————. *The Reformed Catholique: Or, The True Protestant.* 1679.

————. *The Relaps'd Apostate; or notes upon a Presbyterian Pamphlet entitled A Petition for Peace.* 1661. Reprint, 1681.

————. *A Short Answer To A Whole Litter of Libellers.* 1680.

————. *Toleration Discussed; In Two Dialogues.* 1663. Reprint, 1681.

————. *Tyranny and Popery, Lording it Over The Consciences, Lives, Liberties, And Estates Both of King and People.* 1678.

A Letter From A Country Curate To Mr. Henry Care, In Defence of the Seven Bishops. 18 July 1688.

A Letter from a Person of Quality to his Friend concerning His Majesties late Declaration touching the Reasons which moved him to dissolve the Two last Parliaments at Westminster and Oxford. 1688.

A letter to a friend, in answer to A letter to a dissenter, upon occasion of His Majesties late gracious declaration of indulgence. 1687.

A Letter to Mr. C., L.C., J.S. and B.H. 1681.

The Lord Chief Justice Scroggs: His Speech In The Kings-Bench... Together With what was Declared at the same Time... by Mr. Justice Jones, and Mr. Justice Dolbin. 23 October 1679.

The Lord Chief Justice Scroggs: His Speech To the Lord Chancellour. [1678].

A Pair of Spectacles for Mr. Observer; or, Remarks on the phanatical observations on my Lord Petre's Letter to the King. [1688?].

Patrick, John. *Transubstantiation no doctrine of the primitive fathers; being a defense of the Dublin letter herein, against the papist misrepresented and represented, part 2.* 1687.

Pearse, Edward. *The Conformists Plea for the Nonconformists' Or A Just and Compassionate Representation Of The Present State and Condition Of The Non-Conformists.* 1681.

Penn, William. *Good advice to the Church of England, Roman Catholick, and Protestant dissenter. In which it is endeavoured to be made appear that it is their duty, principles & interest to abolish the penal laws and tests.* 1687.

————. *A Letter From a Gentleman in the Country to His Friends in London: Upon the Subject of the Penal Laws and Tests.* 1687.

————. *A Second Letter From a Gentleman in the Country to His Friends in London: Upon the Subject of the Penal Laws and Tests.* April 1687.

————. *A Third Letter From a Gentleman in the Country to His Friends in London: Upon the Subject of the Penal Laws and Tests.* May 1687.

————. *Som Free Reflections Upon Occasion of the Public Discourse about Liberty of Conscience. And the Consequences thereof in this present Conjuncture. In a Letter to a Friend.* 1687.

The Practick Part of the Law: Shewing the Office of an Attorney, In the Courts of Kings-Bench, Common Pleas, and Pleas in the Exchequer. 1681.

The Protestant Cuckold: a new ballad. Being a full and perfect relation how G.H. the protestant-news-forger, caught his beloved wife Ruth in ill circumstances. To the tune of Packington's pound; or Timothy Dash the scriveners apprentice. 1681.

The Reasonableness of Toleration and The Unreasonableness of Penal Laws And Tests: Wherein is prov'd by Scripture, Reason and Antiquity. That Liberty of Conscience is the Undoubted Right of every Man ... And that persecution for meer Religion is Unwarrantable, Unjust, and Destructive to Humane Society. 1687.

A Satyr Against Iniustice: Or Sc——gs upon Sc——gs. [1679].

Scroggs, Sir William. *A Speech Made By Sir William Scrogg, One of His Majesties Sergeants at Law, To the Right Honourable the Lord High*

Chancellor Of England, At his Admission To the Place of One of His Majesties Justices Of the Court of Common-Pleas. 1676.

Several Weighty Quaeries Concerning Heraclitus and the Observator, In A Dialogue Betwixt the Corn-Cutter and Mr. Scruple. 1681.

Sherlock, William. *A short summary of the principal controversies between the Church of England, and the church of Rome.* 1687.

A Short, but Just Account Of The Tryal Of Benjamin Harris, Upon An Information Brought against him For Printing and Vending a late Seditious Book called An Appeal from the Country To the City, For the Preservation of His Majesties Person, Liberty, Property, And The Protestant Religion. 1679 [1680].

A sober Discourse Of The Honest Cavalier With The Popish Couranter: Wherein, The Author of the Dialogue between the Pope and Fanatick vindicates himself to be an hearty Lover of his Prince and Countrey. To Which Is Annexed, a Serious Epistle to Hodge. By a Person of Quality. Principis & Patrie scribere jussit Amor. 1680.

Some Observations Upon the Late Tryals of Sir George Wakeman, Corker, and Marshal, etc. By Tom Ticklefoot, the Taborer, late Clerk to Justice Clodpate. 1679.

Some Queries concerning Liberty of Conscience, directed to William Penn and Henry Care. [1688].

Somers, Sir John. *The Security of English Men's Lives, or the Trust, Power and duty of the Grand Jurys of England.* 1681.

Staveley, Thomas. *The Romish Horseleech: Or, An Impartial Account Of The Intolerable Charge Of Popery To This Nation, In an Historical remembrance of some of those Prodigious summs of money heretofore extorted from all degrees during the exercise of the Papal power here. To which is Annexed an Essay of the Supremacy of the King of England.* 1674.

Stillingfleet, Edward. *The Mischief of Separation. A Sermon Preached at Guild-Hall Chappel, May II. M DC LXXX. Being the First Sunday in Easter-Term., Before the Lord Mayor, etc.* 1680.

Stowe, John. *A Survey of London.* Ed. Charles L. Kingsford. 2 vols. 1603. Reprint, Oxford: Clarendon Press, 1908.

A Supplement to the Popish Courant, Annex'd To The Weekly Pacquet Of Advice from Rome: Friday October 14 1681. Inserted into vol. 3 of *Weekly Pacquet*, after no.71, (14 October 1681). At Bodleian Library.

Three Considerations proposed to Mr. William Pen, Concerning the Validity and Security of his New Magna Charta for Liberty of Conscience, by A. Baptist; which may be worthy the Consideration of all the Quakers, and of all my dissenting Brethren also that have Votes in the Choice of Parliament-Men. 1687.

The Tickler Tickled: Or The Observator Upon the Late Tryals of Sir George Wakeman, etc. Observed. 1679.

Whitby, Daniel. *The Protestant Reconciler.* 1682

Willet, Andrew. *Synopsis Papismi: That Is, A General Viewe Of Papistry: Wherein The Whole Mysterie of Iniquitie, and Summe of Antichristian Doctrine is set downe, which is maintained this day by the Synagogue of Rome, against the Church of Christ.* 1592.

SECONDARY WORKS

Alden, John. 'Pills and Publishing: Some Notes on the English Book Trade, 1660–1715.' *Library,* 5th ser., 8 (1952): 21–37.

Allen, David F. 'Political Clubs in Restoration London.' *Historical Journal* 19 (1976): 561–80.

Almond, Gabriel, and Sidney Verba. *The Civil Culture, Political Attitudes, and Democracy in Five Nations.* Boston: Little, Brown & Co., 1965.

Arber, Edward. *The Term Catalogues, 1668–1709 A.D.; with a number for Easter term, 1711 A.D. A Contemporary Bibliography of English Literature in the Reigns of Charles II, James II, William and Mary and Anne.* 3 vols London: privately printed, 1903.

Ashcraft, Richard. *Revolutionary Politics and Locke's Two Treatises of Government.* Princeton: Princeton Univ. Press, 1986.

Aveling, J.C.J. *The Handle and the Axe: The Catholic Recusants in England from Reformation to Emancipation.* London: Blond & Briggs, 1976.

Backscheider, Paula R. *Daniel Defoe: His Life.* Baltimore: Johns Hopkins Univ. Press, 1989.

Baker, J.H. *An Introduction to English Legal History.* London: Butterworths, 1979.

Beddard, R.A. 'Vincent Alsop and the Emancipation of Restoration Dissent.' *Journal of Ecclesiastical History* 24 (1973): 161–84.

Behrens, B. 'The Whig Theory of the Constitution in the Reign of Charles II.' *Cambridge Historical Journal* 7 (1941): 42–71.

Beier, A. L., and Roger Finlay, eds. *London, 1500–1700: The Making of the Metropolis.* London: Longman, 1986.

Bell, Maureen. 'Women and the Opposition Press after the Restoration.' In *Writing and Radicalism,* ed. J. Lucas, 39–60, 305–18. London:

Longman, 1996.

Birdsall, Paul. '"Non Obstante": A Study in the Dispensing Power of English Kings.' In *Essays in History and Political Theory in Honor of Charles Howard McIlwain*, ed. Carl F. Wittke, 37–76. Cambridge: Harvard Univ. Press, 1936.

Blagden, Cyprian. *The Stationers' Company: A History, 1403–1959*. Stanford: Stanford Univ. Press, 1960.

Blatch, Mervyn. *A Guide to London's Churches*. 2nd edn London: Constable & Co., 1995.

Bonfield, Lloyd, with Richard Smith and Keith Wrightson, eds. *The World We Have Gained: Histories of Population and Social Structure*. Oxford: Basil Blackwell, 1986.

Bossy, John. *The English Catholic Community, 1579–1850*. New York: Oxford Univ. Press, 1976.

Bourne, H.R.F. *English Newspapers: Chapters in the History of Journalism*. 2 vols 1887.

Boyer, Richard E. *English Declarations of Indulgence, 1687 and 1688*. The Hague: Mouton, 1968.

Bronner, Edwin B., and David Fraser, eds *William Penn's Published Writings, 1660–1726: An Interpretive Bibliography*. Vol. 5 of *The Papers of William Penn,* ed. Richard Dunn and Mary Maples Dunn. Philadelphia: Univ. of Pennsylvania Press, 1986.

Brooks, C.W. *Pettyfoggers and Vipers of the Commonwealth: The 'Lower Branch' of the Legal Profession in Early Modern England*. Cambridge: Cambridge Univ. Press, 1986.

Brown, F.C. *Elkanah Settle: His Life and Works*. Chicago: Univ. of Chicago Press, 1910.

Browning, Andrew. *Thomas Osborne, Earl of Danby and Duke of Leeds, 1632–1712*. 3 vols Glasgow: Jackson, Son & Co., Publishers to the University, 1951.

Burke, Peter. *Popular Culture in Early Modern Europe*. London: Temple Smith, 1978.

Capp, Bernard. *Astrology and the Popular Press: English Almanacs, 1500–1800*. London: Faber & Faber, 1979.

Carswell, John. *The Descent on England: A Study of the English Revolution of 1688 and Its European Background*. London: Cresset, 1969.

Carter, Jennifer. 'Law, Courts, and the Constitution.' In *The Restored Monarchy, 1660–1688*, ed. J.R. Jones, 71–93. Totowa, N.J.: Rowman & Littlefield, 1979.

Censer, Jack Richard. *Prelude to Power: The Parisian Radical Press, 1789–91.* Baltimore: Johns Hopkins Univ. Press, 1976.

Champion, J.A.I. *The Pillars of Priestcraft Shaken: The Church of England and Its Enemies, 1660–1730.* Cambridge: Cambridge Univ. Press, 1992.

Chartier, Roger. *The Cultural Uses of Print in Early Modern France.* Trans. Lydia G. Cochrane. Princeton: Princeton Univ. Press, 1987.

Clancy, Thomas H. *A Literary History of the English Jesuits: A Century of Books, 1615–1714.* San Francisco: Catholic Scholars Press, 1996.

Clark, J.C.D. *The Language of Liberty, 1660–1832: Political Discourse and Social Dynamics in the Anglo-American World.* Cambridge: Cambridge Univ. Press, 1994.

Cobb, Gerald. *London City Churches.* 2nd edn London: B.T. Batsford, 1977.

Cockburn, J.S. *A History of English Assizes, 1558–1714.* Cambridge: Cambridge Univ. Press, 1972.

Colbourn, H. Trevor. *The Lamp of Experience: Whig History and the Intellectual Origins of the American Revolution.* Chapel Hill: Univ. of North Carolina Press, 1965.

Cressy, David. *Literacy and the Social Order: Reading and Writing in Tudor and Stuart England.* Cambridge: Cambridge Univ. Press, 1980.

Crist, Timothy. 'Government Control of the Press after the Expiration of the Printing Act in 1679.' *Publishing History* 5 (1979): 49–78.

Curtis, Mark H. 'William Jones: Puritan Printer and Propagandist.' *Library*, 5th ser., 19 (1964): 38–66.

Davis, Natalie Zemon. *Society and Culture in Early Modern France: Eight Essays.* Stanford: Stanford Univ. Press, 1975.

Davis, Richard. 'The 'Presbyterian' Opposition and the Emergence of Party in the House of Lords in the Reign of Charles II.' In *Party and Management in Parliament, 1660–1714*, ed. Clyve Jones, 1–35. Leicester: Leicester Univ. Press, 1984.

De Krey, Gary. 'The First Restoration Crisis: Conscience and Coercion in London, 1667–73.' *Albion* 25 (1993): 565–80.

———. *A Fractured Society: The Politics of London in the First Age of Party, 1688–1715.* Oxford: Clarendon Press, 1985.

———. 'London Radicals and Revolutionary Politics, 1675–1683.' In *The Politics of Religion in Restoration England*, ed. Tim Harris, Paul Seaward and Mark Goldie, 133–62. Oxford: Basil Blackwell, 1990.

———. 'The London Whigs and the Exclusion Crisis Reconsidered.' In *The First Modern Society*, ed. Lee Beier, David Cannadine and James Rosenheim, 457–82. Cambridge: Cambridge Univ. Press, 1989.

————. 'Rethinking the Restoration: Dissenting Cases for Conscience, 1667–1672.' *Historical Journal* 38 (1995): 53–83.

Duckett, Sir George F., ed. *Penal Laws and Test Act: Questions Touching Their Repeal Propounded in 1687–88 by James II., to the Deputy Lieutenants and Magistrates of the counties of beds, berks, Bristol [etc]… from the Original Returns in the Bodleian Library.* 1882.

Dunn, Mary Maples. *William Penn: Politics and Conscience.* Princeton: Princeton Univ. Press, 1967.

Earle, Peter. *The Making of the English Middle Class: Business, Society, and Family Life in London, 1660–1730.* Berkeley and Los Angeles: Univ. of California Press, 1989.

Eisenstein, Elizabeth L. *The Printing Press as an Agent of Change: Communications and Cultural Transformations in Early-Modern Europe.* Cambridge: Cambridge Univ. Press, 1979.

Feiling, Keith. *History of the Tory Party.* Oxford: Clarendon Press, 1924.

Finlay, Roger. *Population and Metropolis: The Demography of London, 1580–1650.* Cambridge: Cambridge Univ. Press, 1981.

Frank, Joseph. *Cromwell's Press Agent: A Critical Biography of Marchamont Nedham, 1620–1678.* Lanham, Md.: Univ. Press of America, 1980.

Fraser, Peter. *The Intelligence of the Secretaries of State.* Cambridge: Cambridge Univ. Press, 1956.

Freist, Dagmar. *Governed by Opinion: Politics, Religion, and the Dynamics of Communication in Stuart London, 1637–1645.* London: I.B. Tauris, 1997.

Furley, O.W. 'The Whig Exclusionists: Pamphlet Literature in the Exclusion Campaign, 1679–81.' *Cambridge Historical Journal* 13 (1957): 19–36.

Goldie, Mark. 'Danby, the Bishops, and the Whigs.' In *The Politics of Religion in Restoration England*, ed. Tim Harris, Paul Seaward and Mark Goldie, 75–105. Oxford: Basil Blackwell, 1990.

————. 'The Hilton Gang and the Purge of London in the 1680's.' In *Politics and the Political Imagination in Later Stuart Britain: Essays Presented to Lois Green Schwoerer*, ed. Howard Nenner, 43–74. Rochester: Univ. of Rochester Press, 1997.

————. 'James II and the Dissenters' Revenge: The Commission of Enquiry of 1688.' *Historical Research: The Bulletin of the Institute of Historical Research* 66 (February 1993): 53–88.

————. 'John Locke and Anglican Royalism.' *Political Studies* 31 (1983): 61–85.

————. 'John Locke, Jonas Proast, and Religious Toleration, 1688–1692.' In *From Toleration to Tractarianism,* ed. J. Walsh, C. Haydon and S. Taylor, 143–71. Cambridge: Cambridge Univ. Press, 1993.

————. 'John Locke's Circle and James II.' *Historical Journal* 35 (1992): 557–86.

————. 'The Revolution of 1689 and the Structure of Political Argument: An Essay and an Annotated Bibliography of Pamphlets on the Allegiance Controversy.' *Bulletin of Research in the Humanities* 83 (1980): 473–563.

Greaves, Richard. *Deliver Us from Evil: The Radical Underground in Britain, 1660–1663.* Oxford: Oxford Univ. Press, 1986.

————. *Enemies under His Feet: Radical and Nonconformists in Britain, 1664–1677.* Stanford: Stanford Univ. Press, 1990.

————. *Secrets of the Kingdom: British Radicals from the Popish Plot to the Revolution of 1688–1689.* Stanford: Stanford Univ. Press, 1992.

Grell, Ole Peter, Jonathan I. Israel, and Nicholas Tyacke, eds. *From Persecution to Toleration: The Glorious Revolution and Religion in England.* Oxford: Clarendon Press, 1991.

Griffiths, Antony. *The Print in Stuart Britain, 1603–1689.* London: British Museum, 1998.

Groenveld, S. 'The Mecca of Authors? State Assemblies and Censorship in the Seventeenth Century Dutch Republic.' In *Too Mighty to Be Free: Censorship and the Press in Britain and The Netherlands,* ed. A.C. Duke and C.A. Tamse. Zutphen, Netherlands: De Walburg Pers, 1987.

Habermas, Jürgen. *The Structural Transformation of the Public Sphere.* Trans. Thomas Burger and Frederick Lawrence. Cambridge: MIT Press, 1989.

Haigh, Robert L. 'New Light on the King's Printing Office, 1680–1730.' *Studies in Bibliography* 8 (1956): 157–67.

Haley, K.H.D. *The First Earl of Shaftesbury.* Oxford: Clarendon Press, 1968.

Halkett, Samuel, and John Laing, comps. *Dictionary of Anonymous and Pseudonymous Literature.* 1926; Reprint, Harlow, Eng.: Longman, 1980.

Hamburger, Philip. 'The Development of the Law of Seditious Libel and the Control of the Press.' *Stanford Law Review* 37 (February 1985): 661–765.

Harris, Tim. *London Crowds in the Reign of Charles II: Propaganda and Politics from the Restoration until the Exclusion Crisis.* Cambridge: Cambridge Univ. Press, 1987.

————. 'The People, the Law, and the Constitution in Scotland and England: A Comparative Approach to the Glorious Revolution.' *Journal of British Studies* 38 (1999): 28–58.

————. 'The Problem of 'Popular Political Culture' in Seventeenth-Century London.' *History of European Ideas* 10 (1989): 43–58.

————. 'What's New about the Restoration?' *Albion* 29 (1997): 187–222.

Harris, Tim, Paul Seaward and Mark Goldie, eds. *The Politics of Religion in Restoration England.* Oxford: Basil Blackwell, 1990.

Harrison, John, and Peter Laslett. *The Library of John Locke.* Oxford: Oxford Univ. Press, 1971.

Hart, W.S. *Index Expurgatorius Anglicanus: or A Descriptive Catalogue of the principal Books printed or Published in England, which have been suppressed, or burnt by The Common Hangman, or censured, or for which the Authors, Printers, or Publishers have been prosecuted.* 1872. Reprint, New York: Burt Franklin, 1969.

Harth, Phillip. *Pen for a Party: Dryden's Tory Propaganda in Its Contexts.* Princeton: Princeton Univ. Press, 1993.

Havighurst, A.F. 'The Judiciary and Politics in the Reign of Charles II.' *Law Quarterly Review* (London) 66 (1950): 62–78, 229–52.

Hellmuth, Eckhart, ed. *The Transformation of Political Culture: England and Germany in the Late Eighteenth Century.* London: German Historical Institute, 1990.

Henning, Basil Duke, ed. *The House of Commons, 1660–1690.* 3 vols London: Published for The History of Parliament by Secker & Warburg, 1983.

Holdsworth, Sir William. *A History of English Law.* 17 vols. London: Methuen, 1903–72.

Hornbeak, Katherine Gee. 'The Complete Letter-Writer in English, 1568–1800.' *Smith College Studies in Modern Languages* 15, nos 3–4 (1934).

Horwitz, Henry. 'Party in a Civic Context: London from the Exclusion Crisis to the Fall of Walpole.' In *Britain in the First Age of Party, 1680–1750: Essays Presented to Geoffrey Holmes,* ed. Clyve Jones Ronceverte, 173–95. London: Hambledon, 1987.

————. 'Protestant Reconciliation in the Exclusion Crisis.' *Journal of Ecclesiastical History* 15 (1964): 201–17.

Hudson, Winthrop S. 'William Penn's *English Liberties:* Tract for Several Times.' *William and Mary Quarterly,* 3rd ser., 26 (1969): 578–85.

Israel, Jonathan I. 'William III and Toleration.' In *From Persecution to Toleration: The Glorious Revolution and Religion in England,* ed. Ole

Peter Grell, Jonathan I. Israel and Nicholas Tyacke, 129–70. Oxford: Clarendon Press, 1991.

————, ed. *The Anglo-Dutch Moment*. Cambridge: Cambridge Univ. Press, 1991.

Jacob, James R. *Henry Stubbe, Radical Protestantism, and the Early Enlightenment*. Cambridge: Cambridge Univ. Press, 1983.

Johns, Adrian. *The Nature of the Book: Print and Knowledge in the Making*. Chicago: Univ. of Chicago Press, 1998.

Jones, George Hilton. *Convergent Forces: Immediate Causes of the Revolution of 1688 in England*. Ames: Iowa State Univ. Press, 1990.

Jones, J.R. *Charles II: Royal Politician*. London: Allen & Unwin, 1987.

————. *The First Whigs: The Politics of the Exclusion Crisis, 1678–1683*. Oxford: Oxford Univ. Press, 1961.

————. 'The Green Ribbon Club.' *Durham University Journal* 49 (1956): 17–20.

————. 'James II's Revolution: Royal Policies, 1686–1692.' In *The Anglo-Dutch Moment,* ed. Jonathan Israel, 47–71. Cambridge: Cambridge Univ. Press, 1991.

————. 'James II's Whig Collaborators.' *Historical Journal* 3 (1960): 65–73.

————. *Liberty Secured? Britain Before and After 1688*. Ed. J.R. Jones. Stanford: Stanford Univ. Press, 1992.

————. *The Revolution of 1688 in England*. London: Weidenfeld & Nicolson, 1972.

Jordain, Violet, ed. *Sir Roger L'Estrange: Selections from the Observator (1681–1687)*. Augustan Reprint Society, 141. Berkeley and Los Angeles: Univ. of California Press for the William Andrew Clark Memorial Library, 1970.

Jouhard, Christian, 'Readability and Persuasion: Political Handbills.' In *The Culture of Print Power and the Uses of Print in Early Modern Europe*, ed. Roger Chartier. Cambridge: Polity Press, 1989.

Keeble, N.H. *The Literary Culture of Nonconformity in Later Seventeenth-Century England*. Athens: Univ. of Georgia Press, 1987.

Kelly, Thomas. *Early Public Libraries: A History of Public Libraries in Great Britain before 1850*. London: Library Association, 1966.

Kenyon, J.P. 'The Acquittal of Sir George Wakeman: 18 July 1679.' *Historical Journal* 14 (1971): 693–708.

————. *The Popish Plot*. London: William Heinemann, 1972.

————. *Revolution Principles: The Politics of Party, 1689–1720*. Cambridge: Cambridge Univ. Press, 1977.

————. *Robert Spencer, Earl of Sunderland.* New York: Longmans, Green, 1958.

Kishlansky, Mark A. *Parliamentary Selection: Social and Political Choice in Early Modern England.* Cambridge: Cambridge Univ. Press, 1986.

Kitchin, Sir George. *Sir Roger L'Estrange: A Contribution to the History of the Press in the Seventeenth Century.* London: Kegan Paul, Trench, Trubner, & Co., 1913.

Knachel, Philip A., ed. *The Case of the Commonwealth of England, Stated by Marchamont Nedham.* Charlottesville: Univ. Press of Virginia for the Folger Shakespeare Library, 1969.

Knights, Mark, 'London's 'Monster' Petition of 1680.' *Historical Journal* 36 (1993): 39–67.

————. 'Petitioning and the Political Theorists: John Locke, Algernon Sidney, and London's 'Monster' Petition of 1680.' *Past and Present,* no.138 (February 1993): 94–111.

————. *Politics and Opinion in Crisis, 1678–1681.* Cambridge: Cambridge Univ. Press, 1994.

Korsten, F.J.M. *Roger North (1651–1734): Virtuoso and Essayist.* Amsterdam: APA-Holland Univ. Press, 1981.

Lacey, Douglas R. *Dissent and Parliamentary Politics in England, 1661–1689: A Study in the Perpetuation and Tempering of Parliamentarianism.* New Brunswick, N.J.: Rutgers Univ. Press, 1969.

Lillywhite, Bryant. *London Coffee Houses: A Reference Book of Coffee Houses of the Seventeenth, Eighteenth, and Nineteenth Centuries.* London: Allen & Unwin, 1963.

M. 'Who was the Author of 'The Modest Enquiry,' etc.' *Notes and Queries,* no.75 (5 April 1851), 264.

Macaulay, Thomas Babington. *History of England from the Accession of James the Second.* Ed. C.H. Firth. 6 vols London: Macmillan, 1913–15.

Maguire, Nancy Klein. *Regicide and Restoration: English Tragicomedy, 1660–1671.* Cambridge: Cambridge Univ. Press, 1992.

Manning, Roger. 'The Origins of the Doctrine of Sedition.' *Albion* 12 (1980): 102–21.

Marshall, John. *John Locke: Resistance, Religion, and Responsibility.* Cambridge: Cambridge Univ. Press, 1994.

Mason, Wilmer G. 'The Annual Output of Wing-listed Titles, 1649–1684.' *Library,* 5th ser., 24 (1974): 219–20.

McDowell, Paula. *The Women of Grub Street: Press, Politics, and Gender in the London Literary Marketplace, 1678–1730.* New York: Clarendon Press, 1998.

McKenzie, D.F. *Stationers' Company Apprentices, 1641–1700.* Oxford: Oxford Univ. Press for the Bibliographical Society, 1974.

Michel, Robert H. 'English Attitudes towards Women, 1640–1700.' *Canadian Journal of History* 13 (1978): 35–60.

Miller, John. *Charles II.* London: Weidenfeld & Nicolson, 1991.

———. 'Charles II and His Parliaments.' *Transactions of the Royal Historical Society,* 5th ser., 32 (1982): 1–23.

———. *James II: A Study in Kingship.* Hove, East Sussex: Wayland, 1978.

———. 'James II and Toleration.' In *By Force or by Default? The Revolution of 1688–89.* ed. E. Cruickshanks, 8–27. Edinburgh: John Donald, 1989.

———. *Popery and Politics in England, 1660–1688.* Cambridge: Cambridge Univ. Press, 1973.

———. 'The Potential for 'Absolutism' in Later Stuart England.' *History* 69 (1984): 187–207.

Monaghan, Frank. 'Benjamin Harris: Printer, Bookseller, and the First American Journalist.' *Colophon* 12 (1932).

Moore, John Robert. '"Robin Hog" Stephens: Messenger of the Press.' *Papers of the Bibliographical Society of America* 50 (1956): 381–87.

Muddiman, J.G. *The King's Journalist, 1659–1689: Studies in the Reign of Charles II.* London: J. Lane, 1923.

Nadelhaft, Jerome. 'The Englishwoman's Sexual Civil War: Feminist Attitudes towards Men, Women, and Marriage, 1650–1740.' *Journal of the History of Ideas* 43 (1982): 555–79.

Nauert, Charles G. Jr. *Agrippa and the Crisis of Renaissance Thought.* Urbana: Univ. of Illinois Press, 1965.

Nelson, Carolyn. 'American Readership of Early British Serials.' In *Serials and Their Readers, 1620–1914,* ed. Robin Myers and Michael Harris, 27–44. Winchester: St Paul's Bibliographies; New Castle, Del.: Oak Knoll Press, 1993.

Nelson, Carolyn, and Matthew Seccombe, eds. *Periodical Publications, 1641–1700: A Survey with Illustrations.* London: Bibliographical Society, 1986.

———, comps. *British Newspapers and Periodicals, 1641–1700: A Short-title Catalogue of Serials Printed in England, Scotland, Ireland, and British America.* New York: Modern Language Association, 1987.

Nenner, Howard. *By Colour of Law.* Chicago: Univ. of Chicago Press, 1977.

————. *The Right to Be King: The Succession to the Crown of England, 1603–1714*. Chapel Hill: Univ. of North Carolina Press, 1995.

————, ed. *Politics and the Political Imagination in Later Stuart Britain: Essays Presented to Lois Green Schwoerer*. Rochester: Univ. of Rochester Press, 1997.

Newton, Theodore F.M. 'The Mask of Heraclitus.' *Harvard Studies and Notes in Philology and Literature* 16 (1934): 145–60.

Ogg, David. *England in the Reign of Charles II*. 3rd edn 2 vols. Oxford: Clarendon Press, 1962.

————. *England in the Reigns of James II and William III*. Oxford: Oxford Univ. Press, 1955.

O'Malley, Thomas. 'Religion and the Newspaper Press, 1660–1685: A Study of the London Gazette.' In *The Press in English Society from the Seventeenth to Nineteenth Centuries*, ed. Michael Harris and Alan Lee, 25–46. Rutherford, N.J.: Fairleigh Dickinson Press, 1986.

Owen, Susan. *Restoration Theatre and Crisis*. Oxford: Oxford Univ. Press, 1996.

Patterson, Annabel. *Censorship and Interpretation: The Conditions of Writing and Reading in Early Modern England*. Madison: Univ. of Wisconsin Press, 1984.

Pincus, Steven C.A. 'From Butterboxes to Wooden Shoes: The Shift in English Popular Sentiment from Anti-Dutch to Anti-French in the 1670s.' *Historical Journal* 38 (1995): 333–62.

Plomer, Henry R., ed. *A Dictionary of the Printers and Booksellers Who Were at Work in England, Scotland, and Ireland from 1641 to 1667*. 1907. Reprint, Oxford: Oxford Univ. Press for the Bibliographical Society, 1968.

Plomer, Henry R., H.G. Aldis, E.R. McC. Dix, G.J. Gray, and R.B. McKerron. *A Dictionary of the Printers and Booksellers Who Were at Work in England, Scotland, and Ireland from 1668 to 1725*. Oxford: Oxford Univ. Press for the Bibliographical Society, 1922.

Pocock, J.G.A. *The Ancient Constitution and the Feudal Law: A Study of English Historical Thought in the Seventeenth Century, A Reissue with a Retrospect*. Cambridge: Cambridge Univ. Press, 1987.

————. *The Machiavellian Moment: Florentine Political Thought and the Atlantic Republican Tradition*. Princeton: Princeton Univ. Press, 1975.

'"Wicked and Turbulent Though It Was": The Restoration Era in Perspective.' In *Politics and the Political Imagination in Later Stuart Britain: Essays Presented to Lois Green Schwoerer*, ed. Howard Nenner, 9–20. Rochester: Univ. of Rochester Press, 1997.

Rahn, Beverly J., ed. *Sir Roger L'Estrange: Citt and Bumpkin (1680)*. Augustan Reprint Society, 117. Berkeley and Los Angeles: Univ. of California Press for the William Andrew Clark Memorial Library, 1965.

Reay, Barry, ed. *Popular Culture in Seventeenth-Century England*. New York: St Martin's, 1985.

Robbins, Caroline. *The Eighteenth-Century English Commonwealthman: Studies in the Transmission, Development, and Circumstance of English Liberal Thought from the Restoration of Charles II until the War with the Thirteen Colonies*. Cambridge: Harvard Univ. Press, 1959.

Rossiter, Clinton Laurence. *Seedtime of the Republic: The Origin of the American Tradition of Political Liberty*. New York: Harcourt, Brace & Co., 1953.

Rostenberg, Leona. *Literary, Political, Scientific, Religious, and Legal Publishing, Printing, and Bookselling in England, 1551–1700: Twelve Studies*. Pref. Donald G. Wing. 2 vols. New York: Burt Franklin, 1965.

Russell, Conrad. 'The Theory of Treason in the Trial of Strafford.' *English Historical Review* 80 (1965): 30–50.

Saunders, J.W. *The Profession of English Letters*. London: Routledge & Kegan Paul; Toronto: Univ. of Toronto Press, 1964.

Schochet, Gordon J. 'Between Lambeth and Leviathan: Samuel Parker on the Church of England and Political Order.' In *Political Discourse in Early Modern Britain: Essays in Honor of John Pocock*, ed. Nicholas Phillipson and Quentin Skinner, 189–208. Cambridge: Cambridge Univ. Press, 1993.

———. 'From Persecution to "Toleration."' In *Liberty Secured? Britain Before and After 1688,* ed. J. R. Jones, 122–57. Stanford: Stanford Univ. Press, 1992.

———. 'Samuel Parker, Religious Diversity, and the Ideology of Persecution.' In *The Margins of Orthodoxy: Heterodox Writing and Cultural Response, 1660–1750*, ed. Roger D. Lund, 119–48. Cambridge: Cambridge Univ. Press, 1995.

———. 'Toleration, Revolution, and Judgment in the Development of Locke's Political Thought.' *Political Science* 40 (1988): 84–96.

Schwoerer, Lois G. 'The Attempted Impeachment of Sir William Scroggs, Lord Chief Justice of the Court of King's Bench, November 1680–March 1681.' *Historical Journal* 38 (1995): 843–74.

———. 'British Lineages and American Choices.' In *The Bill of Rights: Government Proscribed,* ed. Ronald Hoffman and Peter J. Albert, 1–41.

Charlottesville: Univ. Press of Virginia for the United States Capitol Historical Society, 1997.

———. *The Declaration of Rights, 1689.* Baltimore: Johns Hopkins Univ. Press, 1981.

———. 'Liberty of the Press and Public Opinion: 1660–1695.' In *Liberty Secured? Britain Before and After 1688,* ed. J.R. Jones, 199–230. Stanford: Stanford Univ. Press, 1992.

———. 'William, Lord Russell: The Making of a Martyr, 1683–1983.' *Journal of British Studies* 24 (1985): 41–69.

Scott, Jonathan. *Algernon Sidney and the English Republic, 1623–1677.* Cambridge: Cambridge Univ. Press, 1988.

———. *Algernon Sidney and the Restoration Crisis, 1677–1683.* Cambridge: Cambridge Univ. Press, 1991.

Scribner, R.W. *For the Sake of Simple Folk: Popular Propaganda for the German Reformation.* Cambridge: Cambridge Univ. Press, 1981.

Shapiro, Barbara. *Probability and Certainty in Seventeenth-Century England.* Princeton: Princeton Univ. Press, 1984.

Sharpe, Kevin, and Steven N. Zwicker, eds. *Refiguring Revolutions.* Berkeley and Los Angeles: Univ. of California Press, 1998.

Shesgreen, Sean, ed. *The Criers and Hawkers of London: Engravings and Drawings by Marcellus Laroon.* Aldeshot, Hants.: Scolar Press, 1990.

Siebert, Frederick Seaton. *Freedom of the Press in England, 1476–1776: The Rise and Decline of Government Controls.* Urbana: Univ. of Illinois Press, 1952.

Smith, Hilda, and Susan Cardinale, comps. *Women and the Literature of the Seventeenth Century: An Annotated Bibliography Based on Wing's Short-title Catalogue.* New York: Greenwood Press, 1990.

Smith, S.R. 'The Social and Geographical Origins of the London Apprentices, 1630–60.' *Guildhall Miscellany* 4, no.4 (1973): 195–206.

Sowerby, E. Millicent, ed. *Catalogue of the Library of Thomas Jefferson.* 5 vols. Washington, D.C.: Library of Congress, 1952–59.

Speck, W.A. *Reluctant Revolutionaries: Englishmen and the Revolution of 1688.* Oxford: Oxford Univ. Press, 1988.

Spufford, Margaret. 'First Steps in Literacy: The Reading and Writing Experiences of the Humblest Seventeenth-Century Autobiographers.' *Social History* 4 (1979): 407–35.

———. *Small Books and Pleasant Histories.* Cambridge: Cambridge Univ. Press, 1981.

Spurr, John. "'Latitudinarianism" and the Restoration Church.' *Historical Journal* 31 (1988): 61–82.

———. *The Restoration Church of England, 1646–1689.* New Haven: Yale Univ. Press, 1991.

———. 'Schism and the Restoration Church.' *Journal of Ecclesiastical History* 41 (1990): 408–24.

Stater, Victor. *Noble Government: The Stuart Lord Lieutenancy and the Transformation of English Politics.* Athens: Univ. of Georgia Press, 1994.

———. 'Reconstructing the Restoration.' *Journal of British Studies* 29 (1990): 393–401.

Steele, Robert, ed. *A Bibliography of Royal Proclamations of the Tudor and Stuart Sovereigns and of Others Published under Authority, 1485–1714.* 2 vols Oxford: Clarendon Press, 1910.

Stephens, Frederick George. *Catalogue of Political and Personal Satires Preserved in the Department of Prints and Drawings in the British Museum.* 12 vols 1870–1954.

Sutherland, James. *The Restoration Newspaper and Its Development.* Cambridge: Cambridge Univ. Press, 1986.

Swatland, Andrew. *The House of Lords in the Reign of Charles II.* Cambridge: Cambridge Univ. Press, 1996.

Taves, Stuart M. *The Amiable Humorist: A Study of the Comic Theory and Criticism of the Eighteenth and Early Nineteenth Centuries.* Chicago: Univ. of Chicago Press, 1960.

Thomas, Keith. 'The Meaning of Literacy in Early Modern England.' In *The Written Word: Literacy in Transition,* ed. Gerd Baumann, 97–131. Oxford: Oxford Univ. Press, 1986.

———. 'The Place of Laughter in Tudor and Stuart England.' *Times Literary Supplement,* 21 January 1977, 77–81.

Thomas, P. W. *Sir John Berkenhead, 1617–1679: A Royalist Career in Politics and Polemics.* Oxford: Clarendon Press, 1969.

Thornton, John Leonard. *The Chronology of Librarianship: An Introduction to the History of Libraries and Book-collecting.* London: Grafton & Co., 1941.

A Transcript of the Registers of the Worshipful Company of Stationers: From 1640–1708 A.D. 3 vols London: privately printed, 1914.

Treadwell, Michael. 'Lists of Master Printers: The Size of the London Printing Trade, 1637–1723.' In *Aspects of Printing from 1600,* ed. Robin Myers and Michael Harris, 141–70. Oxford: Oxford Polytechnic Press, 1987.

————. 'London Trade Publishers, 1675–1750.' *Library,* 6th ser., 4 (1982): 99–134.

Turner, F.C. *James II.* New York: Macmillan, 1948.

Tyacke, Nicholas. 'The 'Rise of Puritanism' and the Legalizing of Dissent, 1571–1719.' In *From Persecution to Toleration: The Glorious Revolution and Religion in England,* ed. Ole Peter Grell, Jonathan I. Israel, and Nicholas Tyacke, 17–49. Oxford: Clarendon Press, 1991.

Walker, J. 'The Censorship of the Press during the Reign of Charles II.' *History,* n.s., 35 (1950): 219–38.

Walker, R.B. 'The Newspaper Press in the Reign of William III.' *Historical Journal* 17 (1974): 691–709.

Wardroper, John. *Jest upon Jest: A Selection from the Jestbooks and Collections of Merry Tales Published from the Reign of Richard III to George III.* London: Routledge & Kegan Paul, 1970.

Watt, Tessa. *Cheap Print and Popular Piety, 1550–1640.* Cambridge: Cambridge Univ. Press, 1991.

————. 'Publisher, Pedlar, Pot-Poet: The Changing Character of the Broadside Trade, 1550–1640.' In *Spreading the Word: The Distribution Networks of Print, 1550–1850,* ed. Robin Myers and Michael Harris, 61–81. Winchester: St Paul's Bibliographies; Detroit: Omnigraphics, 1990.

Whiteman, Anne, ed., assisted by Mary Clapinson. *The Compton Census of 1676: A Critical Edition.* Records of Social and Economic History, n.s., 10. London: Oxford Univ. Press for the British Academy, 1986.

Williams, J. B. *A History of English Journalism to the Foundation of the Gazette.* London: Longmans, Green, 1908.

————. 'Nathaniel Thompson and the "Popish Plot."' *The Month* (London) 38 (1921): 31–37.

————. 'The Newsbooks and Letters of News of the Restoration.' *English Historical Review* 23 (1908): 252–76.

Willman, Robert. 'The Origins of 'Whig' and 'Tory' in English Political Language.' *Historical Journal* 17 (1974): 247–64.

Wilson, John Harold. *The Court Wits of the Restoration.* Princeton: Princeton Univ. Press, 1948.

Wing, Donald, comp. *Short-title Catalogue, Of Books Printed In England, Scotland, Ireland, Wales, and British America and of English Books Printed In Other Countries.* 2nd. edn Rev. John J. Morrison and Carolyn W. Nelson, eds, and Matthew Seccombe, asst. ed. 4 vols New York: Modern Language Association of America, 1994–98.

Wiseman, Susan. *Drama and Politics in the English Civil War.* Cambridge: Cambridge Univ. Press, 1998.

Wolf, Edwin. *Book Culture of a Colonial American City.* Oxford: Oxford Univ. Press, 1988.

Woolf, Daniel R. 'Narrative Historical Writing in Restoration England: A Preliminary Survey.' In *The Restoration Mind*, ed. W. Gerald Marshall, 207–51. Newark: Univ. of Delaware Press, Associated University Presses, 1997.

Worden, Blair. 'Marchamont Nedham and the Beginnings of English Republicanism, 1649–1656.' In *Republicanism, Liberty, and Commercial Society, 1649–1776*, ed. David Wootton, 45–81. Stanford: Stanford Univ. Press, 1994.

————. 'Milton and Marchamont Nedham.' In *Milton and Republicanism,* ed. David Armitage, Armand Himy, and Quentin Skinner, 156–80. Cambridge: Cambridge Univ. Press, 1995.

Wright, Louis B. *Middle Class Culture in Elizabethan England.* Chapel Hill: Univ. of North Carolina Press, 1935.

Wrigley, Edward A., and Roger S. Schofield. *The Population History of England, 1541–1871: A Reconstruction.* Cambridge: Cambridge Univ. Press, 1989.

Zagorin, Perez. *Ways of Lying: Dissimulation, Persecution, and Conformity in Early Modern Europe.* Cambridge: Harvard Univ. Press, 1990.

Zook, Melinda S. 'Early Whig Ideology, Ancient Constitutionalism, and the Reverend Samuel Johnson.' *Journal of British Studies* 32 (1993): 139–65.

————. *Radical Whigs and Conspiratorial Politics in Late Stuart England.* University Park: Pennsylvania State Univ. Press, 1999.

Zwicker, Steven N. *Lines of Political Authority: Politics and English Literary Culture, 1649–1689.* Ithaca: Cornell Univ. Press, 1993.

————. 'The Paradoxes of Tender Conscience.' *English Literary History* 63 (1996): 851–69.

————. *Refiguring Revolutions.* Ed. Kevin Sharpe and Steven N. Zwicker. Berkeley and Los Angeles: Univ. of California Press, 1998.

DISSERTATIONS

Allen, David F. 'The Crown and the Corporation of London in the Exclusion Crisis, 1678–81.' Cambridge University, 1977.

Botica, Allan Richard. 'Audience, Playhouse and Play in Restoration Theatre, 1660–1710.' Oxford University, 1985.

Colquhoun, Kathleen Mary. '"Issue of the Late Civill Wars": James, Duke of York and the Government of Scotland, 1679–1689.' University of Illinois at Urbana-Champaign, 1992.

Crist, Timothy. 'Francis Smith and the Opposition Press in England, 1660–1688.' Cambridge University, 1977.

Faulkner, Thomas C. 'A Selected Edition of Sir Roger L'Estrange's *Observator.*' University of Wisconsin, 1972.

Hetet, John Stephen Tawhana. 'A Literary Underground in Restoration England: Printers and Dissenters in the Context of Constraints, 1660–1689.' Cambridge University, 1987.

Littlefield, David Joseph. 'The Polemic Art of Sir Roger L'Estrange: A Study of His Political Writings, 1659–1688.' Yale University, 1961.

Marshall, David Norman. 'Protestant Dissent in the Reign of James II.' University of Hull, 1976.

Rahn, Beverly J. 'The Pen and the Plot: Pamphlets of Sir Roger L'Estrange, 1678–1681.' Columbia University, 1975.

List of Illustrations

Front cover: The 'Secretarius', Henry Care (detail). By permission of the Folger Shakespeare Library.

Page 45: Title page of Henry Care's *Weekly Pacquet of Advice from Rome*, volume 1. Care's most widely known publication appeared every week but one from 3 December 1678 to 13 July 1683. The *Popish Courant*, a sheet of jokes and stories demeaning popery and libelling contemporary persons and events, accompanied it. By permission of the Folger Shakespeare Library.

Page 82: Sir William Scroggs (1623-83), Lord Chief Justice of the Court of King's Bench, 1678. Artist unknown, possibly J.M. Wright; by courtesy of the National Portrait Gallery, London.

Page 130-1: *The Committee; Or Popery in Masquerade* (1680), a political print with text by Sir Roger L'Estrange, said to be a 'landmark in the history of English satire'. By permission of the Folger Shakespeare Library.

Page 132: Marginalia from *The Committee; Or Popery in Masquerade* (1680) identifying Henry Care as the 'Secretarius'. A note in Narcissus Luttrell's hand near the couplet 'He deals in Sonnets, Articles, takes Notes,/Frames Histories, Impeachments, enters Votes' reads, 'Touch on Mr. Henry Care'. By permission of the British Library.

Page 159: Sir Roger L'Estrange (1616–1704), appointed surveyor of the press by Charles II, was Care's principal sparring partner in the press. Attributed to J.M. Wright, *c.* 1680; by courtesy of the National Portrait Gallery, London.

Page 246: Title page of Henry Care's *Publick Occurrences Truely Stated*, which appeared under Care's name from February to July 1688 and was continued by Elkanah Settle until October 1688. Folio 34 from *Nichols Newspaper* 7A; with permission of the Bodleian Library, University of Oxford.

Index

If you are interested in purchasing
other books published by Tempus, or in case you have
difficulty finding any Tempus books in your local
bookshop, you can also place orders directly through
our website

www.tempus-publishing.com

or from

BOOKPOST
Freepost, PO Box 29,
Douglas, Isle of Man
IM99 1BQ
Tel 01624 836000
email bookshop@enterprise.net